PENGUIN CLASSICS

ARMY LIFE IN A BLACK REGIMENT

Thomas Wentworth Higginson was born in Cambridge, Massachusetts in 1823. He graduated from Harvard, where his father had been steward, in 1841 and, after a stint teaching school, returned to Cambridge to study at the Harvard Divinity School. In 1847 he became pastor of the First Religious Society of Newburyport and married Mary E. Channing. An ardent abolitionist, he moved to the Free Church in Worcester in 1852 and the following year began writing for the *Atlantic Monthly*. In 1856 he visited "Bloody Kansas" and in 1862 was appointed colonel of the First South Carolina Volunteers, entering the service that would become the basis for *Army Life in a Black Regiment*. In 1862 he also began the correspondence with the reclusive poet Emily Dickinson that would eventually result in the posthumous publication of her poems. After the Civil War Higginson returned to a life of letters. He died in 1911 and was buried in Cambridge.

R. D. Madison teaches English at the U.S. Naval Academy in Annapolis, Maryland. He has edited several works of military and naval history, including Robert Southey's *Life of Nelson* and James Fenimore Cooper's *History of the Navy*, and is the author of a prize-winning play, *Prospect for Freedom: Frederick Douglass and John Brown*, and *Tuckahoe*, a collection of poems based on the early life of Frederick Douglass.

D0366412

ARMY LIFE IN
A BLACK REGIMENT
AND OTHER WRITINGS

THOMAS WENTWORTH HIGGINSON

WITH AN INTRODUCTION
AND NOTES BY
R. D. MADISON

PENGUIN BOOKS

PENGUIN BOOKS
Published by the Penguin Group
Penguin Group (USA) Inc., 375 Hudson Street, New York, New York 10014, U.S.A.
Penguin Group (Canada), 90 Eglinton Avenue East, Suite 700, Toronto,
Ontario, Canada M4P 2Y3 (a division of Pearson Penguin Canada Inc.)
Penguin Books Ltd, 80 Strand, London WC2R 0RL, England
Penguin Ireland, 25 St Stephen's Green, Dublin 2, Ireland (a division of Penguin Books Ltd)
Penguin Group (Australia), 250 Camberwell Road, Camberwell,
Victoria 3124, Australia (a division of Pearson Australia Group Pty Ltd)
Penguin Books India Pvt Ltd, 11 Community Centre, Panchsheel Park, New Delhi – 110 017, India
Penguin Group (NZ), cnr Airborne and Rosedale Roads,
Albany, Auckland 1310, New Zealand (a division of Pearson New Zealand Ltd)
Penguin Books (South Africa) (Pty) Ltd, 24 Sturdee Avenue,
Rosebank, Johannesburg 2196, South Africa

Penguin Books Ltd, Registered Offices: 80 Strand, London WC2R 0RL, England

First published in the United States of America by Fields, Osgood, & Co. 1870
This edition with an introduction and notes by
Robert D. Madison published in Penguin Books 1997

15 14 13 12 11

Introduction and notes copyright © Robert D. Madison, 1997
All rights reserved

Excerpts from Thomas Wentworth Higginson's letters to James T. Fields are reprinted
by permission of the Houghton Library, Harvard University (bMS Am 784).

LIBRARY OF CONGRESS CATALOGING IN PUBLICATION DATA
Higginson, Thomas Wentworth, 1823–1911.
Army life in a Black regiment: and other writings / Thomas
Wentworth Higginson; with an introduction and notes by R. D. Madison.
p.   cm.—(Penguin classics)
Includes bibliographical references and index.
ISBN 0 14 04.3621 9 (pbk)
1. Higginson, Thomas Wentworth, 1823–1911.   2. United States.
Army. Colored Infantry Regiment, 33rd (1864–1866)—Biography.
3. United States. Army—Biography.   4. United States—History—
Civil War, 1861–1865—Participation, Afro-American.   5. United
States—History—Civil War, 1861–1865—Personal narratives.
6. United States—History—Civil War, 1861–1865—Regimental
histories.   7. Soldiers—United States—Biography.   I. Title.
II. Series.
E492.94 1st.H53   1997
973.7′415—dc21   97–7291

Printed in the United States of America
Set in Stempel Garamond

CONTENTS

APPENDIX

INTRODUCTION

Thomas Wentworth Higginson is a writer whose work always pleases but seldom astonishes. And *Army Life in a Black Regiment* belongs to a genre—the regimental history—which seldom even offers much literary pleasure. But as Howard Mumford Jones remarked in his 1960 edition, *Army Life in a Black Regiment* is "a forgotten masterpiece from a neglected literary period by an author who is not supposed to have written masterpieces."

Higginson was born into literary New England on December 22, 1823, and had he been born in another age or another region, would surely have been regarded as a very remarkable man. But he was born just too late to participate fully in the "Newness," as he later called transcendentalism, despite beginning the glorious decade of the eighteen-forties at Harvard College under the reign of President Quincy, with Jones Very as his Greek tutor, and with a cousin named Ellery Channing.

Like his older contemporary Henry David Thoreau, Higginson even put in a stint as a chain-bearer surveying for the railroad, but he did not yet give himself over to wildness. The conventional way to wealth for dreamers of Higginson's day was still Harvard Divinity School, but not wishing to make the plunge, Higginson enrolled merely as a resident graduate, reading the German philosophers and poetry of all ages. His own attempts at poetry were mediocre, except for a few hymns—an early indication that at least in literature his efforts would never wander far from the conventional.

Higginson was not, however, born too late to be caught up in the various reform movements of the nineteenth century. He explored Fourierism, Unitarianism, and above all the struggles for women's rights and the abolition of slavery. In 1846 he finally made up his mind to enter the divinity school and soon began preaching on the inevitable topic of "Clergy and Reform." In 1847, after a long engagement, he married Mary Channing and accepted the call to a pulpit in Newburyport. There he came under the influence—which he no doubt relished—of his near-neighbor,

Quaker poet and abolitionist John Greenleaf Whittier, and the newly formed Free Soil party. The other new influence in Higginson's life at this time was women's rights advocate Lucy Stone, "a little, sweet-looking Quakerish body with the sweetest modest manners, and yet as unshrinking and self-possessed as a loaded cannon" (Higginson 1914, p. 97).

The two-barreled description is significant, for Higginson increasingly advocated (and chose) militant over nonviolent abolitionism, a leaning that would cost him his Newburyport pulpit. In 1851, energized by the rescue of Frederick Jenkins ("Shadrach") in the wake of the Fugitive Slave Law, Higginson joined the Boston Vigilance Committee. An abortive attempt to rescue Thomas Sims, an escaped slave from Savannah, both frustrated Higginson and galvanized him for future action. His church politics, too radical for Newburyport, were welcomed by the Free Church in Worcester, which issued him a call in 1852. Here he became directly involved with the Underground Railroad, and he found this work more to his liking than surveying for the Old Colony line. With renewed self-confidence and a clear vision of his mission, Higginson settled down (if that isn't too tame an image) into becoming one of the significant, if not always visible, movers of the age.

Higginson continued to be involved with women's rights, partly because of and partly in spite of Mary's rapidly declining health. And he continued to admire and to be influenced by Lucy Stone. But in 1854 Higginson's course for the immediate decade was set by the arrest of Anthony Burns under the Fugitive Slave Law.

On a rainy spring night, while most of the vigilance committee were engaged in a protest meeting at Boston's Fanueil Hall, Higginson and a few co-conspirators led a hastily planned attack on the United States courthouse where Burns was being held. With Higginson and an unidentified black man at the head of a battering ram, they broke open the door enough for one man to squeeze through. Higginson would never forget that it was the black man opposite him who immediately jumped through to face the armed guards.

In the melee that followed, a policeman was killed, but the rescue attempt was repulsed. A wounded Higginson and others were recognized and indicted, but never tried—such was the popular resentment towards the Fugitive Slave Law in Massachusetts. Higginson's role in the affair was supported by his congregation and brought him what he considered a welcome notoriety in the cause of freedom.

Meanwhile, his writing had improved, too, and he was being published in *Putnam's Monthly Magazine* in the company of the best writers in the country. But if he was known as a fiery abolitionist in eastern Massachusetts, outside the region he was becoming known, rather, as a spokesman for the healthiness of outdoor pursuits: his *Putnam's* sketches had more to do with mountain climbing than freedom fighting.

But that would come. Returning in 1856 from a voyage to Fayal undertaken for his wife's health, Higginson was greeted by the news of the shocking caning of abolitionist Charles Sumner by South Carolinian Preston Brooks on the floor of the United States Senate and the heightening of troubles in Kansas, where emigrants from the north were endeavoring to keep Kansas free from the spread of slavery. When Higginson became secretary of the Emigrant Aid Society, he decided to make a personal recognizance of the region: "It was decided," he reported, "to send all future emigrants across Iowa and Nebraska, fighting their way, if necessary."

> Our three parties, accordingly, went by that route; the men being provided with rifles, revolvers, and camp equipage. Two of these parties made their rendezvous in Worcester, one under command of my friend Stowell; the third party was formed largely of Maine lumbermen, recruited in a body for the service. I never saw thirty men of finer physique, as they strode through Boston in their red shirts and rough trousers to meet us at the Emigrant Aid Society rooms, which had been kindly lent us for the purpose. The rest of the men came to us singly, from all over New England, some of the best being from Vermont, including Henry Thompson, afterwards John Brown's son-in-law, killed at Harper's Ferry.
>
> (*Cheerful Yesterdays*, 198)

Higginson himself led a party to Kansas in 1856, and for six weeks, as he put it, "my Sharp's rifle, my revolvers,—or, these failing, my own ingenuity and ready wit,—were all the protection

I had. It was a delightful sensation." While in Kansas, he bought a copy of Harriet Beecher Stowe's recently published *Dred: A Tale of the Great Dismal Swamp* and perhaps indulged in visions of leading runaway slaves through the marshes of the South.

When the Kansas troubles died down, Higginson returned his energies to the Free Church, but he kept in close touch with those with whom he had struggled in recent years. Theodore Parkman and Samuel Gridley Howe were friends from the vigilance committee; to these he added George Luther Stearns and Frank Sanborn of the Massachusetts Kansas Committee. Soon after he was in correspondence with another abolitionist who until the Kansas troubles had remained rather obscure: this was John Brown, who in February 1858 wrote Higginson that "Rail Road business on a *somehwat extended* scale is the *identical* object for which I am trying to get means." Higginson met with Brown, whom he described as "simply a high-minded, unselfish, belated Covenanter."

Brown's raid on Harpers Ferry a year and a half later caught his supporters off guard, not only Gerrit Smith, who with Higginson's group had provided material aid to Brown, but also Frederick Douglass himself, with whom Brown had corresponded briefly, and who had pleaded with Brown that Harpers Ferry was "a perfect steel trap." Douglass fled the country; others scattered. Higginson stood firm and dared U.S. marshalls to try to take him out of Worcester. No such attempt was made, and once more Higginson enjoyed basking in glory, however secondhand.

Despite the near-universal unpopularity of Brown's raid in the ensuing year, as disunion approached, public sentiment eventually came to reflect the declaration of Massachusetts Governor John Andrew that "John Brown was right." Higginson, a pen-of-all trades covering saints, water lilies, spiritualism, and women's rights, now began writing for the *Atlantic Monthly*. Founded in 1857 and purchased two years later by the preeminent Boston literary firm of Ticknor & Fields, this magazine was devoted, as its title pages claimed, to literature, art, and politics, and was edited for its first four years by anti-slavery poet James Russell Lowell. Lowell had reacted timidly to Higginson's proposal of an essay about the abolitionist martyr. "Editorially, I am a little afraid of Brown," he wrote Higginson in late October 1859, and Ticknor would be more so. But perhaps I misunderstand you. Anyhow, as long as I edit I want you to write. (*Letters of James Russell Lowell*, I, 298)

Higginson's Brown essay, much revised in the following two months, did not appear in the *Atlantic*, but became the centerpiece of James Redpath's *Public Life of Captain John Brown*.

One strain in Higginson's *Atlantic* essays appropriately descended directly from the Anthony Burns affair: he examined militant resistence to slavery in essays on the Maroons in Jamaica and Surinam, Denmark Vesey, and Nat Turner. In the year of Fort Sumter and the breaking out of civil war, Higginson was still writing about health and the out-of-doors—but his writing also reveals his continued fascination with the idea of a large-scale slave revolt. And Higginson never forgot the lesson in black courage he had learned at the door of the United States courthouse.

In 1861 Higginson published eight essays in the *Atlantic*, including "Nat Turner's Insurrection" (August), a psychological examination of the events of thirty years before. Higginson recognized that the nation had come to a turning point: in this essay he abandons the outspoken and accusatory rhetoric of the abolitionist preacher and quietly and sanely delineates the nature of a slave state in revolution.

Believing open conflict to be unavoidable and immediate, he also was studying war himself. "I find in those days," he later wrote in *Cheerful Yesterdays*, "I read military books; took notes on fortifications, strategy, and the principles of attack and defense." When war broke out, he was offered a commission as major in the Fourth Battalion of Infantry. When he declined, it was given to a schoolmate, Charles Devens, who came out of the war a major general. Higginson's hesitation was due in part to his uncertainty as to whether this was to be an abolition war: he couldn't stand the thought of being ordered to return fugitive slaves to slavery. He continued to practice drill, and when he became convinced that the war would be fought to end slavery, he began raising troops for a regiment.

Early in 1862, however, recruiting was halted. Higginson found solace for this disapointment in his writing for the *Atlantic*, especially in an article entitled "Letter to a Young Contributor" (published in April), which is, otherwise unexpectedly, redolent with martial imagery. This unassuming article, filled with advice to would-be *Atlantic* contributors, turns out to have been the most important essay Higginson wrote, although once more it would lead to fame only by association.

"Are you too deeply occupied to say if my verse is alive?" queried one would-be poet, a timid Emily Dickinson from Amherst. Higginson, always deeply occupied in one thing or another, nevertheless took time out from drill and responded almost immediately, as he recounted many years later in another *Atlantic* essay, "Emily Dickinson's Letters" (October 1891). The unknown poet evidently knew exactly what she was doing: it was no secret that the author of pleasant sketches in the *Atlantic* was also the man from the courthouse door, a confederate of John Brown, and extremely handsome—and had a wife at death's door. Higginson also probably felt that the correspondence could be safe while titillating.

In any case, there was little time for it. In August the Fifty-First Massachusetts began organizing, and Higginson began recruiting as a captain. He had been with this regiment less than a month, however, when he received a letter from Brigadier General Rufus Saxton, military commander of the Department of the South, offering him the colonelcy of the first regiment of emancipated slaves.

Today, Higginson's appointment would probably be regarded as a publicity stunt. Ever since Federal troops had gained control of the Sea Islands on the coast of the Carolinas and Georgia there had been futile attempts to arm the blacks, and it was a remnant of one of these organizations, under the command of then-captain C. T. Trowbridge, that became the nucleus of Higginson's regiment. But Trowbridge was a relative unknown from a regiment of New York Volunteer Engineers. Who would be better at the head of a regiment of escaped slaves than the man who had ridden in Kansas, had flaunted his association with John Brown, and had recently written in the prestigious *Atlantic* about Denmark Vesey and Nat Turner?

It was a match made in heaven, and—at least in Higginson's *Army Life* descriptions—life with his troops in the Sea Islands might itself seem Edenic. But the tone pervading the essays that would become *Army Life* was probably to some extent a literary fiction—at least at first. Esther Hill Hawks, who went to Port Royal, near Beaufort, S.C., as a graduate of the New England Female Medical College, recorded the effect the presence of white Federal troops had immediately produced on the occupied South. Beaufort, she writes,

> was one of the spots of which The "Chivalry" were justly proud—but our crazy solderly [soldiers] made sad havoc with its beauty and its wealth. Much of the rich furniture was stolen by officers and sent north to friends—more of it was wantonly destroyed by the soldiers—apparently for the mere love of destroying. . . . If our soldiers had been content with destroying the rebel property—there might be found excuse for them—but every indignity which human ingenuity could devise was heaped upon the poor negroes, who had hailed their coming so joyfully—and during the first year of our soldiers coming the blacks probably suffered more from their tyrany [sic] and insults, than ever in their lives before.
>
> (*A Woman Doctor's Civil War*, 33)

Hawks goes on to describe rampant sexual exploitation of colored women by both officers and men of the occupying force before General Saxton's influence could be felt throughout the department.

Hawks was there as part of the larger effort to educate and employ freedmen usually referred to as the "Port Royal Experiment." Another participant was Charlotte Forten, a free black born in 1837 in Philadelphia and educated in Massachusetts, whose politically active family brought her into contact with such abolitionists as William Lloyd Garrison and John Greenleaf Whittier. At some risk to herself, she acted on Whittier's hint that she might make herself very useful as a teacher among the newly freed Sea Islanders.

All Massachusetts was watching both experiments at Port Royal—the military one and the educational one—and Whittier had followed with interest the career of his more militant friend Higginson. "I feel the greatest admiration for his heroic self-devotion," he wrote to a friend, "and yet I tremble in view of its peril. He will be a marked man, and especially exposed."

But, if he has work to do under the Divine Providence, his head will be covered in the day of battle. How strange to think of him so fresh, so beautiful in his glorious manhood, with his refinement, culture, and grace—leading that wild African regiment to avenge the wrong of two centuries of slavery! How this one act of his is making his name historic.

(*Letters*, III, 33)

Soon after, Whittier wrote to Forten to urge her to make the acquaintance of Colonel Higginson, "a rare man,—a gentleman, scholar and true friend of the slave." She again acted on his advice, and wrote that she had met him and also happily found that her former physician, Seth Rogers of Worcester, was the surgeon of the regiment.

Forten's proximity to Higginson and her propensity for journalizing make her a unique witness even in a process that was by no means out of the public eye. Higginson, she wrote, "seems to me of all fighting men the one best fitted to command a regiment of colored soldiers." She recalled having seen him as a captain drilling his troops in Worcester: "I never saw him so full of life and energy—entering with his whole soul into his work—without thinking what a splendid general he w'ld make. And that too may come about." A short time after, she was a guest of Dr. Rogers in camp, and although she missed dining with the colonel, he later gave her a tour of his quarters:

Col. H. invited us into his tent—a very nice, almost *homelike* one. I noticed a nice secretary, with writing utensils and "Les Miserables" on it. A *wreath* of beautiful oranges hung against the wall, fronting the door. I wanted to have a good look at this tent; but we were hardly seated when the Dr. and the Col. were called away for a moment. . . . [My] attention was occupied by Col. H. to whom I showed Whittier's poem ["Hymn Sung at Christmas by the Scholars of St. Helena Island"], letter, and photo. "He looks old," he said to me sadly, as he handed back the picture.

(*Journals*, 431–32)

Forten copied sections of her journal as letters to her mentor Whittier in Amesbury, Massachusetts, who tinkered with them and then forwarded them to James T. Fields, since 1861 the editor of the *Atlantic Monthly*. "I am glad thee like 'Life on the Sea Islands,' " Whittier wrote in a postscript to Fields, who published Forten's sketch with a brief preface by Whittier in two parts in the May and June 1864 issues of the *Atlantic*.

That same spring, Higginson had made up his mind to resign his commission, following his near escape from a cannonball (as described in "Up the Edisto") and his consequent failing health. Technically sent north on a furlough, the literally and psychologically shell-shocked Higginson looked forward to returning to the literary life. "Sometimes I think the greater activity in the book-world makes me feel more as if I had been here long enough," he wrote home; "you know when I first came away there was a great stagnation there, and now it seems as if all the wheels were busy again and I must not stay too long away." Years later, in *Cheerful Yesterdays*, he would deny it: "When I left the service, two years of army life, with small access to books, had so far checked the desire for active literary pursuits, on my part, that I should actually have been content not to return to them." But *Les Miserables*, like *Dred*, was not kept simply for its symbolic value.

On July 3 Higginson wrote to Fields asking for anti-slavery novels (presumably to review) and discussed his relationship with the *Atlantic*: "You can say anything you please about my resuming my contributions henceforward, but do not use the word 'regular' as that would seem inconsistent with my duties, should I return to my command, which, however, I do not expect." Despite the perfect opening given by Forten's sketch in the *Atlantic*, it is conceivable that Higginson could not bring himself to write about an experience that, whatever he might say about it later in print, had become unbearable. Maybe Higginson was somewhat nettled that Forten had scooped him with her sketch of the Sea Islands. Kansas crony James Redpath had published the biography of Haitian patriot Toussaint L'Ouverture, the ultimate revolutionary slave, while Higginson was off at war—somewhat diminishing the lasting impact of Higginson's less flamboyant sketches—and now it almost seemed that the market for Port Royal might have been glutted too.

The first essay published after his return, "Regular and Volunteer Officers" (submitted to the *Atlantic* with another unidentified article early in July), skirts personal recollection until its last pages, where the issue of equal pay for the colored soldiers arises. This was a battle Higginson had been fighting all year in the newspapers, and the article is not much more than a rather belated sequel to letters that would later be reprinted as part of the appendix to *Army Life*. It was a rather weak and time-sensitive article, as Higginson acknowledged. "My article on the officers won't very well bear keeping beyond September," he wrote to Fields, "of course I knew it couldn't go into August." (It was published in the *Atlantic* for September.) The other article ("I should like particularly to have them both appear together," he had told Fields) may have disappeared: there is no apparent reason Higginson would have wanted his next published essay to appear with its unrelated predecessor.

On July 29 Higginson sent Fields what may be a third essay: "I send the MS. which I formerly intended to print as anonymous, but now that I have recommenced writing, I don't care for that." This may have been "A Night in the Water," which appeared in the *Atlantic* in October 1864 and which is not only the most remarkable essay in *Army Life* but also one of the most remarkable essays to come out of the entire war. It is, first and foremost, another of Higginson's outdoor sketches—not at all bound by the polemicism of the previous essay nor the more methodical historicity of the three essays of "Leaves from an Officer's Journal" that followed in November, December, and January of 1865. As the first of Higginson's Sea Island essays to appear before the public, it no doubt whetted their appetite for those that followed. But Higginson would not regain the magic of it until "Up the St. Mary's" appeared in April of the next year.

However successful he was at it, the task of writing these essays grated on him. That winter he complained to his former comrade in arms, Seth Rogers:

> I never did anything so distasteful to me. It is a kind of posthumous life, now that that book of my existence is closed. My instinct is always to live in the present and it is hard for me to reproduce my own Past. I do it mainly from a sense of duty and because, until it is done, the way will not seem clear for other things.
>
> (*TWH: The Story of his Life*, 251–52)

Higginson could neither confront his war experience nor escape it. Perhaps in despair he turned to Epictetus, the Greek slave who had become the great teacher of stoicism, and who, Higginson had learned from Redpath, had been the solace of Toussaint, another slave who had liberated his race only to return to prison himself. As an exercise in detachment and restoration of health and soul, Higginson prepared a revision of Elizabeth Carter's translation of the discourses, fragments, and Enchiridion of Epictetus, which appeared in 1865. The middle-aged crusader had decided, in the words of the Quaker Elizabeth Fry that he quoted in his preface to Epictetus, "to follow, not force, Providence."

Nevertheless, he continued to work on his army sketches, sending Fields "Up the St. John's River" in June ("Can you send me $100 on acc't?"). It was published in the September 1865 issue, but the next year saw no Sea Island sketches from Higginson. "I have undertaken a job—to edit the memorial volumes containing lives of those Harvard boys who have died in the war—it will take me a year almost," he wrote to Rogers. Higginson wrote many of the sketches that appeared in the *Harvard Memorial Biographies* (1866), and it was perhaps too much to ask that he continue to reflect on the grimmer aspects of his own war experience as well. But his estimate of the time required was very accurate, for at the very end of the year he was able to write to Fields, "I promised you 'On picket at Port Royal' today & shall mail it today to reach you tomorrow noon. . . . 'On picket' will be 9 pp. I'm sorry but will make it up, by shortness another time." "Out on Picket" would duly appear in the March 1867 *Atlantic*.

However difficult his task, Higginson continued to be an industrious writer and a conscientious proofreader, and in February he wrote to Fields to settle accounts:

Can you send me $200 for my 4th & 5th articles, now in yr. hands? You hv. previously pd. me $300. My next will be "Negro Spirituals." I have sent Howells two bad missprints in my *Out on Picket* which I want corrected if possible.

But a year of concentrated writing for the *Atlantic* (in 1867 Higginson published an essay in every issue except October and November) resulted once again in partial burnout. "Private," he wrote to Fields in August; "I can't agree to write so regularly next year; it [has gone] hard on me this year, & I was obliged to choose themes nearest at hand." After "Up the Edisto" appeared in the August 1867 *Atlantic*, no more Sea Island essays would be published in periodical form until "Some War Scenes Revisited" appeared in the *Atlantic* of July 1878.

Higginson must have known early on that the essays would eventually make a book: his first book, *Outdoor Papers* (1863), was a collection of earlier essays, and *Atlantic Essays* (1871) was probably taking shape in his mind as well. But for two years Higginson's army life was available to the public only in the desultorily presented *Atlantic* essays of the previous several years:

"A Night in the Water"	October 1864
"Leaves from an Officer's Journal I"	November 1864
"Leaves from an Officer's Journal II"	December 1864
"Leaves from an Officer's Journal III"	January 1865
"Up the St. Mary's"	April 1865
"Up the St. John's River"	September 1865
"Out on Picket"	March 1867
"Negro Spirituals"	June 1867
"Up the Edisto"	August 1867

In February 1868 Higginson wrote to Fields about the prospect of the volume:

About my army book, you said it must be ready by Jan. 1 to appear in spring. Now I have had no time & if I went to work at once I could not hv. it ready before Mar 1. wh I suppose wd. be too late for spring. So I think it had better go over till autumn. Perhaps "Army Life in a Black Regiment["] wd. be a good title—better than "Leaves fr. an Officer's Journal" or "The First South Carolina" wh. I had thought of. I see it is semi-officially announced.

But the book wasn't ready for the fall season. Instead, Higginson gave in to the urge to write an autobiographical novel.

I know that this Romance (Malbone) is in me like the statue in the marble, for every little while I catch glimpses of parts of it here and there. I have rather held back from it, but a power within steadily forces me on; the characters are forming themselves more and more . . . and it is so attractive to me that were it to be my ruin in fame and fortune I should still wish to keep on.

(TWH: The Story of His Life, 278)

Malbone ran serially in the *Atlantic* in 1869 and appeared in book form the same year. The experience of writing extended fiction must have been a healthy one, for Higginson was able to return to *Army Life* with renewed energy—although he still found the task distasteful. "Shall I compel myself to it?" he wrote in April.

Finally, though, in a journal entry for September 22 he was able to lay the book to rest:

"Army Life in a Black Regiment" published today. It is amazing how indifferent I feel as to the reception of this book, compared with "Malbone," which was so near my heart. It scarcely awakens the slightest emotion.

(TWH: The Story of His Life, 282)

Nevertheless, the book that had dragged along so begrudgingly had not ended with a whimper. Higginson had slightly rearranged (and in some cases renamed) the chapters, moving "A Night in the Water" to a more appropriate spot following "Out on Picket," and had written another masterpiece in "The Baby of the Regiment," one of four chapters, along with a conclusion, added to the book. A more substantial introduction replaced the three paragraphs that had introduced the first installment of "Leaves" (now "Camp Diary"), while an appendix supplied the usual data pertinent to a regimental history.

If Higginson had been "rather tired of writing," by 1869, the country—according to *Atlantic* reviewer William Dean Howells —was tired of the Negro. Higginson dutifully clipped the Howells review and put it in a folder with other responses to *Army Life*, but surely he must have felt that Howells (who would himself become editor of the *Atlantic* in 1871 and publish his first novel a year later) had missed the point. "When I print a thing like the Driftwood Fire," Higginson had journalized at the beginning of 1867, "which seems to me to have a finer touch in it than anything I ever wrote—I feel as if it were thrown into the sea and as if nobody living cared for it."

> How can a man write who does not enjoy intensely the writing itself as I do? when I first read anything of mine in print, it is with perfect delight—then comes depression and the doubt whether anybody cares for such things and then I let it go, and get interested in something else.
>
> (*TWH: The Story of His Life*, 276)

In his November review, Howells preferred the mundane to the ideal, the "Camp Diary" chapter to "A Night in the Water"; he was struck by "The Baby of the Regiment," but reacted to the whole with what one might call bland enthusiasm—perhaps not an inapt summary of Howells in general—and hardly what Higginson might have felt was due after his years of contributions to the *Atlantic*.

Nevertheless, no other participant in the Civil War had written about it better than Higginson. As a sustained piece of writing, *Army Life in a Black Regiment* drew American Romanticism across the war years and into Reconstruction, into a time when John William De Forest was demythologizing the war in *Miss Ravenel's Conversion* (1867), considered the first novel of American realism. There really weren't any other players of this caliber until Mark Twain and Ambrose Bierce began to redefine the war in the former's "The Private History of a Campaign that Failed" and the latter's short writings late in the century. It may have been De Forest's novel that evoked an uncharacteristic but significant response from Higginson: "After reading a graphic military novel turned to my 'Army Life' and read it with surprise and interest; and with a sort of despair at the comparative emptiness of all other life after that."

Despite the trauma he felt while writing it, Higginson had managed to create in *Army Life* a powerful nostalgic view of the Sea Islands: both book and experience had now faded into a pleasant, if mythical, past. Undoubtedly this was at least partly so because, as Howard Mumford Jones has pointed out, the book Higginson actually wrote is hardly about a war at all. It is, preeminently, a book of Northern escapism, filled with the same indolence and wonder that drew Harriet Beecher Stowe (of all people) to live in the former slave state of Florida following the war. It is the same steamy incertitude that drew painters like Thomas Moran and Frederic Church into the swamps—into what David C. Miller has aptly named the "Elusive Eden." Miller's world is therapeutic, almost, one could say, a Sea Island version of Dr. Rogers's hydropathic cure back in Worcester:

> Letting himself go in this tumescent world, Higginson skirted mental disintegration. . . . Higginson's awareness of the way in which the unconscious dictates his relation to the unknown operates here to transmute into insight and aesthetic pleasure what would otherwise have been merely fear and revulsion.
>
> (*Dark Eden*, 54–55)

Miller's observation may, in fact, have more to do with Higginson's struggle while writing the book than his struggle while living through those scenes he is forced to describe; it is the voice of Epictetus that speaks to us of the difference between the thing itself and our reshaping of it.

Higginson was to live for a half century after his Sea Island days. He never afterward followed the plight of the Negro with as much enthusiasm as he had given to abolition, but his interest in women's rights increased. After the war, he met Helen Hunt (later Jackson) and encouraged her work, and he visited Emily Dickinson in 1870, despairing of ever convincing the shy poet to meet him in Boston. His wife Mary finally died in 1877. With new freedom and renewed health, he visited Harpers Ferry, the scene of John Brown's raid, and his old haunts on the Carolina coast. Less than two years after the death of his first wife, he married Mary Thacher, a niece of Longfellow twenty years younger than himself. A year after that the new Mary delivered Higginson's first child.

He continued to write prolifically and was (as history knows) instrumental in publishing Dickinson's poems after her death in 1886. Still, the loss he recorded in his diary was more personal than literary:

> To Amherst to the funeral of that rare and strange creature Emily
> Dickinson. . . . E.D.'s face a wondrous restoration of youth—she
> is 54 and looked 30, not a gray hair or wrinkle, and perfect peace
> on the beautiful brow. . . . How large a portion of the people who
> have most interested me have passed away.

Despite his fascination with Dickinson, the poem he read at her
funeral was by Emily Brontë.

Higginson became the official historian of Massachusetts in the
Civil War and reprinted *Army Life* as part of his collected works
at the turn of the century. He lived long enough to see Stephen
Crane (who wasn't even alive in 1865) become the great inter-
preter of the Civil War, and if he had any lingering taste for foreign literature (he was always urging Fields to pay more attention
to American books), he might have recognized in the imagery of
Joseph Conrad's *Heart of Darkness* the same riverine wonder he
had encountered thirty years before.

Higginson died on May 9, 1911, at the start of another century
of crusades.

—R. D. Madison

SUGGESTIONS FOR FURTHER READING

The literature of the American Civil War is immense: historical works are listed here only when they bear directly on Thomas Wentworth Higginson or the immediate context of *Army Life in a Black Regiment*.

Allen, William Francis, Charles Pickard Ware, and Lucy McKim Garrison. *Slave Songs of the United States*. 1867. Reprint. Bedford: Applewood Books, n.d.

Blight, David. *Frederick Douglass' Civil War: Keeping Faith in Jubilee*. Baton Rouge: Louisiana State University Press, 1989.

Denison, Frederic. *Shot and Shell: The Third Rhode Island Heavy Artillery Regiment in the Rebellion*. Providence: Third R.I.H. Art. Vet. Association, 1879.

Douglass, Frederick. *Life and Times of Frederick Douglass*. 1892. Reprint. New York: Bonanza Books, n.d.

Edelstein, Tilden G. *Strange Enthusiasm: A Life of Thomas Wentworth Higginson*. New Haven: Yale University Press, 1968.

[Forten, Charlotte]. "Life in the Sea Islands." *Atlantic Monthly* 13 (May and June 1864): 587–96, 666–76.

Grimke, Charlotte Forten. *The Journals of Charlotte Forten Grimke*. Edited by Brenda Stevenson. New York: Oxford University Press, 1988.

Hawks, Esther Hill. *A Woman Doctor's Civil War: Esther Hill Hawks' Diary*. Edited by Gerald Schwarz. Columbia: University of South Carolina Press, 1989.

Higginson, Mary Thatcher. *Letters and Journals of Thomas Wentworth Higginson, 1846–1906*. Boston: Houghton Mifflin Company, 1921.

———. *Thomas Wentworth Higginson: The Story of His Life*. Boston: Houghton Mifflin Company, 1914.

Higginson, Thomas Wentworth. *Army Life in a Black Regiment*. 1869. Edited by E. Franklin Frazier. Boston: Beacon Press, 1962.

———. *Army Life in a Black Regiment*. Edited by Howard

Mumford Jones. East Lansing: Michigan State University Press, 1960.

———. *Army Life in a Black Regiment*. Edited by Howard N. Meyer. New York: W. W. Norton & Company, 1984.

———. *Cheerful Yesterdays*. 1898. Reprint. New York: Arno Press and *The New York Times*, 1968.

———. *The Works of Epictetus*. Boston: Little, Brown, and Company, 1865.

Johnson, Thomas H. *Emily Dickinson: Selected Letters*. Cambridge: Belknap Press of Harvard University Press, 1986.

Meyer, Howard N. *Colonel of the Black Regiment: The Life of Thomas Wentworth Higginson*. New York: W. W. Norton & Company, 1967.

Miller, David C. *Dark Eden: The Swamp in Nineteenth-Century American Culture*. Cambridge: Cambridge University Press, 1989.

Stowe, Harriet Beecher. *A Key to Uncle Tom's Cabin*. London: Sampson Low, Son, & Co., 1853.

Villard, Oswald Garrison. *John Brown 1800–1859: A Biography Fifty Years After*. Boston: Houghton Mifflin Company, 1911.

Wells, Anna Mary. *Dear Preceptor: The Life and Times of Thomas Wentworth Higginson*. Boston: Houghton Mifflin Company, 1963.

Whittier, John Greenleaf. *The Letters of John Greenleaf Whittier*. Edited by John B. Pickard. Vol. 3. Cambridge: The Belknap Press of Harvard University Press, 1975.

Wilson, Edmund. *Patriotic Gore: Studies in the Literature of the American Civil War*. New York: Farrar, Straus and Giroux, 1962.

A NOTE ON THE TEXTS

The text for *Army Life in a Black Regiment* is the first edition, published in 1869 (with an 1870 imprint) by Fields, Osgood, & Co. of Boston, which rearranged and consolidated the *Atlantic Monthly* essays and added several previously unpublished chapters and an appendix.

The text for "A Visit to John Brown's Household in 1859" is reprinted from Higginson's collection *Contemporaries* (Boston: Houghton, Mifflin, 1900), 219–43.

The texts for the remaining four essays in this collection follow their original *Atlantic Monthly* appearance: "Nat Turner's Insurrection," *Atlantic Monthly* 8 (August 1861), 173–87; "Letter to a Young Contributor," *Atlantic Monthly* 9 (April 1862), 401–11; "Some War Scenes Revisited," *Atlantic Monthly* 42 (July 1878), 1–9; "Emily Dickinson's Letters," *Atlantic Monthly* 68 (October 1891), 444–56.

*ARMY LIFE IN
A BLACK REGIMENT* .

CHAPTER I
Introductory

These pages record some of the adventures of the First South Carolina Volunteers,—the first slave regiment mustered into the service of the United States during the late civil war. It was, indeed, the first colored regiment of any kind so mustered, except a portion of the troops raised by Major-General Butler at New Orleans. These scarcely belonged to the same class, however, being recruited from the free colored population of that city, a comparatively self-reliant and educated race. "The darkest of them," said General Butler, "were about the complexion of the late Mr. Webster."

The First South Carolina, on the other hand, contained scarcely a freeman, had not one mulatto in ten, and a far smaller proportion who could read or write when enlisted. The only contemporary regiment of a similar character was the "First Kansas Colored," which began recruiting a little earlier, though it was not mustered in—the usual basis of military seniority—till later.* These were the only colored regiments recruited during the year 1862. The Second South Carolina and the Fifty-Fourth Massachusetts followed early in 1863.

This is the way in which I came to the command of this regiment. One day in November, 1862, I was sitting at dinner with my lieutenants, John Goodell and Luther Bigelow, in the barracks of the Fifty-First Massachusetts, Colonel Sprague, when the following letter was put into my hands:—

BEAUFORT, S. C., November 5, 1862.

My DEAR SIR,—I am organizing the First Regiment of South Carolina Volunteers, with every prospect of success. Your name has been spoken of, in connection with the command of this regiment, by some friends in whose judgment I have confidence. I take great pleasure in offering you the position of Colonel in it,

*See Appendix B.

and hope that you may be induced to accept. I shall not fill the place until I hear from you, or sufficient time shall have passed for me to receive your reply. Should you accept, I enclose a pass for Port Royal, of which I trust you will feel disposed to avail yourself at once.

I am, with sincere regard, yours truly,

R. SAXTON,
Brig.-Genl., Mil. Gov.

Had an invitation reached me to take command of a regiment of Kalmuck Tartars,[1] it could hardly have been more unexpected. I had always looked for the arming of the blacks, and had always felt a wish to be associated with them; had read the scanty accounts of General Hunter's abortive regiment, and had heard rumors of General Saxton's renewed efforts. But the prevalent tone of public sentiment was still opposed to any such attempts; the government kept very shy of the experiment, and it did not seem possible that the time had come when it could be fairly tried.

For myself, I was at the head of a fine company of my own raising, and in a regiment to which I was already much attached. It did not seem desirable to exchange a certainty for an uncertainty; for who knew but General Saxton might yet be thwarted in his efforts by the pro-slavery influence that had still so much weight at head-quarters? It would be intolerable to go out to South Carolina, and find myself, after all, at the head of a mere plantation-guard or a day-school in uniform.

I therefore obtained from the War Department, through Governor Andrew, permission to go and report to General Saxton, without at once resigning my captaincy. Fortunately it took but a few days in South Carolina to make it clear that all was right, and the return steamer took back a resignation of a Massachusetts commission. Thenceforth my lot was cast altogether with the black troops, except when regiments or detachments of white soldiers were also under my command, during the two years following.

These details would not be worth mentioning except as they show this fact: that I did not seek the command of colored troops, but it sought me. And this fact again is only important to my story for this reason, that under these circumstances I naturally viewed the new recruits rather as subjects for discipline than for philanthropy. I had been expecting a war for six years, ever since the Kansas troubles,[2] and my mind had dwelt on military matters more or less during all that time. The best Massachusetts regiments already exhibited a high standard of drill and discipline, and unless these men could be brought tolerably near that standard, the fact of their extreme blackness would afford me, even as a philanthropist, no satisfaction. Fortunately, I felt perfect confidence that they could be so trained,—having happily known, by experience, the qualities of their race, and knowing also that they had home and household and freedom to fight for, besides that abstraction of "the Union." Trouble might perhaps be expected from white officials, though this turned out far less than might have been feared; but there was no trouble to come from the men, I thought, and none ever came. On the other hand, it was a vast experiment of indirect philanthropy, and one on which the result of the war and the destiny of the negro race might rest; and this was enough to tax all one's powers. I had been an abolitionist too long, and had known and loved John Brown[3] too well, not to feel a thrill of joy at last on finding myself in the position where he only wished to be.

In view of all this, it was clear that good discipline must come first; after that, of course, the men must be helped and elevated in all ways as much as possible.

Of discipline there was great need,—that is, of order and regular instruction. Some of the men had already been under fire, but they were very ignorant of drill and camp duty. The officers, being appointed from a dozen different States, and more than as many regiments,—infantry, cavalry, artillery, and engineers,—had all that diversity of methods which so confused our army in those early days. The first need, therefore, was of an unbroken interval of training. During this period, which fortunately lasted nearly two months, I rarely left the camp, and got occasional leisure moments for a fragmentary journal, to send home, recording the many odd or novel aspects of the new experience. Camp-life was a wonderfully strange sensation to almost all volunteer officers, and mine lay among eight hundred men suddenly transformed from slaves into soldiers, and representing a race affectionate, enthusiastic, grotesque, and dramatic beyond all others. Being such, they naturally gave material for description. There is nothing like a diary for freshness,—at least so I think,—and I shall keep to the diary through the days of camp-life, and throw the later experience into another form. Indeed, that matter takes care of itself; diaries and letter-writing stop when field-service begins.

I am under pretty heavy bonds to tell the truth, and only the truth; for those who look back to the newspaper correspondence of that period will see that this particular regiment lived for months in a glare of publicity, such as tests any regiment severely, and certainly prevents all subsequent romancing in its historian. As the scene of the only effort on the Atlantic coast to arm the negro, our camp attracted a continuous stream of visitors, military and civil. A battalion of black soldiers, a spectacle since so common, seemed then the most daring of innovations, and the whole demeanor of this particular regiment was watched with microscopic scrutiny by friends and foes. I felt sometimes as if we were a plant trying to take root, but constantly pulled up to see if we were growing. The slightest camp incidents sometimes came back to us, magnified and distorted, in letters of anxious inquiry from remote parts of the Union. It was no pleasant thing to live under such constant surveillance; but it guaranteed the honesty of any success, while fearfully multiplying the penalties had there been a failure. A single mutiny,—such as has happened in the infancy of a hundred regiments,—a single miniature Bull Run, a stampede of desertions, and it would have been all over with us; the party of distrust would have got the upper hand, and there might not have been, during the whole contest, another effort to arm the negro.

I may now proceed, without farther preparation, to the Diary.

CHAPTER II
Camp Diary

CAMP SAXTON, near Beaufort, S. C.,
November 24, 1862.

Yesterday afternoon we were steaming over a summer sea, the deck level as a parlor-floor, no land in sight, no sail, until at last appeared one light-house, said to be Cape Romaine, and then a line of trees and two distant vessels and nothing more. The sun set, a great illuminated bubble, submerged in one vast bank of rosy suffusion; it grew dark; after tea all were on deck, the people sang hymns; then the moon set, a moon two days old, a curved pencil of light, reclining backwards on a radiant couch which seemed to rise from the waves to receive it; it sank slowly, and the last tip wavered and went down like the mast of a vessel of the skies. Towards morning the boat stopped, and when I came on deck, before six,—

> "The watch-lights glittered on the land,
> The ship-lights on the sea."

Hilton Head lay on one side, the gunboats on the other; all that was raw and bare in the low buildings of the new settlement was softened into picturesqueness by the early light. Stars were still overhead, gulls wheeled and shrieked, and the broad river rippled duskily towards Beaufort.

The shores were low and wooded, like any New England shore; there were a few gunboats, twenty schooners, and some steamers, among them the famous "Planter," which Robert Small, the slave, presented to the nation. The river-banks were soft and graceful, though low, and as we steamed up to Beaufort on the flood-tide this morning, it seemed almost as fair as the smooth and lovely canals which Stedman[1] traversed to meet his negro soldiers in Surinam. The air was cool as at home, yet the foliage seemed green, glimpses of stiff tropical vegetation appeared along the banks, with great clumps of shrubs, whose pale seed-vessels

5

looked like tardy blossoms. Then we saw on a picturesque point an old plantation, with stately magnolia avenue, decaying house, and tiny church amid the woods, reminding me of Virginia; behind it stood a neat encampment of white tents, "and there," said my companion, "is your future regiment."

Three miles farther brought us to the pretty town of Beaufort, with its stately houses amid Southern foliage. Reporting to General Saxton, I had the luck to encounter a company of my destined command, marched in to be mustered into the United States service. They were unarmed, and all looked as thoroughly black as the most faithful philanthropist could desire; there did not seem to be so much as a mulatto among them. Their coloring suited me, all but the legs, which were clad in a lively scarlet, as intolerable to my eyes as if I had been a turkey. I saw them mustered; General Saxton talked to them a little, in his direct, manly way; they gave close attention, though their faces looked impenetrable. Then I conversed with some of them. The first to whom I spoke had been wounded in a small expedition after lumber, from which a party had just returned, and in which they had been under fire and had done very well. I said, pointing to his lame arm,—

"Did you think that was more than you bargained for, my man?"

His answer came promptly and stoutly,—

"I been a-tinking, Mas'r, *dat's jess what I went for.*"

I thought this did well enough for my very first interchange of dialogue with my recruits.

November 27, 1862.

Thanksgiving-Day; it is the first moment I have had for writing during these three days, which have installed me into a new mode of life so thoroughly that they seem three years. Scarcely pausing in New York or in Beaufort, there seems to have been for me but one step from the camp of a Massachusetts regiment to this, and that step over leagues of waves.

It is a holiday wherever General Saxton's proclamation reaches. The chilly sunshine and the pale blue river seem like New England, but those alone. The air is full of noisy drumming, and of gunshots; for the prize-shooting is our great celebration of the day, and the drumming is chronic. My young barbarians are all at play. I look out from the broken windows of this forlorn plantation-house, through avenues of great live-oaks, with their hard, shining leaves, and their branches hung with a universal drapery of soft, long moss, like fringe-trees struck with grayness. Below, the sandy soil, scantly covered with coarse grass, bristles with sharp palmettoes and aloes; all the vegetation is stiff, shining, semi-tropical, with nothing soft or delicate in its texture. Numerous plantation-buildings totter around, all slovenly and unattractive, while the interspaces are filled with all manner of wreck and refuse, pigs, fowls, dogs, and omnipresent Ethiopian infancy. All this is the universal Southern panorama; but five minutes' walk beyond the hovels and the live-oaks will bring one to something so un-Southern that the whole Southern coast at this moment trembles at the suggestion of such a thing,—the camp of a regiment of freed slaves.

One adapts one's self so readily to new surroundings that already the full zest of the novelty seems passing away from my perceptions, and I write these lines in an eager effort to retain all I can. Already I am growing used to the experience, at first so novel, of living among five hundred men, and scarce a white face to be seen,—of seeing them go through all their daily processes, eating, frolicking, talking, just as if they were white. Each day at dress-parade I stand with the customary folding of the arms before a regimental line of countenances so black that I can hardly tell whether the men stand steadily or not; black is every hand which moves in ready cadence as I vociferate, "Battalion! Shoulder arms!" nor is it till the line of white officers moves forward, as parade is dismissed, that I am reminded that my own face is not the color of coal.

The first few days on duty with a new regiment must be devoted almost wholly to tightening reins; in this process one deals chiefly with the officers, and I have as yet had but little personal intercourse with the men. They concern me chiefly in bulk, as so many consumers of rations, wearers of uniforms, bearers of muskets. But as the machine comes into shape, I am beginning to decipher the individual parts. At first, of course, they all looked just alike; the variety comes afterwards, and they are just as distinguishable, the officers say, as so many whites. Most of them are wholly raw, but there are many who have already been for months in camp in the abortive "Hunter Regiment," yet in that loose kind of way which, like average militia training, is a doubtful advantage. I notice that some companies, too, look darker than others, though all are purer African than I expected. This is said to be partly a geographical difference between the South Carolina and Florida men. When the Rebels evacuated this region they probably took with them the house-servants, including most of the mixed blood, so that the residuum seems very black. But the men brought from Fernandina the other day average lighter in complexion, and look more intelligent, and they certainly take wonderfully to the drill.

It needs but a few days to show the absurdity of distrusting the military availability of these people. They have quite as much average comprehension as whites of the need of the thing, as much courage (I doubt not), as much previous knowledge of the gun, and, above all, a readiness of ear and of imitation, which, for purposes of drill, counterbalances any defect of mental training. To learn the drill, one does not want a set of college professors; one wants a squad of eager, active, pliant school-boys; and the more childlike these pupils are the better. There is no trouble about the drill; they will surpass whites in that. As to camp-life, they have little to sacrifice; they are better fed, housed, and clothed than ever in their lives before, and they appear to have few inconvenient vices. They are simple, docile, and affectionate almost to the point of absurdity. The same men who stood fire in open field with perfect coolness, on the late expedition, have come to me blubbering in the most irresistibly ludicrous manner on being transferred from one company in the regiment to another.

In noticing the squad-drills I perceive that the men learn less laboriously than whites that "double, double, toil and trouble,"[2] which is the elementary vexation of the drill-master,—that they more rarely mistake their left for their right,—and are more grave and sedate while under instruction. The extremes of jollity and sobriety, being greater with them, are less liable to be intermingled; these companies can be driven with a looser rein than my former one, for they restrain themselves; but the moment they are dismissed from drill every tongue is relaxed and every ivory tooth visible. This morning I wandered about where the different companies were target-shooting, and their glee was contagious. Such exulting shouts of "Ki! ole man," when some steady old turkey-shooter brought his gun down for an instant's aim, and then unerringly hit the mark; and then, when some unwary youth fired his piece into the ground at half-cock, such infinite guffawing and delight, such rolling over and over on the grass, such dances of ecstasy, as made the "Ethiopian minstrelsy" of the stage appear a feeble imitation.

Evening.—Better still was a scene on which I stumbled to-night. Strolling in the cool moonlight, I was attracted by a brilliant light beneath the trees, and cautiously approached it. A circle of thirty or forty soldiers sat around a roaring fire, while one old uncle, Cato by name, was narrating an interminable tale, to the insatiable delight of his audience. I came up into the dusky background, perceived only by a few, and he still continued. It was a narrative, dramatized to the last degree, of his adventures in escaping from his master to the Union vessels; and even I, who have heard the stories of Harriet Tubman,[3] and such wonderful slave-comedians, never witnessed such a piece of acting. When I came upon the scene he had just come unexpectedly upon a plantation-house, and, putting a bold face upon it, had walked up to the door.

"Den I go up to de white man, berry humble, and say, would he please gib ole man a mouthful for eat?

"He say he must hab de valeration ob half a dollar.

"Den I look berry sorry, and turn for go away.

"Den he say I might gib him dat hatchet I had.

"Den I say" (this in a tragic vein) "dat I must hab dat hatchet for defend myself *from de dogs!*"

[Immense applause, and one appreciating auditor says, chuckling, "Dat was your *arms,* ole man," which brings down the house again.]

"Den he say de Yankee pickets was near by, and I must be very keerful.

"Den I say, 'Good Lord, Mas'r, am dey?' "

Words cannot express the complete dissimulation with which these accents of terror were uttered,—this being precisely the piece of information he wished to obtain.

Then he narrated his devices to get into the house at night and obtain some food,—how a dog flew at him,—how the whole household, black and white, rose in pursuit,—how he scrambled under a hedge and over a high fence, etc.,—all in a style of which Gough[4] alone among orators can give the faintest impression, so thoroughly dramatized was every syllable.

Then he described his reaching the river-side at last, and trying to decide whether certain vessels held friends or foes.

"Den I see guns on board, and sure sartin he Union boat, and I pop my head up. Den I been-a-tink [think] Seceshkey hab guns too, and my head go down again. Den I hide in de bush till morning. Den I open my bundle, and take ole white shirt and tie him on ole pole and wave him, and ebry time de wind blow, I been-a-tremble, and drap down in de bushes,"—because, being between two fires, he doubted whether friend or foe would see his signal first. And so on, with a succession of tricks beyond Molière,[5] of acts of caution, foresight, patient cunning, which were listened to with infinite gusto and perfect comprehension by every listener.

And all this to a bivouac of negro soldiers, with the brilliant fire lighting up their red trousers and gleaming from their shining black faces,—eyes and teeth all white with tumultuous glee. Overhead, the mighty limbs of a great live-oak, with the weird moss swaying in the smoke, and the high moon gleaming faintly through.

Yet to-morrow strangers will remark on the hopeless, impenetrable stupidity in the daylight faces of many of these very men, the solid mask under which Nature has concealed all this wealth of mother-wit. This very comedian is one to whom one might point, as he hoed lazily in a cotton-field, as a being the light of whose brain had utterly gone out; and this scene seems like coming by night upon some conclave of black beetles, and finding them engaged, with green-room and foot-lights, in enacting "Poor Pillicoddy." This is their university; every young Sambo before me, as he turned over the sweet potatoes and peanuts which were roasting in the ashes, listened with reverence to the wiles of the ancient Ulysses, and meditated the same. It is Nature's compensation; oppression simply crushes the upper faculties of the head, and crowds everything into the perceptive organs. Cato, thou reasonest well! When I get into any serious scrape, in an enemy's country, may I be lucky enough to have you at my elbow, to pull me out of it!

The men seem to have enjoyed the novel event of Thanksgiving-Day; they have had company and regimental prize-shootings, a minimum of speeches and a maximum of dinner. Bill of fare: two beef-cattle and a thousand oranges. The oranges cost a cent apiece, and the cattle were Secesh, bestowed by General Saxby, as they all call him.

December 1, 1862.

How absurd is the impression bequeathed by Slavery in regard to these Southern blacks, that they are sluggish and inefficient in labor! Last night, after a hard day's work (our guns and the remainder of our tents being just issued), an order came from Beaufort that we should be ready in the evening to unload a steamboat's cargo of boards, being some of those captured by them a few weeks since, and now assigned for their use. I wondered if the men would grumble at the night-work; but the steamboat arrived by seven, and it was bright moonlight when they went at it. Never have I beheld such a jolly scene of labor. Tugging these wet and heavy boards over a bridge of boats ashore, then across the slimy beach at low tide, then up a steep bank, and all in one great uproar of merriment for two hours. Running most of the time, chattering all the time, snatching the boards from each other's backs as if they were some coveted treasure, getting up eager rivalries between different companies, pouring great choruses of ridicule on the heads of all shirkers, they made the whole scene so enlivening that I gladly stayed out in the moonlight for the whole time to watch it. And all this without any urging or any promised reward, but simply as the most natural way of doing the thing. The steamboat captain declared that they unloaded the ten thousand feet of boards quicker than any white gang could have done it; and they felt it so little, that, when, later in the night, I reproached one whom I found sitting by a camp-fire, cooking a surreptitious opossum, telling him that he ought to be asleep after such a job of work, he answered, with the broadest grin,—

"O no, Cunnel, da's no work at all, Cunnel; dat only jess enough *for stretch we.*"

December 2, 1862.

I believe I have not yet enumerated the probable drawbacks to the success of this regiment, if any. We are exposed to no direct annoyance from the white regiments, being out of their way; and we have as yet no discomforts or privations which we do not share with them. I do not as yet see the slightest obstacle, in the nature of the blacks, to making them good soldiers, but rather the contrary. They take readily to drill, and do not object to discipline; they are not especially dull or inattentive; they seem fully to understand the importance of the contest, and of their share in it. They show no jealousy or suspicion towards their officers.

They do show these feelings, however, towards the Government itself; and no one can wonder. Here lies the drawback to rapid recruiting. Were this a wholly new regiment, it would have been full to overflowing, I am satisfied, ere now. The trouble is in the legacy of bitter distrust bequeathed by the abortive regiment of General Hunter,—into which they were driven like cattle, kept for several months in camp, and then turned off without a shilling, by order of the War Department. The formation of that regiment was, on the whole, a great injury to this one; and the men who came from it, though the best soldiers we have in other respects, are the least sanguine and cheerful; while those who now refuse to enlist have a great influence in deterring others. Our soldiers are constantly twitted by their families and friends with their prospect of risking their lives in the service, and being paid nothing; and it is in vain that we read them the instructions of the Secretary of War to General Saxton, promising them the full pay of soldiers. They only half believe it.*

Another drawback is that some of the white soldiers delight in frightening the women on the plantations with doleful tales of plans for putting us in the front rank in all battles, and such silly talk,—the object being, perhaps, to prevent our being employed on active service at all. All these considerations they feel precisely as white men would,—no less, no more; and it is the comparative

*With what utter humiliation were we, their officers, obliged to confess to them, eighteen months afterwards, that it was their distrust which was wise, and our faith in the pledges of the United States Government which was foolishness!

freedom from such unfavorable influences which makes the Florida men seem more bold and manly, as they undoubtedly do. To-day General Saxton has returned from Fernandina with seventy-six recruits, and the eagerness of the captains to secure them was a sight to see. Yet they cannot deny that some of the very best men in the regiment are South Carolinians.

December 3, 1862.—7 P.M.

What a life is this I lead! It is a dark, mild, drizzling evening, and as the foggy air breeds sand-flies, so it calls out melodies and strange antics from this mysterious race of grown-up children with whom my lot is cast. All over the camp the lights glimmer in the tents, and as I sit at my desk in the open doorway, there come mingled sounds of stir and glee. Boys laugh and shout,—a feeble flute stirs somewhere in some tent, not an officer's,—a drum throbs far away in another,—wild kildeer-plover flit and wail above us, like the haunting souls of dead slave-masters,—and from a neighboring cook-fire comes the monotonous sound of that strange festival, half pow-wow, half prayer-meeting, which they know only as a "shout." These fires are usually enclosed in a little booth, made neatly of palm-leaves and covered in at top, a regular native African hut, in short, such as is pictured in books, and such as I once got up from dried palm-leaves for a fair at home. This hut is now crammed with men, singing at the top of their voices, in one of their quaint, monotonous, endless, negro-Methodist chants, with obscure syllables recurring constantly, and slight variations interwoven, all accompanied with a regular drumming of the feet and clapping of the hands, like castanets. Then the excitement spreads: inside and outside the enclosure men begin to quiver and dance, others join, a circle forms, winding monotonously round some one in the centre; some "heel and toe" tumultuously, others merely tremble and stagger on, others stoop and rise, others whirl, others caper sideways, all keep steadily circling like dervishes; spectators applaud special strokes of skill; my approach only enlivens the scene; the circle enlarges, louder grows the singing, rousing shouts of encouragement come in, half bacchanalian, half devout, "Wake 'em, brudder!" "Stan' up to 'em, brudder!"—and still the ceaseless drumming and clapping, in perfect cadence, goes steadily on. Suddenly there comes a sort of *snap,* and the spell breaks, amid general sighing and laughter. And this not rarely and occasionally, but night after night, while in other parts of the camp the soberest prayers and exhortations are proceeding sedately.

A simple and lovable people, whose graces seem to come by nature, and whose vices by training. Some of the best superintendents confirm the first tales of innocence, and Dr. Zachos[6] told me last night that on his plantation, a sequestered one, "they had absolutely no vices." Nor have these men of mine yet shown any worth mentioning; since I took command I have heard of no man intoxicated, and there has been but one small quarrel. I suppose that scarcely a white regiment in the army shows so little swearing. Take the "Progressive Friends" and put them in red trousers, and I verily believe they would fill a guard-house sooner than these men. If camp regulations are violated, it seems to be usually through heedlessness. They love passionately three things besides their spiritual incantations; namely, sugar, home, and tobacco. This last affection brings tears to their eyes, almost, when they speak of their urgent need of pay; they speak of their last-remembered quid as if it were some deceased relative, too early lost, and to be mourned forever. As for sugar, no white man can drink coffee after they have sweetened it to their liking.

I see that the pride which military life creates may cause the plantation trickeries to diminish. For instance, these men make the most admirable sentinels. It is far harder to pass the camp lines at night than in the camp from which I came; and I have seen none of that disposition to connive at the offences of members of one's own company which is so troublesome among white soldiers. Nor are they lazy, either about work or drill; in all respects they seem better material for soldiers than I had dared to hope.

There is one company in particular, all Florida men, which I certainly think the finest-looking company I ever saw, white or black; they range admirably in size, have remarkable erectness and ease of carriage, and really march splendidly. Not a visitor but notices them; yet they have been under drill only a fortnight, and a part only two days. They have all been slaves, and very few are even mulattoes.

December 4, 1862.

"Dwelling in tents, with Abraham, Isaac, and Jacob."[7] This condition is certainly mine,—and with a multitude of patriarchs beside, not to mention Cæsar and Pompey, Hercules and Bacchus.

A moving life, tented at night, this experience has been mine in civil society, if society be civil before the luxurious forest fires of Maine and the Adirondack, or upon the lonely prairies of Kansas. But a stationary tent life, deliberately going to housekeeping under canvas, I have never had before, though in our barrack life at "Camp Wool" I often wished for it.

The accommodations here are about as liberal as my quarters there, two wall-tents being placed end to end, for office and bedroom, and separated at will by a "fly" of canvas. There is a good board floor and mop-board, effectually excluding dampness and draughts, and everything but sand, which on windy days penetrates everywhere. The office furniture consists of a good desk or secretary, a very clumsy and disastrous settee, and a remarkable chair. The desk is a bequest of the slave-holders, and the settee of the slaves, being ecclesiastical in its origin, and appertaining to the little old church or "praise-house," now used for commissary purposes. The chair is a composite structure: I found a cane seat on a dust-heap, which a black sergeant combined with two legs from a broken bedstead and two more from an oak-bough. I sit on it with a pride of conscious invention, mitigated by profound insecurity. Bedroom furniture, a couch made of gun-boxes covered with condemned blankets, another settee, two pails, a tin cup, tin basin (we prize any tin or wooden ware as savages prize iron), and a valise, regulation size. Seriously considered, nothing more appears needful, unless ambition might crave another chair for company, and, perhaps, something for a wash-stand higher than a settee.

To-day it rains hard, and the wind quivers through the closed canvas, and makes one feel at sea. All the talk of the camp outside is fused into a cheerful and indistinguishable murmur, pierced through at every moment by the wail of the hovering plover. Sometimes a face, black or white, peers through the entrance with some message. Since the light readily penetrates, though the rain cannot, the tent conveys a feeling of charmed security, as if an invisible boundary checked the pattering drops and held the moaning wind. The front tent I share, as yet, with my adjutant; in the inner apartment I reign supreme, bounded in a nutshell, with no bad dreams.

In all pleasant weather the outer "fly" is open, and men pass and repass, a chattering throng. I think of Emerson's Saadi, "As thou sittest at thy door, on the desert's yellow floor,"—for these bare sand-plains, gray above, are always yellow when upturned, and there seems a tinge of Orientalism in all our life.

Thrice a day we go to the plantation-houses for our meals, camp-arrangements being yet very imperfect. The officers board in different messes, the adjutant and I still clinging to the household of William Washington,—William the quiet and the courteous, the pattern of house-servants, William the noiseless, the observing, the discriminating, who knows everything that can be got, and how to cook it. William and his tidy, lady-like little spouse Hetty—a pair of wedded lovers, if ever I saw one—set our table in their one room, half-way between an unglazed window and a large wood-fire, such as is often welcome. Thanks to the adjutant, we are provided with the social magnificence of napkins; while (lest pride take too high a flight) our table-cloth consists of two "New York Tribunes" and a "Leslie's Pictorial." Every steamer brings us a clean table-cloth. Here are we forever supplied with pork and oysters and sweet potatoes and rice and hominy and corn-bread and milk; also mysterious griddle-cakes of corn and pumpkin; also preserves made of pumpkin-chips, and other fanciful productions of Ethiop art. Mr. E. promised the plantation-superintendents who should come down here "all the luxuries of home," and we certainly have much apparent, if little real variety. Once William produced with some palpitation something fricasseed, which he boldly termed chicken; it was very small, and seemed in some undeveloped condition of ante-natal toughness. After the meal he frankly avowed it for a squirrel.

December 5, 1862.

Give these people their tongues, their feet, and their leisure, and they are happy. At every twilight the air is full of singing, talking, and clapping of hands in unison. One of their favorite songs is full of plaintive cadences; it is not, I think, a Methodist tune, and I wonder where they obtained a chant of such beauty.

> "I can't stay behind, my Lord, I can't stay behind!
>   O, my father is gone, my father is gone,
>   My father is gone into heaven, my Lord!
>   I can't stay behind!
> Dere's room enough, room enough,
> Room enough in de heaven for de sojer:
>   Can't stay behind!"

It always excites them to have us looking on, yet they sing these songs at all times and seasons. I have heard this very song dimly droning on near midnight, and, tracing it into the recesses of a cook-house, have found an old fellow coiled away among the pots and provisions, chanting away with his "Can't stay behind, sinner," till I made him leave his song behind.

This evening, after working themselves up to the highest pitch, a party suddenly rushed off, got a barrel, and mounted some man upon it, who said, "Gib anoder song, boys, and I'se gib you a speech." After some hesitation and sundry shouts of "Rise de sing, somebody," and "Stan' up for Jesus, brudder," irreverently put in by the juveniles, they got upon the John Brown song, always a favorite, adding a jubilant verse which I had never before heard,—"We'll beat Beauregard on de clare battlefield." Then came the promised speech, and then no less than seven other speeches by as many men, on a variety of barrels, each orator being affectionately tugged to the pedestal and set on end by his special constituency. Every speech was good, without exception; with the queerest oddities of phrase and pronunciation, there was an invariable enthusiasm, a pungency of statement, and an understanding of the points at issue, which made them all rather thrilling. Those long-winded slaves in "Among the Pines"[8] seemed rather fictitious and literary in comparison. The most eloquent, perhaps, was Corporal Prince Lambkin, just arrived from Fernandina, who evidently had a previous reputation among them. His historical references were very interesting. He reminded them that he had predicted this war ever since Fremont's time,[9] to which some of the crowd assented; he gave a very intelligent account of that Presidential campaign, and then described most impressively the secret anxiety of the slaves in Florida to know all about President Lincoln's election, and told how they all refused to work on the fourth of March, expecting their freedom to date from that day. He finally brought out one of the few really impressive appeals for the American flag that I have ever heard. "Our mas'rs dey hab lib under de flag, dey got dere wealth under it, and ebryting beautiful for dere chilen. Under it dey hab grind us up, and put us in dere pocket for money. But de fus' minute dey tink dat ole flag mean freedom for we colored people, dey pull it right down, and run up de rag ob dere own." (Immense applause). "But we'll neber desert de ole flag, boys, neber; we hab lib under it for *eighteen hundred sixty-two years,* and we'll die for it now." With which overpowering discharge of chronology-at-long-range, this most effective of stump-speeches closed. I see already with relief that there will be small demand in this regiment for harangues from the officers; give the men an empty barrel for a stump, and they will do their own exhortation.

December 11, 1862.

Haroun Alraschid,[10] wandering in disguise through his imperial streets, scarcely happened upon a greater variety of groups than I, in my evening strolls among our own camp-fires.

Beside some of these fires the men are cleaning their guns or rehearsing thei.. .... .. others, smoking in silence their very ... tobacco,—beside others, telling sto- ...ter over the broadest mimicry, in ...ich the officers come in for a full ..." is always within hearing, with its ...d its castanet-like clapping of the ...prayer-meetings, with pious invo- ...oned out" from memory by the ... sort of wailing chant. Elsewhere, ...*versazioni* around fires, with a woman for queen of the circle,—her Nubian face, gay headdress, gilt necklace, and white teeth, all resplendent in the glowing light. Sometimes the woman is spelling slow monosyllables out of a primer, a feat which always commands all ears,—they rightly recognizing a mighty spell, equal to the overthrowing of monarchs, in the magic assonance of *cat, hat, pat, bat,* and the rest of it. Elsewhere, it is some solitary old cook, some aged Uncle Tiff, with enormous spectacles, who is perusing a hymn-book by the light of a pine splinter, in his deserted cooking booth of palmetto leaves. By another fire there is an actual dance, red-legged soldiers doing right-and-left, and "now-lead-de-lady-ober," to the music of a violin which is rather artistically played, and which may have guided the steps, in other days, of Barnwells and Hugers. And yonder is a stump-orator perched on his barrel, pouring out his exhortations to fidelity in war and in religion. To-night for the first time I have heard an harangue in a different strain, quite saucy, sceptical, and defiant, appealing to them in a sort of French materialistic style, and claiming some personal experience of warfare. "You don't know notin' about it, boys. You tink you's brave enough; how you tink, if you stan' clar in de open field,—here you, and dar de Secesh? You's got to hab de right ting inside o' you. You must hab it 'served [preserved] in you, like dese yer sour plums dey 'serve in de barr'l; you's got to harden it down inside o' you, or it's notin'." Then he hit hard at the religionists: "When a man's got de sperit ob de Lord in him, it weakens him all out, can't hoe de corn." He had a great deal of broad sense in his speech; but presently some others began praying vociferously close by, as if to drown this free-thinker, when at last he exclaimed, "I mean to fight de war through, an' die a good sojer wid de last kick,—dat's *my* prayer!" and suddenly jumped off the barrel. I was quite interested at discovering this reverse side of the temperament, the devotional side preponderates so enormously, and the greatest scamps kneel and groan in their prayer-meetings with such entire zest. It shows that there is some individuality developed among them, and that they will not become too exclusively pietistic.

Their love of the spelling-book is perfectly inexhaustible,—they stumbling on by themselves, or the blind leading the blind, with the same pathetic patience which they carry into everything. The chaplain is getting up a schoolhouse, where he will soon teach them as regularly as he can. But the alphabet must always be a very incidental business in a camp.

December 14.

Passages from prayers in the camp:—

"Let me so lib dat when I die I shall *hab manners,* dat I shall know what to say when I see my Heabenly Lord."

"Let me lib wid de musket in one hand an' de Bible in de

oder,—dat if I die at de muzzle ob de musket, die in de water, die on de land, I may know I hab de bressed Jesus in my hand, an' hab no fear."

"I hab lef' my wife in de land o' bondage; my little ones dey say eb'ry night, Whar is my fader? But when I die, when de bressed mornin' rises, when I shall stan' in de glory, wid one foot on de water an' one foot on de land, den, O Lord, I shall see my wife an' my little chil'en once more."

These sentences I noted down, as best I could, beside the glimmering camp-fire last night. The same person was the hero of a singular little *contre-temps* at a funeral in the afternoon. It was our first funeral. The man had died in hospital, and we had chosen a picturesque burial-place above the river, near the old church, and beside a little nameless cemetery, used by generations of slaves. It was a regular military funeral, the coffin being draped with the American flag, the escort marching behind, and three volleys fired over the grave. During the services there was singing, the chaplain deaconing out the hymn in their favorite way. This ended, he announced his text,—"This poor man cried, and the Lord heard him, and delivered him out of all his trouble." Instantly, to my great amazement, the cracked voice of the chorister was uplifted, intoning the text, as if it were the first verse of another hymn. So calmly was it done, so imperturbable were all the black countenances, that I half began to conjecture that the chaplain himself intended it for a hymn, though I could imagine no prospective rhyme for *trouble* unless it were approximated by *debbil*,—which is, indeed, a favorite reference, both with the men and with his Reverence. But the chaplain, peacefully awaiting, gently repeated his text after the chant, and to my great relief the old chorister waived all further recitative, and let the funeral discourse proceed.

Their memories are a vast bewildered chaos of Jewish history and biography; and most of the great events of the past, down to the period of the American Revolution, they instinctively attribute to Moses. There is a fine bold confidence in all their citations, however, and the record never loses piquancy in their hands, though strict accuracy may suffer. Thus, one of my captains, last Sunday, heard a colored exhorter at Beaufort proclaim, "Paul may plant, *and may polish wid water,* but it won't do," in which the sainted Apollos would hardly have recognized himself.

Just now one of the soldiers came to me to say that he was about to be married to a girl in Beaufort, and would I lend him a dollar and seventy-five cents to buy the wedding outfit? It seemed as if matrimony on such moderate terms ought to be encouraged in these days; and so I responded to the appeal.

December 16.

To-day a young recruit appeared here, who had been the slave of Colonel Sammis, one of the leading Florida refugees. Two white companions came with him, who also appeared to be retainers of the Colonel, and I asked them to dine. Being likewise refugees, they had stories to tell, and were quite agreeable: one was English born, the other Floridian, a dark, sallow Southerner, very well bred. After they had gone, the Colonel himself appeared, I told him that I had been entertaining his white friends, and after a while he quietly let out the remark,—

"Yes, one of those white friends of whom you speak is a boy raised on one of my plantations; he has travelled with me to the North, and passed for white, and he always keeps away from the negroes."

Certainly no such suspicion had ever crossed my mind.

I have noticed one man in the regiment who would easily pass for white,—a little sickly drummer, aged fifty at least, with brown eyes and reddish hair, who is said to be the son of one of our commodores. I have seen perhaps a dozen persons as fair, or fairer, among fugitive slaves, but they were usually young children. It touched me far more to see this man, who had spent more than half a lifetime in this low estate, and for whom it now seemed too late to be anything but a "nigger." This offensive word, by the way, is almost as common with them as at the North, and far more common than with well-bred slaveholders. They have meekly accepted it. "Want to go out to de nigger houses, Sah," is the universal impulse of sociability, when they wish to cross the lines. "He hab twenty house-servants, an' two hundred head o' nigger," is a still more degrading form of phrase, in which the epithet is limited to the field-hands, and they estimated like so many cattle. This want of self-respect of course interferes with the authority of the non-commissioned officers, which is always difficult to sustain, even in white regiments. "He need n't try to play de white man ober me," was the protest of a soldier against his corporal the other day. To counteract this I have often to remind them that they do not obey their officers because they are white, but because they are their officers; and guard duty is an admirable school for this, because they readily understand that the sergeant or corporal of the guard has for the time more authority than any commissioned officer who is not on duty. It is necessary also for their superiors to treat the non-commissioned officers with careful courtesy, and I often caution the line officers never to call them "Sam" or "Will," nor omit the proper handle to their names. The value of the habitual courtesies of the regular army is exceedingly apparent with these men: an officer of polished manners can wind them round his finger, while white soldiers seem rather to prefer a certain roughness. The demeanor of my men to each other is very courteous, and yet I see none of that sort of upstart conceit which is sometimes offensive among free negroes at the North, the dandy-barber strut. This is an agreeable surprise, for I feared that freedom and regimentals would produce precisely that.

They seem the world's perpetual children, docile, gay, and lovable, in the midst of this war for freedom on which they have intelligently entered. Last night, before "taps," there was the greatest noise in camp that I had ever heard, and I feared some riot. On going out, I found the most tumultuous sham-fight proceeding in total darkness, two companies playing like boys, beating tin cups for drums. When some of them saw me they seemed a little dismayed, and came and said, beseechingly,—"Cunnel, Sah, you hab no objection to we playin', Sah?"—which objection I disclaimed; but soon they all subsided, rather to my regret, and scattered merrily. Afterward I found that some other officer had told them that I considered the affair too noisy, so that I felt a mild self-reproach when one said, "Cunnel, wish you had let we play a little longer, Sah." Still I was not sorry, on the whole; for these sham-fights between companies would in some regiments lead to real ones, and there is a latent jealousy here between the Florida and South Carolina men, which sometimes makes me anxious.

The officers are more kind and patient with the men than I should expect, since the former are mostly young, and drilling tries the temper; but they are aided by hearty satisfaction in the results already attained. I have never yet heard a doubt expressed among the officers as to the *superiority* of these men to white troops in aptitude for drill and discipline, because of their imitativeness and docility, and the pride they take in the service. One captain said to me to-day, "I have this afternoon taught my men to load-in-nine-times, and they do it better than we did it in my former company in three months." I can personally testify that one of our best lieutenants, an Englishman, taught a part of his company the essential movements of the "school for skirmishers" in a single lesson of two hours, so that they did them very passably, though I feel bound to discourage such haste. However, I "formed square" on the third battalion drill. Three fourths of drill consist of attention, imitation, and a good ear for time; in the other fourth, which consists of the application of principles, as, for instance, performing by the left flank some movement before learned by the right, they are perhaps slower than better educated men. Having belonged to five different drill-clubs before entering the army, I certainly ought to know something of the resources of human awkwardness, and I can honestly say that they astonish me by the facility with which they do things. I expected much harder work in this respect.

The habit of carrying burdens on the head gives them erectness of figure, even where physically disabled. I have seen a woman, with a brimming water-pail balanced on her head, or perhaps a cup, saucer, and spoon, stop suddenly, turn round, stoop to pick up a missile, rise again, fling it, light a pipe, and go through many evolutions with either hand or both, without spilling a drop. The pipe, by the way, gives an odd look to a well-dressed young girl on Sunday, but one often sees that spectacle. The passion for tobacco among our men continues quite absorbing, and I have piteous appeals for some arrangement by which they can buy it on credit, as we have yet no sutler. Their imploring, "Cunnel, we can't *lib* widout it, Sah," goes to my heart; and as they cannot read, I cannot even have the melancholy satisfaction of supplying them with the excellent anti-tobacco tracts of Mr. Trask.

December 19.

Last night the water froze in the adjutant's tent, but not in mine. To-day has been mild and beautiful. The blacks say they do not feel the cold so much as the white officers do, and perhaps it is so, though their health evidently suffers more from dampness. On the other hand, while drilling on very warm days, they have seemed to suffer more from the heat than their officers. But they dearly love fire, and at night will always have it, if possible, even on the minutest scale,—a mere handful of splinters, that seems hardly more efficacious than a friction-match. Probably this is a natural habit for the short-lived coolness of an out-door country; and then there is something delightful in this rich pine, which burns like a tar-barrel. It was, perhaps, encouraged by the masters, as the only cheap luxury the slaves had at hand.

As one grows more acquainted with the men, their individualities emerge; and I find, first their faces, then their characters, to be as distinct as those of whites. It is very interesting the desire they show to do their duty, and to improve as soldiers; they evidently think about it, and see the importance of the thing; they say to me that we white men cannot stay and be their leaders always and that they must learn to depend on themselves, or else relapse into their former condition.

Beside the superb branch of uneatable bitter oranges which decks my tent-pole, I have to-day hung up a long bough of finger-sponge, which floated to the river-bank. As winter advances, butterflies gradually disappear: one species (a *Vanessa*) lingers; three others have vanished since I came. Mocking-birds are abundant, but rarely sing; once or twice they have reminded me of the red thrush, but are inferior, as I have always thought. The colored people all say that it will be much cooler; but my officers do not think so, perhaps because last winter was so unusually mild,—with only one frost, they say.

December 20.

Philoprogenitiveness is an important organ for an officer of colored troops; and I happen to be well provided with it. It seems to be the theory of all military usages, in fact, that soldiers are to be treated like children; and these singular persons, who never know their own age till they are past middle life, and then choose a birthday with such precision,—"Fifty year old, Sah, de fus' last April,"—prolong the privilege of childhood.

I am perplexed nightly for countersigns,—their range of proper names is so distressingly limited, and they make such amazing work of every new one. At first, to be sure, they did not quite recognize the need of any variation: one night some officer asked a sentinel whether he had the countersign yet, and was indignantly answered, "Should tink I hab 'em, hab 'em for a fortnight"; which seems a long epoch for that magic word to hold out. To-night I thought I would have "Fredericksburg," in honor of Burnside's reported victory, using the rumor quickly, for fear of a contradiction. Later, in comes a captain, gets the countersign for his own use, but presently returns, the sentinel having pronounced it incorrect. On inquiry, it appears that the sergeant of the guard, being weak in geography, thought best to substitute the more familiar word, "Crockery-ware"; which was, with perfect gravity, confided to all the sentinels, and accepted without question. O life! what is the fun of fiction beside thee?

I should think they would suffer and complain these cold nights; but they say nothing, though there is a good deal of coughing. I should fancy that the scarlet trousers must do something to keep them warm, and wonder that they dislike them so much, when they are so much like their beloved fires. They certainly multiply firelight in any case. I often notice that an infinitesimal flame, with one soldier standing by it, looks like quite a respectable conflagration, and it seems as if a group of them must dispel dampness.

December 21.

To a regimental commander no book can be so fascinating as the consolidated Morning Report, which is ready about nine, and tells how many in each company are sick, absent, on duty, and so on. It is one's newspaper and daily mail; I never grow tired of it. If a single recruit has come in, I am always eager to see how he looks on paper.

To-night the officers are rather depressed by rumors of Burnside's being defeated, after all. I am fortunately equable and undepressible; and it is very convenient that the men know too little of the events of the war to feel excitement or fear. They know

General Saxton and me,—"de General" and "de Cunnel,"—and seem to ask no further questions. We are the war. It saves a great deal of trouble, while it lasts, this childlike confidence; nevertheless, it is our business to educate them to manhood, and I see as yet no obstacle. As for the rumor, the world will no doubt roll round, whether Burnside is defeated or succeeds.

Christmas Day.

"We'll fight for liberty
Till de Lord shall call us home;
We'll soon be free
Till de Lord shall call us home."

This is the hymn which the slaves at Georgetown, South Carolina, were whipped for singing when President Lincoln was elected. So said a little drummer-boy, as he sat at my tent's edge last night and told me his story; and he showed all his white teeth as he added, "Dey tink 'de Lord' meant for say de Yankees."

Last night, at dress-parade, the adjutant read General Saxton's Proclamation for the New Year's Celebration. I think they understood it, for there was cheering in all the company-streets afterwards. Christmas is the great festival of the year for this people; but, with New Year's coming after, we could have no adequate programme for to-day, and so celebrated Christmas Eve with pattern simplicity. We omitted, namely, the mystic curfew which we call "taps," and let them sit up and burn their fires, and have their little prayer-meetings as late as they desired; and all night, as I waked at intervals, I could hear them praying and "shouting" and clattering with hands and heels. It seemed to make them very happy, and appeared to be at least an innocent Christmas dissipation, as compared with some of the convivialities of the "superior race" hereabouts.

December 26.

The day passed with no greater excitement for the men than target-shooting, which they enjoyed. I had the private delight of the arrival of our much-desired surgeon and his nephew, the captain, with letters and news from home. They also bring the good tidings that General Saxton is not to be removed, as had been reported.

Two different stands of colors have arrived for us, and will be presented at New Year's,—one from friends in New York, and the other from a lady in Connecticut. I see that "Frank Leslie's Illustrated Weekly" of December 20th has a highly imaginative picture of the muster-in of our first company, and also of a skirmish on the late expedition.

I must not forget the prayer overheard last night by one of the captains: "O Lord! when I tink ob dis Kismas and las' year de Kismas. Las' Kismas he in de Secesh, and notin' to eat but grits, and no salt in 'em. Dis year in de camp, and too much victual!" This "too much" is a favorite phrase out of their grateful hearts, and did not in this case denote an excess of dinner,—as might be supposed,—but of thanksgiving.

December 29.

Our new surgeon has begun his work most efficiently: he and the chaplain have converted an old gin-house into a comfortable hospital, with ten nice beds and straw pallets. He is now, with a hearty professional faith, looking round for somebody to put into it. I am afraid the regiment will accommodate him; for, although he declares that these men do not sham sickness, as he expected, their catarrh is an unpleasant reality. They feel the dampness very much, and make such a coughing at dress-parade, that I have urged him to administer a dose of cough-mixture, all round, just before that pageant. Are the colored race *tough?* is my present anxiety; and it is odd that physical insufficiency, the only discouragement not thrown in our way by the newspapers, is the only discouragement which finds any place in our minds. They are used to sleeping indoors in winter, herded before fires, and so they feel the change. Still, the regiment is as healthy as the average, and experience will teach us something.*

---

*A second winter's experience removed all this solicitude, for they learned to take care of themselves. During the first February the sick-list averaged about ninety, during the second about thirty,—this being the worst month in the year for blacks.

December 30.

On the first of January we are to have a slight collation, ten oxen or so, barbecued,—or not properly barbecued, but roasted whole. Touching the length of time required to "do" an ox, no two housekeepers appear to agree. Accounts vary from two hours to twenty-four. We shall happily have enough to try all gradations of roasting, and suit all tastes, from Miss A.'s to mine. But fancy me proffering a spare-rib, well done, to some fair lady! What ever are we to do for spoons and forks and plates? Each soldier has his own, and is sternly held responsible for it by "Army Regulations." But how provide for the multitude? Is it customary, I ask you, to help to tenderloin with one's fingers? Fortunately, the Major is to see to that department. Great are the advantages of military discipline: for anything perplexing, detail a subordinate.

New Year's Eve.

My housekeeping at home is not, perhaps, on any very extravagant scale. Buying beefsteak, I usually go to the extent of two or three pounds. Yet when, this morning at daybreak, the quartermaster called to inquire how many cattle I would have killed for roasting, I turned over in bed, and answered composedly, "Ten, —and keep three to be fatted."

Fatted, quotha! Not one of the beasts at present appears to possess an ounce of superfluous flesh. Never were seen such lean kine. As they swing on vast spits, composed of young trees, the firelight glimmers through their ribs, as if they were great lanterns. But no matter, they are cooking,—nay, they are cooked.

One at least is taken off to cool, and will be replaced tomorrow to warm up. It was roasted three hours, and well done, for I tasted it. It is so long since I tasted fresh beef that forgetfulness is possible; but I fancied this to be successful. I tried to imagine that I liked the Homeric repast, and certainly the whole thing has been far more agreeable than was to be expected. The doubt now is, whether I have made a sufficient provision for my household. I should have roughly guessed that ten beeves would feed as many million people, it has such a stupendous sound; but General Saxton predicts a small social party of five thousand, and we fear that meat will run short, unless they prefer bone. One of the cattle is so small, we are hoping it may turn out veal.

For drink we aim at the simple luxury of molasses-and-water, a barrel per company, ten in all. Liberal housekeepers may like to know that for a barrel of water we allow three gallons of molasses, half a pound of ginger, and a quart of vinegar,—this last being a new ingredient for my untutored palate, though all the rest are amazed at my ignorance. Hard bread, with more molasses, and a dessert of tobacco, complete the festive repast, destined to cheer, but not inebriate.

On this last point, of inebriation, this is certainly a wonderful camp. For us it is absolutely omitted from the list of vices. I have never heard of a glass of liquor in the camp, nor of any effort either to bring it in or to keep it out. A total absence of the circulating medium might explain the abstinence,—not that it seems to have that effect with white soldiers,—but it would not explain the silence. The craving for tobacco is constant, and not to be allayed, like that of a mother for her children; but I have never heard whiskey even wished for, save on Christmas-Day, and then only by one man, and he spoke with a hopeless ideal sighing, as one alludes to the Golden Age. I am amazed at this total omission of the most inconvenient of all camp appetites. It certainly is not the result of exhortation, for there has been no occasion for any, and even the pledge would scarcely seem efficacious where hardly anybody can write.

I do not think there is a great visible eagerness for tomorrow's festival: it is not their way to be very jubilant over anything this side of the New Jerusalem. They know also that those in this Department are nominally free already, and that the practical freedom has to be maintained, in any event, by military success. But they will enjoy it greatly, and we shall have a multitude of people.

January 1, 1863 (evening).

A happy New Year to civilized people,—mere white folks. Our festival has come and gone, with perfect success, and our good General has been altogether satisfied. Last night the great fires were kept smouldering in the pit, and the beeves were cooked more or less, chiefly more,—during which time they had to be carefully watched, and the great spits turned by main force. Happy were the merry fellows who were permitted to sit up all night, and watch the glimmering flames that threw a thousand fantastic shadows among the great gnarled oaks. And such a chattering as I was sure to hear whenever I awoke that night!

My first greeting to-day was from one of the most stylish sergeants, who approached me with the following little speech, evidently the result of some elaboration:—

"I tink myself happy, dis New Year's Day, for salute my own Cunnel. Dis day las' year I was servant to a Cunnel ob Secesh; but now I hab de privilege for salute my own Cunnel."

That officer, with the utmost sincerity, reciprocated the sentiment.

About ten o'clock the people began to collect by land, and also by water,—in steamers sent by General Saxton for the purpose; and from that time all the avenues of approach were thronged. The multitude were chiefly colored women, with gay handkerchiefs on their heads, and a sprinkling of men, with that peculiarly respectable look which these people always have on Sundays and holidays. There were many white visitors also,—ladies on horseback and in carriages, superintendents and teachers, officers, and cavalry-men. Our companies were marched to the neighborhood of the platform, and allowed to sit or stand, as at the Sunday services; the platform was occupied by ladies and dignitaries, and by the band of the Eighth Maine, which kindly volunteered for the occasion; the colored people filled up all the vacant openings in the beautiful grove around, and there was a cordon of mounted visitors beyond. Above, the great live-oak branches and their trailing moss; beyond the people, a glimpse of the blue river.

The services began at half past eleven o'clock, with prayer by our chaplain, Mr. Fowler, who is always, on such occasions, simple, reverential, and impressive. Then the President's Proclamation was read by Dr. W. H. Brisbane, a thing infinitely appropriate, a South Carolinian addressing South Carolinians; for he was reared among these very islands, and here long since emancipated his own slaves. Then the colors were presented to us by the Rev. Mr. French, a chaplain who brought them from the donors in New York. All this was according to the programme. Then followed an incident so simple, so touching, so utterly unexpected and startling, that I can scarcely believe it on recalling, though it gave the key-note to the whole day. The very moment the speaker had ceased, and just as I took and waved the flag, which now for the first time meant anything to these poor people, there suddenly arose, close beside the platform, a strong male voice (but rather cracked and elderly), into which two women's voices instantly blended, singing, as if by an impulse that could no more be repressed than the morning note of the song-sparrow.—

> "My Country, 't is of thee,
> Sweet land of liberty,
> Of thee I sing!"

People looked at each other, and then at us on the platform, to see whence came this interruption, not set down in the bills. Firmly and irrepressibly the quavering voices sang on, verse after verse; others of the colored people joined in; some whites on the platform began, but I motioned them to silence. I never saw anything so electric; it made all other words cheap; it seemed the choked voice of a race at last unloosed. Nothing could be more wonderfully unconscious; art could not have dreamed of a tribute to the day of jubilee that should be so affecting; history will not believe it; and when I came to speak of it, after it was ended, tears were everywhere. If you could have heard how quaint and innocent it was! Old Tiff and his children might have sung it; and close before me was a little slave-boy, almost white, who seemed to belong to the party, and even he must join in. Just think of it!—the first day they had ever had a country, the first flag they had ever seen which promised anything to their people, and here, while mere spectators stood in silence, waiting for my stupid words, these simple souls burst out in their lay, as if they were by their own hearths at home! When they stopped, there was nothing to do for it but to speak, and I went on; but the life of the whole day was in those unknown people's song.

Receiving the flags, I gave them into the hands of two fine-looking men, jet black, as color-guard, and they also spoke, and very effectively,—Sergeant Prince Rivers and Corporal Robert Sutton. The regiment sang "Marching Along," and then General Saxton spoke, in his own simple, manly way, and Mrs. Francis D. Gage spoke very sensibly to the women, and Judge Stickney, from Florida, added something; then some gentlemen sang an ode, and the regiment the John Brown song, and then they went to their beef and molasses. Everything was very orderly, and they seemed to have a very gay time. Most of the visitors had far to go, and so dispersed before dress-parade, though the band stayed to enliven it. In the evening we had letters from home, and General Saxton had a reception at his house, from which I excused myself; and so ended one of the most enthusiastic and happy gatherings I ever knew. The day was perfect, and there was nothing but success.

I forgot to say, that, in the midst of the services, it was announced that General Fremont was appointed Commander-in-Chief,—an announcement which was received with immense cheering, as would have been almost anything else, I verily believe, at that moment of high tide. It was shouted across by the pickets above,—a way in which we often receive news, but not always trustworthy.

January 3, 1863.

Once, and once only, thus far, the water has frozen in my tent; and the next morning showed a dense white frost outside. We have still mocking-birds and crickets and rosebuds, and occasional noonday baths in the river, though the butterflies have vanished, as I remember to have observed in Fayal, after December. I have been here nearly six weeks without a rainy day; one or two slight showers there have been, once interrupting a drill, but never dress-parade. For climate, by day, we might be among the isles of Greece,—though it may be my constant familiarity with the names of her sages which suggests that impression. For instance, a voice just now called, near my tent,—"Cato, whar 's Plato?"

The men have somehow got the impression that it is essential to the validity of a marriage that they should come to me for permission, just as they used to go to the master; and I rather encourage these little confidences, because it is so entertaining to hear them. "Now, Cunnel," said a faltering swain the other day, "I want for get me one good lady," which I approved, especially the limitation as to number. Afterwards I asked one of the bridegroom's friends whether he thought it a good match. "O yes, Cunnel," said he, in all the cordiality of friendship, "John's gwine for marry Venus." I trust the goddess will prove herself a better lady than she appeared during her previous career upon this planet. But this naturally suggests the isles of Greece again.

January 7.

On first arriving, I found a good deal of anxiety among the officers as to the increase of desertions, that being the rock on which the "Hunter Regiment" split. Now this evil is very nearly stopped, and we are every day recovering the older absentees. One of the very best things that have happened to us was the half-accidental shooting of a man who had escaped from the guard-house, and was wounded by a squad sent in pursuit. He has since died; and this very evening another man, who escaped with him, came and opened the door of my tent, after being five days in the woods, almost without food. His clothes were in rags, and he was nearly starved, poor foolish fellow, so that we can almost dispense with further punishment. Severe penalties would be wasted on these people, accustomed as they have been to the most violent passions on the part of white men; but a mild inexorableness tells on them, just as it does on any other children. It is something utterly new to them, and it is thus far perfectly efficacious. They have a great deal of pride as soldiers, and a very little of severity goes a great way, if it be firm and consistent. This is very encouraging.

The single question which I asked of some of the plantation superintendents, on the voyage, was, "Do these people appreciate *justice*?" If they did it was evident that all the rest would be easy. When a race is degraded beyond that point it must be very hard to deal with them; they must mistake all kindness for indulgence, all strictness for cruelty. With these freed slaves there is no such trouble, not a particle: let an officer be only just and firm, with a cordial, kindly nature, and he has no sort of difficulty. The plantation superintendents and teachers have the same experience, they say; but we have an immense advantage in the military organization, which helps in two ways: it increases their self-respect, and it gives us an admirable machinery for discipline, thus improving both the fulcrum and the lever.

The wounded man died in the hospital, and the general verdict seemed to be, "Him brought it on heself." Another soldier died of pneumonia on the same day, and we had the funerals in the evening. It was very impressive. A dense mist came up, with a moon behind it, and we had only the light of pine-splinters, as the procession wound along beneath the mighty, moss-hung branches of the ancient grove. The groups around the grave, the dark faces, the red garments, the scattered lights, the misty boughs, were weird and strange. The men sang one of their own wild chants. Two crickets sang also, one on either side, and did not cease their little monotone, even when the three volleys were fired above the graves. Just before the coffins were lowered, an old man whispered to me that I must have their position altered,—the heads must be towards the west; so it was done,— though they are in a place so veiled in woods that either rising or setting sun will find it hard to spy them.

We have now a good regimental hospital, admirably arranged in a deserted gin-house,—a fine well of our own digging, within the camp lines,—a full allowance of tents, all floored,—a wooden cook-house to every company, with sometimes a palmetto mess-house beside,—a substantial wooden guard-house, with a fireplace five feet "in de clar," where the men off duty can dry themselves and sleep comfortably in bunks afterwards. We have also a great circular school-tent, made of condemned canvas, thirty feet in diameter, and looking like some of the Indian lodges I saw in Kansas. We now meditate a regimental bakery. Our aggregate has increased from four hundred and ninety to seven hundred and forty, besides a hundred recruits now waiting at St. Augustine, and we have practised through all the main movements in battalion drill.

Affairs being thus prosperous, and yesterday having been six weeks since my last and only visit to Beaufort, I rode in, glanced at several camps, and dined with the General. It seemed absolutely like re-entering the world; and I did not fully estimate my past seclusion till it occurred to me, as a strange and novel phenomenon, that the soldiers at the other camps were white.

January 8.

This morning I went to Beaufort again, on necessary business, and by good luck happened upon a review and drill of the white regiments. The thing that struck me most was that same absence of uniformity, in minor points, that I noticed at first in my own officers. The best regiments in the Department are represented among my captains and lieutenants, and very well represented too; yet it has cost much labor to bring them to any uniformity in their drill. There is no need of this; for the prescribed "Tactics" approach perfection; it is never left discretionary in what place an officer shall stand, or in what words he shall give his order. All variation would seem to imply negligence. Yet even West Point occasionally varies from the "Tactics,"—as, for instance, in requiring the line officers to face down the line, when each is giving the order to his company. In our strictest Massachusetts regiments this is not done.

It needs an artist's eye to make a perfect drill-master. Yet the small points are not merely a matter of punctilio; for, the more perfectly a battalion is drilled on the parade-ground, the more quietly it can be handled in action. Moreover, the great need of uniformity is this: that, in the field, soldiers of different companies, and even of different regiments, are liable to be intermingled, and a diversity of orders may throw everything into confusion. Confusion means Bull Run.

I wished my men at the review to-day; for, amidst all the rattling and noise of artillery and the galloping of cavalry, there was only one infantry movement that we have not practised, and that was done by only one regiment, and apparently considered quite a novelty, though it is easily taught,—forming square by Casey's method: forward on centre.

It is really just as easy to drill a regiment as a company,—perhaps easier, because one has more time to think; but it is just as essential to be sharp and decisive, perfectly clear-headed, and to put life into the men. A regiment seems small when one has learned how to handle it, a mere handful of men; and I have no doubt that a brigade or a division would soon appear equally small. But to handle either *judiciously*,—ah, that is another affair!

So of governing; it is as easy to govern a regiment as a school or a factory, and needs like qualities,—system, promptness, patience, tact; moreover, in a regiment one has the aid of the admirable machinery of the army, so that I see very ordinary men who succeed very tolerably.

Reports of a six months' armistice are rife here, and the thought is deplored by all. I cannot believe it; yet sometimes one feels very anxious about the ultimate fate of these poor people. After the experience of Hungary,[11] one sees that revolutions may go backward; and the habit of injustice seems so deeply impressed upon the whites, that it is hard to believe in the possibility of anything better. I dare not yet hope that the promise of the President's Proclamation will be kept. For myself I can be indifferent, for the experience here has been its own daily and hourly reward; and the adaptedness of the freed slaves for drill and discipline is now thoroughly demonstrated, and must soon be universally acknowledged. But it would be terrible to see this regiment disbanded or defrauded.

January 12.

Many things glide by without time to narrate them. On Saturday we had a mail with the President's Second Message of Emancipation, and the next day it was read to the men. The words themselves did not stir them very much, because they have been often told that they were free, especially on New Year's Day, and, being unversed in politics, they do not understand, as well as we do, the importance of each additional guaranty. But the chaplain spoke to them afterwards very effectively, as usual; and then I proposed to them to hold up their hands and pledge themselves to be faithful to those still in bondage. They entered heartily into this, and the scene was quite impressive, beneath the great oak-branches. I heard afterwards that only one man refused to raise his hand, saying bluntly that his wife was out of slavery with him, and he did not care to fight. The other soldiers of his company were very indignant, and shoved him about among them while marching back to their quarters, calling him "Coward." I was glad of their exhibition of feeling, though it is very possible that the one who had thus the moral courage to stand alone among his comrades might be more reliable, on a pinch, than some who yielded a more ready assent. But the whole response, on their part, was very hearty, and will be a good thing to which to hold them hereafter, at any time of discouragement or demoralization,— which was my chief reason for proposing it. With their simple natures it is a great thing to tie them to some definite committal;

they never forget a marked occurrence, and never seem disposed to evade a pledge.

It is this capacity of honor and fidelity which gives me such entire faith in them as soldiers. Without it all their religious demonstration would be mere sentimentality. For instance, every one who visits the camp is struck with their bearing as sentinels. They exhibit, in this capacity, not an upstart conceit, but a steady, conscientious devotion to duty. They would stop their idolized General Saxton, if he attempted to cross their beat contrary to orders: I have seen them. No feeble or incompetent race could do this. The officers tell many amusing instances of this fidelity, but I think mine the best.

It was very dark the other night,—an unusual thing here,—and the rain fell in torrents; so I put on my India-rubber suit, and went the rounds of the sentinels, incognito, to test them. I can only say that I shall never try such an experiment again, and have cautioned my officers against it. 'T is a wonder I escaped with life and limb,—such a charging of bayonets and clicking of gun-locks. Sometimes I tempted them by refusing to give any countersign, but offering them a piece of tobacco, which they could not accept without allowing me nearer than the prescribed bayonet's distance. Tobacco is more than gold to them, and it was touching to watch the struggle in their minds; but they always did their duty at last, and I never could persuade them. One man, as if wishing to crush all his inward vacillations at one fell stroke, told me stoutly that he never used tobacco, though I found next day that he loved it as much as any one of them. It seemed wrong thus to tamper with their fidelity; yet it was a vital matter to me to know how far it could be trusted, out of my sight. It was so intensely dark that not more than one or two knew me, even after I had talked with the very next sentinel, especially as they had never seen me in India-rubber clothing, and I can always disguise my voice. It was easy to distinguish those who did make the discovery; they were always conscious and simpering when their turn came; while the others were stout and irreverent till I revealed myself, and then rather cowed and anxious, fearing to have offended.

It rained harder and harder, and when I had nearly made the

rounds I had had enough of it, and, simply giving the countersign to the challenging sentinel, undertook to pass within the lines.

"Halt!" exclaimed this dusky man and brother, bringing down his bayonet, "de countersign not correck."

Now the magic word, in this case, was "Vicksburg," in honor of a rumored victory. But as I knew that these hard names became quite transformed upon their lips, "Carthage" being familiarized into Cartridge, and "Concord" into Corn-cob, how could I possibly tell what shade of pronunciation my friend might prefer for this particular proper name?

"Vicksburg," I repeated, blandly, but authoritatively, endeavoring, as zealously as one of Christy's Minstrels, to assimilate my speech to any supposed predilection of the Ethiop vocal organs.

"Halt dar! Countersign not correck," was the only answer.

The bayonet still maintained a position which, in a military point of view, was impressive.

I tried persuasion, orthography, threats, tobacco, all in vain. I could not pass in. Of course my pride was up; for was I to defer to an untutored African on a point of pronunciation? Classic shades of Harvard, forbid! Affecting scornful indifference, I tried to edge away, proposing to myself to enter the camp at some other point, where my elocution would be better appreciated. Not a step could I stir.

"Halt!" shouted my gentleman again, still holding me at his bayonet's point, and I wincing and halting.

I explained to him the extreme absurdity of this proceeding, called his attention to the state of the weather, which, indeed, spoke for itself so loudly that we could hardly hear each other speak, and requested permission to withdraw. The bayonet, with mute eloquence, refused the application.

There flashed into my mind, with more enjoyment in the retrospect than I had experienced at the time, an adventure on a lecturing tour in other years, when I had spent an hour in trying to scramble into a country tavern, after bed-time, on the coldest night of winter. On that occasion I ultimately found myself stuck midway in the window, with my head in a temperature of 80°, and my heels in a temperature of −10°, with a heavy window-sash pinioning the small of my back. However, I had got safe out of that dilemma, and it was time to put an end to this one.

"Call the corporal of the guard," said I, at last, with dignity, unwilling either to make a night of it or to yield my incognito.

"Corporal ob de guard!" he shouted, lustily,—"Post Number Two!" while I could hear another sentinel chuckling with laughter. This last was a special guard, placed over a tent, with a prisoner in charge. Presently he broke silence.

"Who am dat?" he asked, in a stage whisper. "Am he a buckra [white man]?"

"Dunno whether he been a buckra or not," responded, doggedly, my Cerberus in uniform; "but I's bound to keep him here till de corporal ob de guard come."

Yet, w̲h̲e̲n̲ that dignitary arrived, and I revealed myself, poor Number _____ transfixed with terror, and seemed to look _____ execution. Of course I praised _____ mplimented him before the gua _____ ain; and the whole affair was ve _____ if Satan himself should approa _____ ney will take him for "de Cunn _____ erity.

January 13.

In many ways the childish nature of this people shows itself. I have just had to make a change of officers in a company which has constantly complained, and with good reason, of neglect and improper treatment. Two excellent officers have been assigned to them; and yet they sent a deputation to me in the evening, in a state of utter wretchedness. "We's bery grieved dis evening, Cunnel; 'pears like we could n't bear it, to lose de Cap'n and de Lieutenant, all two togeder." Argument was useless; and I could only fall back on the general theory, that I knew what was best for them, which had much more effect; and I also could cite the instance of another company, which had been much improved by a new captain, as they readily admitted. So with the promise that the new officers should not be "savage to we," which was the one thing they deprecated, I assuaged their woes. Twenty-four hours have passed, and I hear them singing most merrily all down that company street.

I often notice how their griefs may be dispelled, like those of children, merely by permission to utter them: if they can tell their sorrows, they go away happy, even without asking to have anything done about them. I observe also a peculiar dislike of all *intermediate* control: they always wish to pass by the company officer, and deal with me personally for everything. General Saxton notices the same thing with the people on the plantations as regards himself. I suppose this proceeds partly from the old habit of appealing to the master against the overseer. Kind words would cost the master nothing, and he could easily put off any non-fulfilment upon the overseer. Moreover, the negroes have acquired such constitutional distrust of white people, that it is perhaps as much as they can do to trust more than one person at a time. Meanwhile this constant personal intercourse is out of the question in a well-ordered regiment; and the remedy for it is to introduce by degrees more and more of system, so that their immediate officers will become all-sufficient for the daily routine.

It is perfectly true (as I find everybody takes for granted) that the first essential for an officer of colored troops is to gain their confidence. But it is equally true, though many persons do not appreciate it, that the admirable methods and proprieties of the regular army are equally available for all troops, and that the sublimest philanthropist, if he does not appreciate this, is unfit to command them.

Another childlike attribute in these men, which is less agreeable, is a sort of blunt insensibility to giving physical pain. If they are cruel to animals, for instance, it always reminds me of children pulling off flies' legs, in a sort of pitiless, untaught, experimental way. Yet I should not fear any wanton outrage from them. After all their wrongs, they are not really revengeful; and I would far rather enter a captured city with them than with white troops, for they would be more subordinate. But for mere physical suffering they would have no fine sympathies. The cruel things they have seen and undergone have helped to blunt them; and if I ordered them to put to death a dozen prisoners, I think they would do it without remonstrance.

Yet their religious spirit grows more beautiful to me in living longer with them; it is certainly far more so than at first, when it seemed rather a matter of phrase and habit. It influences them both on the negative and the positive side. That is, it cultivates the feminine virtues first,—makes them patient, meek, resigned. This is very evident in the hospital; there is nothing of the restless, defiant habit of white invalids. Perhaps, if they had more of this, they would resist disease better. Imbued from childhood with the habit of submission, drinking rough every pore that other-world trust which is the their songs, they can endure everything. This relieved to find that their religion stive side also,—gives zeal, enerle fanatics, if I chose; but I dosentially Mohammedan, perhapnd I feel the same de-gree of Turkish command,—that is, on, not tending towards agreemenon. Their philosophizing is of-ten the higcism; and our dear surgeon declares that they aral transcendentalists. The white camps seem rough and selar, after this; and I hear our men talk about "a religious army," "a Gospel army," in their prayer-meetings. They are certainly evangelizing the chaplain, who was rather a heretic at the beginning; at least, this is his own admission. We have re-cruits on their way from St. Augustine, where the negroes are chiefly Roman Catholics; and it will be interesting to see how their type of character combines with that elder creed.

It is time for rest; and I have just looked out into the night, where the eternal stars shut down, in concave protection, over the yet glimmering camp, and Orion hangs above my tent-door, giv-ing to me the sense of strength and assurance which these simple children obtain from their Moses and the Prophets. Yet external Nature does its share in their training; witness that most poetic of all their songs, which always reminds me of the "Lyke-Wake Dirge" in the "Scottish Border Minstrelsy,"[12]

> "I know moon-rise, I know star-rise;
>   Lay dis body down.
> I walk in de moonlight, I walk in de starlight,
>   To lay dis body down.

I'll walk in de graveyard, I'll walk through de graveyard,
 To lay dis body down.
I'll lie in de grave and stretch out my arms;
 Lay dis body down.
I go to de Judgment in de evening ob de day
 When I lay dis body down;
And my soul and your soul will meet in de day
 When I lay dis body down."

January 14.

In speaking of the military qualities of the blacks, I should add, that the only point where I am disappointed is one I have never seen raised by the most incredulous newspaper critics,—namely, their physical condition. To be sure they often look magnificently to my gymnasium-trained eye; and I always like to observe them when bathing,—such splend' muscular development, set off by that smooth coatin'   tissue which makes them, like the South-Sea I'   n more muscular than they are. Th'   n than those of whites, the sur-
                              her and far more free from hair.
                        ; pneumonia and pleurisy are
                              easily made ill,—and easily
                              organizations again. Guard-
du   pparently; and double-quick
mo   them coughing badly. But then
it is   that this is their sickly season, from January to M   that their healthy season will come in summer, when the whites break down. Still my conviction of the physical superiority of more highly civilized races is strengthened on the whole, not weakened, by observing them. As to availability for military drill and duty in other respects, the only question I ever hear debated among the officers is, whether they are equal or superior to whites. I have never heard it suggested that they were inferior, although I expected frequently to hear such complaints from hasty or unsuccessful officers.

Of one thing I am sure, that their best qualities will be wasted by merely keeping them for garrison duty. They seem peculiarly fitted for offensive operations, and especially for partisan warfare; they have so much dash and such abundant resources, combined with such an Indian-like knowledge of the country and its ways. These traits have been often illustrated in expeditions sent after deserters. For instance, I despatched one of my best lieutenants and my best sergeant with a squad of men to search a certain plantation, where there were two separate negro villages. They went by night, and the force was divided. The lieutenant took one set of huts, the sergeant the other. Before the lieutenant had reached his first house, every man in the village was in the woods, innocent and guilty alike. But the sergeant's mode of operation was thus described by a corporal from a white regiment who happened to be in one of the negro houses. He said that not a sound was heard until suddenly a red leg appeared in the open doorway, and a voice outside said, "Rally." Going to the door, he observed a similar pair of red legs before every hut, and not a person was allowed to go out, until the quarters had been thoroughly searched, and the three deserters found. This was managed by Sergeant Prince Rivers, our color-sergeant, who is provost-sergeant also, and has entire charge of the prisoners and of the daily policing of the camp. He is a man of distinguished appearance, and in old times was the crack coachman of Beaufort, in which capacity he once drove Beauregard from this plantation to Charleston, I believe. They tell me that he was once allowed to present a petition to the Governor of South Carolina in behalf of slaves, for the redress of certain grievances; and that a placard, offering two thousand dollars for his recapture, is still to be seen by the wayside between here and Charleston. He was a sergeant in the old "Hunter Regiment," and was taken by General Hunter to New York last spring, where the *chevrons* on his arm brought a mob upon him in Broadway, whom he kept off till the police interfered. There is not a white officer in this regiment who has more administrative ability, or more absolute authority over the men; they do not love him, but his mere presence has controlling power over them. He writes well enough to prepare for me a daily report of his duties in the camp; if his education reached a higher point, I see no reason why he should not command the Army of the Potomac. He is jet-black, or rather, I should say, *wine-black;* his complexion, like that of others of my darkest men, having a sort of rich, clear depth, without a trace of sootiness, and to my eye very handsome. His features are tolerably regular, and full of command, and his figure superior to that of any of our white officers,—being six feet high, perfectly proportioned, and of apparently inexhaustible strength and activity. His gait is like a panther's; I never saw such a tread. No anti-slavery novel has described a man of such marked ability. He makes Toussaint[13] perfectly intelligible; and if there should ever be a black monarchy in South Carolina, he will be its king.

January 15.

This morning is like May. Yesterday I saw bluebirds and a butterfly; so this winter of a fortnight is over. I fancy there is a trifle less coughing in the camp. We hear of other stations in the Department where the mortality, chiefly from yellow fever, has been frightful. Dr. ——— is rubbing his hands professionally over the fearful tales of the surgeon of a New York regiment, just from Key West, who has had two hundred cases of the fever. "I suppose he is a skilful, highly educated man," said I. "Yes," he responded with enthusiasm. "Why, he had seventy deaths!"—as if that proved his superiority past question.

January 19.

> "And first, sitting proud as a king on his throne,
> At the head of them all rode Sir Richard Tyrone."

But I fancy that Sir Richard felt not much better satisfied with his following than I to-day. J. R. L.[14] said once that nothing was quite so good as turtle-soup, except mock-turtle; and I have heard officers declare that nothing was so stirring as real war, except some exciting parade. To-day, for the first time, I marched the whole regiment through Beaufort and back,—the first appearance of such a novelty on any stage. They did march splendidly; this all admit. M———'s[15] prediction was fulfilled: "Will not ——— be in bliss? A thousand men, every one as black as a coal!" I confess it. To look back on twenty broad double-ranks of men (for they marched by platoons),—every polished musket having a black face beside it, and every face set steadily to the front,—a regiment of freed slaves marching on into the future,—it was something to remember; and when they returned through the same streets, marching by the flank, with guns at a "support," and each man covering his file-leader handsomely, the effect on the eye was almost as fine. The band of the Eighth Maine joined us at the entrance of the town, and escorted us in. Sergeant Rivers said ecstatically afterwards, in describing the affair, "And when dat band wheel in before us, and march on,—my God! I quit dis world altogeder." I wonder if he pictured to himself the many dusky regiments, now unformed, which I seemed to see marching up behind us, gathering shape out of the dim air.

I had cautioned the men, before leaving camp, not to be staring about them as they marched, but to look straight to the front, every man; and they did it with their accustomed fidelity, aided by the sort of spontaneous eye-for-effect which is in all their melodramatic natures. One of them was heard to say exultingly afterwards, "We did n't look to de right nor to de leff. I did n't see notin' in Beaufort. Eb'ry step was worth a half a dollar." And they all marched as if it were so. They knew well that they were marching through throngs of officers and soldiers who had drilled as many months as we had drilled weeks, and whose eyes would readily spy out every defect. And I must say, that, on the whole, with a few trivial exceptions, those spectators behaved in a manly and courteous manner, and I do not care to write down all the handsome things that were said. Whether said or not, they were deserved; and there is no danger that our men will not take sufficient satisfaction in their good appearance. I was especially amused at one of our recruits, who did not march in the ranks, and who said, after watching the astonishment of some white soldiers, "De buckra sojers look like a man who been-a-steal a sheep,"—that is, I suppose, sheepish.

After passing and repassing through the town, we marched to the parade-ground, and went through an hour's drill, forming squares and reducing them, and doing other things which look hard on paper, and are perfectly easy in fact; and we were to have been reviewed by General Saxton, but he had been unexpectedly called to Ladies Island, and did not see us at all, which was the only thing to mar the men's enjoyment. Then we marched back to camp (three miles), the men singing the "John Brown Song," and all manner of things,—as happy creatures as one can well conceive.

It is worth mentioning, before I close, that we have just received an article about "Negro Troops," from the London Spectator, which is so admirably true to our experience that it seems as if written by one of us. I am confident that there never has been, in any American newspaper, a treatment of the subject so discriminating and so wise.

January 21.

To-day brought a visit from Major-General Hunter and his staff, by General Saxton's invitation,—the former having just arrived in the Department. I expected them at dress-parade, but they came during battalion drill, rather to my dismay, and we were caught in our old ____. It was our first review, and I dare say we did tole____ ____urse it seemed to me that the men never app____ ____ as one always thinks a party at one's ____ the guests seem to enjoy it, because ____ every little thing that goes wrong. ____al Hunter made the men a little ____ them that he wished there were ____ ____Saxton spoke to them afterwards, ____muskets were on their way for col____ ____cheered both the generals lustily; and they ____ ____ntary afterwards, though I knew that the regiment c____ ____ have appeared nearly so well as on its visit to Beaufort. I suppose I felt like some anxious mamma whose children have accidentally appeared at dancing-school in their old clothes.

General Hunter promises us all we want,—pay when the funds arrive, Springfield rifled muskets, and blue trousers. Moreover, he has graciously consented that we should go on an expedition along the coast, to pick up cotton, lumber, and, above all, recruits. I declined an offer like this just after my arrival, because the regiment was not drilled or disciplined, not even the officers; but it is all we wish for now.

> "What care I how black I be?
> Forty pounds will marry me,"

quoth Mother Goose. Forty *rounds* will marry us to the American Army, past divorcing, if we can only use them well. Our success or failure may make or mar the prospects of colored troops. But it is well to remember in advance that military success is really less satisfactory than any other, because it may depend on a moment's turn of events, and that may be determined by some trivial thing, neither to be anticipated nor controlled. Napoleon ought to have won at Waterloo by all reasonable calculations; but who cares? All that one can expect is, to do one's best, and to take with equanimity the fortune of war.

CHAPTER III
Up the St. Mary's

If Sergeant Rivers was a natural king among my dusky soldiers, Corporal Robert Sutton was the natural prime-minister. If not in all respects the ablest, he was the wisest man in our ranks. As large, as powerful, and as black as our good-looking Color-Sergeant, but more heavily built and with less personal beauty, he had a more massive brain and a far more meditative and systematic intellect. Not yet grounded even in the spelling-book, his modes of thought were nevertheless strong, lucid, and accurate; and he yearned and pined for intellectual companionship beyond all ignorant men whom I have ever met. I believe that he would have talked all day and all night, for days together, to any officer who could instruct him, until his companion, at least, fell asleep exhausted. His comprehension of the whole problem of Slavery was more thorough and far-reaching than that of any Abolitionist, so far as its social and military aspects went; in that direction I could teach him nothing, and he taught me much. But it was his methods of thought which always impressed me chiefly: superficial brilliancy he left to others, and grasped at the solid truth.

Of course his interest in the war and in the regiment was unbounded; he did not take to drill with especial readiness, but he was insatiable of it, and grudged every moment of relaxation. Indeed, he never had any such moments; his mind was at work all the time, even when he was singing hymns, of which he had endless store. He was not, however, one of our leading religionists, but his moral code was solid and reliable, like his mental processes. Ignorant as he was, the "years that bring the philosophic mind" had yet been his, and most of my young officers seemed boys beside him. He was a Florida man, and had been chiefly employed in lumbering and piloting on the St. Mary's River, which divides Florida from Georgia. Down this stream he had escaped in a "dug-out," and after thus finding the way, had returned (as had not a few of my men in other cases) to bring away wife and child. "I would n't have leff my child, Cunnel," he said, with an emphasis that sounded the depths of his strong nature. And up this same river he was always imploring to be allowed to guide an expedition.

Many other men had rival propositions to urge, for they gained self-confidence from drill and guard-duty, and were growing impatient of inaction. "Ought to go to work, Sa,—don't believe in we lyin' in camp eatin' up de perwisions." Such were the quaint complaints, which I heard with joy. Looking over my note-books of that period, I find them filled with topographical memoranda, jotted down by a flickering candle, from the evening talk of the men,—notes of vulnerable points along the coast, charts of rivers, locations of pickets. I prized these conversations not more for what I thus learned of the country than for what I learned of the men. One could thus measure their various degrees of accuracy and their average military instinct; and I must say that in every respect, save the accurate estimate of distances, they stood the test well. But no project took my fancy so much, after all, as that of the delegate from the St. Mary's River.

The best peg on which to hang an expedition in the Department of the South, in those days, was the promise of lumber. Dwelling in the very land of Southern pine, the Department authorities had to send North for it, at a vast expense. There was reported to be plenty in the enemy's country, but somehow the colored soldiers were the only ones who had been lucky enough to obtain any, thus far, and the supply brought in by our men, after flooring the tents of the white regiments and our own, was running low. An expedition of white troops, four companies, with two steamers and two schooners, had lately returned empty-handed, after a week's foraging; and now it was our turn. They said the mills were all burned; but should we go up the St. Mary's, Corporal Sutton was prepared to offer more lumber than we had transportation to carry. This made the crowning charm of his suggestion. But there is never any danger of erring on the side of secrecy, in a military department; and I resolved to avoid all undue publicity for our plans, by not finally deciding on any until we should get outside the bar. This was happily approved by my superior officers, Major-General Hunter and Brigadier-General Saxton; and I was accordingly permitted to take three steamers, with four hundred and sixty-two officers and men, and two or three invited guests, and go down the coast on my own responsibility. We were, in short, to win our spurs; and if, as among the Araucanians,[1] our spurs were made of lumber, so much the better. The whole history of the Department of the South had been defined as "a military picnic," and now we were to take our share of the entertainment.

It seemed a pleasant share, when, after the usual vexations and delays, we found ourselves (January 23, 1863) gliding down the full waters of Beaufort River, the three vessels having sailed at different hours, with orders to rendezvous at St. Simon's Island, on the coast of Georgia. Until then, the flag-ship, so to speak, was to be the "Ben De Ford," Captain Hallett,—this being by far the largest vessel, and carrying most of the men. Major Strong was in command upon the "John Adams," an army gunboat, carrying a thirty-pound Parrott gun, two ten-pound Parrotts, and an eight-inch howitzer. Captain Trowbridge (since promoted Lieutenant-Colonel of the regiment) had charge of the famous "Planter," brought away from the Rebels by Robert Small; she carried a ten-pound Parrott gun, and two howitzers. The John Adams was our main reliance. She was an old East Boston ferry-boat, a "double-ender," admirable for riverwork, but unfit for sea-service. She drew seven feet of water; the Planter drew only four; but the latter was very slow, and being obliged to go to St. Simon's by an inner passage, would delay us from the beginning. She delayed us so much, before the end, that we virtually parted company, and her career was almost entirely separated from our own.

From boyhood I have had a fancy for boats, and have seldom been without a share, usually more or less fractional, in a rather indeterminate number of punts and wherries. But when, for the first time, I found myself at sea as Commodore of a fleet of armed steamers,—for even the Ben De Ford boasted a six-pounder or so,—it seemed rather an unexpected promotion. But it is a characteristic of army life, that one adapts one's self, as coolly as in a dream, to the most novel responsibilities. One sits on court-martial, for instance, and decides on the life of a fellow-creature, without being asked any inconvenient questions as to previous knowledge of Blackstone;[2] and after such an experience, shall one shrink from wrecking a steamer or two in the cause of the nation? So I placidly accepted my naval establishment, as if it were a new form of boat-club, and looked over the charts, balancing between one river and another, as if deciding whether to pull up or down Lake Quinsigamond.[3] If military life ever contemplated the exercise of the virtue of humility under any circumstances, this would perhaps have been a good opportunity to begin its practice. But as the "Regulations" clearly contemplated nothing of the kind, and as I had never met with any precedent which looked in that direction, I had learned to check promptly all such weak proclivities.

Captain Hallett proved the most frank and manly of sailors, and did everything for our comfort. He was soon warm in his praises of the demeanor of our men, which was very pleasant to hear, as this was the first time that colored soldiers in any number had been conveyed on board a transport, and I know of no place where a white volunteer appears to so much disadvantage. His mind craves occupation, his body is intensely uncomfortable, the daily emergency is not great enough to call out his heroic qualities, and he is apt to be surly, discontented, and impatient even of sanitary rules. The Southern black soldier, on the other hand, is seldom sea-sick (at least, such is my experience), and, if properly managed, is equally contented, whether idle or busy; he is, moreover, so docile that all needful rules are executed with cheerful acquiescence, and the quarters can therefore be kept clean and wholesome. Very forlorn faces were soon visible among the officers in the cabin, but I rarely saw such among the men.

Pleasant still seemed our enterprise, as we anchored at early morning in the quiet waters of St. Simon's Sound, and saw the light fall softly on the beach and the low bluffs, on the picturesque plantation-houses which nestled there, and the graceful naval vessels that lay at anchor before us. When we afterwards landed the air had that peculiar Mediterranean translucency which Southern islands wear; and the plantation we visited had the loveliest tropical garden, though tangled and desolate, which I have ever seen in the South. The deserted house was embowered in great blossoming shrubs, and filled with hyacinthine odors, among which predominated that of the little Chickasaw roses which everywhere bloomed and trailed around. There were fig-trees and date-palms, crape-myrtles and wax-myrtles, Mexican agaves and English ivies, japonicas, bananas, oranges, lemons, oleanders, jonquils, great cactuses, and wild Florida lilies. This was not the plantation which Mrs. Kemble[4] has since made historic, although that was on the same island; and I could not waste much sentiment over it, for it had belonged to a Northern renegade, Thomas Butler King. Yet I felt then, as I have felt a hundred times since, an emotion of heart-sickness at this desecration of a homestead,—and especially when, looking from a bare upper window of the empty house upon a range of broad, flat, sunny roofs, such as children love to play on, I thought how that place might have been loved by yet innocent hearts, and I mourned anew the sacrilege of war.

I had visited the flag-ship Wabash ere we left Port Royal Harbor, and had obtained a very kind letter of introduction from Admiral Dupont, that stately and courtly potentate, elegant as one's ideal French marquis; and under these credentials I received polite attention from the naval officers at St. Simon's,—Acting Volunteer Lieutenant Budd, of the gunboat Potomska, and Acting Master Moses, of the barque Fernandina. They made valuable suggestions in regard to the different rivers along the coast, and gave vivid descriptions of the last previous trip up the St. Mary's undertaken by Captain Stevens, U. S. N., in the gunboat Ottawa, when he had to fight his way past batteries at every bluff in descending the narrow and rapid stream. I was warned that no resistance would be offered to the ascent, but only to our return; and was further cautioned against the mistake, then common, of underrating the courage of the Rebels. "It proved impossible to dislodge those fellows from the banks," my informant said; "they had dug rifle-pits, and swarmed like hornets, and when fairly silenced in one direction they were sure to open upon us from another." All this sounded alarming, but it was nine months since the event had happened; and although nothing had gone up the river meanwhile, I counted on less resistance now. And something must be risked anywhere.

We were delayed all that day in waiting for our consort, and improved our time by verifying certain rumors about a quantity of new railroad-iron which was said to be concealed in the abandoned Rebel forts on St. Simon's and Jekyll Islands, and which would have much value at Port Royal, if we could only unearth it. Some of our men had worked upon these very batteries, so that they could easily guide us; and by the additional discovery of a large flat-boat we were enabled to go to work in earnest upon the removal of the treasure. These iron bars, surmounted by a dozen feet of sand, formed an invulnerable roof for the magazines and bomb-proofs of the fort, and the men enjoyed demolishing them far more than they had relished their construction. Though the day was the 24th of January, 1863, the sun was very oppressive upon the sands; but all were in the highest spirits, and worked with the greatest zeal. The men seemed to regard these massive bars as their first trophies; and if the rails had been wreathed with roses, they could not have been got out in more holiday style. Nearly a hundred were obtained that day, besides a quantity of five-inch plank with which to barricade the very conspicuous pilot-houses of the John Adams.

Still another day we were delayed, and could still keep at this work, not neglecting some foraging on the island, from which horses, cattle, and agricultural implements were to be removed, and the few remaining colored families transferred to Fernandina. I had now become quite anxious about the missing steamboat, as the inner passage, by which alone she could arrive, was exposed at certain points to fire from Rebel batteries, and it would have been unpleasant to begin with a disaster. I remember that, as I stood on deck, in the still and misty evening, listening with strained senses for some sound of approach, I heard a low continuous noise from the distance, more wild and desolate than anything in my memory can parallel. It came from within the vast girdle of mist, and seemed like the cry of a myriad of lost souls upon the horizon's verge; it was Dante become audible: and yet it was but the accumulated cries of innumerable sea-fowl at the entrance of the outer bay.

Late that night the Planter arrived. We left St. Simon's on the following morning, reached Fort Clinch by four o'clock, and there transferring two hundred men to the very scanty quarters of the John Adams, allowed the larger transport to go into Fernandina, while the two other vessels were to ascend the St. Mary's River, unless (as proved inevitable in the end) the defects in the boiler of the Planter should oblige her to remain behind. That night I proposed to make a sort of trial-trip up stream, as far as

Township Landing, some fifteen miles, there to pay our respects to Captain Clark's company of cavalry, whose camp was reported to lie near by. This was included in Corporal Sutton's programme, and seemed to me more inviting, and far more useful to the men, than any amount of mere foraging. The thing really desirable appeared to be to get them under fire as soon as possible, and to teach them, by a few small successes, the application of what they had learned in camp.

I had ascertained that the camp of this company lay five miles from the landing, and was accessible by two roads, one of which was a lumber-path, not commonly used, but which Corporal Sutton had helped to construct, and along which he could easily guide us. The plan was to go by night, surround the house and negro cabins at the landing (to prevent an alarm from being given), then to take the side path, and if all went well, to surprise the camp; but if they got notice of our approach, through their pickets, we should, at worst, have a fight, in which the best man must win.

The moon was bright, and the river swift, but easy of navigation thus far. Just below Township I landed a small advance force, to surround the houses silently. With them went Corporal Sutton; and when, after rounding the point, I went on shore with a larger body of men, he met me with a silent chuckle of delight, and with the information that there was a negro in a neighboring cabin who had just come from the Rebel camp, and could give the latest information. While he hunted up this valuable auxiliary, I mustered my detachment, winnowing out the men who had coughs (not a few), and sending them ignominiously on board again: a process I had regularly to perform, during this first season of catarrh, on all occasions where quiet was needed. The only exception tolerated at this time was in the case of one man who offered a solemn pledge, that, if unable to restrain his cough, he would lie down on the ground, scrape a little hole, and cough into it unheard. The ingenuity of this proposition was irresistible, and the eager patient was allowed to pass muster.

It was after midnight when we set off upon our excursion. I had about a hundred men, marching by the flank, with a small advanced guard, and also a few flankers, where the ground permitted. I put my Florida company at the head of the column, and had by my side Captain Metcalf, an excellent officer, and Sergeant McIntyre, his first sergeant. We plunged presently into pine woods, whose resinous smell I can still remember. Corporal Sutton marched near me, with his captured negro guide, whose first fear and sullenness had yielded to the magic news of the President's Proclamation, then just issued, of which Governor Andrew had sent me a large printed supply;—we seldom found men who could read it, but they all seemed to feel more secure when they held it in their hands. We marched on through the woods, with no sound but the peeping of the frogs in a neighboring marsh, and the occasional yelping of a dog, as we passed the hut of some "cracker." This yelping always made Corporal Sutton uneasy; dogs are the detective officers of Slavery's police.

We had halted once or twice to close up the ranks, and had marched some two miles, seeing and hearing nothing more. I had got all I could out of our new guide, and was striding on, rapt in pleasing contemplation. All had gone so smoothly that I had merely to fancy the rest as being equally smooth. Already I fancied our little detachment bursting out of the woods, in swift surprise, upon the Rebel quarters,—already the opposing commander, after hastily firing a charge or two from his revolver (of course above my head), had yielded at discretion, and was gracefully tendering, in a stage attitude, his unavailing sword,—when suddenly—

There was a trampling of feet among the advanced guard as they came confusedly to a halt, and almost at the same instant a more ominous sound, as of galloping horses in the path before us. The moonlight outside the woods gave that dimness of atmosphere within which is more bewildering than darkness, because the eyes cannot adapt themselves to it so well. Yet I fancied, and others aver, that they saw the leader of an approaching party mounted on a white horse and reining up in the pathway; others, again, declare that he drew a pistol from the holster and took aim; others heard the words, "Charge in upon them! Surround them!" But all this was confused by the opening rifle-shots of our advanced guard, and, as clear observation was impossible, I made the men fix their bayonets and kneel in the cover on each side the pathway, and I saw with delight the brave fellows, with Sergeant McIntyre at their head, settling down in the grass as coolly and warily as if wild turkeys were the only game. Perhaps at the first shot a man fell at my elbow. I felt it no more than if a tree had fallen,—I was so busy watching my own men and the enemy, and planning what to do next. Some of our soldiers, misunderstanding the order, "Fix bayonets," were actually *charging* with them, dashing off into the dim woods, with nothing to charge at but the vanishing tail of an imaginary horse,—for we could really see nothing. This zeal I noted with pleasure, and also with anxiety, as our greatest danger was from confusion and scattering; and for infantry to pursue cavalry would be a novel enterprise. Captain Metcalf stood by me well in keeping the men steady, as did Assistant Surgeon Minor, and Lieutenant, now Captain, Jackson. How the men in the rear were behaving I could not tell,—not so coolly, I afterwards found, because they were more entirely bewildered, supposing, until the shots came, that the column had simply halted for a moment's rest, as had been done once or twice before. They did not know who or where their assailants might be, and the fall of the man beside me created a hasty rumor that I was killed, so that it was on the whole an alarming experience for them. They kept together very tolerably, however, while our assailants, dividing, rode along on each side through the open pine-barren, firing into our ranks, but mostly over the heads of the men. My soldiers in turn fired rapidly,—too rapidly, being yet beginners,—and it was evident that, dim as it was, both sides had opportunity to do some execution.

I could hardly tell whether the fight had lasted ten minutes or an hour, when, as the enemy's fire had evidently ceased or slackened, I gave the order to cease firing. But it was very difficult at first to make them desist: the taste of gunpowder was too intoxicating. One of them was heard to mutter, indignantly, "Why de Cunnel order *Cease firing,* when de Secesh blazin' away at de rate ob ten dollar a day?" Every incidental occurrence seemed somehow to engrave itself upon my perceptions, without interrupting the main course of thought. Thus I know, that, in one of the pauses of the affair, there came wailing through the woods a cracked female voice, as if calling back some stray husband who had run out to join in the affray, "John, John, are you going to leave me, John? Are you going to let me and the children be killed,

John?" I suppose the poor thing's fears of gunpowder were very genuine; but it was such a wailing squeak, and so infinitely ludicrous, and John was probably ensconced so very safely in some hollow tree, that I could see some of the men showing all their white teeth in the very midst of the fight. But soon this sound, with all others, had ceased, and left us in peaceful possession of the field.

I have made the more of this little affair because it was the first stand-up fight in which my men had been engaged, though they had been under fire, in an irregular way, in their small early expeditions. To me personally the event was of the greatest value: it had given us all an opportunity to test each other, and our abstract surmises were changed into positive knowledge. Hereafter it was of small importance what nonsense might be talked or written about colored troops; so long as mine did not flinch, it made no difference to me. My brave young officers, themselves mostly new to danger, viewed the matter much as I did; and yet we were under bonds of life and death to form a correct opinion, which was more than could be said of the Northern editors, and our verdict was proportionately of greater value.

I was convinced from appearances that we had been victorious, so far, though I could not suppose that this would be the last of it. We knew neither the numbers of the enemy, nor their plans, nor their present condition: whether they had surprised us or whether we had surprised them was all a mystery. Corporal Sutton was urgent to go on and complete the enterprise. All my impulses said the same thing; but then I had the most explicit injunctions from General Saxton to risk as little as possible in this first enterprise, because of the fatal effect on public sentiment of even an honorable defeat. We had now an honorable victory, so far as it went; the officers and men around me were in good spirits, but the rest of the column might be nervous; and it seemed so important to make the first fight an entire success, that I thought it wiser to let well alone; nor have I ever changed this opinion. For one's self, Montrose's[5] verse may be well applied, "To win or lose it all." But one has no right to deal thus lightly with the fortunes of a race, and that was the weight which I always felt as resting on our action. If my raw infantry force had stood unflinchingly a night-surprise from "de hoss cavalry," as they reverentially termed them, I felt that a good beginning had been made. All hope of surprising the enemy's camp was now at an end; I was willing and ready to fight the cavalry over again, but it seemed wiser that we, not they, should select the ground.

Attending to the wounded, therefore, and making as we best could stretchers for those who were to be carried, including the remains of the man killed at the first discharge (Private William Parsons of Company G), and others who seemed at the point of death, we marched through the woods to the landing,—expecting at every moment to be involved in another fight. This not occurring, I was more than ever satisfied that we had won a victory; for it was obvious that a mounted force would not allow a detachment of infantry to march two miles through open woods by night without renewing the fight, unless they themselves had suffered a good deal. On arrival at the landing, seeing that there was to be no immediate affray, I sent most of the men on board, and called for volunteers to remain on shore with me and hold the plantation-house till morning. They eagerly offered; and I was glad to see them, when posted as sentinels by Lieutenants Hyde and Jackson, who stayed with me, pace their beats as steadily and challenge as coolly as veterans, though of course there was some powder wasted on imaginary foes. Greatly to my surprise, however, we had no other enemies to encounter. We did not yet know that we had killed the first lieutenant of the cavalry, and that our opponents had retreated to the woods in dismay, without daring to return to their camp. This at least was the account we heard from prisoners afterwards, and was evidently the tale current in the neighborhood, though the statements published in Southern newspapers did not correspond. Admitting the death of Lieutenant Jones, the Tallahassee Floridian of February 14th stated that "Captain Clark, finding the enemy in strong force, fell back with his command to camp, and removed his ordnance and commissary and other stores, with twelve negroes on their way to the enemy, captured on that day."

In the morning, my invaluable surgeon, Dr. Rogers, sent me his report of killed and wounded; and I have been since permitted to make the following extracts from his notes: "One man killed instantly by ball through the heart, and seven wounded, one of whom will die. Braver men never lived. One man with two bullet-holes through the large muscles of the shoulders and neck brought off from the scene of action, two miles distant, two muskets; and not a murmur has escaped his lips. Another, Robert Sutton, with three wounds,—one of which, being on the skull, may cost him his life,—would not report himself till compelled to do so by his officers. While dressing his wounds, he quietly talked of what they had done, and of what they yet could do. To-day I have had the Colonel *order* him to obey me. He is perfectly quiet and cool, but takes this whole affair with the religious bearing of a man who realizes that freedom is sweeter than life. Yet another soldier did not report himself at all, but remained all night on guard, and possibly I should not have known of his having had a buck-shot in his shoulder, if some duty requiring a sound shoulder had not been required of him to-day." This last, it may be added, had persuaded a comrade to dig out the buck-shot, for fear of being ordered on the sick-list. And one of those who were carried to the vessel—a man wounded through the lungs—asked only if I were safe, the contrary having been reported. An officer may be pardoned some enthusiasm for such men as these.

The anxious night having passed away without an attack, another problem opened with the morning. For the first time, my officers and men found themselves in possession of an enemy's abode; and though there was but little temptation to plunder, I knew that I must here begin to draw the line. I had long since resolved to prohibit absolutely all indiscriminate pilfering and wanton outrage, and to allow nothing to be taken or destroyed but by proper authority. The men, to my great satisfaction, entered into this view at once, and so did (perhaps a shade less readily, in some cases) the officers. The greatest trouble was with the steamboat hands, and I resolved to let them go ashore as little as possible. Most articles of furniture were already, however, before our visit, gone from the plantation-house, which was now used only as a picket-station. The only valuable article was a piano-forte, for which a regular packing-box lay invitingly ready outside. I had made up my mind, in accordance with the orders given to naval commanders in that department,* to burn all picket-stations, and all villages from which I should be covertly attacked, and nothing else; and as this house was destined to the flames, I should have left the piano in it, but for the seductions of that box. With such a receptacle all ready, even to the cover, it would have seemed like flying in the face of Providence not to put the piano in. I ordered it removed, therefore, and afterwards presented it to the school for colored children at Fernandina. This I mention because it was the only article of property I ever took, or knowingly suffered to be taken, in the enemy's country, save for legitimate military uses, from first to last; nor would I have taken this, but for the thought of the school, and, as aforesaid, the temptation of the box. If any other officer has been more rigid, with equal opportunities, let him cast the first stone.[6]

I think the zest with which the men finally set fire to the house at my order was enhanced by this previous abstemiousness; but there is a fearful fascination in the use of fire, which every child knows in the abstract, and which I found to hold true in the practice. On our way down river we had opportunity to test this again.

The ruined town of St. Mary's had at that time a bad reputation, among both naval and military men. Lying but a short distance above Fernandina, on the Georgia side, it was occasionally visited by our gunboats. I was informed that the only residents of the town were three old women, who were apparently kept there as spies,—that, on our approach, the aged crones would come out and wave white handkerchiefs,—that they would receive us hospitably, profess to be profoundly loyal, and exhibit a portrait of Washington,—that they would solemnly assure us that no Rebel pickets had been there for many weeks,—but that in the adjoining yard we should find fresh horse-tracks, and that we should be fired upon by guerillas the moment we left the wharf. My officers had been much excited by these tales; and I had as-

*"It is my desire to avoid the destruction of private property, unless used for picket or guard-stations, or for other military purposes, by the enemy. . . . Of course, if fired upon from any place, it is your duty, if possible, to destroy it."—*Letter of* ADMIRAL DUPONT, *commanding South Atlantic Squadron, to* LIEUTENANT-COMMANDER HUGHES *of United States Gunboat Mohawk, Fernandina Harbor.*

sured them that, if this programme were literally carried out, we would straightway return and burn the town, or what was left of it, for our share. It was essential to show my officers and men that, while rigid against irregular outrage, we could still be inexorable against the enemy.

We had previously planned to stop at this town, on our way down river, for some valuable lumber which we had espied on a wharf; and gliding down the swift current, shelling a few bluffs as we passed, we soon reached it. Punctual as the figures in a panorama appeared the old ladies with their white handkerchiefs. Taking possession of the town, much of which had previously been destroyed by the gunboats, and stationing the color-guard, to their infinite delight, in the cupola of the most conspicuous house, I deployed skirmishers along the exposed suburb, and set a detail of men at work on the lumber. After a stately and decorous interview with the queens of society of St. Mary's,—is it Scott[7] who says that nothing improves the manners like piracy?—I peacefully withdrew the men when the work was done. There were faces of disappointment among the officers,—for all felt a spirit of mischief after the last night's adventure,—when, just as we had fairly swung out into the stream and were under way, there came, like the sudden burst of a tropical tornado, a regular little hail-storm of bullets into the open end of the boat, driving every gunner in an instant from his post, and surprising even those who were looking to be surprised. The shock was but for a second; and though the bullets had pattered precisely like the sound of hail upon the iron cannon, yet nobody was hurt. With very respectable promptness, order was restored, our own shells were flying into the woods from which the attack proceeded, and we were steaming up to the wharf again, according to promise.

Who shall describe the theatrical attitudes assumed by the old ladies as they reappeared at the front-door,—being luckily out of direct range,—and set the handkerchiefs in wilder motion than ever? They brandished them, they twirled them after the manner of the domestic mop, they clasped their hands, handkerchiefs included. Meanwhile their friends in the wood popped away steadily at us, with small effect; and occasionally an invisible field-piece thundered feebly from another quarter, with equally invisible results. Reaching the wharf, one company, under Lieutenant (now Captain) Danilson, was promptly deployed in search of our assailants, who soon grew silent. Not so the old ladies, when I announced to them my purpose, and added, with extreme regret, that, as the wind was high, I should burn only that half of the town which lay to leeward of their house, which did not, after all, amount to much. Between gratitude for this degree of mercy, and imploring appeals for greater, the treacherous old ladies manœuvred with clasped hands and demonstrative handkerchiefs around me, impairing the effect of their eloquence by constantly addressing me as "Mr. Captain"; for I have observed, that, while the sternest officer is greatly propitiated by attributing to him a rank a little higher than his own, yet no one is ever mollified by an error in the opposite direction. I tried, however, to disregard such low considerations, and to strike the correct mean between the sublime patriot and the unsanctified incendiary, while I could find no refuge from weak contrition save in greater and greater depths of courtesy; and so melodramatic became our interview that some of the soldiers still maintain that "dem dar ole Secesh women been a-gwine for kiss de Cunnel," before we ended. But of this monstrous accusation I wish to register an explicit denial, once for all.

Dropping down to Fernandina unmolested after this affair, we were kindly received by the military and naval commanders,— Colonel Hawley, of the Seventh Connecticut (now Brigadier-General Hawley), and Lieutenant-Commander Hughes, of the gunboat Mohawk. It turned out very opportunely that both of these officers had special errands to suggest still farther up the St. Mary's, and precisely in the region where I wished to go. Colonel Hawley showed me a letter from the War Department, requesting him to ascertain the possibility of obtaining a supply of brick for Fort Clinch from the brickyard which had furnished the original materials, but which had not been visited since the perilous river-trip of the Ottawa. Lieutenant Hughes wished to obtain information for the Admiral respecting a Rebel steamer,—the Berosa,—said to be lying somewhere up the river, and awaiting her chance to run the blockade. I jumped at the opportunity. Berosa and brickyard,—both were near Woodstock, the former home of Corporal Sutton; he was ready and eager to pilot us up the river; the moon would be just right that evening, setting at 3h. 19m. A.M.; and our boat was precisely the one to undertake the expedition. Its double-headed shape was just what was needed in that swift and crooked stream; the exposed pilot-houses had been tolerably barricaded with the thick planks from St. Simon's; and we further obtained some sand-bags from Fort Clinch, through the aid of Captain Sears, the officer in charge, who had originally suggested the expedition after brick. In return for this aid, the Planter was sent back to the wharf at St. Mary's, to bring away a considerable supply of the same precious article, which we had observed near the wharf. Meanwhile the John Adams was coaling from naval supplies, through the kindness of Lieutenant Hughes; and the Ben De Ford was taking in the lumber which we had yesterday brought down. It was a great disappointment to be unable to take the latter vessel up the river; but I was unwillingly convinced that, though the depth of water might be sufficient, yet her length would be unmanageable in the swift current and sharp turns. The Planter must also be sent on a separate cruise, as her weak and disabled machinery made her useless for my purpose. Two hundred men were therefore transferred, as before, to the narrow hold of the John Adams, in addition to the company permanently stationed on board to work the guns. At seven o'clock on the evening of January 29th, beneath a lovely moon, we steamed up the river.

Never shall I forget the mystery and excitement of that night. I know nothing in life more fascinating than the nocturnal ascent of an unknown river, leading far into an enemy's country, where one glides in the dim moonlight between dark hills and meadows, each turn of the channel making it seem like an inland lake, and cutting you off as by a barrier from all behind,—with no sign of human life, but an occasional picket-fire left glimmering beneath the bank, or the yelp of a dog from some low-lying plantation. On such occasions every nerve is strained to its utmost tension; all dreams of romance appear to promise immediate fulfilment; all lights on board the vessel are obscured, loud voices are hushed; you fancy a thousand men on shore, and yet see nothing; the lonely river, unaccustomed to furrowing keels, lapses by the vessel with a treacherous sound; and all the senses are merged in a sort of anxious trance. Three times I have had in full perfection this fascinating experience; but that night was the first, and its zest was the keenest. It will come back to me in dreams, if I live a thousand years.

I feared no attack during our ascent,—that danger was for our return; but I feared the intricate navigation of the river, though I did not fully know, till the actual experience, how dangerous it was. We passed without trouble far above the scene of our first fight,—the Battle of the Hundred Pines, as my officers had baptized it; and ever, as we ascended, the banks grew steeper, the current swifter, the channel more tortuous and more encumbered with projecting branches and drifting wood. No piloting less skilful than that of Corporal Sutton and his mate, James Bezzard, could have carried us through, I thought; and no side-wheel steamer less strong than a ferry-boat could have borne the crash and force with which we struck the wooded banks of the river. But the powerful paddles, built to break the Northern ice, could crush the Southern pine as well; and we came safely out of entanglements that at first seemed formidable. We had the tide with us, which makes steering far more difficult; and, in the sharp angles of the river, there was often no resource but to run the bow boldly on shore, let the stern swing round, and then reverse the motion. As the reversing machinery was generally out of order, the engineer stupid or frightened, and the captain excited, this involved moments of tolerably concentrated anxiety. Eight times we grounded in the upper waters, and once lay aground for half an hour; but at last we dropped anchor before the little town of Woodstock, after moon-set and an hour before daybreak, just as I had planned, and so quietly that scarcely a dog barked, and not a soul in the town, as we afterwards found, knew of our arrival.

As silently as possible, the great flat-boat which we had brought from St. Simon's was filled with men. Major Strong was sent on shore with two companies,—those of Captain James and Captain Metcalf,—with instructions to surround the town quietly, allow no one to leave it, molest no one, and hold as temporary prisoners every man whom he found. I watched them push off into the darkness, got the remaining force ready to land, and then paced the deck for an hour in silent watchfulness, waiting for rifle-shots. Not a sound came from the shore, save the barking of dogs and the morning crow of cocks; the time seemed interminable; but when daylight came, I landed, and found a pair of scarlet trousers pacing on their beat before every house in the village, and a small squad of prisoners, stunted and forlorn as Falstaff's ragged regiment,[8] already in hand. I observed with delight the good demeanor of my men towards these folorn Anglo-Saxons, and towards the more tumultuous women. Even one soldier, who threatened to throw an old termagant into the river, took care to append the courteous epithet "Madam."

I took a survey of the premises. The chief house, a pretty one with picturesque outbuildings, was that of Mrs. A., who owned the mills and lumber-wharves adjoining. The wealth of these wharves had not been exaggerated. There was lumber enough to freight half a dozen steamers, and I half regretted that I had agreed to take down a freight of bricks instead. Further researches made me grateful that I had already explained to my men the difference between public foraging and private plunder. Along the river-bank I found building after building crowded with costly furniture, all neatly packed, just as it was sent up from St. Mary's when that town was abandoned. Pianos were a drug; china, glass-ware, mahogany, pictures, all were here. And here were my men, who knew that their own labor had earned for their masters these luxuries, or such as these; their own wives and children were still sleeping on the floor, perhaps, at Beaufort or Fernandina; and yet they submitted, almost without a murmur, to the enforced abstinence. Bed and bedding for our hospitals they might take from those store-rooms,—such as the surgeon selected,—also an old flag which we found in a corner, and an old field-piece (which the regiment still possesses),—but after this the doors were closed and left unmolested. It cost a struggle to some of the men, whose wives were destitute, I know; but their pride was very easily touched, and when this abstinence was once recognized as a rule, they claimed it as an honor, in this and all succeeding expeditions. I flatter myself that, if they had once been set upon wholesale plundering, they would have done it as thoroughly as their betters; but I have always been infinitely grateful, both for the credit and for the discipline of the regiment,—as well as for the men's subsequent lives,—that the opposite method was adopted.

When the morning was a little advanced, I called on Mrs. A., who received me in quite a stately way at her own door with "To

what am I indebted for the honor of this visit, Sir?" The foreign
name of the family, and the tropical look of the buildings, made
it seem (as, indeed, did all the rest of the adventure) like a chapter
out of "Amyas Leigh";[9] but as I had happened to hear that the
lady herself was a Philadelphian, and her deceased husband a
New-Yorker, I could not feel even that modicum of reverence
due to sincere Southerners. However, I wished to present my credentials; so, calling up my companion, I said that I believed she
had been previously acquainted with Corporal Robert Sutton? I
never saw a finer bit of unutterable indignation than came over
the face of my hostess, as she slowly recognized him. She drew
herself up, and dropped out the monosyllables of her answer as
if they were so many drops of nitric acid. "Ah," quoth my lady,
"*we* called him Bob!"

It was a group for a painter. The whole drama of the war
seemed to reverse itself in an instant, and my tall, well-dressed,
imposing, philosophic Corporal dropped down the immeasurable
depth into a mere plantation "Bob" again. So at least in my imagination; not to that person himself. Too essentially dignified in
his nature to be moved by words where substantial realities were
in question, he simply turned from the lady, touched his hat to
me, and asked if I would wish to see the slave-jail, as he had the
keys in his possession.

If he fancied that I was in danger of being overcome by blandishments, and needed to be recalled to realities, it was a master-
stroke.

I must say that, when the door of that villanous edifice was
thrown open before me, I felt glad that my main interview with
its lady proprietor had passed before I saw it. It was a small building, like a Northern corn-barn, and seemed to have as prominent
and as legitimate a place among the outbuildings of the establishment. In the middle of the door was a large staple with a rusty
chain, like an ox-chain, for fastening a victim down. When the
door had been opened after the death of the late proprietor, my
informant said, a man was found padlocked in that chain. We
found also three pairs of stocks of various construction, two of
which had smaller as well as larger holes, evidently for the feet of
women or children. In a building near by we found something
far more complicated, which was perfectly unintelligible till the

men explained all its parts: a machine so contrived that a person once imprisoned in it could neither sit, stand, nor lie, but must support the body half raised, in a position scarcely endurable. I have since bitterly reproached myself for leaving this piece of in-genuity behind; but it would have cost much labor to remove it, and to bring away the other trophies seemed then enough. I re-member the unutterable loathing with which I leaned against the door of that prison-house; I had thought myself seasoned to any conceivable horrors of Slavery, but it seemed as if the visible pres-ence of that den of sin would choke me. Of course it would have been burned to the ground by us, but that this would have in-volved the sacrifice of every other building and all the piles of lumber, and for the moment it seemed as if the sacrifice would be righteous. But I forbore, and only took as trophies the instru-ments of torture and the keys of the jail.

We found but few colored people in this vicinity; some we brought away with us, and an old man and woman preferred to remain. All the white males whom we found I took as hostages, in order to shield us, if possible, from attack on our way down river, explaining to them that they would be put on shore when the dangerous points were passed. I knew that their wives could easily send notice of this fact to the Rebel forces along the river. My hostages were a forlorn-looking set of "crackers," far inferior to our soldiers in *physique*, and yet quite equal, the latter declared, to the average material of the Southern armies. None were in uni-form, but this proved nothing as to their being soldiers. One of them, a mere boy, was captured at his own door, with gun in hand. It was a fowling-piece, which he used only, as his mother plaintively assured me, "to shoot little birds with." As the guile-less youth had for this purpose loaded the gun with eighteen buck-shot, we thought it justifiable to confiscate both the weapon and the owner, in mercy to the birds.

We took from this place, for the use of the army, a flock of some thirty sheep, forty bushels of rice, some other provisions, tools, oars, and a little lumber, leaving all possible space for the bricks which we expected to obtain just below. I should have gone farther up the river, but for a dangerous boom which kept back a great number of logs in a large brook that here fell into the St. Mary's; the stream ran with force, and if the Rebels had wit enough to do it, they might in ten minutes so choke the river with drift-wood as infinitely to enhance our troubles. So we dropped down stream a mile or two, found the very brickyard from which Fort Clinch had been constructed,—still stored with bricks, and seemingly unprotected. Here Sergeant Rivers again planted his standard, and the men toiled eagerly, for several hours, in loading our boat to the utmost with the bricks. Meanwhile we questioned black and white witnesses, and learned for the first time that the Rebels admitted a repulse at Township Landing, and that Lieutenant Jones and ten of their number were killed,—though this I fancy to have been an exaggeration. They also declared that the mysterious steamer Berosa was lying at the head of the river, but was a broken-down and worthless affair, and would never get to sea. The result has since proved this; for the vessel subsequently ran the blockade and foundered near shore, the crew barely escaping with their lives. I had the pleasure, as it happened, of being the first person to forward this information to Admiral Dupont, when it came through the pickets, many months after,—thus concluding my report on the Berosa.

Before the work at the yard was over the pickets reported mounted men in the woods near by, as had previously been the report at Woodstock. This admonished us to lose no time; and as we left the wharf, immediate arrangements were made to have the gun-crews all in readiness, and to keep the rest of the men below, since their musketry would be of little use now, and I did not propose to risk a life unnecessarily. The chief obstacle to this was their own eagerness; penned down on one side, they popped up on the other; their officers, too, were eager to see what was going on, and were almost as hard to cork down as the men. Add to this, that the vessel was now very crowded, and that I had to be chiefly on the hurricane-deck with the pilots. Captain Clifton, master of the vessel, was brave to excess, and as much excited as the men; he could no more be kept in the little pilot-house than they below; and when we had passed one or two bluffs, with no sign of an enemy, he grew more and more irrepressible, and exposed himself conspicuously on the upper deck. Perhaps we all were a little lulled by apparent safety; for myself, I lay down for a moment on a settee in a state-room, having been on my feet, almost without cessation, for twenty-four hours.

Suddenly there swept down from a bluff above us, on the Georgia side, a mingling of shout and roar and rattle as of a tornado let loose; and as a storm of bullets came pelting against the sides of the vessel, and through a window, there went up a shrill answering shout from our own men. It took but an instant for me to reach the gun-deck. After all my efforts the men had swarmed once more from below, and already, crowding at both ends of the boat, were loading and firing with inconceivable rapidity, shouting to each other, "Nebber gib it up!" and of course having no steady aim, as the vessel glided and whirled in the swift current. Meanwhile the officers in charge of the large guns had their crews in order, and our shells began to fly over the bluffs, which, as we now saw, should have been shelled in advance, only that we had to economize ammunition. The other soldiers I drove below, almost by main force, with the aid of their officers, who behaved exceedingly well, giving the men leave to fire from the open port-holes which lined the lower deck, almost at the water's level. In the very midst of the *mêlée* Major Strong came from the upper deck, with a face of horror, and whispered to me, "Captain Clifton was killed at the first shot by my side."

If he had said that the vessel was on fire the shock would hardly have been greater. Of course, the military commander on board a steamer is almost as helpless as an unarmed man, so far as the risks of water go. A seaman must command there. In the hazardous voyage of last night, I had learned, though unjustly, to distrust every official on board the steamboat except this excitable, brave, warm-hearted sailor; and now, among these added dangers, to lose him! The responsibility for his life also thrilled me; he was not among my soldiers, and yet he was killed. I thought of his wife and children, of whom he had spoken; but one learns to think rapidly in war, and, cautioning the Major to silence, I went up to the hurricane-deck and drew in the helpless body, that it should be safe from further desecration, and then looked to see where we were.

We were now gliding past a safe reach of marsh, while our assailants were riding by cross-paths to attack us at the next bluff. It was Reed's Bluff where we were first attacked, and Scrubby Bluff, I think, was next. They were shelled in advance, but swarmed manfully to the banks again as we swept round one of the sharp angles of the stream beneath their fire. My men were now pretty well imprisoned below in the hot and crowded hold, and actually fought each other, the officers afterwards said, for places at the open port-holes, from which to aim. Others implored to be landed, exclaiming that they "supposed de Cunnel knew best," but it was "mighty mean" to be shut up down below, when they might be "fightin' de Secesh *in de clar field.*" This clear field, and no favor, was what they thenceforward sighed for. But in such difficult navigation it would have been madness to think of landing, although one daring Rebel actually sprang upon the large boat which we towed astern, where he was shot down by one of our sergeants. This boat was soon after swamped and abandoned, then taken and repaired by the Rebels at a later date, and finally, by a piece of dramatic completeness, was seized by a party of fugitive slaves, who escaped in it to our lines, and some of whom enlisted in my own regiment.

It has always been rather a mystery to me why the Rebels did not fell a few trees across the stream at some of the many sharp angles where we might so easily have been thus imprisoned. This, however, they did not attempt, and with the skilful pilotage of our trusty Corporal,—philosophic as Socrates through all the din, and occasionally relieving his mind by taking a shot with his rifle through the high port-holes of the pilot-house,—we glided safely on. The steamer did not ground once on the descent, and the mate in command, Mr. Smith, did his duty very well. The plank sheathing of the pilot-house was penetrated by few bullets, though struck by so many outside that it was visited as a curiosity after our return; and even among the gun-crews, though they had no protection, not a man was hurt. As we approached some wooded bluff, usually on the Georgia side, we could see galloping along the hillside what seemed a regiment of mounted riflemen, and could see our shell scatter them ere we approached. Shelling did not, however, prevent a rather fierce fusilade from our old friends of Captain Clark's company at Waterman's Bluff, near Township Landing; but even this did no serious damage, and this was the last.

It was of course impossible, while thus running the gauntlet, to put our hostages ashore, and I could only explain to them that they must thank their own friends for their inevitable detention.

I was by no means proud of their forlorn appearance, and besought Colonel Hawley to take them off my hands; but he was sending no flags of truce at that time, and liked their looks no better than I did. So I took them to Port Royal, where they were afterwards sent safely across the lines. Our men were pleased at taking them back with us, as they had already said, regretfully, "S'pose we leave dem Secesh at Fernandina, General Saxby won't see 'em,"—as if they were some new natural curiosity, which indeed they were. One soldier further suggested the expediency of keeping them permanently in camp, to be used as marks for the guns of the relieved guard every morning. But this was rather an ebullition of fancy than a sober proposition.

Against these levities I must put a piece of more tragic eloquence, which I took down by night on the steamer's deck from the thrilling harangue of Corporal Adam Allston, one of our most gifted prophets, whose influence over the men was unbounded. "When I heard," he said, "de bombshell a-screamin' troo de woods like de Judgment Day, I said to myself, 'If my head was took off to-night, dey could n't put my soul in de torments, perceps [except] God was my enemy!' And when de rifle-bullets came whizzin' across de deck, I cried aloud, 'God help my congregation! Boys, load and fire!' "

I must pass briefly over the few remaining days of our cruise. At Fernandina we met the Planter, which had been successful on her separate expedition, and had destroyed extensive salt-works at Crooked River, under charge of the energetic Captain Trowbridge, efficiently aided by Captain Rogers. Our commodities being in part delivered at Fernandina, our decks being full, coal nearly out, and time up, we called once more at St. Simon's Sound, bringing away the remainder of our railroad-iron, with some which the naval officers had previously disinterred, and then steamed back to Beaufort. Arriving there at sunrise (February 2, 1863), I made my way with Dr. Rogers to General Saxton's bedroom, and laid before him the keys and shackles of the slave-prison, with my report of the good conduct of the men,—as Dr. Rogers remarked, a message from heaven and another from hell.

Slight as this expedition now seems among the vast events of the war, the future student of the newspapers of that day will find that it occupied no little space in their columns, so intense was

the interest which then attached to the novel experiment of em-
ploying black troops. So obvious, too, was the value, during this
raid, of their local knowledge and their enthusiasm, that it was
impossible not to find in its successes new suggestions for the war.
Certainly I would not have consented to repeat the enterprise with
the bravest white troops, leaving Corporal Sutton and his mates
behind, for I should have expected to fail. For a year after our
raid the Upper St. Mary's remained unvisited, till in 1864 the large
force with which we held Florida secured peace upon its banks;
then Mrs. A. took the oath of allegiance, the Government bought
her remaining lumber, and the John Adams again ascended with
a detachment of my men under Lieutenant Parker, and brought a
portion of it to Fernandina. By a strange turn of fortune, Corporal
Sutton (now Sergeant) was at this time in jail at Hilton Head,
under sentence of court-martial for an alleged act of mutiny,—an
affair in which the general voice of our officers sustained him and
condemned his accusers, so that he soon received a full pardon,
and was restored in honor to his place in the regiment, which he
has ever since held.

Nothing can ever exaggerate the fascinations of war, whether
on the largest or smallest scale. When we settled down into camp-
life again, it seemed like a butterfly's folding its wings to re-enter
the chrysalis. None of us could listen to the crack of a gun without
recalling instantly the sharp shots that spilled down from the
bluffs of the St. Mary's, or hear a sudden trampling of horsemen
by night without recalling the sounds which startled us on the
Field of the Hundred Pines. The memory of our raid was preserved in the camp by many legends of adventure, growing vaster
and more incredible as time wore on,—and by the morning appeals to the surgeon of some veteran invalids, who could now cut
off all reproofs and suspicions with "Doctor, I 's been a sickly
pusson eber since de *expeditious*." But to me the most vivid re-
membrancer was the flock of sheep which we had "lifted." The
Post Quartermaster discreetly gave us the charge of them, and
they filled a gap in the landscape and in the larder,—which last
had before presented one unvaried round of impenetrable beef.
Mr. Obadiah Oldbuck,[10] when he decided to adopt a pastoral life,
and assumed the provisional name of Thyrsis, never looked upon
his flocks and herds with more unalloyed contentment than I

upon that fleecy family. I had been familiar, in Kansas, with the metaphor by which the sentiments of an owner were credited to his property, and had heard of a proslavery colt and an antislavery cow. The fact that these sheep were but recently converted from "Secesh" sentiments was their crowning charm. Methought they frisked and fattened in the joy of their deliverance from the shadow of Mrs. A.'s slave-jail, and gladly contemplated translation into mutton-broth for sick or wounded soldiers. The very slaves who once, perchance, were sold at auction with yon aged patriarch of the flock, had now asserted their humanity, and would devour him as hospital rations. Meanwhile our shepherd bore a sharp bayonet without a crook, and I felt myself a peer of Ulysses and Rob Roy,[11]—those sheep-stealers of less elevated aims,—when I met in my daily rides these wandering trophies of our wider wanderings.

CHAPTER IV

Up the St. John's

There was not much stirring in the Department of the South early in 1863, and the St. Mary's expedition had afforded a new sensation. Of course the few officers of colored troops, and a larger number who wished to become such, were urgent for further experiments in the same line; and the Florida tax-commissioners were urgent likewise. I well remember the morning when, after some preliminary correspondence, I steamed down from Beaufort, S. C., to Hilton Head, with General Saxton, Judge S., and one or two others, to have an interview on the matter with Major-General Hunter, then commanding the Department.

Hilton Head, in those days, seemed always like some foreign military station in the tropics. The long, low, white buildings, with piazzas and verandas on the waterside; the general impression of heat and lassitude, existence appearing to pulsate only with the sea-breeze; the sandy, almost impassable streets; and the firm, level beach, on which everybody walked who could get there: all these suggested Jamaica or the East Indies. Then the head-quarters at the end of the beach, the Zouave sentinels, the successive anterooms, the lounging aids, the good-natured and easy General,—easy by habit and energetic by impulse,—all had a certain air of Southern languor, rather picturesque, but perhaps not altogether bracing. General Hunter received us, that day, with his usual kindliness; there was a good deal of pleasant chat; Miles O'Reilly[1] was called in to read his latest verses; and then we came to the matter in hand.

Jacksonville, on the St. John's River, in Florida, had been already twice taken and twice evacuated; having been occupied by Brigadier-General Wright, in March, 1862, and by Brigadier-General Brannan, in October of the same year. The second evacuation was by Major-General Hunter's own order, on the avowed ground that a garrison of five thousand was needed to hold the place, and that this force could not be spared. The present proposition was to take and hold it with a brigade of less than a thousand men, carrying, however, arms and uniforms for twice that number, and a month's rations. The claim was, that there were fewer rebel troops in the Department than formerly, and that the St. Mary's expedition had shown the advantage possessed by colored troops, in local knowledge, and in the confidence of the loyal blacks. It was also urged, that it was worth while to risk something, in the effort to hold Florida, and perhaps bring it back into the Union.

My chief aim in the negotiation was to get the men into action, and that of the Florida Commissioners to get them into Florida. Thus far coinciding, we could heartily co-operate; and though General Hunter made some reasonable objections, they were yielded more readily than I had feared; and finally, before half our logical ammunition was exhausted, the desired permission was given, and the thing might be considered as done.

We were now to leave, as we supposed forever, the camp which had thus far been our home. Our vast amount of surplus baggage made a heavy job in the loading, inasmuch as we had no wharf, and everything had to be put on board by means of flat-boats. It was completed by twenty-four hours of steady work; and after some of the usual uncomfortable delays which wait on military expeditions, we were at last afloat.

I had tried to keep the plan as secret as possible, and had requested to have no definite orders, until we should be on board ship. But this larger expedition was less within my own hands than was the St. Mary's affair, and the great reliance for concealment was on certain counter reports, ingeniously set afloat by some of the Florida men. These reports rapidly swelled into the most enormous tales, and by the time they reached the New York newspapers, the expedition was "a great volcano about bursting, whose lava will burn, flow, and destroy,"—"the sudden appearance in arms of no less than five thousand negroes,"—"a liberating host,"—"not the phantom, but the reality, of servile insurrection." What the undertaking actually was may be best seen in the instructions which guided it.*

In due time, after touching at Fernandina, we reached the difficult bar of the St. John's, and were piloted safely over. Admiral Dupont had furnished a courteous letter of introduction,* and we were cordially received by Commander Duncan of the Norwich, and Lieutenant Watson, commanding the Uncas. Like all officers on blockade duty, they were impatient of their enforced inaction, and gladly seized the opportunity for a different service. It was

---

*HEAD-QUARTERS, BEAUFORT, S. C.,
MARCH 5, 1863.

COLONEL,—You will please proceed with your command, the First and Second Regiments South Carolina Volunteers, which are now embarked upon the steamers John Adams, Boston, and Burnside, to Fernandina, Florida.

Relying upon your military skill and judgment, I shall give you no special directions as to your procedure after you leave Fernandina. I expect, however, that you will occupy Jacksonville, Florida, and intrench yourselves there.

The main objects of your expedition are to carry the proclamation of freedom to the enslaved; to call all loyal men into the service of the United States; to occupy as much of the State of Florida as possible with the forces under your command; and to neglect no means consistent with the usages of civilized warfare to weaken, harass, and annoy those who are in rebellion against the Government of the United States.

Trusting that the blessing of our Heavenly Father will rest upon your noble enterprise,

I am yours, sincerely,
R. SAXTON,
Brig.-Gen., Mil. Gov. Dept. of the South.

Colonel Higginson, Comdg. Expeditionary Corps.

*FLAG SHIP WABASH,
PORT ROYAL HARBOR, S. C., March 6, 1863.
SIR,—I am informed by Major-General Hunter that he is sending Colonel Higginson on an important mission in the southerly part of his Department.

I have not been made acquainted with the objects of this mission, but any assistance that you can offer Colonel Higginson, which will not interfere with your other duties, you are authorized to give.

Respectfully your obedient servant,
S. F. DUPONT,
Rear-Adm. Comdg. S. Atl. Block. Squad.

To the Senior Officer present at the different Blockading Stations on the Coast of Georgia and Florida.

some time since they had ascended as high as Jacksonville, for their orders were strict, one vessel's coal was low, the other was in infirm condition, and there were rumors of cotton-clads and torpedoes. But they gladly agreed to escort us up the river, so soon as our own armed gunboat, the John Adams, should arrive,—she being unaccountably delayed.

We waited twenty-four hours for her, at the sultry mouth of that glassy river, watching the great pelicans which floated lazily on its tide, or sometimes shooting one, to admire the great pouch, into which one of the soldiers could insert his foot, as into a boot. "He hold one quart," said the admiring experimentalist. "Hi! boy," retorted another quickly, "neber you bring dat quart measure in *my* peck o' corn." The protest came very promptly, and was certainly fair; for the strange receptacle would have held nearly a gallon.

We went on shore, too, and were shown a rather pathetic little garden, which the naval officers had laid out, indulging a dream of vegetables. They lingered over the little microscopic sprouts, pointing them out tenderly, as if they were cradled babies. I have often noticed this touching weakness, in gentlemen of that profession, on lonely stations.

We wandered among the bluffs, too, in the little deserted hamlet once called "Pilot Town." The ever-shifting sand had in some cases almost buried the small houses, and had swept around others a circular drift, at a few yards' distance, overtopping their eaves, and leaving each the untouched citadel of this natural redoubt. There was also a dismantled lighthouse, an object which always seems the most dreary symbol of the barbarism of war, when one considers the national beneficence which reared and kindled it. Despite the service rendered by this once brilliant light, there were many wrecks which had been strown upon the beach, victims of the most formidable of the Southern river-bars. As I stood with my foot on the half-buried ribs of one of these vessels,—so distinctly traced that one might almost fancy them human,—the old pilot, my companion, told me the story of the wreck. The vessel had formerly been in the Cuba trade; and her owner, an American merchant residing in Havana, had christened her for his young daughter. I asked the name, and was startled to recognize that of a favorite young cousin of mine, beside the bones of whose representative I was thus strangely standing, upon this lonely shore.

It was well to have something to relieve the anxiety naturally felt at the delay of the John Adams,—anxiety both for her safety and for the success of our enterprise. The Rebels had repeatedly threatened to burn the whole of Jacksonville, in case of another attack, as they had previously burned its mills and its great hotel. It seemed as if the news of our arrival must surely have travelled thirty miles by this time. All day we watched every smoke that rose among the wooded hills, and consulted the compass and the map, to see if that sign announced the doom of our expected home. At the very last moment of the tide, just in time to cross the bar that day, the missing vessel arrived; all anxieties vanished; I transferred my quarters on board, and at two the next morning we steamed up the river.

Again there was the dreamy delight of ascending an unknown stream, beneath a sinking moon, into a region where peril made fascination. Since the time of the first explorers, I suppose that those Southern waters have known no sensations so dreamy and so bewitching as those which this war has brought forth. I recall, in this case, the faintest sensations of our voyage, as Ponce de Leon[2] may have recalled those of his wandering search, in the same soft zone, for the secret of the mystic fountain. I remember how, during that night, I looked for the first time through a powerful night-glass. It had always seemed a thing wholly inconceivable, that a mere lens could change darkness into light; and as I turned the instrument on the preceding gunboat, and actually discerned the man at the wheel and the officers standing about him,—all relapsing into vague gloom again at the withdrawal of the glass,—it gave a feeling of childish delight. Yet it seemed only in keeping with the whole enchantment of the scene; and had I been some Aladdin,[3] convoyed by genii or giants, I could hardly have felt more wholly a denizen of some world of romance.

But the river was of difficult navigation; and we began to feel sometimes, beneath the keel, that ominous, sliding, grating, treacherous arrest of motion which makes the heart shudder, as the vessel does. There was some solicitude about torpedoes, also,—a peril which became a formidable thing, one year later, in the very channel where we found none. Soon one of our consorts grounded, then another, every vessel taking its turn, I believe, and then in turn getting off, until the Norwich lay hopelessly stranded, for that tide at least, a few miles below Jacksonville, and out of sight of the city, so that she could not even add to our dignity by her visible presence from afar.

This was rather a serious matter, as the Norwich was our main naval reliance, the Uncas being a small steamer of less than two hundred tons, and in such poor condition that Commander Duncan, on finding himself aground, at first quite declined to trust his consort any farther alone. But, having got thus far, it was plainly my duty to risk the remainder with or without naval assistance; and this being so, the courageous officer did not long object, but allowed his dashing subordinate to steam up with us to the city. This left us one naval and one army gunboat; and, fortunately, the Burnside, being a black propeller, always passed for an armed vessel among the Rebels, and we rather encouraged that pleasing illusion.

We had aimed to reach Jacksonville at daybreak; but these mishaps delayed us, and we had several hours of fresh, early sunshine, lighting up the green shores of that lovely river, wooded to the water's edge, with sometimes an emerald meadow, opening a vista to some picturesque house,—all utterly unlike anything we had yet seen in the South, and suggesting rather the Penobscot or Kennebec.⁴ Here and there we glided by the ruins of some sawmill burned by the Rebels on General Wright's approach; but nothing else spoke of war, except, perhaps, the silence. It was a delicious day, and a scene of fascination. Our Florida men were wild with delight; and when we rounded the point below the city, and saw from afar its long streets, its brick warehouses, its white cottages, and its overshadowing trees,—all peaceful and undisturbed by flames,—it seemed, in the men's favorite phrase, "too much good," and all discipline was merged, for the moment, in a buzz of ecstasy.

The city was still there for us, at any rate; though none knew what perils might be concealed behind those quiet buildings. Yet there were children playing on the wharves; careless men, here and there, lounged down to look at us, hands in pockets; a few women came to their doors, and gazed listlessly upon us, shading their eyes with their hands. We drew momently nearer, in silence and with breathless attention. The gunners were at their posts, and the men in line. It was eight o'clock. We were now directly opposite the town: yet no sign of danger was seen; not a rifle-shot was heard; not a shell rose hissing in the air. The Uncas rounded to, and dropped anchor in the stream; by previous agreement, I steamed to an upper pier of the town, Colonel Montgomery to a lower one; the little boat-howitzers were run out upon the wharves, and presently to the angles of the chief streets; and the pretty town was our own without a shot. In spite of our detention, the surprise had been complete, and not a soul in Jacksonville had dreamed of our coming.

The day passed quickly, in eager preparations for defence; the people could or would give us no definite information about the Rebel camp, which was, however, known to be near, and our force did not permit our going out to surprise it. The night following was the most anxious I ever spent. We were all tired out; the companies were under arms, in various parts of the town, to be ready for an attack at any moment. My temporary quarters were beneath the loveliest grove of linden-trees, and as I reclined, half-dozing, the mocking-birds sang all night like nightingales,—their notes seeming to trickle down through the sweet air from amid the blossoming boughs. Day brought relief and the sense of due possession, and we could see what we had won.

Jacksonville was now a United States post again: the only post on the main-land in the Department of the South. Before the war it had three or four thousand inhabitants, and a rapidly growing lumber-trade, for which abundant facilities were evidently provided. The wharves were capacious, and the blocks of brick warehouses along the lower street were utterly unlike anything we had yet seen in that region, as were the neatness and thrift everywhere visible. It had been built up by Northern enterprise, and much of the property was owned by loyal men. It had been a great resort for invalids, though the Rebels had burned the large hotel which once accommodated them. Mills had also been burned; but the dwelling-houses were almost all in good condition. The quarters for the men were admirable; and I took official possession of the handsome brick house of Colonel Sunderland, the established head-quarters through every occupation, whose accommodating flag-staff had literally and repeatedly changed its colors. The seceded Colonel, reputed author of the State ordinance of Secession, was a New-Yorker by birth, and we found his law-card, issued when in practice in Easton, Washington County, New York. He certainly had good taste in planning the inside of a house, though time had impaired its condition. There was a neat office with ample bookcases and no books, a billiard-table with no balls, gas-fixtures without gas, and a bathing-room without water. There was a separate building for servants' quarters, and a kitchen with every convenience, even to a few jars of lingering pickles. On the whole, there was an air of substance and comfort about the town, quite alien from the picturesque decadence of Beaufort.

The town rose gradually from the river, and was bounded on the rear by a long, sluggish creek, beyond which lay a stretch of woods, affording an excellent covert for the enemy, but without great facilities for attack, as there were but two or three fords and bridges. This brook could easily be held against a small force, but could at any time and at almost any point be readily crossed by a large one. North of the town the land rose a little, between the river and the sources of the brook, and then sank to a plain, which had been partially cleared by a previous garrison. For so small a force as ours, however, this clearing must be extended nearer to the town; otherwise our lines would be too long for our numbers.

This deficiency in numbers at once became a source of serious anxiety. While planning the expedition, it had seemed so important to get the men a foothold in Florida that I was willing to risk everything for it. But this important post once in our possession, it began to show some analogies to the proverbial elephant in the lottery. To hold it permanently with nine hundred men was not, perhaps, impossible, with the aid of a gunboat (I had left many of my own regiment sick and on duty in Beaufort, and Colonel Montgomery had as yet less than one hundred and fifty); but to hold it, and also to make forays up the river, certainly required a larger number. We came in part to recruit, but had found scarcely an able-bodied negro in the city; all had been removed farther up, and we must certainly contrive to follow them. I was very unwilling to have, as yet, any white troops under my command, with the blacks. Finally, however, being informed by Judge S. of a conversation with Colonel Hawley, commanding at Fernandina, in which the latter had offered to send four companies and a light battery to swell our force,—in view of the aid given to his position by this more advanced post, I decided to authorize the energetic Judge to go back to Fernandina and renew the negotiation, as the John Adams must go thither at any rate for coal.

Meanwhile all definite display of our force was avoided; dress-parades were omitted; the companies were so distributed as to tell for the utmost; and judicious use was made, here and there, of empty tents. The gunboats and transports moved impressively up and down the river, from time to time. The disposition of pickets was varied each night to perplex the enemy, and some advantage taken of his distrust, which might be assumed as equalling our own. The citizens were duly impressed by our supply of ammunition, which was really enormous, and all these things soon took effect. A loyal woman, who came into town, said that the Rebel scouts, stopping at her house, reported that there were "sixteen hundred negroes all over the woods, and the town full of them besides." "It was of no use to go in. General Finnegan had driven them into a bad place once, and should not do it again." "They had lost their captain and their best surgeon in the first skirmish, and if the Savannah people wanted the negroes driven away, they might come and do it themselves." Unfortunately, we knew that they could easily come from Savannah at any time, as there was railroad communication nearly all the way; and every time we heard the steam-whistle, the men were convinced of their arrival. Thus we never could approach to any certainty as to their numbers, while they could observe, from the bluffs, every steamboat that ascended the river.

To render our weak force still more available, we barricaded the approaches to the chief streets by constructing barriers or felling trees. It went to my heart to sacrifice, for this purpose, several of my beautiful lindens; but it was no time for æsthetics. As the giants lay on the ground, still scenting the air with their abundant bloom, I used to rein up my horse and watch the children playing hide-and-seek among their branches, or some quiet cow grazing at the foliage. Nothing impresses the mind in war like some occasional object or association that belongs apparently to peace alone.

Among all these solicitudes, it was a great thing that one particular anxiety vanished in a day. On the former expedition the men were upon trial as to their courage; now they were to endure another test, as to their demeanor as victors. Here were five hundred citizens, nearly all white, at the mercy of their former slaves. To some of these whites it was the last crowning humiliation, and they were, or professed to be, in perpetual fear. On the other hand, the most intelligent and lady-like woman I saw, the wife of a Rebel captain, rather surprised me by saying that it seemed pleasanter to have these men stationed there, whom they had known all their lives, and who had generally borne a good character, than to be in the power of entire strangers. Certainly the men deserved the confidence, for there was scarcely an exception to their good behavior. I think they thoroughly felt that their honor and dignity were concerned in the matter, and took too much pride in their character as soldiers,—to say nothing of higher motives,—to tarnish it by any misdeeds. They watched their officers vigilantly and even suspiciously, to detect any disposition towards compromise; and so long as we pursued a just course it was evident that they could be relied on. Yet the spot was pointed out to me where two of our leading men had seen their brothers hanged by Lynch law; many of them had private wrongs to avenge; and they all had utter disbelief in all pretended loyalty, especially on the part of the women.

One citizen alone was brought to me in a sort of escort of honor by Corporal Prince Lambkin,—one of the color-guard, and one of our ablest men,—the same who had once made a speech in camp, reminding his hearers that they had lived under the American flag for eighteen hundred and sixty-two years, and ought to live and die under it. Corporal Lambkin now introduced his man, a German, with the highest compliment in his power, "He hab true colored-man heart." Surrounded by mean, cajoling, insinuating white men and women who were all that and worse, I was quite ready to appreciate the quality he thus proclaimed. A colored-man heart, in the Rebel States, is a fair synonyme for a loyal heart, and it is about the only such synonyme. In this case, I found afterwards that the man in question, a small grocer, had been an object of suspicion to the whites from his readiness to lend money to the negroes, or sell to them on credit; in which, perhaps, there may have been some mixture of self-interest with benevolence.

I resort to a note-book of that period, well thumbed and pocket-worn, which sometimes received a fragment of the day's experience.

"March 16, 1863.

"Of course, droll things are constantly occurring. Every white man, woman, and child is flattering, seductive, and professes Union sentiment; every black ditto believes that every white ditto is a scoundrel, and ought to be shot, but for good order and military discipline. The Provost Marshal and I steer between them as blandly as we can. Such scenes as succeed each other! Rush of indignant Africans. A white man, in woman's clothes, has been seen to enter a certain house,—undoubtedly a spy. Further evidence discloses the Roman Catholic priest, a peaceful little Frenchman, in his professional apparel.—Anxious female enters. Some sentinel has shot her cow by mistake for a Rebel. The United States cannot think of paying the desired thirty dollars. Let her go to the Post-Quartermaster and select a cow from his herd. If there is none to suit her (and, indeed, not one of them gave a drop of milk,—neither did hers), let her wait till the next lot comes in,—that is all.—Yesterday's operations gave the following total yield: Thirty 'contrabands,' eighteen horses, eleven cattle, ten saddles and bridles, and one new army-wagon. At this rate we shall soon be self-supporting *cavalry*.

"Where complaints are made of the soldiers, it almost always turns out that the women have insulted them most grossly, swearing at them, and the like. One unpleasant old Dutch woman came in, bursting with wrath, and told the whole narrative of her blameless life, diversified with sobs:—

" 'Last January I ran off two of my black people from St. Mary's to Fernandina,' (sob,)—'then I moved down there myself, and at Lake City I lost six women and a boy,' (sob,)—'then I stopped at Baldwin for one of the wenches to be confined,' (sob,)—'then I brought them all here to live in a Christian country' (sob, sob). 'Then the blockheads' [blockades, that is, gunboats] 'came, and they all ran off with the blockheads,' (sob, sob, sob,) 'and left me, an old lady of forty-six, obliged to work for a living.' (Chaos of sobs, without cessation.)

"But when I found what the old sinner had said to the soldiers I rather wondered at their self-control in not throttling her."

Meanwhile skirmishing went on daily in the outskirts of the town. There was a fight on the very first day, when our men killed, as before hinted, a Rebel surgeon, which was oddly metamorphosed in the Southern newspapers into their killing one of ours, which certainly never happened. Every day, after this, they appeared in small mounted squads in the neighborhood, and exchanged shots with our pickets, to which the gunboats would contribute their louder share, their aim being rather embarrassed by the woods and hills. We made reconnoissances, too, to learn the country in different directions, and were apt to be fired upon during these. Along the farther side of what we called the "Debatable Land" there was a line of cottages, hardly superior to negro huts, and almost all empty, where the Rebel pickets resorted, and from whose windows they fired. By degrees all these nests were broken up and destroyed, though it cost some trouble to do it, and the hottest skirmishing usually took place around them.

Among these little affairs was one which we called "Company K's Skirmish," because it brought out the fact that this company, which was composed entirely of South Carolina men, and had never shone in drill or discipline, stood near the head of the regiment for coolness and courage,—the defect of discipline showing itself only in their extreme unwillingness to halt when once let loose. It was at this time that the small comedy of the Goose occurred,—an anecdote which Wendell Phillips[5] has since made his own.

One of the advancing line of skirmishers, usually an active fellow enough, was observed to move clumsily and irregularly. It soon appeared that he had encountered a fine specimen of the domestic goose, which had surrendered at discretion. Not wishing to lose it, he could yet find no way to hold it but between his legs; and so he went on, loading, firing, advancing, halting, always with the goose writhing and struggling and hissing in this natural pair of stocks. Both happily came off unwounded, and retired in good order at the signal, or some time after it; but I have hardly a cooler thing to put on record.

Meanwhile, another fellow left the field less exultingly; for, after a thoroughly courageous share in the skirmish, he came blubbering to his captain, and said,—

"Cappen, make Cæsar gib me my cane."

It seemed that, during some interval of the fighting, he had helped himself to an armful of Rebel sugar-cane, such as they all delighted in chewing. The Roman hero, during another pause, had confiscated the treasure; whence these tears of the returning warrior. I never could accustom myself to these extraordinary interminglings of manly and childish attributes.

Our most untiring scout during this period was the chaplain of my regiment,—the most restless and daring spirit we had, and now exulting in full liberty of action. He it was who was daily permitted to stray singly where no other officer would have been allowed to go, so irresistible was his appeal, "You know I am only a chaplain." Methinks I see our regimental saint, with pistols in belt and a Ballard rifle slung on shoulder, putting spurs to his steed, and cantering away down some questionable wood-path, or returning with some tale of Rebel haunt discovered, or store of foraging. He would track an enemy like an Indian, or exhort him, when apprehended, like an early Christian. Some of our devout soldiers shook their heads sometimes over the chaplain's little eccentricities.

"Woffor Mr. Chapman made a preacher for?" said one of them, as usual transforming his title into a patronymic. "He's *de fightingest more Yankee* I eber see in all my days."

And the criticism was very natural, though they could not deny that, when the hour for Sunday service came, Mr. F. commanded the respect and attention of all. That hour never came, however, on our first Sunday in Jacksonville; we were too busy and the men too scattered; so the chaplain made his accustomed foray beyond the lines instead.

"Is it not Sunday?" slyly asked an unregenerate lieutenant.

"Nay," quoth his Reverence, waxing fervid; "it is the Day of Judgment."

This reminds me of a raid up the river, conducted by one of our senior captains, an enthusiast whose gray beard and prophetic manner always took me back to the Fifth-Monarchy[6] men. He was most successful that day, bringing back horses, cattle, provisions, and prisoners; and one of the latter complained bitterly to me of being held, stating that Captain R. had promised him speedy liberty. But that doughty official spurned the imputation of such weak blandishments, in this day of triumphant retribution.

"Promise him!" said he, "I promised him nothing but the Day of Judgment and Periods of Damnation!"

Often since have I rolled beneath my tongue this savory and solemn sentence, and I do not believe that since the days of the Long Parliament there has been a more resounding anathema.

In Colonel Montgomery's hands these up-river raids reached the dignity of a fine art. His conceptions of foraging were rather more Western and liberal than mine, and on these excursions he fully indemnified himself for any undue abstinence demanded of him when in camp. I remember being on the wharf, with some naval officers, when he came down from his first trip. The steamer seemed an animated hen-coop. Live poultry hung from the foremast shrouds, dead ones from the mainmast, geese hissed from the binnacle, a pig paced the quarter-deck, and a duck's wings were seen fluttering from a line which was wont to sustain duck-trousers. The naval heroes, mindful of their own short rations, and taking high views of one's duties in a conquered country, looked at me reproachfully, as who should say, "Shall these things be?" In a moment or two the returning foragers had landed.

"Captain ——," said Montgomery, courteously, "would you allow me to send a remarkably fine turkey for your use on board ship?"

"Lieutenant ——," said Major Corwin, "may I ask your acceptance of a pair of ducks for your mess?"

Never did I behold more cordial relations between army and navy than sprang into existence at those sentences. So true it is, as Charles Lamb[7] says, that a single present of game may diffuse kindly sentiments through a whole community.

These little trips were called "rest"; there was no other rest during those ten days. An immense amount of picket and fatigue duty had to be done. Two redoubts were to be built to command the Northern Valley; all the intervening grove, which now afforded lurking-ground for a daring enemy, must be cleared away; and a few houses must be reluctantly razed for the same purpose.

The fort on the left was named Fort Higginson, and that built by my own regiment, in return, Fort Montgomery. The former was necessarily a hasty work, and is now, I believe, in ruins; the latter was far more elaborately constructed, on lines well traced by the Fourth New Hampshire during the previous occupation. It did great credit to Captain Trowbridge, of my regiment (formerly of the New York Volunteer Engineers), who had charge of its construction.

How like a dream seems now that period of daily skirmishes and nightly watchfulness! The fatigue was so constant that the days hurried by. I felt the need of some occasional change of ideas, and having just received from the North Mr. Brook's beautiful translation of Jean Paul's "Titan,"[8] I used to retire to my bedroom for some ten minutes every afternoon, and read a chapter or two. It was more refreshing than a nap, and will always be to me one of the most fascinating books in the world, with this added association. After all, what concerned me was not so much the fear of an attempt to drive us out and retake the city,—for that would be against the whole policy of the Rebels in that region,—as of an effort to fulfil their threats and burn it, by some nocturnal dash. The most valuable buildings belonged to Union men, and the upper part of the town, built chiefly of resinous pine, was combustible to the last degree. In case of fire, if the wind blew towards the river, we might lose steamers and all. I remember regulating my degree of disrobing by the direction of the wind; if it blew from the river, it was safe to make one's self quite comfortable; if otherwise, it was best to conform to Suwarrow's[9] idea of luxury, and take off one spur.

So passed our busy life for ten days. There were no tidings of reinforcements, and I hardly knew whether I wished for them,— or rather, I desired them as a choice of evils; for our men were giving out from overwork, and the recruiting excursions, for which we had mainly come, were hardly possible. At the utmost, I had asked for the addition of four companies and a light battery. Judge of my surprise when two infantry regiments successively arrived! I must resort to a scrap from the diary. Perhaps diaries are apt to be thought tedious; but I would rather read a page of one, whatever the events described, than any more deliberate narrative,—it gives glimpses so much more real and vivid.

"Head-quarters, Jacksonville,
March 20, 1863, Midnight.

"For the last twenty-four hours we have been sending women and children out of town, in answer to a demand by flag of truce, with a threat of bombardment. [N. B. I advised them not to go, and the majority declined doing so.] It was designed, no doubt, to intimidate; and in our ignorance of the force actually outside, we have had to recognize the possibility of danger, and work hard at our defences. At any time, by going into the outskirts, we can have a skirmish, which is nothing but fun; but when night closes in over a small and weary garrison, there sometimes steals into my mind, like a chill, that most sickening of all sensations, the anxiety of a commander. This was the night generally set for an attack, if any, though I am pretty well satisfied that they have not strength to dare it, and the worst they could probably do is to burn the town. But to-night, instead of enemies, appear friends, —our devoted civic ally, Judge S., and a whole Connecticut regiment, the Sixth, under Major Meeker; and though the latter are aground, twelve miles below, yet they enable one to breathe more freely. I only wish they were black; but now I have to show, not only that blacks can fight, but that they and white soldiers can act in harmony together."

That evening the enemy came up for a reconnoissance, in the deepest darkness, and there were alarms all night. The next day the Sixth Connecticut got afloat, and came up the river; and two days after, to my continued amazement, arrived a part of the Eighth Maine, under Lieutenant-Colonel Twichell. This increased my command to four regiments, or parts of regiments, half white and half black. Skirmishing had almost ceased,—our defences being tolerably complete, and looking from without much more effective than they really were. We were safe from any attack by a small force, and hoped that the enemy could not spare a large one from Charleston or Savannah. All looked bright without, and gave leisure for some small anxieties within.

It was the first time in the war (so far as I know) that white and black soldiers had served together on regular duty. Jealousy was still felt towards even the officers of colored regiments, and any difficult contingency would be apt to bring it out. The white soldiers, just from shipboard, felt a natural desire to stray about the town; and no attack from an enemy would be so disastrous as the slightest collision between them and the black provost-guard. I shudder, even now, to think of the train of consequences, bearing on the whole course of subsequent national events, which one such mishap might then have produced. It is almost impossible for us now to remember in what a delicate balance then hung the whole question of negro enlistments, and consequently of Slavery. Fortunately for my own serenity, I had great faith in the intrinsic power of military discipline, and also knew that a common service would soon produce mutual respect among good soldiers; and so it proved. But the first twelve hours of this mixed command were to me a more anxious period than any outward alarms had created.

Let us resort to the note-book again.

"JACKSONVILLE, March 22, 1863.

"It is Sunday; the bell is ringing for church, and Rev. Mr. F., from Beaufort, is to preach. This afternoon our good quartermaster establishes a Sunday-school for our little colony of 'contrabands,' now numbering seventy.

"Sunday Afternoon.

"The bewildering report is confirmed; and in addition to the Sixth Connecticut, which came yesterday, appears part of the Eighth Maine. The remainder, with its colonel, will be here tomorrow, and, report says, Major-General Hunter. Now my hope is that we may go to some point higher up the river, which we can hold for ourselves. There are two other points [Magnolia and Pilatka], which, in themselves, are as favorable as this, and, for getting recruits, better. So I shall hope to be allowed to go. To take posts, and then let white troops garrison them,—that is my programme.

"What makes the thing more puzzling is, that the Eighth Maine has only brought ten days' rations, so that they evidently are not to stay here; and yet where they go, or why they come, is a puzzle. Meanwhile we can sleep sound o' nights; and if the black and white babies do not quarrel and pull hair, we shall do very well."

Colonel Rust, on arriving, said frankly that he knew nothing of the plans prevailing in the Department, but that General Hunter was certainly coming soon to act for himself; that it had been reported at the North, and even at Port Royal, that we had all been captured and shot (and, indeed, I had afterwards the pleasure of reading my own obituary in a Northern Democratic journal), and that we certainly needed reinforcements; that he himself had been sent with orders to carry out, so far as possible, the original plans of the expedition; that he regarded himself as only a visitor, and should remain chiefly on shipboard,—which he did. He would relieve the black provost-guard by a white one, if I approved,—which I certainly did. But he said that he felt bound to give the chief opportunities of action to the colored troops,— which I also approved, and which he carried out, not quite to the satisfaction of his own eager and daring officers.

I recall one of these enterprises, out of which we extracted a good deal of amusement; it was baptized the Battle of the Clothes-Lines. A white company was out scouting in the woods behind the town, with one of my best Florida men for a guide; and the captain sent back a message that he had discovered a Rebel camp with twenty-two tents, beyond a creek, about four miles away; the officers and men had been distinctly seen, and it would be quite possible to capture it. Colonel Rust at once sent me out with two hundred men to do the work, recalling the original scouts, and disregarding the appeals of his own eager officers. We marched through the open pine woods, on a delightful afternoon, and met the returning party. Poor fellows! I never shall forget the longing eyes they cast on us, as we marched forth to the field of glory, from which they were debarred. We went three or four miles out, sometimes halting to send forward a scout, while I made all the men lie down in the long, thin grass and beside the fallen trees, till one could not imagine that there was a person there. I remember how picturesque the effect was, when, at the signal, all rose again, like Roderick Dhu's[10] men, and the green wood appeared suddenly populous with armed life. At a certain point forces were divided, and a detachment was sent round the head of the creek, to flank the unsuspecting enemy; while we of the main body, stealing with caution nearer and nearer, through ever denser woods, swooped down at last in triumph upon a solitary farm-house,—where the family-washing had been hung out to dry! This was the "Rebel camp"!

It is due to Sergeant Greene, my invaluable guide, to say that he had from the beginning discouraged any high hopes of a crossing of bayonets. He had early explained that it was not he who claimed to have seen the tents and the Rebel soldiers, but one of the officers,—and had pointed out that our undisturbed approach was hardly reconcilable with the existence of a hostile camp so near. This impression had also pressed more and more upon my own mind, but it was our business to put the thing beyond a doubt. Probably the place may have been occasionally used for a picket-station, and we found fresh horse-tracks in the vicinity, and there was a quantity of iron bridle-bits in the house, of which no clear explanation could be given; so that the armed men may not have been wholly imaginary. But camp there was none. After enjoying to the utmost the fun of the thing, therefore, we borrowed the only horse on the premises, hung all the bits over his neck, and as I rode him back to camp, they clanked like broken chains. We were joined on the way by our dear and devoted surgeon, whom I had left behind as an invalid, but who had mounted his horse and ridden out alone to attend to our wounded, his green sash looking quite in harmony with the early spring verdure of those lovely woods. So came we back in triumph, enjoying the joke all the more because some one else was responsible. We mystified the little community at first, but soon let out the secret, and witticisms abounded for a day or two, the mildest of which was the assertion that the author of the alarm must have been "three sheets in the wind."

Another expedition was of more exciting character. For several days before the arrival of Colonel Rust a reconnoissance had been planned in the direction of the enemy's camp, and he finally consented to its being carried out. By the energy of Major Corwin, of the Second South Carolina Volunteers, aided by Mr. Holden, then a gunner on the Paul Jones, and afterwards made captain of the same regiment, one of the ten-pound Parrott guns had been mounted on a hand-car, for use on the railway. This it was now proposed to bring into service. I took a large detail of men from the two white regiments and from my own, and had instructions to march as far as the four-mile station on the railway, if possible, examine the country, and ascertain if the Rebel camp had been removed, as was reported, beyond that distance. I was forbidden going any farther from camp, or attacking the Rebel camp, as my force comprised half our garrison, and should the town meanwhile be attacked from some other direction, it would be in great danger.

I never shall forget the delight of that march through the open pine barren, with occasional patches of uncertain swamp. The Eighth Maine, under Lieutenant-Colonel Twichell, was on the right, the Sixth Connecticut, under Major Meeker, on the left, and my own men, under Major Strong, in the centre, having in charge the cannon, to which they had been trained. Mr. Heron, from the John Adams, acted as gunner. The mounted Rebel pickets retired before us through the woods, keeping usually beyond range of the skirmishers, who in a long line—white, black, white—were deployed transversely. For the first time I saw the two colors fairly alternate on the military chessboard; it had been the object of much labor and many dreams, and I liked the pattern at last. Nothing was said about the novel fact by anybody,—it all seemed to come as matter-of-course; there appeared to be no mutual distrust among the men, and as for the officers, doubtless "each crow thought its own young the whitest,"—I certainly did, although doing full justice to the eager courage of the Northern portion of my command. Especially I watched with pleasure the fresh delight of the Maine men, who had not, like the rest, been previously in action, and who strode rapidly on with their long legs, irresistibly recalling, as their gaunt, athletic frames and sunburnt faces appeared here and there among the pines, the lumber regions of their native State, with which I was not unfamiliar.

We passed through a former camp of the Rebels, from which everything had been lately removed; but when the utmost permitted limits of our reconnoissance were reached, there were still no signs of any other camp, and the Rebel cavalry still kept provokingly before us. Their evident object was to lure us on to their own stronghold, and had we fallen into the trap, it would perhaps have resembled, on a smaller scale, the Olustee of the following year. With a good deal of reluctance, however, I caused the recall to be sounded, and, after a slight halt, we began to retrace our steps.

Straining our eyes to look along the reach of level railway which stretched away through the pine barren, we began to see certain ominous puffs of smoke, which might indeed proceed from some fire in the woods, but were at once set down by the men as coming from the mysterious locomotive battery which the Rebels were said to have constructed. Gradually the smoke grew denser, and appeared to be moving up along the track, keeping pace with our motion, and about two miles distant. I watched it steadily through a field-glass from our own slowly moving battery: it seemed to move when we moved and to halt when we halted. Sometimes in the dim smoke I caught a glimpse of something blacker, raised high in the air like the threatening head of some great gliding serpent. Suddenly there came a sharp puff of lighter smoke that seemed like a forked tongue, and then a hollow report, and we could see a great black projectile hurled into the air, and falling a quarter of a mile away from us, in the woods. I did not at once learn that this first shot killed two of the Maine men, and wounded two more. This was fired wide, but the numerous shots which followed were admirably aimed, and seldom failed to fall or explode close to our own smaller battery.

It was the first time that the men had been seriously exposed to artillery fire,—a danger more exciting to the ignorant mind than any other, as this very war has shown.* So I watched them anxiously. Fortunately there were deep trenches on each side the

---

*Take this for an example: "The effect was electrical. The Rebels were the best men in Ford's command, being Lieutenant-Colonel Showalter's Californians, and they are brave men. They had dismounted and sent their horses to the rear, and were undoubtedly determined upon a desperate fight, and their superior numbers made them confident of success. But they never fought with artillery, and a cannon has more terror for them than ten thousand rifles and all the wild Camanches on the plains of Texas. At first glimpse of the shining brass monsters there was a visible wavering in the determined front of the enemy, and as the shells came screaming over their heads the scare was complete. They broke ranks, fled for their horses, scrambled on the first that came to hand, and skedaddled in the direction of Brownsville."—*New York Evening Post*, September 25, 1864.

railway, with many stout, projecting roots, forming very tolerable bomb-proofs for those who happened to be near them. The enemy's gun was a sixty-four-pound Blakely, as we afterward found, whose enormous projectiles moved very slowly and gave ample time to cover,—insomuch, that, while the fragments of shell fell all around and amongst us, not a man was hurt. This soon gave the men the most buoyant confidence, and they shouted with childish delight over every explosion.

The moment a shell had burst or fallen unburst, our little gun was invariably fired in return, and that with some precision, so far as we could judge, its range also being nearly as great. For some reason they showed no disposition to overtake us, in which attempt their locomotive would have given them an immense advantage over our heavy hand-car, and their cavalry force over our infantry. Nevertheless, I rather hoped that they would attempt it, for then an effort might have been made to cut them off in the rear by taking up some rails. As it was, this was out of the question, though they moved slowly, as we moved, keeping always about two miles away. When they finally ceased firing we took up the rails beyond us before withdrawing, and thus kept the enemy from approaching so near the city again. But I shall never forget that Dantean[11] monster, rearing its black head amid the distant smoke, nor the solicitude with which I watched for the puff which meant danger and looked round to see if my chickens were all under cover. The greatest peril, after all, was from the possible dismounting of our gun, in which case we should have been very apt to lose it, if the enemy had showed any dash. There may be other such tilts of railway artillery on record during the war; but if so, I have not happened to read of them, and so have dwelt the longer on this.

This was doubtless the same locomotive battery which had previously fired more than once upon the town,—running up within two miles and then withdrawing, while it was deemed inexpedient to destroy the railroad, on our part, lest it might be needed by ourselves in turn. One night, too, the Rebel threat had been fulfilled, and they had shelled the town with the same battery. They had the range well, and every shot fell near the post headquarters. It was exciting to see the great Blakely shell, showing a light as it rose, and moving slowly towards us like a comet, then exploding and scattering its formidable fragments. Yet, strange to say, no serious harm was done to life or limb, and the most formidable casualty was that of a citizen who complained that a shell had passed through the wall of his bedroom, and carried off his mosquito curtain in its transit.

Little knew we how soon these small entertainments would be over. Colonel Montgomery had gone up the river with his two companies, perhaps to remain permanently; and I was soon to follow. On Friday, March 27th, I wrote home: "The Burnside has gone to Beaufort for rations, and the John Adams to Fernandina for coal; we expect both back by Sunday, and on Monday I hope to get the regiment off to a point farther up,—Magnolia, thirty-five miles, or Pilatka, seventy-five,—either of which would be a good post for us. General Hunter is expected every day, and it is strange he has not come." The very next day came an official order recalling the whole expedition, and for the third time evacuating Jacksonville.

A council of military and naval officers was at once called (though there was but one thing to be done), and the latter were even more disappointed and amazed than the former. This was especially the case with the senior naval officer, Captain Steedman, a South-Carolinian by birth, but who had proved himself as patriotic as he was courteous and able, and whose presence and advice had been of the greatest value to me. He and all of us felt keenly the wrongfulness of breaking the pledges which we had been authorized to make to these people, and of leaving them to the mercy of the Rebels once more. Most of the people themselves took the same view, and eagerly begged to accompany us on our departure. They were allowed to bring their clothing and furniture also, and at once developed that insane mania for aged and valueless trumpery which always seizes upon the human race, I believe, in moments of danger. With the greatest difficulty we selected between the essential and the non-essential, and our few transports were at length loaded to the very water's edge on the morning of March 29th,—Colonel Montgomery having by this time returned from up-river, with sixteen prisoners, and the fruits of foraging in plenty.

And upon that last morning occurred an act on the part of some of the garrison most deeply to be regretted, and not to be excused by the natural indignation at their recall,—an act which, through the unfortunate eloquence of one newspaper correspondent, rang through the nation,—the attempt to burn the town. I fortunately need not dwell much upon it, as I was not at the time in command of the post,—as the white soldiers frankly took upon themselves the whole responsibility,—and as all the fires were made in the wooden part of the city, which was occupied by them, while none were made in the brick part, where the colored soldiers were quartered. It was fortunate for our reputation that the newspaper accounts generally agreed in exculpating us from all share in the matter;* and the single exception, which one correspondent asserted, I could never verify, and do not believe to have existed. It was stated by Colonel Rust, in his official report, that some twenty-five buildings in all were burned, and I doubt if the actual number was greater; but this was probably owing in part to a change of wind, and did not diminish the discredit of the transaction. It made our sorrow at departure no less, though it infinitely enhanced the impressiveness of the scene.

The excitement of the departure was intense. The embarkation was so laborious that it seemed as if the flames must be upon us before we could get on board, and it was also generally expected that the Rebel skirmishers would be down among the houses, wherever practicable, to annoy us to the utmost, as had been the case at the previous evacuation. They were, indeed, there, as we afterwards heard, but did not venture to molest us. The sight and roar of the flames, and the rolling clouds of smoke, brought home to the impressible minds of the black soldiers all their favorite imagery of the Judgment-Day; and those who were not too much depressed by disappointment were excited by the spectacle, and sang and exhorted without ceasing.

With heavy hearts their officers floated down the lovely river, which we had ascended with hopes so buoyant; and from that day

---

*"The colored regiments had nothing at all to do with it; they behaved with propriety throughout."—*Boston Journal Correspondence*. ("Carleton.")

"The negro troops took no part whatever in the perpetration of this Vandalism."—*New York Tribune Correspondence*. ("N.P.")

"We know not whether we are most rejoiced or saddened to observe, by the general concurrence of accounts, that the negro soldiers had nothing to do with the barbarous act."—*Boston Journal Editorial*, April 10, 1863.

to this, the reasons for our recall have never been made public. It was commonly attributed to proslavery advisers, acting on the rather impulsive nature of Major-General Hunter, with a view to cut short the career of the colored troops, and stop their recruiting. But it may have been simply the scarcity of troops in the Department, and the renewed conviction at head-quarters that we were too few to hold the post alone. The latter theory was strengthened by the fact that, when General Seymour reoccupied Jacksonville, the following year, he took with him twenty thousand men instead of one thousand,—and the sanguinary battle of Olustee found him with too few.

CHAPTER V
Out on Picket

One can hardly imagine a body of men more disconsolate than a regiment suddenly transferred from an adventurous life in the enemy's country to the quiet of a sheltered camp, on safe and familiar ground. The men under my command were deeply dejected when, on a most appropriate day,—the First of April, 1863,—they found themselves unaccountably recalled from Florida, that region of delights which had seemed theirs by the right of conquest. My dusky soldiers, who based their whole walk and conversation strictly on the ancient Israelites, felt that the prophecies were all set at naught, and that they were on the wrong side of the Red Sea; indeed, I fear they regarded even me as a sort of reversed Moses, whose Pisgah[1] fronted in the wrong direction. Had they foreseen how the next occupation of the Promised Land was destined to result, they might have acquiesced with more of their wonted cheerfulness. As it was, we were very glad to receive, after a few days of discontented repose on the very ground where we had once been so happy, an order to go out on picket at Port Royal Ferry, with the understanding that we might remain there for some time.

This picket station was regarded as a sort of military picnic by the regiments stationed at Beaufort, South Carolina; it meant blackberries and oysters, wild roses and magnolias, flowery lanes instead of sandy barrens, and a sort of guerilla existence in place of the camp routine. To the colored soldiers especially, with their love of country life, and their extensive personal acquaintance on the plantations, it seemed quite like a Christmas festival. Besides, they would be in sight of the enemy, and who knew but there might, by the blessing of Providence, be a raid or a skirmish? If they could not remain on the St. John's River, it was something to dwell on the Coosaw. In the end they enjoyed it as much as they expected, and though we "went out" several times subsequently, until it became an old story, the enjoyment never waned.

And as even the march from the camp to the picket lines was something that could not possibly have been the same for any white regiment in the service, it is worth while to begin at the beginning and describe it.

A regiment ordered on picket was expected to have reveille at daybreak, and to be in line for departure by sunrise. This delighted our men, who always took a childlike pleasure in being out of bed at any unreasonable hour; and by the time I had emerged, the tents were nearly all struck, and the great wagons were lumbering into camp to receive them, with whatever else was to be transported. The first rays of the sun must fall upon the line of these wagons, moving away across the wide parade-ground, followed by the column of men, who would soon outstrip them. But on the occasion which I especially describe the sun was shrouded, and, when once upon the sandy plain, neither camp nor town nor river could be seen in the dimness; and when I rode forward and looked back there was only visible the long, moving, shadowy column, seeming rather awful in its snake-like advance. There was a swaying of flags and multitudinous weapons that might have been camels' necks for all one could see, and the whole thing might have been a caravan upon the desert. Soon we debouched upon the "Shell Road," the wagon-train drew on one side into the fog, and by the time the sun appeared the music ceased, the men took the "route step," and the fun began.

The "route step" is an abandonment of all military strictness, and nothing is required of the men but to keep four abreast, and not lag behind. They are not required to keep step, though, with the rhythmical ear of our soldiers, they almost always instinctively did so; talking and singing are allowed, and of this privilege, at least, they eagerly availed themselves. On this day they were at the top of exhilaration. There was one broad grin from one end of the column to the other; it might soon have been a caravan of elephants instead of camels, for the ivory and the blackness; the chatter and the laughter almost drowned the tramp of feet and the clatter of equipments. At cross-roads and plantation gates the colored people thronged to see us pass; every one found a friend and a greeting. "How you do, aunty?" "Huddy (how d' ye), Budder Benjamin?" "How you find yourself dis mornin', Tittawisa (Sister Louisa)?" Such salutations rang out to everybody, known or un-

known. In return, venerable, kerchiefed matrons courtesied laboriously to every one, with an unfailing "Bress de Lord,
budder." Grave little boys, blacker than ink, shook hands with
our laughing and utterly unmanageable drummers, who greeted
them with this sure word of prophecy, "Dem's de drummers for
de nex' war!" Pretty mulatto girls ogled and coquetted, and made
eyes, as Thackeray[2] would say, at half the young fellows in the
battalion. Meantime the singing was brisk along the whole column, and when I sometimes reined up to see them pass, the chant
of each company, entering my ear, drove out from the other ear
the strain of the preceding. Such an odd mixture of things, military
and missionary, as the successive waves of song drifted by! First,
"John Brown," of course; then, "What make old Satan for follow
me so?" then, "Marching Along"; then, "Hold your light on Canaan's shore"; then, "When this cruel war is over" (a new favorite,
sung by a few); yielding presently to a grand burst of the favorite
marching song among them all, and one at which every step instinctively quickened, so light and jubilant its rhythm,—

> "All true children gwine in de wilderness,
> Gwine in de wilderness, gwine in de wilderness,
> True believers gwine in de wilderness,
> To take away de sins ob de world,"—

ending in a "Hoigh!" after each verse,—a sort of Irish yell. For
all the songs, but especially for their own wild hymns, they constantly improvised simple verses, with the same odd mingling,—
the little facts of to-day's march being interwoven with the depths
of theological gloom, and the same jubilant chorus annexed to all;
thus,—

> "We're gwine to de Ferry,
>   De bell done ringing;
> Gwine to de landing,
>   De bell done ringing;
> Trust, believer,
>   O, de bell done ringing;
> Satan's behind me,
>   De bell done ringing;
> 'T is a misty morning,

> De bell done ringing;
> O de road am sandy,
>   De bell done ringing;
> Hell been open,
>   De bell done ringing";—

and so on indefinitely.

The little drum-corps kept in advance, a jolly crew, their drums slung on their backs, and the drum-sticks perhaps balanced on their heads. With them went the officers' servant-boys, more uproarious still, always ready to lend their shrill treble to any song. At the head of the whole force there walked, by some self-imposed preeminence, a respectable elderly female, one of the company laundresses, whose vigorous stride we never could quite overtake, and who had an enormous bundle balanced on her head, while she waved in her hand, like a sword, a long-handled tin dipper. Such a picturesque medley of fun, war, and music I believe no white regiment in the service could have shown; and yet there was no straggling, and a single tap of the drum would at any moment bring order out of this seeming chaos. So we marched our seven miles out upon the smooth and shaded road,—beneath jasmine clusters, and great pine-cones dropping, and great bunches of misletoe still in bloom among the branches. Arrived at the station, the scene soon became busy and more confused; wagons were being unloaded, tents pitched, water brought, wood cut, fires made, while the "field and staff" could take possession of the abandoned quarters of their predecessors, and we could look round in the lovely summer morning to "survey our empire and behold our home."

The only thoroughfare by land between Beaufort and Charleston is the "Shell Road," a beautiful avenue, which, about nine miles from Beaufort, strikes a ferry across the Coosaw River. War abolished the ferry, and made the river the permanent barrier between the opposing picket lines. For ten miles, right and left, these lines extended, marked by well-worn footpaths, following the endless windings of the stream; and they never varied until nearly the end of the war. Upon their maintenance depended our whole foothold on the Sea Islands; and upon that again finally depended

the whole campaign of Sherman. But for the services of the colored troops, which finally formed the main garrison of the Department of the South, the Great March would never have been
performed.

There was thus a region ten or twelve miles square of which I
had exclusive military command. It was level, but otherwise broken and bewildering to the last degree. No road traversed it, properly speaking, but the Shell Road. All the rest was a wild medley
of cypress swamp, pine barren, muddy creek, and cultivated plantation, intersected by interminable lanes and bridle-paths, through
which we must ride day and night, and which our horses soon
knew better than ourselves. The regiment was distributed at different stations, the main force being under my immediate command, at a plantation close by the Shell Road, two miles from the
ferry, and seven miles from Beaufort. Our first picket duty was
just at the time of the first attack on Charleston, under Dupont
and Hunter; and it was generally supposed that the Confederates
would make an effort to recapture the Sea Islands. My orders were
to watch the enemy closely, keep informed as to his position and
movements, attempt no advance, and, in case any were attempted
from the other side, to delay it as long as possible, sending instant
notice to head-quarters. As to the delay, that could be easily guaranteed. There were causeways on the Shell Road which a single
battery could hold against a large force; and the plantations were
everywhere so intersected by hedges and dikes that they seemed
expressly planned for defence. Although creeks wound in and out
everywhere, yet these were only navigable at high tide, and at all
other times were impassable marshes. There were but few posts
where the enemy were within rifle range, and their occasional
attacks at those points were soon stopped by our enforcement of
a pithy order from General Hunter, "Give them as good as they
send." So that, with every opportunity for being kept on the alert,
there was small prospect of serious danger; and all promised an
easy life, with only enough of care to make it pleasant. The picket
station was therefore always a coveted post among the regiments,
combining some undeniable importance with a kind of relaxation;
and as we were there three months on our first tour of duty, and
returned there several times afterwards, we got well acquainted

with it. The whole region always reminded me of the descriptions of La Vendée, and I always expected to meet Henri Larocheja-quelein[3] riding in the woods.

How can I ever describe the charm and picturesqueness of that summer life? Our house possessed four spacious rooms and a piazza; around it were grouped sheds and tents; the camp was a little way off on one side, the negro-quarters of the plantation on the other; and all was immersed in a dense mass of waving and murmuring locust-blossoms. The spring days were always lovely, while the evenings were always conveniently damp; so that we never shut the windows by day, nor omitted our cheerful fire by night. Indoors, the main head-quarters seemed like the camp of some party of young engineers in time of peace, only with a little female society added, and a good many martial associations thrown in. A large, low, dilapidated room, with an immense fire-place, and with window-panes chiefly broken, so that the sashes were still open even when closed,—such was our home. The walls were scrawled with capital charcoal sketches by R. of the Fourth New Hampshire, and with a good map of the island and its wood-paths by C. of the First Massachusetts Cavalry. The room had the picturesqueness which comes everywhere from the natural grouping of articles of daily use,—swords, belts, pistols, rifles, field-glasses, spurs, canteens, gauntlets,—while wreaths of gray moss above the windows, and a pelican's wing three feet long over the high mantel-piece, indicated more deliberate decoration. This, and the whole atmosphere of the place, spoke of the refining pres-ence of agreeable women; and it was pleasant when they held their little court in the evening, and pleasant all day, with the different visitors who were always streaming in and out,—officers and sol-diers on various business; turbaned women from the plantations, coming with complaints or questionings; fugitives from the main-land to be interrogated; visitors riding up on horseback, their hands full of jasmine and wild roses; and the sweet sunny air all perfumed with magnolias and the Southern pine. From the neigh-boring camp there was a perpetual low hum. Louder voices and laughter re-echoed, amid the sharp sounds of the axe, from the pine woods; and sometimes, when the relieved pickets were dis-charging their pieces, there came the hollow sound of dropping rifle-shots, as in skirmishing,—perhaps the most unmistakable and fascinating association that war bequeaths to the memory of the ear.

Our domestic arrangements were of the oddest description. From the time when we began housekeeping by taking down the front-door to complete therewith a little office for the surgeon on the piazza, everything seemed upside down. I slept on a shelf in the corner of the parlor, bequeathed me by Major F., my jovial predecessor, and, if I waked at any time, could put my head through the broken window, arouse my orderly, and ride off to see if I could catch a picket asleep. We used to spell the word *picquet*, because that was understood to be the correct thing, in that Department at least; and they used to say at post head-quarters that as soon as the officer in command of the outposts grew negligent, and was guilty of a *k*, he was ordered in immediately. Then the arrangements for ablution were peculiar. We fitted up a bathing-place in a brook, which somehow got appropriated at once by the company laundresses; but I had my revenge, for I took to bathing in the family wash-tub. After all, however, the kitchen department had the advantage, for they used my solitary napkin to wipe the mess-table. As for food, we found it impossible to get chickens, save in the immature shape of eggs; fresh pork was prohibited by the surgeon, and other fresh meat came rarely. We could, indeed, hunt for wild turkeys, and even deer, but such hunting was found only to increase the appetite, without corresponding supply. Still we had our luxuries,—large, delicious drum-fish, and alligator steaks,—like a more substantial fried halibut,—which might have afforded the theme for Charles Lamb's dissertation on Roast Pig, and by whose aid "for the first time in our lives we tasted *crackling*." The post bakery yielded admirable bread; and for vegetables and fruit we had very poor sweet potatoes, and (in their season) an unlimited supply of the largest blackberries. For beverage, we had the vapid milk of that region, in which, if you let it stand, the water sinks instead of the cream's rising; and the delicious sugar-cane syrup, which we had brought from Florida, and which we drank at all hours. Old Floridians say that no one is justified in drinking whiskey, while he can get cane-juice; it is sweet and spirited, without cloying, foams like ale, and there were little spots on the ceiling of the dining-room where our lively beverage had popped out its cork. We kept it in a whiskey-bottle; and as whiskey itself was absolutely prohibited among us, it was amusing to see the surprise of our military visitors when this innocent substitute was brought in. They usually liked it in the end, but, like the old Frenchwoman over her glass of water, wished that it were a sin to give it a relish. As the foaming beakers of molasses and water were handed round, the guests would make with them the courteous little gestures of polite imbibing, and would then quaff the beverage, some with gusto, others with a slight after-look of dismay. But it was a delicious and cooling drink while it lasted; and at all events was the best and the worst we had.

We used to have reveille at six, and breakfast about seven; then the mounted couriers began to arrive from half a dozen different directions, with written reports of what had happened during the night,—a boat seen, a picket fired upon, a battery erecting. These must be consolidated and forwarded to head-quarters, with the daily report of the command,—so many sick, so many on detached service, and all the rest. This was our morning newspaper, our Herald and Tribune; I never got tired of it. Then the couriers must be furnished with countersign and instructions, and sent off again. Then we scattered to our various rides, all disguised as duty; one to inspect pickets, one to visit a sick soldier, one to build a bridge or clear a road, and still another to head-quarters for ammunition or commissary stores. Galloping through green lanes, miles of triumphal arches of wild roses,—roses pale and large and fragrant, mingled with great boughs of the white cornel, fantastic masses, snowy surprises,—such were our rides, ranging from eight to fifteen and even twenty miles. Back to a late dinner with our various experiences, and perhaps specimens to match,—a thunder-snake, eight feet long; a live opossum, with the young clinging to the natural pouch; an armful of great white, scentless pond-lilies. After dinner, to the tangled garden for rosebuds or early magnolias, whose cloying fragrance will always bring back to me the full zest of those summer days; then dress-parade and a little drill as the day grew cool. In the evening, tea; and then the piazza or the fireside, as the case might be,—chess, cards,—perhaps a little music by aid of the assistant surgeon's melodeon, a few pages of Jean Paul's "Titan," almost my only book, and carefully husbanded,—perhaps a mail, with its infinite felicities. Such was our day.

Night brought its own fascinations, more solitary and profound. The darker they were, the more clearly it was our duty to visit the pickets. The paths that had grown so familiar by day seemed a wholly new labyrinth by night; and every added shade of darkness seemed to shift and complicate them all anew, till at last man's skill grew utterly baffled, and the clew must be left to the instinct of the horse. Riding beneath the solemn starlight, or soft, gray mist, or densest blackness, the frogs croaking, the strange "chuckwill's-widow" droning his ominous note above my head, the mocking-bird dreaming in music, the great Southern fireflies rising to the tree-tops, or hovering close to the ground like glow-worms, till the horse raised his hoops to avoid them; through pine woods and cypress swamps, or past sullen brooks, or white tents, or the dimly seen huts of sleeping negroes; down to the glimmering shore, where black statues leaned against trees or stood alert in the pathways;—never, in all the days of my life, shall I forget the magic of those haunted nights.

We had nocturnal boat service, too, for it was a part of our instructions to obtain all possible information about the enemy's position; and we accordingly, as usual in such cases, incurred a great many risks that harmed nobody, and picked up much information which did nobody any good. The centre of these nightly reconnoissances, for a long time, was the wreck of the George Washington, the story of whose disaster is perhaps worth telling.

Till about the time when we went on picket, it had been the occasional habit of the smaller gunboats to make the circuit of Port Royal Island,—a practice which was deemed very essential to the safety of our position, but which the Rebels effectually stopped, a few days after our arrival, by destroying the army gunboat George Washington with a single shot from a light battery. I was roused soon after daybreak by the firing, and a courier soon came dashing in with the particulars. Forwarding these hastily to Beaufort (for we had then no telegraph), I was soon at the scene of action, five miles away. Approaching, I met on the picket paths man after man who had escaped from the wreck across a half-mile of almost impassable marsh. Never did I see such objects,—some stripped to their shirts, some fully clothed, but all having every garment literally pasted to their bodies with mud. Across the river, the Rebels were retiring, having done their work, but were still shelling, from greater and greater distances, the wood through which I rode. Arrived at the spot nearest the wreck (a point opposite to what we called the Brickyard Station), I saw the burning vessel aground beyond a long stretch of marsh, out of which the forlorn creatures were still floundering. Here and there in the mud and reeds we could see the laboring heads, slowly advancing, and could hear excruciating cries from wounded men in the more distant depths. It was the strangest mixture of war and Dante and Robinson Crusoe.[4] Our energetic chaplain coming up, I sent him with four men, under a flag of truce, to the place whence the worst cries proceeded, while I went to another part of the marsh. During that morning we got them all out, our last achievement being the rescue of the pilot, an immense negro with a wooden leg,—an article so particularly unavailable for mud travelling, that it would have almost seemed better, as one of the men suggested, to cut the traces, and leave it behind.

A naval gunboat, too, which had originally accompanied this vessel, and should never have left it, now came back and took off the survivors, though there had been several deaths from scalding and shell. It proved that the wreck was not aground after all, but at anchor, having foolishly lingered till after daybreak, and having thus given time for the enemy to bring down their guns. The first shot had struck the boiler, and set the vessel on fire; after which the officer in command had raised a white flag, and then escaped with his men to our shore; and it was for this flight in the wrong direction that they were shelled in the marshes by the Rebels. The case furnished in this respect some parallel to that of the Kearsage and Alabama,[5] and it was afterwards cited, I believe, officially or unofficially, to show that the Rebels had claimed the right to punish, in this case, the course of action which they approved in Semmes. I know that they always asserted thenceforward that the detachment on board the George Washington had become rightful prisoners of war, and were justly fired upon when they tried to escape.

This was at the time of the first attack on Charleston, and the noise of this cannonading spread rapidly thither, and brought four regiments to reinforce Beaufort in a hurry, under the impression that the town was already taken, and that they must save what remnants they could. General Saxton, too, had made such capital plans for defending the post that he could not bear not to have it attacked; so, while the Rebels brought down a force to keep us from taking the guns off the wreck, I was also supplied with a section or two of regular artillery, and some additional infantry, with which to keep them from it; and we tried to "make believe very hard," and rival the Charleston expedition on our own island. Indeed, our affair came to about as much,—nearly nothing,—and lasted decidedly longer; for both sides nibbled away at the guns, by night, for weeks afterward, though I believe the mud finally got them,—at least, we did not. We tried in vain to get the use of a steamboat or floating derrick of any kind; for it needed more mechanical ingenuity than we possessed to transfer anything so heavy to our small boats by night, while by day we did not go near the wreck in anything larger than a "dug-out."

One of these nocturnal visits to the wreck I recall with peculiar gusto, because it brought back that contest with catarrh and coughing among my own warriors which had so ludicrously beset me in Florida. It was always fascinating to be on those forbidden waters by night, stealing out with muffled oars through the creeks and reeds, our eyes always strained for other voyagers, our ears listening breathlessly to all the marsh sounds,—black-fish splashing, and little wakened reed-birds that fled wailing away over the dim river, equally safe on either side. But it always appeared to the watchful senses that we were making noise enough to be heard at Fort Sumter; and somehow the victims of catarrh seemed always the most eager for any enterprise requiring peculiar caution. In this case I thought I had sifted them beforehand; but as soon as we were afloat, one poor boy near me began to wheeze, and I turned upon him in exasperation. He saw his danger, and meekly said, "I won't cough, Cunnel!" and he kept his word. For two mortal hours he sat grasping his gun, with never a chirrup. But two unfortunates in the bow of the boat developed symptoms which I could not suppress; so, putting in at a picket station, with some risk I dumped them in mud knee-deep, and embarked a substitute, who after the first five minutes absolutely coughed louder than both the others united. Handkerchiefs, blankets, over-coats, suffocation in its direst forms, were all tried in vain, but apparently the Rebel pickets slept through it all, and we explored the wreck in safety. I think they were asleep, for certainly across the level marshes there came a nasal sound, as of the "Conthiev-eracy" in its slumbers. It may have been a bull-frog, but it sounded like a human snore.

Picket life was of course the place to feel the charm of natural beauty on the Sea Islands. We had a world of profuse and tangled vegetation around us, such as would have been a dream of delight to me, but for the constant sense of responsibility and care which came between. Amid this preoccupation, Nature seemed but a mirage, and not the close and intimate associate I had before known. I pressed no flowers, collected no insects or birds' eggs, made no notes on natural objects, reversing in these respects all previous habits. Yet now, in the retrospect, there seems to have been infused into me through every pore the voluptuous charm of the season and the place; and the slightest corresponding sound or odor now calls back the memory of those delicious days. Being afterwards on picket at almost every season, I tasted the sensations of all; and though I hardly then thought of such a result, the associations of beauty will remain forever.

In February, for instance,—though this was during a later pe-riod of picket service,—the woods were usually draped with that "net of shining haze" which marks our Northern May; and the house was embowered in wild-plum-blossoms, small, white, profuse, and tenanted by murmuring bees. There were peach-blossoms, too, and the yellow jasmine was opening its multitu-dinous buds, climbing over tall trees, and waving from bough to bough. There were fresh young ferns and white bloodroot in the edges of woods, matched by snowdrops in the garden, beneath budded myrtle and *Petisporum*. In this wilderness the birds were busy; the two main songsters being the mocking-bird and the cardinal-grosbeak, which monopolized all the parts of our more varied Northern orchestra save the tender and liquid notes, which in South Carolina seemed unattempted except by some stray blue-bird. Jays were as loud and busy as at the North in autumn; there were sparrows and wrens; and sometimes I noticed the shy and whimsical chewink.

From this early spring-time onward, there seemed no great difference in atmospheric sensations, and only a succession of bloom. After two months one's notions of the season grew bewildered, just as very early rising bewilders the day. In the army one is perhaps roused after a bivouac, marches before daybreak, halts, fights, somebody is killed, a long day's life has been lived, and after all it is not seven o'clock, and breakfast is not ready. So when we had lived in summer so long as hardly to remember winter, it suddenly occurred to us that it was not yet June. One escapes at the South that mixture of hunger and avarice which is felt in the Northern summer, counting each hour's joy with the sad consciousness that an hour is gone. The compensating loss is in missing those soft, sweet, liquid sensations of the Northern spring, that burst of life and joy, those days of heaven that even April brings; and this absence of childhood in the year creates a feeling of hardness in the season, like that I have suggested in the melody of the Southern birds. It seemed to me also that the woods had not those pure, clean, *innocent* odors which so abound in the New England forest in early spring; but there was something luscious, voluptuous, almost oppressively fragrant about the magnolias, as if they belonged not to Hebe, but to Magdalen.[6]

Such immense and lustrous butterflies I had never seen but in dreams; and not even dreams had prepared me for sand-flies. Almost too small to be seen, they inflicted a bite which appeared larger than themselves,—a positive wound, more torturing than that of a mosquito, and leaving more annoyance behind. These tormentors elevated dress-parade into the dignity of a military engagement. I had to stand motionless, with my head a mere nebula of winged atoms, while tears rolled profusely down my face, from mere muscular irritation. Had I stirred a finger, the whole battalion would have been slapping its cheeks. Such enemies were, however, a valuable aid to discipline, on the whole, as they abounded in the guard-house, and made that institution an object of unusual abhorrence among the men.

The presence of ladies and the homelike air of everything, made the picket station a very popular resort while we were there. It was the one agreeable ride from Beaufort, and we often had a dozen people unexpectedly to dinner. On such occasions there was sometimes mounting in hot haste, and an eager search among the outlying plantations for additional chickens and eggs, or through the company kitchens for some of those villanous tin cans which everywhere marked the progress of our army. In those cans, so far as my observation went, all fruits relapsed into a common acidulation, and all meats into a similarity of tastelessness; while the "condensed milk" was best described by the men, who often unconsciously stumbled on a better joke than they knew, and always spoke of it as *condemned* milk.

We had our own excursions too,—to the Barnwell plantations, with their beautiful avenues and great live-oaks, the perfection of Southern beauty,—to Hall's Island, debatable ground, close under the enemy's fire, where half-wild cattle were to be shot, under military precautions, like Scottish moss-trooping,[7]—or to the ferry, where it was fascinating to the female mind to scan the Rebel pickets through a field-glass. Our horses liked the by-ways far better than the level hardness of the Shell Road, especially those we had brought from Florida, which enjoyed the wilderness as if they had belonged to Marion's men.[8] They delighted to feel the long sedge brush their flanks, or to gallop down the narrow wood-paths, leaping the fallen trees, and scaring the bright little lizards which shot across our track like live rays broken from the sunbeams. We had an abundance of horses, mostly captured and left in our hands by some convenient delay of the post quarter-master. We had also two side-saddles, which, not being munitions of war, could not properly (as we explained) be transferred like other captured articles to the general stock; otherwise the P. Q. M. (a married man) would have showed no unnecessary delay in their case. For miscellaneous accommodation was there not an ambulance,—that most inestimable of army conveniences, equally ready to carry the merry to a feast or the wounded from a fray. "Ambulance" was one of those words, rather numerous, which Ethiopian lips were not framed by Nature to articulate. Only the highest stages of colored culture could compass it; on the tongue of the many it was transformed mystically as "amulet," or ambitiously as "epaulet," or in culinary fashion as "omelet." But it was our experience that an ambulance under any name jolted equally hard.

Besides these divertisements, we had more laborious vocations,—a good deal of fatigue, and genuine though small alarms.

The men went on duty every third day at furthest, and the officers nearly as often,—most of the tours of duty lasting twenty-four hours, though the stream was considered to watch itself tolerably well by daylight. This kind of responsibility suited the men; and we had already found, as the whole army afterwards acknowledged, that the constitutional watchfulness and distrustfulness of the colored race made them admirable sentinels. Soon after we went on picket, the commanding general sent an aid, with a cavalry escort, to visit all the stations, without my knowledge. They spent the whole night, and the officer reported that he could not get within thirty yards of any post without a challenge. This was a pleasant assurance for me; since our position seemed so secure, compared with Jacksonville, that I had feared some relaxation of vigilance, while yet the safety of all depended on our thorough discharge of duty.

Jacksonville had also seasoned the men so well that they were no longer nervous, and did not waste much powder on false alarms. The Rebels made no formal attacks, and rarely attempted to capture pickets. Sometimes they came stealing through the creeks in "dug-outs," as we did on their side of the water, and occasionally an officer of ours was fired upon while making his rounds by night. Often some boat or scow would go adrift, and sometimes a mere dark mass of river-weed would be floated by the tide past the successive stations, eliciting a challenge and perhaps a shot from each. I remember the vivid way in which one of the men stated to his officer the manner in which a faithful picket should do his duty, after challenging, in case a boat came in sight. "Fus' ting I shoot, and den I shoot, and den I shoot again. Den I creep-creep up near de boat, and see who dey in 'em; and s'pose anybody pop up he head, den I shoot again. S'pose I fire my forty rounds. I tink he hear at de camp and send more mans,"—which seemed a reasonable presumption. This soldier's name was Paul Jones, a daring fellow, quite worthy of his namesake.

In time, however, they learned quieter methods, and would wade far out in the water, there standing motionless at last, hoping to surround and capture these floating boats, though, to their great disappointment, the prize usually proved empty. On one occasion they tried a still profounder strategy; for an officer visiting the pickets after midnight, and hearing in the stillness a portentous snore from the end of the causeway (our most important station), straightway hurried to the point of danger, with wrath in his soul. But the sergeant of the squad came out to meet him, imploring silence, and explaining that they had seen or suspected a boat hovering near, and were feigning sleep in order to lure and capture those who would entrap them.

The one military performance at the picket station of which my men were utterly intolerant was an occasional flag of truce, for which this was the appointed locality. These farces, for which it was our duty to furnish the stock actors, always struck them as being utterly despicable, and unworthy the serious business of war. They felt, I suppose, what Mr. Pickwick[9] felt, when he heard his counsel remark to the counsel for the plaintiff, that it was a very fine morning. It goaded their souls to see the young officers from the two opposing armies salute each other courteously, and interchange cigars. They despised the object of such negotiations, which was usually to send over to the enemy some family of Rebel women who had made themselves quite intolerable on our side, but were not above collecting a subscription among the Union officers, before departure, to replenish their wardrobes. The men never showed disrespect to these women by word or deed, but they hated them from the bottom of their souls. Besides, there was a grievance behind all this. The Rebel order remained unrevoked which consigned the new colored troops and their officers to a felon's death, if captured; and we all felt that we fought with ropes round our necks. "Dere 's no flags ob truce for us," the men would contemptuously say. "When de Secesh fight de *Fus' Souf*" (First South Carolina), "he fight in earnest." Indeed, I myself took it as rather a compliment when the commander on the other side—though an old acquaintance of mine in Massachusetts and in Kansas—at first refused to negotiate through me or my officers,—a refusal which was kept up, greatly to the enemy's inconvenience, until our men finally captured some of the opposing pickets, and their friends had to waive all scruples in order to send them supplies. After this there was no trouble, and I think that the first Rebel officer in South Carolina who officially met any officer of colored troops under a flag of truce was Captain John C. Calhoun. In Florida we had been so recognized long before; but that was when they wished to frighten us out of Jacksonville.

Such was our life on picket at Port Royal,—a thing whose memory is now fast melting into such stuff as dreams are made of.[10] We stayed there more than two months at that time; the first attack on Charleston exploded with one puff, and had its end; General Hunter was ordered North, and the busy Gilmore reigned in his stead; and in June, when the blackberries were all eaten, we were summoned, nothing loath, to other scenes and encampments new.[11]

CHAPTER VI

A Night in the Water

Yes, that was a pleasant life on picket, in the delicious early summer of the South, and among the endless flowery forests of that blossoming isle. In the retrospect I seem to see myself adrift upon a horse's back amid a sea of roses. The various outposts were within a six-mile radius, and it was one long, delightful gallop, day and night. I have a faint impression that the moon shone steadily every night for two months; and yet I remember certain periods of such dense darkness that in riding through the wood-paths it was really unsafe to go beyond a walk, for fear of branches above and roots below; and one of my officers was once shot at by a Rebel scout who stood unperceived at his horse's bridle.

To those doing outpost-duty on an island, however large, the main-land has all the fascination of forbidden fruit, and on a scale bounded only by the horizon. Emerson says that every house looks ideal until we enter it,—and it is certainly so, if it be just the other side of the hostile lines. Every grove in that blue distance appears enchanted ground, and yonder loitering gray-back leading his horse to water in the farthest distance, makes one thrill with a desire to hail him, to shoot at him, to capture him, to do anything to bridge this inexorable dumb space that lies between. A boyish feeling, no doubt, and one that time diminishes, without effacing; yet it is a feeling which lies at the bottom of many rash actions in war, and of some brilliant ones. For one, I could never quite outgrow it, though restricted by duty from doing many foolish things in consequence, and also restrained by reverence for certain confidential advisers whom I had always at hand, and who considered it their mission to keep me always on short rations of personal adventure. Indeed, most of that sort of entertainment in the army devolves upon scouts detailed for the purpose, volunteer aides-de-camp and newspaper-reporters,—other officers being expected to be about business more prosaic.

All the excitements of war are quadrupled by darkness; and as

I rode along our outer lines at night, and watched the glimmering flames which at regular intervals starred the opposite river-shore, the longing was irresistible to cross the barrier of dusk, and see whether it were men or ghosts who hovered round those dying embers. I had yielded to these impulses in boat-adventures by night,—for it was a part of my instructions to obtain all possible information about the Rebel outposts,—and fascinating indeed it was to glide along, noiselessly paddling, with a dusky guide, through the endless intricacies of those Southern marshes, scaring the reed-birds, which wailed and fled away into the darkness, and penetrating several miles into the interior, between hostile fires, where discovery might be death. Yet there were drawbacks as to these enterprises, since it is not easy for a boat to cross still water, even on the darkest night, without being seen by watchful eyes; and, moreover, the extremes of high and low tide transform so completely the whole condition of those rivers that it needs very nice calculation to do one's work at precisely the right time. To vary the experiment, I had often thought of trying a personal reconnoissance by swimming, at a certain point, whenever circumstances should make it an object.

The opportunity at last arrived, and I shall never forget the glee with which, after several postponements, I finally rode forth, a little before midnight, on a night which seemed made for the purpose. I had, of course, kept my own secret, and was entirely alone. The great Southern fireflies were out, not haunting the low ground merely, like ours, but rising to the loftiest tree-tops with weird illumination, and anon hovering so low that my horse often stepped the higher to avoid them. The dewy Cherokee roses brushed my face, the solemn "Chuckwill's-widow" croaked her incantation, and the rabbits raced phantom-like across the shadowy road. Slowly in the darkness I followed the well-known path to the spot where our most advanced outposts were stationed, holding a causeway which thrust itself far out across the separating river,—thus fronting a similar causeway on the other side, while a channel of perhaps three hundred yards, once traversed by a ferry-boat, rolled between. At low tide this channel was the whole river, with broad, oozy marshes on each side; at high tide the marshes were submerged, and the stream was a mile wide. This was the point which I had selected. To ascertain the numbers and position of the picket on the opposite causeway was my first object, as it was a matter on which no two of our officers agreed.

To this point, therefore, I rode, and dismounting, after being duly challenged by the sentinel at the causeway-head, walked down the long and lonely path. The tide was well up, though still on the flood, as I desired; and each visible tuft of marsh-grass might, but for its motionlessness, have been a prowling boat. Dark as the night had appeared, the water was pale, smooth, and phosphorescent, and I remember that the phrase "wan water," so familiar in the Scottish ballads, struck me just then as peculiarly appropriate, though its real meaning is quite different. A gentle breeze, from which I had hoped for a ripple, had utterly died away, and it was a warm, breathless Southern night. There was no sound but the faint swash of the coming tide, the noises of the reed-birds in the marshes, and the occasional leap of a fish; and it seemed to my overstrained ear as if every footstep of my own must be heard for miles. However, I could have no more postponements, and the thing must be tried now or never.

Reaching the farther end of the causeway, I found my men couched, like black statues, behind the slight earthwork there constructed. I expected that my proposed immersion would rather bewilder them, but knew that they would say nothing, as usual. As for the lieutenant on that post, he was a steady, matter-of-fact, perfectly disciplined Englishman, who wore a Crimean medal, and never asked a superfluous question in his life. If I had casually remarked to him, "Mr. Hooper, the General has ordered me on a brief personal reconnoissance to the Planet Jupiter, and I wish you to take care of my watch, lest it should be damaged by the Precession of the Equinoxes," he would have responded with a brief "All right, Sir," and a quick military gesture, and have put the thing in his pocket. As it was, I simply gave him the watch, and remarked that I was going to take a swim.

I do not remember ever to have experienced a greater sense of exhilaration than when I slipped noiselessly into the placid water, and struck out into the smooth, eddying current for the opposite shore. The night was so still and lovely, my black statues looked so dream-like at their posts behind the low earthwork, the opposite arm of the causeway stretched so invitingly from the Rebel main, the horizon glimmered so low around me,—for it always appears lower to a swimmer than even to an oarsman,—that I seemed floating in some concave globe, some magic crystal, of which I was the enchanted centre. With each little ripple of my steady progress all things hovered and changed; the stars danced and nodded above; where the stars ended the great Southern fire-flies began; and closer than the fireflies, there clung round me a halo of phosphorescent sparkles from the soft salt water.

Had I told any one of my purpose, I should have had warnings and remonstrances enough. The few negroes who did not believe in alligators believed in sharks; the sceptics as to sharks were or-thodox in respect to alligators; while those who rejected both had private prejudices as to snapping-turtles. The surgeon would have threatened intermittent fever, the first assistant rheumatism, and the second assistant congestive chills; non-swimmers would have predicted exhaustion, and swimmers cramp; and all this before coming within bullet-range of any hospitalities on the other shore. But I knew the folly of most alarms about reptiles and fishes; man's imagination peoples the water with many things which do not belong there, or prefer to keep out of his way, if they do; fevers and congestions were the surgeon's business, and I always kept people to their own department; cramp and exhaustion were dangers I could measure, as I had often done; bullets were a more substantial danger, and I must take the chance,—if a loon could dive at the flash, why not I? If I were once ashore, I should have to cope with the Rebels on their own ground, which they knew better than I; but the water was my ground, where I, too, had been at home from boyhood.

I swam as swiftly and softly as I could, although it seemed as if water never had been so still before. It appeared impossible that anything uncanny should hide beneath that lovely mirror; and yet when some floating wisp of reeds suddenly coiled itself around my neck, or some unknown thing, drifting deeper, coldly touched my foot, it caused that undefinable shudder which every swimmer knows, and which especially comes over one by night. Sometimes a slight sip of brackish water would enter my lips,—for I naturally tried to swim as low as possible,—and then would follow a slight gasping and contest against choking, that seemed to me a perfect convulsion; for I suppose the tendency to choke and sneeze is always enhanced by the circumstance that one's life may depend

on keeping still, just as yawning becomes irresistible where to
yawn would be social ruin, and just as one is sure to sleep in
church, if one sits in a conspicuous pew. At other times, some
unguarded motion would create a splashing which seemed, in the
tension of my senses, to be loud enough to be heard at Richmond,
although it really mattered not, since there are fishes in those rivers which make as much noise on special occasions as if they were
misguided young whales.

As I drew near the opposite shore, the dark causeway projected
more and more distinctly, to my fancy at least, and I swam more
softly still, utterly uncertain as to how far, in the stillness of air
and water, my phosphorescent course could be traced by eye or
ear. A slight ripple would have saved me from observation, I was
more than ever sure, and I would have whistled for a fair wind as
eagerly as any sailor, but that my breath was worth to me more
than anything it was likely to bring. The water became smoother
and smoother, and nothing broke the dim surface except a few
clumps of rushes and my unfortunate head. The outside of this
member gradually assumed to its inside a gigantic magnitude; it
had always annoyed me at the hatter's from a merely animal big-
ness, with no commensurate contents to show for it, and now I
detested it more than ever. A physical feeling of turgescence and
congestion in that region, such as swimmers often feel, probably
increased the impression. I thought with envy of the Aztec children, of the headless horseman of Sleepy Hollow, of Saint Somebody[1] with his head tucked under his arm. Plotinus[2] was less
ashamed of his whole body than I of this inconsiderate and stupid
appendage. To be sure, I might swim for a certain distance under
water. But that accomplishment I had reserved for a retreat, for I
knew that the longer I stayed down the more surely I should have
to snort like a walrus when I came up again, and to approach an
enemy with such a demonstration was not to be thought of.

Suddenly a dog barked. We had certain information that a pack
of hounds was kept at a Rebel station a few miles off, on purpose
to hunt runaways, and I had heard from the negroes almost fabulous accounts of the instinct of these animals. I knew that, although water baffled their scent, they yet could recognize in some
manner the approach of any person across water as readily as by
land; and of the vigilance of all dogs by night every traveller

among Southern plantations has ample demonstration. I was now so near that I could dimly see the figures of men moving to and fro upon the end of the causeway, and could hear the dull knock, when one struck his foot against a piece of timber.

As my first object was to ascertain whether there were sentinels at that time at that precise point, I saw that I was approaching the end of my experiment. Could I have once reached the causeway unnoticed, I could have lurked in the water beneath its projecting timbers, and perhaps made my way along the main shore, as I had known fugitive slaves to do, while coming from that side. Or had there been any ripple on the water, to confuse the aroused and watchful eyes, I could have made a circuit and approached the causeway at another point, though I had already satisfied myself that there was only a narrow channel on each side of it, even at high tide, and not, as on our side, a broad expanse of water. Indeed, this knowledge alone was worth all the trouble I had taken, and to attempt much more than this, in the face of a curiosity already roused, would have been a waste of future opportunities. I could try again, with the benefit of this new knowledge, on a point where the statements of the negroes had always been contradictory.

Resolving, however, to continue the observation a very little longer, since the water felt much warmer than I had expected, and there was no sense of chill or fatigue, I grasped at some wisps of straw or rushes that floated near, gathering them round my face a little, and then drifting nearer the wharf in what seemed a sort of eddy was able, without creating further alarm, to make some additional observations on points which it is not best now to particularize. Then, turning my back upon the mysterious shore which had thus far lured me, I sank softly below the surface, and swam as far as I could under water.

During this unseen retreat, I heard, of course, all manner of gurglings and hollow reverberations, and could fancy as many rifle-shots as I pleased. But on rising to the surface all seemed quiet, and even I did not create as much noise as I should have expected. I was now at a safe distance, since the enemy were always chary of showing their boats, and always tried to convince us they had none. What with absorbed attention first, and this submersion afterwards, I had lost all my bearings but the stars, having been long out of sight of my original point of departure. However, the difficulties of the return were nothing; making a slight allowance for the flood-tide, which could not yet have turned, I should soon regain the place I had left. So I struck out freshly against the smooth water, feeling just a little stiffened by the exertion, and with an occasional chill running up the back of the neck, but with no nips from sharks, no nudges from alligators, and not a symptom of fever-and-ague.

Time I could not, of course, measure,—one never can in a novel position; but, after a reasonable amount of swimming, I began to look, with a natural interest, for the pier which I had quitted. I noticed, with some solicitude, that the woods along the friendly shore made one continuous shadow, and that the line of low bushes on the long causeway could scarcely be relieved against them, yet I knew where they ought to be, and the more doubtful I felt about it, the more I put down my doubts, as if they were unreasonable children. One can scarcely conceive of the alteration made in familiar objects by bringing the eye as low as the horizon, especially by night; to distinguish foreshortening is impossible, and every low near object is equivalent to one higher and more remote. Still I had the stars; and soon my eye, more practised, was enabled to select one precise line of bushes as that which marked the causeway, and for which I must direct my course.

As I swam steadily, but with some sense of fatigue, towards this phantom-line, I found it difficult to keep my faith steady and my progress true; everything appeared to shift and waver, in the uncertain light. The distant trees seemed not trees, but bushes, and the bushes seemed not exactly bushes, but might, after all, be distant trees. Could I be so confident that, out of all that low stretch of shore, I could select the one precise point where the friendly causeway stretched its long arm to receive me from the water? How easily (some tempter whispered at my ear) might one swerve a little, on either side, and be compelled to flounder over half a mile of oozy marsh on an ebbing tide, before reaching our own shore and that hospitable volley of bullets with which it would probably greet me! Had I not already (thus the tempter continued) been swimming rather unaccountably far, supposing me on a straight track for that inviting spot where my sentinels and my drapery were awaiting my return?

Suddenly I felt a sensation as of fine ribbons drawn softly across my person, and I found myself among some rushes. But what business had rushes there, or I among them? I knew that there was not a solitary spot of shoal in the deep channel where I supposed myself swimming, and it was plain in an instant that I had somehow missed my course, and must be getting among the marshes. I felt confident, to be sure, that I could not have widely erred, but was guiding my course for the proper side of the river. But whether I had drifted above or below the causeway I had not the slightest clew to tell.

I pushed steadily forward, with some increasing sense of lassitude, passing one marshy islet after another, all seeming strangely out of place, and sometimes just reaching with my foot a soft tremulous shoal which gave scarce the shadow of a support, though even that shadow rested my feet. At one of these moments of stillness it suddenly occurred to my perception (what nothing but this slight contact could have assured me, in the darkness) that I was in a powerful current, and that this current set *the wrong way*. Instantly a flood of new intelligence came. Either I had unconsciously turned and was rapidly nearing the Rebel shore,—a suspicion which a glance at the stars corrected,—or else it was the tide itself which had turned, and which was sweeping me down the river with all its force, and was also sucking away at every moment the narrowing water from that treacherous expanse of mud out of whose horrible miry embrace I had lately helped to rescue a ship-wrecked crew.

Either alternative was rather formidable. I can distinctly remember that for about one half-minute the whole vast universe appeared to swim in the same watery uncertainty in which I floated. I began to doubt everything, to distrust the stars, the line of low bushes for which I was wearily striving, the very land on which they grew, if such visionary things could be rooted anywhere. Doubts trembled in my mind like the weltering water, and that awful sensation of having one's feet unsupported, which benumbs the spent swimmer's heart, seemed to clutch at mine, though not yet to enter it. I was more absorbed in that singular sensation of nightmare, such as one may feel equally when lost by land or by water, as if one's own position were all right, but the place looked for had somehow been preternaturally abolished out of the universe. At best, might not a man in the water lose all his power of direction, and so move in an endless circle until he sank exhausted? It required a deliberate and conscious effort to keep my brain quite cool. I have not the reputation of being of an excitable temperament, but the contrary; yet I could at that moment see my way to a condition in which one might become insane in an instant. It was as if a fissure opened somewhere, and I saw my way into a mad-house; then it closed, and everything went on as before. Once in my life I had obtained a slight glimpse of the same sensation, and then, too, strangely enough, while swimming,—in the mightiest ocean-surge into which I had ever dared plunge my mortal body. Keats[3] hints at the same sudden emotion, in a wild poem written among the Scottish mountains. It was not the distinctive sensation which drowning men are said to have, that spasmodic passing in review of one's whole personal history. I had no well-defined anxiety, felt no fear, was moved to no prayer, did not give a thought to home or friends; only it swept over me, as with a sudden tempest, that, if I meant to get back to my own camp, I must keep my wits about me. I must not dwell on any other alternative, any more than a boy who climbs a precipice must look down. Imagination had no business here. That way madness lay.[4] There was a shore somewhere before me, and I must get to it, by the ordinary means, before the ebb laid bare the flats, or swept me below the lower bends of the stream. That was all.

Suddenly a light gleamed for an instant before me, as if from a house in a grove of great trees upon a bank; and I knew that it came from the window of a ruined plantation-building, where our most advanced outposts had their head-quarters. The flash revealed to me every point of the situation. I saw at once where I was, and how I got there: that the tide had turned while I was swimming, and with a much briefer interval of slack-water than I had been led to suppose,—that I had been swept a good way down stream, and was far beyond all possibility of regaining the point I had left. Could I, however, retain my strength to swim one or two hundred yards farther, of which I had no doubt,—

and if the water did not ebb too rapidly, of which I had more fear,—then I was quite safe. Every stroke took me more and more out of the power of the current, and there might even be an eddy to aid me. I could not afford to be carried down much farther, for there the channel made a sweep toward the wrong side of the river; but there was now no reason why I should not reach land. I could dismiss all fear, indeed, except that of being fired upon by our own sentinels, many of whom were then new recruits, and with the usual disposition to shoot first and investigate afterwards.

I found myself swimming in shallow and shallower water, and the flats seemed almost bare when I neared the shore, where the great gnarled branches of the live-oaks hung far over the muddy bank. Floating on my back for noiselessness, I paddled rapidly in with my hands, expecting momentarily to hear the challenge of the picket, and the ominous click so likely to follow. I knew that some one should be pacing to and fro, along that beat, but could not tell at what point he might be at that precise moment. Besides, there was a faint possibility that some chatty corporal might have carried the news of my bath thus far along the line, and they might be partially prepared for this unexpected visitor. Suddenly, like another flash, came the quick, quaint challenge,—

"Halt! Who's go dar?"

"F-f-friend with the c-c-countersign," retorted I, with chilly, but conciliatory energy, rising at full length out of the shallow water, to show myself a man and a brother.[5]

"Ac-vance, friend, and give de countersign," responded the literal soldier, who at such a time would have accosted a spirit of light or goblin damned with no other formula.

I advanced and gave it, he recognizing my voice at once. And then and there, as I stood, a dripping ghost, beneath the trees before him, the unconscionable fellow, wishing to exhaust upon me the utmost resources of military hospitality, deliberately presented arms!

Now a soldier on picket, or at night, usually presents arms to nobody; but a sentinel on camp-guard by day is expected to perform that ceremony to anything in human shape that has two rows of buttons. Here was a human shape, but so utterly buttonless that it exhibited not even a rag to which a button could by any earthly possibility be appended, buttonless even potentially;

and my blameless Ethiopian presented arms to even this. Where, then, are the theories of Carlyle,[6] the axioms of "Sartor Resartus," the inability of humanity to conceive "a naked Duke of Windlestraw addressing a naked House of Lords"? Cautioning my adherent, however, as to the proprieties suitable for such occasions thenceforward, I left him watching the river with renewed vigilance, and awaiting the next merman who should report himself.

Finding my way to the building, I hunted up a sergeant and a blanket, got a fire kindled in the dismantled chimney, and sat before it in my single garment, like a moist but undismayed Choctaw, until horse and clothing could be brought round from the causeway. It seemed strange that the morning had not yet dawned, after the uncounted periods that must have elapsed; but when the wardrobe arrived I looked at my watch and found that my night in the water had lasted precisely one hour.

Galloping home, I turned in with alacrity, and without a drop of whiskey, and waked a few hours after in excellent condition. The rapid changes of which that Department has seen so many—and, perhaps, to so little purpose—soon transferred us to a different scene. I have been on other scouts since then, and by various processes, but never with a zest so novel as was afforded by that night's experience. The thing soon got wind in the regiment, and led to only one ill consequence, so far as I know. It rather suppressed a way I had of lecturing the officers on the importance of reducing their personal baggage to a minimum. They got a trick of congratulating me, very respectfully, on the thoroughness with which I had once conformed my practice to my precepts.

CHAPTER VII
Up the Edisto

In reading military history, one finds the main interest to lie, undoubtedly, in the great campaigns, where a man, a regiment, a brigade, is but a pawn in the game. But there is a charm also in the more free and adventurous life of partisan warfare, where, if the total sphere be humbler, yet the individual has more relative importance, and the sense of action is more personal and keen. This is the reason given by the eccentric Revolutionary biographer, Weems,[1] for writing the Life of Washington first, and then that of Marion. And there were, certainly, in the early adventures of the colored troops in the Department of the South, some of the same elements of picturesqueness that belonged to Marion's band, on the same soil, with the added feature that the blacks were fighting for their personal liberties, of which Marion had helped to deprive them.

It is stated by Major-General Gillmore, in his "Siege of Charleston," as one of the three points in his preliminary strategy, that an expedition was sent up the Edisto River to destroy a bridge on the Charleston and Savannah Railway. As one of the early raids of the colored troops, this expedition may deserve narration, though it was, in a strategic point of view, a disappointment. It has already been told, briefly and on the whole with truth, by Greeley[2] and others, but I will venture on a more complete account.

The project dated back earlier than General Gillmore's siege, and had originally no connection with that movement. It had been formed by Captain Trowbridge and myself in camp, and was based on facts learned from the men. General Saxton and Colonel W. W. H. Davis, the successive post-commanders, had both favored it. It had been also approved by General Hunter, before his sudden removal, though he regarded the bridge as a secondary affair, because there was another railway communication between the two cities. But as my main object was to obtain permission to go, I tried to make the most of all results which might follow, while it was very clear that the raid would harass and confuse the enemy, and be the means of bringing away many of the slaves. General Hunter had, therefore, accepted the project mainly as a stroke for freedom and black recruits; and General Gillmore, because anything that looked toward action found favor in his eyes, and because it would be convenient to him at that time to effect a diversion, if nothing more.

It must be remembered that, after the first capture of Port Royal, the outlying plantations along the whole Southern coast were abandoned, and the slaves withdrawn into the interior. It was necessary to ascend some river for thirty miles in order to reach the black population at all. This ascent could only be made by night, as it was a slow process, and the smoke of a steamboat could be seen for a great distance. The streams were usually shallow, winding, and muddy, and the difficulties of navigation were such as to require a full moon and a flood tide. It was really no easy matter to bring everything to bear, especially as every projected raid must be kept a secret so far as possible. However, we were now somewhat familiar with such undertakings, half military, half naval, and the thing to be done on the Edisto was precisely what we had proved to be practicable on the St. Mary's and the St. John's,—to drop anchor before the enemy's door some morning at daybreak, without his having dreamed of our approach.

Since a raid made by Colonel Montgomery up the Combahee, two months before, the vigilance of the Rebels had increased. But we had information that upon the South Edisto, or Pon-Pon River, the rice plantations were still being actively worked by a large number of negroes, in reliance on obstructions placed at the mouth of that narrow stream, where it joins the main river, some twenty miles from the coast. This point was known to be further protected by a battery of unknown strength, at Wiltown Bluff, a commanding and defensible situation. The obstructions consisted of a row of strong wooden piles across the river; but we convinced ourselves that these must now be much decayed, and that Captain Trowbridge, an excellent engineer officer, could remove them by the proper apparatus. Our proposition was to man the John Adams, an armed ferry-boat, which had before done us much service,—and which has now reverted to the pursuits of peace, it is said, on the East Boston line,—to ascend in this to Wiltown Bluff, silence the battery, and clear a passage through the obstructions. Leaving the John Adams to protect this point, we could then ascend the smaller stream with two light-draft boats, and perhaps burn the bridge, which was ten miles higher, before the enemy could bring sufficient force to make our position at Wiltown Bluff untenable.

The expedition was organized essentially upon this plan. The smaller boats were the Enoch Dean,—a river steamboat, which carried a ten-pound Parrott gun, and a small howitzer,—and a little mosquito of a tug, the Governor Milton, upon which, with the greatest difficulty, we found room for two twelve-pound Armstrong guns, with their gunners, forming a section of the First Connecticut Battery, under Lieutenant Clinton, aided by a squad from my own regiment, under Captain James. The John Adams carried, if I remember rightly, two Parrott guns (of twenty and ten pounds calibre) and a howitzer or two. The whole force of men did not exceed two hundred and fifty.

We left Beaufort, S.C., on the afternoon of July 9th, 1863. In former narrations I have sufficiently described the charm of a moonlight ascent into a hostile country, upon an unknown stream, the dark and silent banks, the rippling water, the wail of the reed-birds, the anxious watch, the breathless listening, the veiled lights, the whispered orders. To this was now to be added the vexation of an insufficient pilotage, for our negro guide knew only the upper river, and, as it finally proved, not even that, while, to take us over the bar which obstructed the main stream, we must borrow a pilot from Captain Dutch, whose gunboat blockaded that point. This active naval officer, however, whose boat expeditions had penetrated all the lower branches of those rivers, could supply our want, and we borrowed from him not only a pilot, but a surgeon, to replace our own, who had been prevented by an accident from coming with us. Thus accompanied, we steamed over the bar in safety, had a peaceful ascent, passed the island of Jehossee,—the fine estate of Governor Aiken, then left undisturbed by both sides,—and fired our first shell into the camp at Wiltown Bluff at four o'clock in the morning.

The battery—whether fixed or movable we knew not—met us

with a promptness that proved very short-lived. After three shots it was silent, but we could not tell why. The bluff was wooded, and we could see but little. The only course was to land, under cover of the guns. As the firing ceased and the smoke cleared away, I looked across the rice-fields which lay beneath the bluff. The first sunbeams glowed upon their emerald levels, and on the blossoming hedges along the rectangular dikes. What were those black dots which everywhere appeared? Those moist meadows had become alive with human heads, and along each narrow path came a straggling file of men and women, all on a run for the river-side. I went ashore with a boat-load of troops at once. The landing was difficult and marshy. The astonished negroes tugged us up the bank, and gazed on us as if we had been Cortez and Columbus. They kept arriving by land much faster than we could come by water; every moment increased the crowd, the jostling, the mutual clinging, on that miry foothold. What a scene it was! With the wild faces, eager figures, strange garments, it seemed, as one of the poor things reverently suggested, "like notin' but de judgment day." Presently they began to come from the houses also, with their little bundles on their heads; then with larger bundles. Old women, trotting on the narrow paths, would kneel to pray a little prayer, still balancing the bundle; and then would suddenly spring up, urged by the accumulating procession behind, and would move on till irresistibly compelled by thankfulness to dip down for another invocation. Reaching us, every human being must grasp our hands, amid exclamations of "Bress you, mas'r," and "Bress de Lord," at the rate of four of the latter ascriptions to one of the former. Women brought children on their shoulders; small black boys carried on their backs little brothers equally inky, and, gravely depositing them, shook hands. Never had I seen human beings so clad, or rather so unclad, in such amazing squalidness and destitution of garments. I recall one small urchin without a rag of clothing save the basque waist of a lady's dress, bristling with whalebones, and worn wrong side before, beneath which his smooth ebony legs emerged like those of an ostrich from its plumage. How weak is imagination, how cold is memory, that I ever cease, for a day of my life, to see before me the picture of that astounding scene!

Yet at the time we were perforce a little impatient of all this piety, protestation, and hand-pressing; for the vital thing was to ascertain what force had been stationed at the bluff, and whether it was yet withdrawn. The slaves, on the other hand, were too much absorbed in their prospective freedom to aid us in taking any further steps to secure it. Captain Trowbridge, who had by this time landed at a different point, got quite into despair over the seeming deafness of the people to all questions. "How many soldiers are there on the bluff?" he asked of the first-comer.

"Mas'r," said the man, stuttering terribly, "I c-c-c—"

"Tell me how many soldiers there are!" roared Trowbridge, in his mighty voice, and all but shaking the poor old thing, in his thirst for information.

"O mas'r," recommenced in terror the incapacitated witness, "I c-c-carpenter!" holding up eagerly a little stump of a hatchet, his sole treasure, as if his profession ought to excuse him from all military opinions.

I wish that it were possible to present all this scene from the point of view of the slaves themselves. It can be most nearly done, perhaps, by quoting the description given of a similar scene on the Combahee River, by a very aged man, who had been brought down on the previous raid, already mentioned. I wrote it down in tent, long after, while the old man recited the tale, with much gesticulation, at the door; and it is by far the best glimpse I have ever had, through a negro's eyes, at these wonderful birthdays of freedom.

"De people was all a hoein', mas'r," said the old man. "Dey was a hoein' in the rice-field, when de gunboats come. Den ebry man drap dem hoe, and leff de rice. De mas'r he stand and call, 'Run to de wood for hide! Yankee come, sell you to Cuba! run for hide!' Ebry man he run, and, my God! run all toder way!

"Mas'r stand in de wood, peep, peep, faid for truss [afraid to trust]. He say, 'Run to de wood!' and ebry man run by him, straight to de boat.

"De brack sojer so presumptious, dey come right ashore, hold up dere head. Fus' ting I know, dere was a barn, ten tousand bushel rough rice, all in a blaze, den mas'r's great house, all crack-lin' up de roof. Did n't I keer for see 'em blaze? Lor, mas'r, did n't care notin' at all, *I was gwine to de boat*."

Doré's[3] Don Quixote could not surpass the sublime absorption in which the gaunt old man, with arm uplifted, described this stage of affairs, till he ended in a shrewd chuckle, worthy of Sancho Panza.[4] Then he resumed.

"De brack sojers so presumptious!" This he repeated three times, slowly shaking his head in an ecstasy of admiration. It flashed upon me that the apparition of a black soldier must amaze those still in bondage, much as a butterfly just from the chrysalis might astound his fellow-grubs. I inwardly vowed that my soldiers, at least, should be as "presumptious" as I could make them. Then he went on.

"Ole woman and I go down to de boat; den dey say behind us, 'Rebels comin'! Rebels comin'!' Ole woman say, 'Come ahead, come plenty ahead!' I hab notin' on but my shirt and pantaloon; ole woman one single frock he hab on, and one handkerchief on he head; I leff all-two my blanket and run for de Rebel come, and den dey did n't come, did n't truss for come.

"Ise eighty-eight year old, mas'r. My ole Mas'r Lowndes keep all de ages in a big book, and when we come to age ob sense we mark em down ebry year, so I know. Too ole for come? Mas'r joking. Neber too ole for leave de land o'bondage. I old, but great good for chil'en, gib tousand tank ebry day. Young people can go through, *force* [forcibly], mas'r, but de ole folk mus' go slow."

Such emotions as these, no doubt, were inspired by our arrival, but we could only hear their hasty utterance in passing; our duty being, with the small force already landed, to take possession of the bluff. Ascending, with proper precautions, the wooded hill, we soon found ourselves in the deserted camp of a light battery, amid scattered equipments and suggestions of a very unattractive breakfast. As soon as possible, skirmishers were thrown out through the woods to the farther edge of the bluff, while a party searched the houses, finding the usual large supply of furniture and pictures,—brought up for safety from below,—but no soldiers. Captain Trowbridge then got the John Adams beside the row of piles, and went to work for their removal.

Again I had the exciting sensation of being within the hostile lines,—the eager explorations, the doubts, the watchfulness, the listening for every sound of coming hoofs. Presently a horse's tread was heard in earnest, but it was a squad of our own men bringing in two captured cavalry soldiers. One of these, a sturdy fellow, submitted quietly to his lot, only begging that, whenever we should evacuate the bluff, a note should be left behind stating that he was a prisoner. The other, a very young man, and a member of the "Rebel Troop," a sort of Cadet corps among the Charleston youths, came to me in great wrath, complaining that the corporal of our squad had kicked him after he had surrendered. His air of offended pride was very rueful, and it did indeed seem a pathetic reversal of fortunes for the two races. To be sure, the youth was a scion of one of the foremost families of South Carolina, and when I considered the wrongs which the black race had encountered from those of his blood, first and last, it seemed as if the most scrupulous Recording Angel might tolerate one final kick to square the account. But I reproved the corporal, who respectfully disclaimed the charge, and said the kick was an incident of the scuffle. It certainly was not their habit to show such poor malice; they thought too well of themselves.

His demeanor seemed less lofty, but rather piteous, when he implored me not to put him on board any vessel which was to ascend the upper stream, and hinted, by awful implications, the danger of such ascent. This meant torpedoes, a peril which we treated, in those days, with rather mistaken contempt. But we found none on the Edisto, and it may be that it was only a foolish attempt to alarm us.

Meanwhile, Trowbridge was toiling away at the row of piles, which proved easier to draw out than to saw asunder, either work being hard enough. It took far longer than we had hoped, and we saw noon approach and the tide rapidly fall, taking with it, inch by inch, our hopes of effecting a surprise at the bridge. During this time, and indeed all day, the detachments on shore, under Captains Whitney and Sampson, were having occasional skirmishes with the enemy, while the colored people were swarming to the shore, or running to and fro like ants, with the poor treasures of their houses. Our busy Quartermaster, Mr. Bingham— who died afterwards from the overwork of that sultry day—was transporting the refugees on board the steamer, or hunting up bales of cotton, or directing the burning of rice-houses, in accordance with our orders. No dwelling-houses were destroyed or plundered by our men,—Sherman's "bummers" not having yet arrived,—though I asked no questions as to what the plantation negroes might bring in their great bundles. One piece of property, I must admit, seemed a lawful capture,—a United States dress-sword, of the old pattern, which had belonged to the Rebel general who afterwards gave the order to bury Colonel Shaw "with his niggers." That I have retained, not without some satisfaction, to this day.

A passage having been cleared at last, and the tide having turned by noon, we lost no time in attempting the ascent, leaving the bluff to be held by the John Adams, and by the small force on shore. We were scarcely above the obstructions, however, when the little tug went aground, and the Enoch Dean, ascending a mile farther, had an encounter with a battery on the right,—perhaps our old enemy,—and drove it back. Soon after, she also ran aground, a misfortune of which our opponent strangely took no advantage; and, on getting off, I thought it best to drop down to the bluff again, as the tide was still hopelessly low. None can tell, save those who have tried them, the vexations of those muddy Southern streams, navigable only during a few hours of flood-tide.

After waiting an hour, the two small vessels again tried the ascent. The enemy on the right had disappeared; but we could now see, far off on our left, another light battery moving parallel with the river, apparently to meet us at some upper bend. But for the present we were safe, with the low rice-fields on each side of us; and the scene was so peaceful, it seemed as if all danger were done. For the first time, we saw in South Carolina blossoming river-banks and low emerald meadows, that seemed like New England. Everywhere there were the same rectangular fields, smooth canals, and bushy dikes. A few negroes stole out to us in dugouts, and breathlessly told us how others had been hurried away by the overseers. We glided safely on, mile after mile. The day was unutterably hot, but all else seemed propitious. The men had their combustibles all ready to fire the bridge, and our hopes were unbounded.

But by degrees the channel grew more tortuous and difficult, and while the little Milton glided smoothly over everything, the Enoch Dean, my own boat, repeatedly grounded. On every occasion of especial need, too, something went wrong in her machinery,—her engine being constructed on some wholly new patent, of which, I should hope, this trial would prove entirely sufficient. The black pilot, who was not a soldier, grew more and more bewildered, and declared that it was the channel, not his brain, which had gone wrong; the captain, a little elderly man, sat wringing his hands in the pilot-box; and the engineer appeared to be mingling his groans with those of the diseased engine. Meanwhile I, in equal ignorance of machinery and channel, had to give orders only justified by minute acquaintance with both. So I navigated on general principles, until they grounded us on a mudbank, just below a wooded point, and some two miles from the bridge of our destination. It was with a pang that I waved to Major Strong, who was on the other side of the channel in a tug, not to risk approaching us, but to steam on and finish the work, if he could.

Short was his triumph. Gliding round the point, he found himself instantly engaged with a light battery of four or six guns, doubtless the same we had seen in the distance. The Milton was within two hundred and fifty yards. The Connecticut men fought their guns well, aided by the blacks, and it was exasperating for us to hear the shots, while we could see nothing and do nothing. The scanty ammunition of our bow gun was exhausted, and the gun in the stern was useless, from the position in which we lay. In vain we moved the men from side to side, rocking the vessel, to dislodge it. The heat was terrific that August afternoon; I remember I found myself constantly changing places, on the scorched deck, to keep my feet from being blistered. At last the officer in charge of the gun, a hardy lumberman from Maine, got the stern of the vessel so far round that he obtained the range of the battery through the cabin windows, "but it would be necessary," he coolly added, on reporting to me this fact, "to shoot away the corner of the cabin." I knew that this apartment was newly painted and gilded, and the idol of the poor captain's heart; but it was plain that even the thought of his own upholstery could not make the poor soul more wretched than he was. So I bade Captain Dolly blaze away, and thus we took our hand in the little game, though at a sacrifice.

It was of no use. Down drifted our little consort round the point, her engine disabled and her engineer killed, as we afterwards found, though then we could only look and wonder. Still pluckily firing, she floated by upon the tide, which had now just turned; and when, with a last desperate effort, we got off, our engine had one of its impracticable fits, and we could only follow her. The day was waning, and all its range of possibility had lain within the limits of that one tide.

All our previous expeditions had been so successful it now seemed hard to turn back; the river-banks and rice-fields, so beautiful before, seemed only a vexation now. But the swift current bore us on, and after our Parthian shots had died away, a new discharge of artillery opened upon us, from our first antagonist of the morning, which still kept the other side of the stream. It had taken up a strong position on another bluff, almost out of range of the John Adams, but within easy range of us. The sharpest contest of the day was before us. Happily the engine and engineer were now behaving well, and we were steering in a channel already traversed, and of which the dangerous points were known. But we had a long, straight reach of river before us, heading directly toward the battery, which, having once got our range, had only to keep it, while we could do nothing in return. The Rebels certainly served their guns well. For the first time I discovered that there were certain compensating advantages in a slightly built craft, as compared with one more substantial; the missiles never lodged in the vessel, but crashed through some thin partition as if it were paper, to explode beyond us, or fall harmless in the water. Splintering, the chief source of wounds and death in wooden ships, was thus entirely avoided; the danger was that our machinery might be disabled, or that shots might strike below the water-line and sink us.

This, however, did not happen. Fifteen projectiles, as we afterwards computed, passed through the vessel or cut the rigging. Yet few casualties occurred, and those instantly fatal. As my orderly stood leaning on a comrade's shoulder, the head of the latter was shot off. At last I myself felt a sudden blow in the side, as if from some prize-fighter, doubling me up for a moment, while I sank upon a seat. It proved afterwards to have been produced by the grazing of a ball, which, without tearing a garment, had yet made a large part of my side black and blue, leaving a sensation of paralysis which made it difficult to stand. Supporting myself on Captain Rogers, I tried to comprehend what had happened, and

I remember being impressed by an odd feeling that I had now got my share, and should henceforth be a great deal safer than any of the rest. I am told that this often follows one's first experience of a wound.

But this immediate contest, sharp as it was, proved brief; a turn in the river enabled us to use our stern gun, and we soon glided into the comparative shelter of Wiltown Bluff. There, however, we were to encounter the danger of shipwreck, superadded to that of fight. When the passage through the piles was first cleared, it had been marked by stakes, lest the rising tide should cover the remaining piles, and make it difficult to run the passage. But when we again reached it, the stakes had somehow been knocked away, the piles were just covered by the swift current, and the little tug-boat was aground upon them. She came off easily, however, with our aid, and, when we in turn essayed the passage, we grounded also, but more firmly. We getting off at last, and making the passage, the tug again became lodged, when nearly past danger, and all our efforts proved powerless to pull her through. I therefore dropped down below, and sent the John Adams to her aid, while I superintended the final recall of the pickets, and the embarkation of the remaining refugees.

While thus engaged, I felt little solicitude about the boats above. It was certain that the John Adams could safely go close to the piles on the lower side, that she was very strong, and that the other was very light. Still, it was natural to cast some anxious glances up the river, and it was with surprise that I presently saw a canoe descending, which contained Major Strong. Coming on board, he told me with some excitement that the tug could not possibly be got off, and he wished for orders.

It was no time to consider whether it was not his place to have given orders, instead of going half a mile to seek them. I was by this time so far exhausted that everything seemed to pass by me as by one in a dream; but I got into a boat, pushed up stream, met presently the John Adams returning, and was informed by the officer in charge of the Connecticut battery that he had abandoned the tug, and—worse news yet—that his guns had been thrown overboard. It seemed to me then, and has always seemed, that this sacrifice was utterly needless, because, although the captain of the John Adams had refused to risk his vessel by going near enough to receive the guns, he should have been compelled to do so. Though the thing was done without my knowledge, and beyond my reach, yet, as commander of the expedition, I was technically responsible. It was hard to blame a lieutenant when his senior had shrunk from a decision, and left him alone; nor was it easy to blame Major Strong, whom I knew to be a man of personal courage, though without much decision of character. He was subsequently tried by court-martial and acquitted, after which he resigned, and was lost at sea on his way home.

The tug, being thus abandoned, must of course be burned to prevent her falling into the enemy's hands. Major Strong went with prompt fearlessness to do this, at my order; after which he remained on the Enoch Dean, and I went on board the John Adams, being compelled to succumb at last, and transfer all remaining responsibility to Captain Trowbridge. Exhausted as I was, I could still observe, in a vague way, the scene around me. Every available corner of the boat seemed like some vast auction-room of second-hand goods. Great piles of bedding and bundles lay on every side, with black heads emerging and black forms reclining in every stage of squalidness. Some seemed ill, or wounded, or asleep, others were chattering eagerly among themselves, singing, praying, or soliloquizing on joys to come. "Bress de Lord," I heard one woman say, "I spec' I get salt victual now,—notin' but fresh victual dese six months, but Ise get salt victual now,"—thus reversing, under pressure of the salt-embargo, the usual anticipations of voyagers.

Trowbridge told me, long after, that, on seeking a fan for my benefit, he could find but one on board. That was in the hands of a fat old "aunty," who had just embarked, and sat on an enormous bundle of her goods, in everybody's way, fanning herself vehemently, and ejaculating, as her gasping breath would permit, "Oh! Do, Jesus! Oh! Do, Jesus!" when the captain abruptly disarmed her of the fan, and left her continuing her pious exercises.

Thus we glided down the river in the waning light. Once more we encountered a battery, making five in all; I could hear the guns of the assailants, and could not distinguish the explosion of their shells from the answering throb of our own guns. The kind Quartermaster kept bringing me news of what occurred, like Rebecca[5] in Front-de-Bœuf's castle, but discreetly withholding any actual casualties. Then all faded into safety and sleep; and we reached Beaufort in the morning, after thirty-six hours of absence. A kind friend, who acted in South Carolina a nobler part amid tragedies than in any of her early stage triumphs, met us with an ambulance at the wharf, and the prisoners, the wounded, and the dead were duly attended.

The reader will not care for any personal record of convalescence; though, among the general military laudations of whiskey, it is worth while to say that one life was saved, in the opinion of my surgeons, by an habitual abstinence from it, leaving no food for peritoneal inflammation to feed upon. The able-bodied men who had joined us were sent to aid General Gillmore in the trenches, while their families were established in huts and tents on St. Helena Island. A year after, greatly to the delight of the regiment, in taking possession of a battery which they had helped to capture on James Island, they found in their hands the selfsame guns which they had seen thrown overboard from the Governor Milton. They then felt that their account with the enemy was squared, and could proceed to further operations.

Before the war, how great a thing seemed the rescue of even one man from slavery; and since the war has emancipated all, how little seems the liberation of two hundred! But no one then knew how the contest might end; and when I think of that morning sunlight, those emerald fields, those thronging numbers, the old women with their prayers, and the little boys with their living burdens, I know that the day was worth all it cost, and more.

CHAPTER VIII

The Baby of the Regiment

We were in our winter camp on Port Royal Island. It was a lovely November morning, soft and spring-like; the mocking-birds were singing, and the cotton-fields still white with fleecy pods. Morning drill was over, the men were cleaning their guns and singing very happily; the officers were in their tents, reading still more happily their letters just arrived from home. Suddenly I heard a knock at my tent-door, and the latch clicked. It was the only latch in camp, and I was very proud of it, and the officers always clicked it as loudly as possible, in order to gratify my feelings. The door opened, and the Quartermaster thrust in the most beaming face I ever saw.

"Colonel," said he, "there are great news for the regiment. My wife and baby are coming by the next steamer!"

"Baby!" said I, in amazement. "Q. M., you are beside yourself." (We always called the Quartermaster Q.M. for shortness.) "There was a pass sent to your wife, but nothing was ever said about a baby. Baby indeed!"

"But the baby was included in the pass," replied the triumphant father-of-a-family. "You don't suppose my wife would come down here without her baby! Besides, the pass itself permits her to bring necessary baggage, and is not a baby six months old necessary baggage?"

"But, my dear fellow," said I, rather anxiously, "how can you make the little thing comfortable in a tent, amidst these rigors of a South Carolina winter, when it is uncomfortably hot for drill at noon, and ice forms by your bedside at night?"

"Trust me for that," said the delighted papa, and went off whistling. I could hear him telling the same news to three others, at least, before he got to his own tent.

That day the preparations began, and soon his abode was a wonder of comfort. There were posts and rafters, and a raised floor, and a great chimney, and a door with hinges,—every luxury except a latch, and that he could not have, for mine was the last that could be purchased. One of the regimental carpenters was employed to make a cradle, and another to make a bedstead high enough for the cradle to go under. Then there must be a bit of red carpet beside the bedstead, and thus the progress of splendor went on. The wife of one of the colored sergeants was engaged to act as nursery-maid. She was a very respectable young woman; the only objection to her being that she smoked a pipe. But we thought that perhaps Baby might not dislike tobacco; and if she did, she would have excellent opportunities to break the pipe in pieces.

In due time the steamer arrived, and Baby and her mother were among the passengers. The little recruit was soon settled in her new cradle, and slept in it as if she had never known any other. The sergeant's wife soon had her on exhibition through the neighborhood, and from that time forward she was quite a queen among us. She had sweet blue eyes and pretty brown hair, with round, dimpled cheeks, and that perfect dignity which is so beautiful in a baby. She hardly ever cried, and was not at all timid. She would go to anybody, and yet did not encourage any romping from any but the most intimate friends. She always wore a warm long-sleeved scarlet cloak with a hood, and in this costume was carried or "toted," as the soldiers said, all about the camp. At "guard-mounting" in the morning, when the men who are to go on guard duty for the day are drawn up to be inspected, Baby was always there, to help inspect them. She did not say much, but she eyed them very closely, and seemed fully to appreciate their bright buttons. Then the Officer-of-the-Day, who appears at guard-mounting with his sword and sash, and comes afterwards to the Colonel's tent for orders, would come and speak to Baby on his way, and receive her orders first. When the time came for drill she was usually present to watch the troops; and when the drum beat for dinner she liked to see the long row of men in each company march up to the cook-house, in single file, each with tin cup and plate.

During the day, in pleasant weather, she might be seen in her nurse's arms, about the company streets, the centre of an admiring circle, her scarlet costume looking very pretty amidst the shining black cheeks and neat blue uniforms of the soldiers. At "dress-parade," just before sunset, she was always an attendant. As I stood before the regiment, I could see the little spot of red out of the corner of my eye, at one end of the long line of men; and I looked with so much interest for her small person, that, instead of saying at the proper time, "Attention, Battalion! Shoulder arms!"—it is a wonder that I did not say, "Shoulder babies!"

Our little lady was very impartial, and distributed her kind looks to everybody. She had not the slightest prejudice against color, and did not care in the least whether her particular friends were black or white. Her especial favorites, I think, were the drummer-boys, who were not my favorites by any means, for they were a roguish set of scamps, and gave more trouble than all the grown men in the regiment. I think Annie liked them because they were small, and made a noise, and had red caps like her hood, and red facings on their jackets, and also because they occasionally stood on their heads for her amusement. After dress-parade the whole drum-corps would march to the great flag-staff, and wait till just sunset-time, when they would beat "the retreat," and then the flag would be hauled down,—a great festival for Annie. Sometimes the Sergeant-Major would wrap her in the great folds of the flag, after it was taken down, and she would peep out very prettily from amidst the stars and stripes, like a new-born Goddess of Liberty.

About once a month, some inspecting officer was sent to the camp by the general in command, to see to the condition of everything in the regiment, from bayonets to buttons. It was usually a long and tiresome process, and, when everything else was done, I used to tell the officer that I had one thing more for him to inspect, which was peculiar to our regiment. Then I would send for Baby to be exhibited, and I never saw an inspecting officer, old or young, who did not look pleased at the sudden appearance of the little, fresh, smiling creature,—a flower in the midst of war. And Annie in her turn would look at them, with the true baby dignity in her face,—that deep, earnest look which babies often have, and which people think so wonderful when Raphael[1] paints it, although they might often see just the same expression in the faces of their own darlings at home.

Meanwhile Annie seemed to like the camp style of housekeeping very much. Her father's tent was double, and he used the front apartment for his office, and the inner room for parlor and bed-room; while the nurse had a separate tent and wash-room behind all. I remember that, the first time I went there in the evening, it was to borrow some writing-paper; and while Baby's mother was hunting for it in the front tent, I heard a great cooing and mur-muring in the inner room. I asked if Annie was still awake, and her mother told me to go in and see. Pushing aside the canvas door, I entered. No sign of anybody was to be seen; but a variety of soft little happy noises seemed to come from some unseen cor-ner. Mrs. C. came quietly in, pulled away the counterpane of her own bed, and drew out the rough cradle where lay the little dam-sel, perfectly happy, and wider awake than anything but a baby possibly can be. She looked as if the seclusion of a dozen family bedsteads would not be enough to discourage her spirits, and I saw that camp life was likely to suit her very well.

A tent can be kept very warm, for it is merely a house with a thinner wall than usual; and I do not think that Baby felt the cold much more than if she had been at home that winter. The great trouble is, that a tent-chimney, not being built very high, is apt to smoke when the wind is in a certain direction; and when that happens it is hardly possible to stay inside. So we used to build the chimneys of some tents on the east side, and those of others on the west, and thus some of the tents were always comfortable. I have seen Baby's mother running in a hard rain, with little Red-Riding-Hood[2] in her arms, to take refuge with the Adjutant's wife, when every other abode was full of smoke; and I must admit that there were one or two windy days that season when nobody could really keep warm, and Annie had to remain ignominiously in her cradle, with as many clothes on as possible, for almost the whole time.

The Quartermaster's tent was very attractive to us in the eve-ning. I remember that once, on passing near it after nightfall, I heard our Major's fine voice singing Methodist hymns within, and Mrs. C.'s sweet tones chiming in. So I peeped through the outer door. The fire was burning very pleasantly in the inner tent, and the scrap of new red carpet made the floor look quite magnificent. The Major sat on a box, our surgeon on a stool; "Q.M." and his wife, and the Adjutant's wife, and one of the captains, were all sitting on the bed, singing as well as they knew how; and the baby was under the bed. Baby had retired for the night, was overshadowed, suppressed, sat upon; the singing went on, and she had wandered away into her own land of dreams, nearer to heaven, perhaps, than any pitch their voices could attain. I went in, and joined the party. Presently the music stopped, and another officer was sent for, to sing some particular song. At this pause the invisible innocent waked a little, and began to cluck and coo.

"It's the kitten," exclaimed somebody.

"It's my baby!" exclaimed Mrs. C. triumphantly, in that tone of unfailing personal pride which belongs to young mothers.

The people all got up from the bed for a moment, while Annie was pulled from beneath, wide awake and placid as usual; and she sat in one lap or another during the rest of the concert, sometimes winking at the candle, but usually listening to the songs, with a calm and critical expression, as if she could make as much noise as any of them, whenever she saw fit to try. Not a sound did she make, however, except one little soft sneeze, which led to an immediate flood-tide of red shawl, covering every part of her but the forehead. But I soon hinted that the concert had better be ended, because I knew from observation that the small damsel had carefully watched a regiment̲a̲l̲ ̲i̲ ̲ ̲ ̲ ̲ ̲ ̲ ̲ ̲ ̲ ̲ ̲ ̲ ̲ ̲ ̲ ̲n that day, and that an interval ̲ ̲ ̲ ̲ ̲

Annie did not long remain ̲ ̲ ̲ ̲ ̲ ̲ ̲ ̲ ̲ ̲ ̲ ̲ ̲ ̲ y, on going out to the stables to ̲ ̲ ̲ ̲ ̲ ̲ ̲ ̲ ̲ ̲ ̲ ̲ ̲ ̲ ̲ ̲f baby-talk, addressed by some ̲ ̲ ̲ ̲ ̲ ̲ ̲ ̲ ̲ ̲ ̲ ̲ ̲ ̲ g round the corner of a tent, I ̲ ̲ ̲ ̲ ̲ ̲ ̲ ̲ ̲ ̲ ̲ ̲ ̲ ̲ ̲ d something black and round, l̲y̲ ̲ ̲ ̲ ̲ ̲ ̲ ̲ ̲ ̲ ̲ ̲ ̲ ̲ ̲ ̲ ̲, with which he was playing very ̲ ̲ ̲ ̲ ̲ ̲ ̲ ̲ ̲ ̲ ̲ ̲ ̲ ̲ ̲, a plump, shiny thing, younge̲r̲ ̲ ̲ ̲ ̲ ̲ ̲ ̲ ̲ ̲ ̲ ̲ ̲ ̲ ̲ d merrier picture than the happy father frolicking with his child, while the mother stood quietly by. This was Baby Number Two, and she stayed in camp several weeks, the two innocents meeting each other every day, in the placid indifference that belonged to their years; both were happy little healthy things, and it never seemed to cross their minds that there was any difference in their complexions. As I said before, Annie was not troubled by any prejudice in regard to color, nor do I suppose that the other little maiden was.

Annie enjoyed the tent-life very much; but when we were sent out on picket soon after, she enjoyed it still more. Our head-quarters were at a deserted plantation house, with one large parlor, a dining-room, and a few bedrooms. Baby's father and mother had a room up stairs, with a stove whose pipe went straight out at the window. This was quite comfortable, though half the windows were broken, and there was no glass and no glazier to mend them. The windows of the large parlor were in much the same condition, though we had an immense fireplace, where we had a bright fire whenever it was cold, and always in the evening. The walls of this room were very dirty, and it took our ladies several days to cover all the unsightly places with wreaths and hangings of evergreen. In this performance Baby took an active part. Her duties consisted in sitting in a great nest of evergreen, pulling and fingering the fragrant leaves, and occasionally giving a little cry of glee when she had accomplished some piece of decided mischief.

There was less entertainment to be found in the camp itself at this time; but the household at head-quarters was larger than Baby had been accustomed to. We had a great deal of company, moreover, and she had quite a gay life of it. She usually made her appearance in the large parlor soon after breakfast; and to dance her for a few moments in our arms was one of the first daily duties of each one. Then the morning reports began to arrive from the different outposts,—a mounted officer or courier coming in from each place, dismounting at the door, and clattering in with jingling arms and spurs, each a new excitement for Annie. She usually got some attention from any officer who came, receiving with her wonted dignity any daring caress. When the messengers had ceased to be interesting, there were always the horses to look at, held or tethered under the trees beside the sunny piazza. After the various couriers had been received, other messengers would be despatched to the town, seven miles away, and Baby had all the excitement of their mounting and departure. Her father was often one of the riders, and would sometimes seize Annie for a good-by kiss, place her on the saddle before him, gallop her round the house once or twice, and then give her back to her nurse's arms again. She was perfectly fearless, and such boisterous attentions never frightened her, nor did they ever interfere with her sweet, infantine self-possession.

After the riding-parties had gone, there was the piazza still for entertainment, with a sentinel pacing up and down before it; but Annie did not enjoy the sentinel, though his breastplate and buttons shone like gold, so much as the hammock which always hung swinging between the pillars. It was a pretty hammock, with great open meshes; and she delighted to lie in it, and have the netting closed above her, so that she could only be seen through the apertures. I can see her now, the fresh little rosy thing, in her blue and scarlet wrappings, with one round and dimpled arm thrust forth through the netting, and the other grasping an armful of blushing roses and fragrant magnolias. She looked like those pretty French bas-reliefs of Cupids imprisoned in baskets, and peeping through. That hammock was a very useful appendage; it was a couch for us, a cradle for Baby, a nest for the kittens; and we had, moreover, a little hen, which tried to roost there every night.

When the mornings were colder, and the stove up stairs smoked the wrong way, Baby was brought down in a very incomplete state of toilet, and finished her dressing by the great fire. We found her bare shoulders very becoming, and she was very much interested in her own little pink toes. After a very slow dressing, she had a still slower breakfast out of a tin cup of warm milk, of which she generally spilt a good deal, as she had much to do in watching everybody who came into the room, and seeing that there was no mischief done. Then she would be placed on the floor, on our only piece of carpet, and the kittens would be brought in for her to play with.

We had, at different times, a variety of pets, of whom Annie did not take much notice. Sometimes we had young partridges, caught by the drummer-boys in trap-cages. The children called them "Bob and Chloe," because the first notes of the male and female sound like those names. One day I brought home an opossum, with her blind bare little young clinging to the droll pouch where their mothers keep them. Sometimes we had pretty green lizards, their color darkening or deepening, like that of chameleons, in light or shade. But the only pets that took Baby's fancy were the kittens. They perfectly delighted her, from the first moment she saw them; they were the only things younger than herself that she had ever beheld, and the only things softer than themselves that her small hands had grasped. It was astonishing to see how much the kittens would endure from her. They could scarcely be touched by any one else without mewing; but when Annie seized one by the head and the other by the tail, and rubbed them violently together, they did not make a sound. I suppose that a baby's grasp is really soft, even if it seems ferocious, and so it gives less pain than one would think. At any rate, the little animals had the best of it very soon; for they entirely outstripped Annie in learning to walk, and they could soon scramble away beyond her reach, while she sat in a sort of dumb despair, unable to comprehend why anything so much smaller than herself should be so much nimbler. Meanwhile, the kittens would sit up and look at her with the most provoking indifference, just out of arm's length, until some of us would take pity on the young lady, and toss her furry playthings back to her again. "Little baby," she learned to call them; and these were the very first words she spoke.

Baby had evidently a natural turn for war, further cultivated by an intimate knowledge of drills and parades. The nearer she came to actual conflict the better she seemed to like it, peaceful as her own little ways might be. Twice, at least, while she was with us on picket, we had alarms from the Rebel troops, who would bring down cannon to the opposite side of the Ferry, about two miles beyond us, and throw shot and shell over upon our side. Then the officer at the Ferry would think that there was to be an attack made, and couriers would be sent, riding to and fro, and the men would all be called to arms in a hurry, and the ladies at head-quarters would all put on their best bonnets and come down stairs, and the ambulance would be made ready to carry them to a place of safety before the expected fight. On such occasions Baby was in all her glory. She shouted with delight at being suddenly uncribbed and thrust into her little scarlet cloak, and brought down stairs, at an utterly unusual and improper hour, to a piazza with lights and people and horses and general excitement. She crowed and gurgled and made gestures with her little fists, and screamed out what seemed to be her advice on the military situation, as freely as if she had been a newspaper editor. Except that it was rather difficult to understand her precise directions, I do not know but the whole Rebel force might have been captured through her plans. And at any rate, I should much rather obey her orders than those of some generals whom I have known; for she at least meant no harm, and would lead one into no mischief.

However, at last the danger, such as it was, would be all over, and the ladies would be induced to go peacefully to bed again; and Annie would retreat with them to her ignoble cradle, very much disappointed, and looking vainly back at the more martial scene below. The next morning she would seem to have forgotten all about it, and would spill her bread and milk by the fire as if nothing had happened.

I suppose we hardly knew, at the time, how large a part of the sunshine of our daily lives was contributed by dear little Annie. Yet, when I now look back on that pleasant Southern home, she seems as essential a part of it as the mocking-birds or the magnolias, and I cannot convince myself that in returning to it I should not find her there. But Annie went back, with the spring, to her Northern birthplace, and then passed away from this earth before her little feet had fairly learned to tread its paths; and when I meet her next it must be in some world where there is triumph without armies, and where innocence is trained in scenes of peace. I know, however, that her little life, short as it seemed, was a blessing to us all, giving a perpetual image of serenity and sweetness, recalling the lovely atmosphere of far-off homes, and holding us by unsuspected ties to whatsoever things were pure.[3]

CHAPTER IX
Negro Spirituals

The war brought to some of us, besides its direct experiences, many a strange fulfilment of dreams of other days. For instance, the present writer had been a faithful student of the Scottish ballads, and had always envied Sir Walter the delight of tracing them out amid their own heather, and of writing them down piecemeal from the lips of aged crones. It was a strange enjoyment, therefore, to be suddenly brought into the midst of a kindred world of unwritten songs, as simple and indigenous as the Border Minstrelsy, more uniformly plaintive, almost always more quaint, and often as essentially poetic.

This interest was rather increased by the fact that I had for many years heard of this class of songs under the name of "Negro Spirituals," and had even heard some of them sung by friends from South Carolina. I could now gather on their own soil these strange plants, which I had before seen as in museums alone. True, the individual songs rarely coincided; there was a line here, a chorus there,—just enough to fix the class, but this was unmistakable. It was not strange that they differed, for the range seemed almost endless, and South Carolina, Georgia, and Florida seemed to have nothing but the generic character in common, until all were mingled in the united stock of camp-melodies.

Often in the starlit evening I have returned from some lonely ride by the swift river, or on the plover-haunted barrens, and, entering the camp, have silently approached some glimmering fire, round which the dusky figures moved in the rhythmical barbaric dance the negroes call a "shout," chanting, often harshly, but always in the most perfect time, some monotonous refrain. Writing down in the darkness, as I best could,—perhaps with my hand in the safe covert of my pocket,—the words of the song, I have afterwards carried it to my tent, like some captured bird or insect, and then, after examination, put it by. Or, summoning one of the men at some period of leisure,—Corporal Robert Sutton, for instance, whose iron memory held all the details of a song as if it were a ford or a forest,—I have completed the new specimen by supplying the absent parts. The music I could only retain by ear, and though the more common strains were repeated often enough to fix their impression, there were others that occurred only once or twice.

The words will be here given, as nearly as possible, in the original dialect; and if the spelling seems sometimes inconsistent, or the misspelling insufficient, it is because I could get no nearer. I wished to avoid what seems to me the only error of Lowell's "Biglow Papers"[1] in respect to dialect,—the occasional use of an extreme misspelling, which merely confuses the eye, without taking us any closer to the peculiarity of sound.

The favorite song in camp was the following,—sung with no accompaniment but the measured clapping of hands and the clatter of many feet. It was sung perhaps twice as often as any other. This was partly due to the fact that it properly consisted of a chorus alone, with which the verses of other songs might be combined at random.

I. HOLD YOUR LIGHT

"Hold your light, Brudder Robert,—
    Hold your light,
Hold your light on Canaan's shore.

"What make ole Satan for follow me so?
Satan ain't got notin' for do wid me.
    Hold your light,
    Hold your light,
Hold your light on Canaan's shore."

This would be sung for half an hour at a time, perhaps each person present being named in turn. It seemed the simplest primitive type of "spiritual." The next in popularity was almost as elementary, and, like this, named successively each one of the circle. It was, however, much more resounding and convivial in its music.

II. BOUND TO GO

"Jordan River, I'm bound to go,
    Bound to go, bound to go,—
Jordan River, I'm bound to go,
    And bid 'em fare ye well.

"My Brudder Robert, I'm bound to go,
    Bound to go," &c.

"My Sister Lucy, I'm bound to go,
    Bound to go," &c.

Sometimes it was "tink 'em" (think them) "fare ye well." The *ye* was so detached that I thought at first it was "very" or "vary well."

Another picturesque song, which seemed immensely popular, was at first very bewildering to me. I could not make out the first words of the chorus, and called it the "Romandàr," being reminded of some Romaic song which I had formerly heard. That association quite fell in with the Orientalism[2] of the new tent-life.

III. ROOM IN THERE

"O, my mudder is gone! my mudder is gone!
My mudder is gone into heaven, my Lord!
        I can't stay behind!
Dere's room in dar, room in dar,
Room in dar, in de heaven, my Lord!
        I can't stay behind!
Can't stay behind, my dear,
        I can't stay behind!

"O, my fader is gone!" &c.

"O, de angels are gone!" &c.

"O, I'se been on de road! I 'se been on de road!
I 'se been on de road into heaven, my Lord!
        I can't stay behind!
O, room in dar, room in dar,

> Room in dar, in de heaven, my Lord!
>   I can't stay behind!"

By this time every man within hearing, from oldest to youngest, would be wriggling and shuffling, as if through some magic piper's bewitchment; for even those who at first affected contemptuous indifference would be drawn into the vortex erelong.

Next to these in popularity ranked a class of songs belonging emphatically to the Church Militant, and available for camp purposes with very little strain upon their symbolism. This, for instance, had a true companion-in-arms heartiness about it, not impaired by the feminine invocation at the end.

IV. HAIL MARY

> "One more valiant soldier here,
>   One more valiant soldier here,
>   One more valiant soldier here,
>   To help me bear de cross.
>   O hail, Mary, hail!
>   Hail, Mary, hail!
>   Hail, Mary, hail!
>   To help me bear de cross."

I fancied that the original reading might have been "soul," instead of "soldier,"—with some other syllable inserted to fill out the metre,—and that the "Hail, Mary," might denote a Roman Catholic origin, as I had several men from St. Augustine who held in a dim way to that faith. It was a very ringing song, though not so grandly jubilant as the next, which was really impressive as the singers pealed it out, when marching or rowing or embarking.

V. MY ARMY CROSS OVER

> "My army cross over,
>   My army cross over,
>   O, Pharaoh's army drownded!
>   My army cross over.

"We'll cross de mighty river,
    My army cross over;
We'll cross de river Jordan,
    My army cross over;
We'll cross de danger water,
    My army cross over;
We'll cross de mighty Myo,
    My army cross over. *(Thrice.)*
    O, Pharaoh's army drownded!
    My army cross over."

I could get no explanation of the "mighty Myo," except that one of the old men thought it meant the river of death. Perhaps it is an African word. In the Cameroon dialect, "Mawa" signifies "to die."

The next also has a military ring about it, and the first line is well matched by the music. The rest is conglomerate, and one or two lines show a more Northern origin. "Done" is a Virginia shibboleth, quite distinct from the "been" which replaces it in South Carolina. Yet one of their best choruses, without any fixed words, was, "De bell done ringing," for which, in proper South Carolina dialect, would have been substituted, "De bell been a-ring." This refrain may have gone South with our army.

VI. RIDE IN, KIND SAVIOUR

"Ride in, kind Saviour!
    No man can hinder me.
O, Jesus is a mighty man!
    No man, &c.
We're marching through Virginny fields.
    No man, &c.
O, Satan is a busy man,
    No man, &c.
And he has his sword and shield,
    No man, &c.
O, old Secesh done come and gone!
    No man can hinder me."

Sometimes they substituted "hinder *we*," which was more spicy to the ear, and more in keeping with the usual head-over-heels arrangement of their pronouns.

Almost all their songs were thoroughly religious in their tone, however quaint their expression, and were in a minor key, both as to words and music. The attitude is always the same, and, as a commentary on the life of the race, is infinitely pathetic. Nothing but patience for this life,—nothing but triumph in the next. Sometimes the present predominates, sometimes the future; but the combination is always implied. In the following, for instance, we hear simply the patience.

VII. THIS WORLD ALMOST DONE

"Brudder, keep your lamp trimmin' and a-burnin',
 Keep your lamp trimmin' and a-burnin',
 Keep your lamp trimmin' and a-burnin',
  For dis world most done.
So keep your lamp, &c.
  Dis world most done."

But in the next, the final reward of patience is proclaimed as plaintively.

VIII. I WANT TO GO HOME

"Dere's no rain to wet you,
 O, yes, I want to go home.
Dere's no sun to burn you,
 O, yes, I want to go home;
O, push along, believers,
 O, yes, &c.
Dere's no hard trials,
 O, yes, &c.
Dere's no whips a-crackin',
 O, yes, &c.
My brudder on de wayside,
 O, yes, &c.
O, push along, my brudder,
 O, yes, &c.

Where dere's no stormy weather,
   O, yes, &c.
Dere's no tribulation,
   O, yes, &c.

This next was a boat-song, and timed well with the tug of the oar.

IX. THE COMING DAY

"I want to go to Canaan,
I want to go to Canaan,
I want to go to Canaan,
   To meet 'em at de comin' day.
O, remember, let me go to Canaan, *(Thrice.)*
   To meet 'em, &c.
O brudder, let me go to Canaan, *(Thrice.)*
   To meet 'em, & c.
My brudder, you—oh!—remember, *(Thrice.)*
   To meet 'em at de comin' day."

The following begins with a startling affirmation, yet the last line quite outdoes the first. This, too, was a capital boat-song.

X. ONE MORE RIVER

"O, Jordan bank was a great old bank,
   Dere ain't but one more river to cross.
We have some valiant soldier here,
   Dere ain't, &c.
O, Jordan stream will never run dry,
   Dere ain't, &c.
Dere's a hill on my leff, and he catch on my right,
   Dere ain't but one more river to cross."

I could get no explanation of this last riddle, except, "Dat mean, if you go on de leff, go to 'struction, and if you go on de right, go to God, for sure."

In others, more of spiritual conflict is implied, as in this next.

XI. O THE DYING LAMB!

"I wants to go where Moses trod,
　　O de dying Lamb!
For Moses gone to de promised land,
　　O de dying Lamb!
To drink from springs dat never run dry,
　　O, &c.
Cry O my Lord!
　　O, &c.
Before I'll stay in hell one day,
　　O, &c.
I'm in hopes to pray my sins away,
　　O, &c.
Cry O my Lord!
　　O, &c.
Brudder Moses promised for be dar too,
　　O, &c.
To drink from streams dat never run dry,
　　O de dying Lamb!"

In the next, the conflict is at its height, and the lurid imagery of the Apocalypse is brought to bear. This book, with the books of Moses, constituted their Bible; all that lay between, even the narratives of the life of Jesus, they hardly cared to read or to hear.

XII. DOWN IN THE VALLEY

"We'll run and never tire,
We'll run and never tire,
We'll run and never tire,
　　Jesus set poor sinners free.
Way down in de valley,
　　Who will rise and go with me?
You've heern talk of Jesus,
　　Who set poor sinners free.

"De lightnin' and de flashin'
De lightnin' and de flashin',
De lightnin' and de flashin',
　　Jesus set poor sinners free.

> I can't stand the fire. *(Thrice.)*
>   Jesus set poor sinners free,
> De green trees a-flamin'. *(Thrice.)*
>   Jesus set poor sinners free,
>   Way down in de valley,
>   Who will rise and go with me?
>   You've heern talk of Jesus
>   Who set poor sinners free."

"De valley" and "de lonesome valley" were familiar words in their religious experience. To descend into that region implied the same process with the "anxious-seat" of the camp-meeting. When a young girl was supposed to enter it, she bound a handkerchief by a peculiar knot over her head, and made it a point of honor not to change a single garment till the day of her baptism, so that she was sure of being in physical readiness for the cleansing rite, whatever her spiritual mood might be. More than once, in noticing a damsel thus mystically kerchiefed, I have asked some dusky attendant its meaning, and have received the unfailing answer,— framed with their usual indifference to the genders of pronouns, —"He in de lonesome valley, sa."

The next gives the same dramatic conflict, while its detached and impersonal refrain gives it strikingly the character of the Scotch and Scandinavian ballads.

XIII. CRY HOLY

> "Cry holy, holy!
>   Look at de people dat is born of God.
> And I run down de valley, and I run down to pray,
>   Says, look at de people dat is born of God.
> When I get dar, Cappen Satan was dar,
>   Says, look at, &c.
> Says, young man, young man, dere's no use for pray,
>   Says, look at, &c.
> For Jesus is dead, and God gone away,
>   Says, look at, &c.
> And I made him out a liar, and I went my way,
>   Says, look at, &c.
>   Sing holy, holy!

"O, Mary was a woman, and he had a one Son,
    Says, look at, &c.
And de Jews and de Romans had him hung,
    Says, look at, &c.
        Cry holy, holy!

"And I tell you, sinner, you had better had pray,
    Says, look at, &c.
For hell is a dark and dismal place,
    Says, look at, &c.
And I tell you, sinner, and I would n't go dar!
    Says, look at, &c.
        Cry holy, holy!"

Here is an infinitely quaint description of the length of the heavenly road:—

XIV. O'ER THE CROSSING

"Yonder's my old mudder,
    Been a-waggin' at de hill so long.
It's about time she'll cross over;
    Get home bimeby.
Keep prayin', I do believe
    We're a long time waggin' o'er de crossin'.
Keep prayin', I do believe
    We'll get home to heaven bimeby.

"Hear dat mournful thunder
    Roll from door to door,
Calling home God's children;
    Get home bimeby.
Little chil'en, I do believe
    We're a long time, &c.
Little chil'en, I do believe
    We'll get home, &c.

"See dat forked lightnin'
    Flash from tree to tree,
Callin' home God's chil'en;
    Get home bimeby.
True believer, I do believe

We're a long time, &c.
O brudders, I do believe,
    We'll get home to heaven bimeby."

One of the most singular pictures of future joys, and with a
fine flavor of hospitality about it, was this:—

XV. WALK 'EM EASY

"O, walk 'em easy round de heaven,
Walk 'em easy round de heaven,
Walk 'em easy round de heaven,
    Dat all de people may join de band.
Walk 'em easy round de heaven. *(Thrice.)*
    O, shout glory till 'em join dat band!"

The chorus was usually the greater part of the song, and often
came in paradoxically, thus:—

XVI. O YES, LORD

"O, must I be like de foolish mans?
        O yes, Lord!
Will build de house on de sandy hill.
        O yes, Lord!
I'll build my house on Zion hill,
        O yes, Lord!
No wind nor rain can blow me down,
        O yes, Lord!"

The next is very graceful and lyrical, and with more variety of
rhythm than usual:—

XVII. BOW LOW, MARY

"Bow low, Mary, bow low, Martha,
    For Jesus come and lock de door,
    And carry de keys away.
Sail, sail, over yonder,
    And view de promised land.

> For Jesus come, &c.
> Weep, O Mary, bow low, Martha,
> > For Jesus come, &c.
> Sail, sail, my true believer;
> Sail, sail, over yonder;
> Mary, bow low, Martha, bow low,
> > For Jesus come and lock de door
> > And carry de keys away."

But of all the "spirituals" that which surprised me the most, I think,—perhaps because it was that in which external nature furnished the images most directly,—was this. With all my experience of their ideal ways of speech, I was startled when first I came on such a flower of poetry in that dark soil.

XVIII. I KNOW MOON-RISE

> "I know moon-rise, I know star-rise,
> > Lay dis body down.
> I walk in de moonlight, I walk in de starlight,
> > To lay dis body down.
> I'll walk in de graveyard, I'll walk through de graveyard,
> > To lay dis body down.
> I'll lie in de grave and stretch out my arms;
> > Lay dis body down.
> I go to de judgment in de evenin' of de day,
> > When I lay dis body down;
> And my soul and your soul will meet in de day
> > When I lay dis body down."

"I'll lie in de grave and stretch out my arms." Never, it seems to me, since man first lived and suffered, was his infinite longing for peace uttered more plaintively than in that line.

The next is one of the wildest and most striking of the whole series: there is a mystical effect and a passionate striving throughout the whole. The Scriptural struggle between Jacob and the angel, which is only dimly expressed in the words, seems all uttered in the music. I think it impressed my imagination more powerfully than any other of these songs.

XIX. WRESTLING JACOB

"O wrestlin' Jacob, Jacob, day's a-breakin';
  I will not let thee go!
O wrestlin' Jacob, Jacob, day's a-breakin';
  He will not let me go!
O, I hold my brudder wid a tremblin' hand;
  I would not let him go!
I hold my sister wid a tremblin' hand;
  I would not let her go!

"O, Jacob do hang from a tremblin' limb,
  He would not let him go!
O, Jacob do hang from a tremblin' limb;
  De Lord will bless my soul.
O wrestlin' Jacob, Jacob," &c.

Of "occasional hymns," properly so called, I noticed but one, a funeral hymn for an infant, which is sung plaintively over and over, without variety of words.

XX. THE BABY GONE HOME

"De little baby gone home,
  De little baby gone home,
  De little baby gone along,
    For to climb up Jacob's ladder.
  And I wish I'd been dar,
  I wish I'd been dar,
  I wish I'd been dar, my Lord,
    For to climb up Jacob's ladder."

Still simpler is this, which is yet quite sweet and touching.

XXI. JESUS WITH US

"He have been wid us, Jesus,
  He still wid us, Jesus,
  He will be wid us, Jesus,
    Be wid us to the end."

The next seemed to be a favorite about Christmas time, when meditations on "de rollin' year" were frequent among them.

XXII. LORD, REMEMBER ME

"O do, Lord, remember me!
   O do, Lord, remember me!
  O, do remember me, until de year roll round!
   Do, Lord, remember me!

"If you want to die like Jesus died,
   Lay in de grave,
  You would fold your arms and close your eyes
   And die wid a free good will.

"For Death is a simple ting,
   And he go from door to door,
  And he knock down some, and he cripple up some,
   And he leave some here to pray.

"O do, Lord, remember me!
   O do, Lord, remember me!
  My old fader's gone till de year roll round;
   Do, Lord, remember me!"

The next was sung in such an operatic and rollicking way that it was quite hard to fancy it a religious performance, which, however, it was. I heard it but once.

XXIII. EARLY IN THE MORNING

"I meet little Rosa early in de mornin',
   O Jerusalem! early in de mornin';
  And I ax her, How you do, my darter?
   O Jerusalem! early in de mornin'.

"I meet my mudder early in de mornin',
   O Jerusalem! &c.
  And I ax her, How you do, my mudder?
   O Jerusalem! &c.

"I meet Brudder Robert early in de mornin',
   O Jerusalem! &c.
And I ax him, How you do, my sonny?
   O Jerusalem! &c.

"I meet Tittawisa early in de mornin',
   O Jerusalem! &c.
And I ax her, How you do, my darter?
   O Jerusalem!" &c.

"Tittawisa" means "Sister Louisa." In songs of this class the name of every person present successively appears.

Their best marching song, and one which was invaluable to lift their feet along, as they expressed it, was the following. There was a kind of spring and *lilt* to it, quite indescribable by words.

XXIV. GO IN THE WILDERNESS

"Jesus call you. Go in de wilderness,
   Go in de wilderness, go in de wilderness,
Jesus call you.   Go in de wilderness
   To wait upon de Lord.
Go wait upon de Lord,
Go wait upon de Lord,
Go wait upon de Lord, my God,
   He take away de sins of de world.

"Jesus a-waitin'.   Go in de wilderness,
   Go, &c.
All dem chil'en go in de wilderness
   To wait upon de Lord."

The next was one of those which I had heard in boyish days, brought North from Charleston. But the chorus alone was identical; the words were mainly different, and those here given are quaint enough.

XXV. BLOW YOUR TRUMPET, GABRIEL

"O, blow your trumpet, Gabriel,
   Blow your trumpet louder;

And I want dat trumpet to blow me home
To my new Jerusalem.

"De prettiest ting dat ever I done
Was to serve de Lord when I was young.
So blow your trumpet, Gabriel, &c.

"O, Satan is a liar, and he conjure too,
And if you don't mind, he'll conjure you.
So blow your trumpet, Gabriel, &c.

"O, I was lost in de wilderness,
King Jesus hand me de candle down.
So blow your trumpet, Gabriel," &c.

The following contains one of those odd transformations of
proper names with which their Scriptural citations were often en-
riched. It rivals their text, "Paul may plant, and may polish wid
water," which I have elsewhere quoted, and in which the sainted
Apollos would hardly have recognized himself.

XXVI. IN THE MORNING

"In de mornin',
In de mornin',
Chil'en? Yes, my Lord!
Don't you hear de trumpet sound?
If I had a-died when I was young,
I never would had de race for run.
Don't you hear de trumpet sound?

"O Sam and Peter was fishin' in de sea,
And dey drop de net and follow my Lord.
Don't you hear de trumpet sound?

"Dere's a silver spade for to dig my grave
And a golden chain for to let me down.
Don't you hear de trumpet sound?
In de mornin',
In de mornin',

Chil'en?   Yes, my Lord!
Don't you hear de trumpet sound?"

These golden and silver fancies remind one of the King of
Spain's daughter in "Mother Goose," and the golden apple, and
the silver pear, which are doubtless themselves but the vestiges of
some simple early composition like this. The next has a humbler
and more domestic style of fancy.

XXVII. FARE YE WELL

"My true believers, fare ye well,
   Fare ye well, fare ye well,
Fare ye well, by de grace of God,
   For I'm going home.

Massa Jesus give me a little broom
   For to sweep my heart clean,
And I will try, by de grace of God,
   To win my way home."

Among the songs not available for marching, but requiring the
concentrated enthusiasm of the camp, was "The Ship of Zion," of
which they had three wholly distinct versions, all quite exuberant
and tumultuous.

XXVIII. THE SHIP OF ZION

"Come along, come along,
   And let us go home,
O, glory, hallelujah?
Dis de ole ship o' Zion,
   Halleloo! Halleloo!
Dis de ole ship o' Zion,
   Hallelujah!

"She has landed many a tousand,
She can land as many more.
   O, glory, hallelujah! &c.

"Do you tink she will be able
For to take us all home?
   O, glory, hallelujah! &c.

"You can tell 'em I'm a comin',
   Halleloo! Halleloo!
You can tell 'em I'm a comin',
   Hallelujah!
Come along, come along," &c.

XXIX. THE SHIP OF ZION (Second version.)

"Dis de good ole ship o' Zion,
Dis de good ole ship o' Zion,
Dis de good ole ship o' Zion,
   And she's makin' for de Promise Land.
She hab angels for de sailors, (Thrice.)
   And she's, &c.
And how you know dey's angels? (Thrice.)
   And she's, &c.
Good Lord, shall I be one? (Thrice.)
   And she's, &c.

"Dat ship is out a-sailin', sailin', sailin',
   And she's, &c.
She's a-sailin' mighty steady, steady, steady,
   And she's, &c.
She'll neither reel nor totter, totter, totter,
   And she's, &c.
She's a-sailin' away cold Jordan, Jordan, Jordan,
   And she's, &c.
King Jesus is de captain, captain, captain,
   And she's makin' for de Promise Land."

XXX. THE SHIP OF ZION (Third version.)

"De Gospel ship is sailin',
   Hosann—sann.
O, Jesus is de captain,
   Hosann—sann.
De angels are de sailors,
   Hosann—sann.

O, is your bundle ready?
  Hosann—sann.
O, have you got your ticket?
  Hosann—sann."

This abbreviated chorus is given with unspeakable unction.

The three just given are modifications of an old camp-meeting melody; and the same may be true of the three following, although I cannot find them in the Methodist hymn-books. Each, however, has its characteristic modifications, which make it well worth giving. In the second verse of this next, for instance, "Saviour" evidently has become "soldier."

XXXI. SWEET MUSIC

"Sweet music in heaven,
  Just beginning for to roll.
Don't you love God?
  Glory, hallelujah!

"Yes, late I heard my soldier say,
Come, heavy soul, I am de way.
  Don't you love God?
  Glory, hallelujah!

"I'll go and tell to sinners round
What a kind Saviour I have found.
  Don't you love God?
  Glory, hallelujah!

"My grief my burden long has been,
Because I was not cease from sin.
  Don't you love God?
  Glory, hallelujah!"

XXXII. GOOD NEWS

"O, good news! O, good news!
De angels brought de tidings down,
  Just comin' from de trone.

"As grief from out my soul shall fly,
    Just comin' from de trone;
I'll shout salvation when I die,
    Good news, O, good news!
    Just comin' from de trone.

"Lord, I want to go to heaven when I die,
    Good news, O, good news! &c.

"De white folks call us a noisy crew,
    Good news, O, good news!
But dis I know, we are happy too,
    Just comin' from de trone."

XXXIII. THE HEAVENLY ROAD

"You may talk of my name as much as you please,
    And carry my name abroad,
But I really do believe I'm a child of God
    As I walk in de heavenly road.
O, won't you go wid me? *(Thrice.)*
    For to keep our garments clean.

"O Satan is a mighty busy ole man,
    And roll rocks in my way;
But Jesus is my bosom friend,
    And roll 'em out of de way.
O, won't you go wid me? *(Thrice.)*
    For to keep our garments clean.

"Come, my brudder, if you never did pray,
    I hope you may pray to-night;
For I really believe I'm a child of God
    As I walk in de heavenly road.
O, won't you," &c.

Some of the songs had played an historic part during the war.
For singing the next, for instance, the negroes had been put in jail
in Georgetown, S.C., at the outbreak of the Rebellion. "We'll
soon be free" was too dangerous an assertion; and though the
chant was an old one, it was no doubt sung with redoubled

emphasis during the new events. "De Lord will call us home," was evidently thought to be a symbolical verse; for, as a little drummer-boy explained to me, showing all his white teeth as he sat in the moonlight by the door of my tent, "Dey tink *de Lord* mean for say *de Yankees.*"

XXXIV. WE'LL SOON BE FREE

"We'll soon be free,
We'll soon be free,
We'll soon be free,
   When de Lord will call us home.
My brudder, how long,
My brudder, how long,
My brudder, how long,
   'Fore we done sufferin' here?
It won't be long *(Thrice.)*
   'Fore de Lord will call us home.
We'll walk de miry road *(Thrice.)*
   Where pleasure never dies.
We'll walk de golden street *(Thrice.)*
   Where pleasure never dies.
My brudder, how long *(Thrice.)*
   'Fore we done sufferin' here?
We'll soon be free *(Thrice.)*
   When Jesus sets me free.
We'll fight for liberty *(Thrice.)*
   When de Lord will call us home."

The suspicion in this case was unfounded, but they had another song to which the Rebellion had actually given rise. This was composed by nobody knew whom,—though it was the most recent, doubtless, of all these "spirituals,"—and had been sung in secret to avoid detection. It is certainly plaintive enough. The peck of corn and pint of salt were slavery's rations.

XXXV. MANY THOUSAND GO

"No more peck o' corn for me,
   No more, no more,—

> No more peck o' corn for me,
>   Many tousand go.
>
> "No more driver's lash for me, *(Twice.)*
>   No more, &c.
>
> "No more pint o' salt for me, *(Twice.)*
>   No more, &c.
>
> "No more hundred lash for me, *(Twice.)*
>   No more, &c.
>
> "No more mistress' call for me,
>   No more, no more,—
> No more mistress' call for me,
>   Many tousand go."

Even of this last composition, however, we have only the approximate date and know nothing of the mode of composition. Allan Ramsay[3] says of the Scotch songs, that, no matter who made them, they were soon attributed to the minister of the parish whence they sprang. And I always wondered, about these, whether they had always a conscious and definite origin in some leading mind, or whether they grew by gradual accretion, in an almost unconscious way. On this point I could get no information, though I asked many questions, until at last, one day when I was being rowed across from Beaufort to Ladies' Island, I found myself, with delight, on the actual trail of a song. One of the oarsmen, a brisk young fellow, not a soldier, on being asked for his theory of the matter, dropped out a coy confession. "Some good sperituals," he said, "are start jess out o' curiosity. I been a-raise a sing, myself, once."

My dream was fulfilled, and I had traced out, not the poem alone, but the poet. I implored him to proceed.

"Once we boys," he said, "went for tote some rice and de nigger-driver he keep a-callin' on us; and I say, 'O, de ole nigger-driver!' Den anudder said, 'Fust ting my mammy tole me was, notin' so bad as nigger-driver.' Den I made a sing, just puttin' a word, and den anudder word."

Then he began singing, and the men, after listening a moment, joined in the chorus, as if it were an old acquaintance, though they evidently had never heard it before. I saw how easily a new "sing" took root among them.

XXXVI. THE DRIVER

"O, de ole nigger-driver!
  O, gwine away!
Fust ting my mammy tell me,
  O, gwine away!
Tell me 'bout de nigger-driver,
  O, gwine away!
Nigger-driver second devil,
  O, gwine away!
Best ting for do he driver,
  O, gwine away!
Knock he down and spoil he labor,
  O, gwine away!"

It will be observed that, although this song is quite secular in its character, yet its author called it a "spiritual." I heard but two songs among them, at any time, to which they would not, perhaps, have given this generic name. One of these consisted simply in the endless repetition—after the manner of certain college songs —of the mysterious line,—

"Rain fall and wet Becky Lawton."

But who Becky Lawton was, and why she should or should not be wet, and whether the dryness was a reward or a penalty, none could say. I got the impression that, in either case, the event was posthumous, and that there was some tradition of grass not growing over the grave of a sinner; but even this was vague, and all else vaguer.

The other song I heard but once, on a morning when a squad of men came in from picket duty, and chanted it in the most rousing way. It had been a stormy and comfortless night, and the picket station was very exposed. It still rained in the morning when I strolled to the edge of the camp, looking out for the men, and wondering how they had stood it. Presently they came striding along the road, at a great pace, with their shining rubber blankets worn as cloaks around them, the rain streaming from these and from their equally shining faces, which were almost all upon the broad grin, as they pealed out this remarkable ditty:—

HANGMAN JOHNNY

"O, dey call me Hangman Johnny!
          O, ho! O, ho!
But I never hang nobody,
          O, hang, boys, hang!
O, dey call me Hangman Johnny!
          O, ho! O, ho!
But we'll all hang togedder,
          O, hang, boys, hang!"

My presence apparently checked the performance of another verse, beginning, "De buckra 'list for money," apparently in reference to the controversy about the pay-question, then just beginning, and to the more mercenary aims they attributed to the white soldiers. But "Hangman Johnny" remained always a myth as inscrutable as "Becky Lawton."

As they learned all their songs by ear, they often strayed into wholly new versions, which sometimes became popular, and entirely banished the others. This was amusingly the case, for instance, with one phrase in the popular camp-song of "Marching Along," which was entirely new to them until our quartermaster taught it to them, at my request. The words, "Gird on the armor," were to them a stumbling-block, and no wonder, until some ingenious ear substituted, "Guide on de army," which was at once accepted, and became universal.

"We'll guide on de army, and be marching along"

is now the established version on the Sea Islands.

These quaint religious songs were to the men more than a source of relaxation; they were a stimulus to courage and a tie to heaven. I never overheard in camp a profane or vulgar song. With the trifling exceptions given, all had a religious motive, while the

most secular melody could not have been more exciting. A few
youths from Savannah, who were comparatively men of the
world, had learned some of the "Ethiopian Minstrel" ditties, im-
ported from the North. These took no hold upon the mass; and,
on the other hand, they sang reluctantly, even on Sunday, the long
and short metres of the hymn-books, always gladly yielding to
the more potent excitement of their own "spirituals." By these
they could sing themselves, as had their fathers before them, out
of the contemplation of their own low estate, into the sublime
scenery of the Apocalypse. I remember that this minor-keyed pathos used to seem to me almost too sad to dwell upon, while
slavery seemed destined to last for generations; but now that their
patience has had its perfect work, history cannot afford to lose
this portion of its record. There is no parallel instance of an op-
pressed race thus sustained by the religious sentiment alone. These
songs are but the vocal expression of the simplicity of their faith
and the sublimity of their long resignation.

CHAPTER X
Life at Camp Shaw

The Edisto expedition cost me the health and strength of several years. I could say, long after, in the words of one of the men, "I'se been a sickly person, eber since de expeditious." Justice to a strong constitution and good habits compels me, however, to say that, up to the time of my injury, I was almost the only officer in the regiment who had not once been off duty from illness. But at last I had to yield, and went North for a month.

We heard much said, during the war, of wounded officers who stayed unreasonably long at home. I think there were more instances of those who went back too soon. Such at least was my case. On returning to the regiment I found a great accumulation of unfinished business; every member of the field and staff was prostrated by illness or absent on detailed service; two companies had been sent to Hilton Head on fatigue duty, and kept there unexpectedly long: and there was a visible demoralization among the rest, especially from the fact that their pay had just been cut down, in violation of the express pledges of the government. A few weeks of steady sway made all right again; and during those weeks I felt a perfect exhilaration of health, followed by a month or two of complete prostration, when the work was done. This passing, I returned to duty, buoyed up by the fallacious hope that the winter months would set me right again.

We had a new camp on Port Royal Island, very pleasantly situated, just out of Beaufort. It stretched nearly to the edge of a shelving bluff, fringed with pines and overlooking the river; below the bluff was a hard, narrow beach, where one might gallop a mile and bathe at the farther end. We could look up and down the curving stream, and watch the few vessels that came and went. Our first encampment had been lower down that same river, and we felt at home.

The new camp was named Camp Shaw, in honor of the noble young officer who had lately fallen at Fort Wagner, under circumstances which had endeared him to all the men. As it happened, they had never seen him, nor was my regiment ever placed within immediate reach of the Fifty-Fourth Massachusetts. This I always regretted, feeling very desirous to compare the military qualities of the Northern and Southern blacks. As it was, the Southern regiments with which the Massachusetts troops were brigaded were hardly a fair specimen of their kind, having been raised chiefly by drafting, and, for this and other causes, being afflicted with perpetual discontent and desertion.

We had, of course, looked forward with great interest to the arrival of these new colored regiments, and I had ridden in from the picket-station to see the Fifty-Fourth. Apart from the peculiarity of its material, it was fresh from my own State, and I had relatives and acquaintances among its officers. Governor Andrew, who had formed it, was an old friend, and had begged me, on departure from Massachusetts, to keep him informed as to our experiment. I had good reason to believe that my reports had helped to prepare the way for this new battalion, and I had sent him, at his request, some hints as to its formation.*

*COMMONWEALTH OF MASSACHUSETTS,
Executive Department,
Boston, February 5, 1863.

To COL. T. W. HIGGINSON, *Commanding 1st Regt. S. C. Vols.,*
Port Royal Id., S. C.

COLONEL,—I am under obligations to you for your very interesting letter of January 19th, which I considered to be too important in its testimony to the efficiency of colored troops to be allowed to remain hidden on my files. I therefore placed some portions of it in the hands of Hon. Stephen M. Weld, of Jamaica Plain, for publication, and you will find enclosed the newspaper slip from the "Journal" of February 3d, in which it appeared. During a recent visit at Washington I have obtained permission from the Department of War to enlist colored troops as part of the Massachusetts quota, and I am about to begin to organize a colored infantry regiment, to be numbered the "54th Massachusetts Volunteers."

I shall be greatly obliged by any suggestions which your experience may afford concerning it, and I am determined that it shall serve as a model, in the high character of its officers and the thorough discipline of its men, for all subsequent corps of the like material.

Please present to General Saxton the assurances of my respectful regard.

I have the honor to be, respectfully and obediently yours,

JOHN A. ANDREW,
Governor of Massachusetts.

In the streets of Beaufort I had met Colonel Shaw, riding with his lieutenant-colonel and successor, Edward Hallowell, and had gone back with them to share their first meal in camp. I should have known Shaw anywhere by his resemblance to his kindred, nor did it take long to perceive that he shared their habitual truthfulness and courage. Moreover, he and Hallowell had already got beyond the commonplaces of inexperience, in regard to colored troops, and, for a wonder, asked only sensible questions. For instance, he admitted the mere matter of courage to be settled, as regarded the colored troops, and his whole solicitude bore on this point,—Would they do as well in line-of-battle as they had already done in more irregular service, and on picket and guard duty? Of this I had, of course, no doubt, nor, I think, had he; though I remember his saying something about the possibility of putting them between two fires in case of need, and so cutting off their retreat. I should never have thought of such a project, but I could not have expected him to trust them as I did, until he had been actually under fire with them. That, doubtless, removed all his anxieties, if he really had any.

This interview had occurred on the 4th of June. Shaw and his regiment had very soon been ordered to Georgia, then to Morris Island; Fort Wagner had been assaulted, and he had been killed. Most of the men knew about the circumstances of his death, and many of them had subscribed towards a monument for him,—a project which originated with General Saxton, and which was finally embodied in the "Shaw School-house" at Charleston. So it gave us all pleasure to name this camp for him, as its predecessor had been named for General Saxton.

The new camp was soon brought into good order. The men had great ingenuity in building screens and shelters of light poles, filled in with the gray moss from the live-oaks. The officers had vestibules built in this way, before all their tents; the cooking-places were walled round in the same fashion; and some of the wide company-streets had sheltered sidewalks down the whole line of tents. The sergeant on duty at the entrance of the camp had a similar bower, and the architecture culminated in a "Praise-House" for school and prayer-meetings, some thirty feet in diameter. As for chimneys and flooring, they were provided with that magic and invisible facility which marks the second year of a regiment's life.

That officer is happy who, besides a constitutional love of adventure, has also a love for the details of camp life, and likes to bring them to perfection. Nothing but a hen with her chickens about her can symbolize the content I felt on getting my scattered companies together, after some temporary separation on picket or fatigue duty. Then we went to work upon the nest. The only way to keep a camp in order is to set about everything as if you expected to stay there forever; if you stay, you get the comfort of it; if ordered away in twenty-four hours, you forget all wasted labor in the excitement of departure. Thus viewed, a camp is a sort of model farm or bit of landscape gardening; there is always some small improvement to be made, a well, more shade against the sun, an increased vigilance in sweeping. Then it is pleasant to take care of the men, to see them happy, to hear them purr.

Then the duties of inspection and drill, suspended during active service, resume their importance with a month or two of quiet. It really costs unceasing labor to keep a regiment in perfect condition and ready for service. The work is made up of minute and endless details, like a bird's pruning her feathers or a cat's licking her kittens into their proper toilet. Here are eight hundred men, every one of whom, every Sunday morning at farthest, must be perfectly *soigné*[1] in all personal properties; he must exhibit himself provided with every article of clothing, buttons, shoe-strings, hooks and eyes, company letter, regimental number, rifle, bayonet, bayonet-scabbard, cap-pouch, cartridge-box, cartridge-box belt, cartridge-box belt-plate, gun-sling, canteen, haversack, knapsack, packed according to rule, forty cartridges, forty percussion caps; and every one of these articles polished to the highest brightness or blackness as the case may be, and moreover hung or slung or tied or carried in precisely the correct manner.

What a vast and formidable housekeeping is here, my patriotic sisters! Consider, too, that every corner of the camp is to be kept absolutely clean and ready for exhibition at the shortest notice; hospital, stables, guard-house, cook-houses, company tents, must all be brought to perfection, and every square inch of this "farm of four acres" must look as smooth as an English lawn, twice a day. All this, beside the discipline and the drill and the regimental and company books, which must keep rigid account of all these details; consider all this, and then wonder no more that officers and men rejoice in being ordered on active service, where a few strokes of the pen will dispose of all this multiplicity of trappings as "expended in action" or "lost in service."

For one, the longer I remained in service, the better I appreciated the good sense of most of the regular army niceties. True, these things must all vanish when the time of action comes, but it is these things that have prepared you for action. Of course, if you dwell on them only, military life becomes millinery life alone. Kinglake[2] says that the Russian Grand-Duke Constantine, contemplating his beautiful toy-regiments, said that he dreaded war, for he knew that it would spoil the troops. The simple fact is, that a soldier is like the weapon he carries; service implies soiling, but you must have it clean in advance, that when soiled it may be of some use.

The men had that year a Christmas present which they enjoyed to the utmost,—furnishing the detail, every other day, for provost-guard duty in Beaufort. It was the only military service which they had ever shared within the town, and it moreover gave a sense of self-respect to be keeping the peace of their own streets. I enjoyed seeing them put on duty those mornings; there was such a twinkle of delight in their eyes, though their features were immovable. As the "reliefs" went round, posting the guard, under charge of a corporal, one could watch the black sentinels successively dropped and the whites picked up,—gradually changing the complexion, like Lord Somebody's black stockings which became white stockings,—till at last there was only a squad of white soldiers obeying the "Support Arms! Forward, March!" of a black corporal.

Then, when once posted, they glorified their office, you may be sure. Discipline had grown rather free-and-easy in the town about that time, and it is said that the guard-house never was so full within human memory as after their first tour of duty. I remember hearing that one young reprobate, son of a leading Northern philanthropist in those parts, was much aggrieved at being taken to the lock-up merely because he was found drunk in the streets. "Why," said he, "the white corporals always showed me the way home." And I can testify that, after an evening party, some weeks later, I heard with pleasure the officers asking eagerly for the countersign. "Who has the countersign?" said they. "The darkeys are on guard to-night, and we must look out for our lives." Even after a Christmas party at General Saxton's, the guard at the door very properly refused to let the ambulance be brought round from the stable for the ladies because the driver had not the countersign.

One of the sergeants of the guard, on one of these occasions, made to one who questioned his authority an answer that could hardly have been improved. The questioner had just been arrested for some offence.

"Know what dat mean?" said the indignant sergeant, pointing to the chevrons on his own sleeve. "Dat mean *Guv'ment*." Volumes could not have said more, and the victim collapsed. The thing soon settled itself, and nobody remembered to notice whether the face beside the musket of a sentinel were white or black. It meant Government, all the same.

The men were also indulged with several raids on the mainland, under the direction of Captain J. E. Bryant, of the Eighth Maine, the most experienced scout in that region, who was endeavoring to raise by enlistment a regiment of colored troops. On one occasion Captains Whitney and Heasley, with their companies, penetrated nearly to Pocataligo, capturing some pickets and bringing away all the slaves of a plantation,—the latter operation being entirely under the charge of Sergeant Harry Williams (Co. K), without the presence of any white man. The whole command was attacked on the return by a rebel force, which turned out to be what was called in those regions a "dog-company," consisting of mounted riflemen with half a dozen trained bloodhounds. The men met these dogs with their bayonets, killed four or five of their old tormentors with great relish, and brought away the carcass of one. I had the creature skinned, and sent the skin to New York to be stuffed and mounted, meaning to exhibit it at the Sanitary Commission Fair in Boston; but it spoiled on the passage. These quadruped allies were not originally intended as "dogs of war,"[3] but simply to detect fugitive slaves, and the men were delighted at this confirmation of their tales of dog-companies, which some of the officers had always disbelieved.

Captain Bryant, during his scouting adventures, had learned to outwit these bloodhounds, and used his skill in eluding escape, during another expedition of the same kind. He was sent with Captain Metcalf's company far up the Combahee River to cut the telegraphic wires and intercept despatches. Our adventurous chaplain and a telegraphic operator went with the party. They ascended the river, cut the wires, and read the despatches for an hour or two. Unfortunately, the attached wire was too conspicuously hung, and was seen by a passenger on the railway train in passing. The train was stopped and a swift stampede followed; a squad of cavalry was sent in pursuit, and our chaplain, with Lieutenant Osborn, of Bryant's projected regiment, were captured; also one private,—the first of our men who had ever been taken prisoners. In spite of an agreement at Washington to the contrary, our chaplain was held as prisoner of war, the only spiritual adviser in uniform, so far as I know, who had that honor. I do not know but his reverence would have agreed with Scott's pirate-lieutenant,[4] that it was better to live as plain Jack Bunce than die as Frederick Altamont; but I am very sure that he would rather have been kept prisoner to the close of the war, as a combatant, than have been released on parole as a non-resistant.

After his return, I remember, he gave the most animated accounts of the whole adventure, of which he had enjoyed every instant, from the first entrance on the enemy's soil to the final capture. I suppose we should all like to tap the telegraphic wires anywhere and read our neighbor's messages, if we could only throw round this process the dignity of a Sacred Cause. This was what our good chaplain had done, with the same conscientious zest with which he had conducted his Sunday foraging in Florida. But he told me that nothing so impressed him on the whole trip as the sudden transformation in the black soldier who was taken prisoner with him. The chaplain at once adopted the policy, natural to him, of talking boldly and even defiantly to his captors, and commanding instead of beseeching. He pursued the same policy always and gained by it, he thought. But the negro adopted the diametrically opposite policy, also congenial to his crushed race,—all the force seemed to go out of him, and he surrendered himself like a tortoise to be kicked and trodden upon at their will. This manly, well-trained soldier at once became a slave again, asked no questions, and, if any were asked, made meek and conciliatory answers. He did not know, nor did any of us know, whether he would be treated as a prisoner of war, or shot, or sent to a rice-plantation. He simply acted according to the traditions of his race, as did the chaplain on his side. In the end the soldier's cunning was vindicated by the result; he escaped, and rejoined us in six months, while the chaplain was imprisoned for a year.

The men came back very much exhausted from this expedition, and those who were in the chaplain's squad narrowly escaped with their lives. One brave fellow had actually not a morsel to eat for four days, and then could keep nothing on his stomach for two days more, so that his life was despaired of; and yet he brought all his equipments safe into camp. Some of these men had led such wandering lives, in woods and swamps, that to hunt them was like hunting an otter; shyness and concealment had grown to be their second nature.

After these little episodes came two months of peace. We were clean, comfortable, quiet, and consequently discontented. It was therefore with eagerness that we listened to a rumor of a new Florida expedition, in which we might possibly take a hand.

CHAPTER XI

Florida Again?

Let me revert once more to my diary, for a specimen of the sharp changes and sudden disappointments that may come to troops in service. But for a case or two of varioloid[1] in the regiment, we should have taken part in the battle of Olustee, and should have had (as was reported) the right of the line. At any rate we should have shared the hard knocks and the glory, which were distributed pretty freely to the colored troops then and there. The diary will give, better than can any continuous narrative, our ups and downs of expectation in those days.

"CAMP SHAW, BEAUFORT, S.C.,
February 7, 1864.

"Great are the uncertainties of military orders! Since our recall from Jacksonville we have had no such surprises as came to us on Wednesday night. It was our third day of a new tour of duty at the picket station. We had just got nicely settled,—men well tented, with good floors, and in high spirits, officers at out-stations all happy, Mrs.——coming to stay with her husband, we at head-quarters just in order, house cleaned, moss-garlands up, camellias and jessamines in the tin washbasins, baby in bliss;—our usual run of visitors had just set in, two Beaufort captains and a surgeon had just risen from a late dinner after a flag of truce, General Saxton and his wife had driven away but an hour or two before, we were all sitting about busy, with a great fire blazing, Mrs. D. had just remarked triumphantly, 'Last time I had but a mouthful here, and now I shall be here three weeks'—when—

"In dropped, like a bombshell, a despatch announcing that we were to be relieved by the Eighth Maine, the next morning, as General Gillmore had sent an order that we should be ready for departure from Beaufort at any moment.

"Conjectures, orders, packing, sending couriers to outstations, were the employments of the evening; the men received the news with cheers, and we all came in next morning."

"February 11, 1864.

"For three days we have watched the river, and every little steamboat that comes up for coal brings out spy-glasses and conjectures, and 'Dar's de Fourf New Hampshire,'—for when that comes, it is said, we go. Meanwhile we hear stirring news from Florida, and the men are very impatient to be off. It is remarkable how much more thoroughly they look at things as soldiers than last year, and how much less as home-bound men,—the South-Carolinians, I mean, for of course the Floridians would naturally wish to go to Florida.

"But in every way I see the gradual change in them, sometimes with a sigh, as parents watch their children growing up and miss the droll speeches and the confiding ignorance of childhood. Sometimes it comes over me with a pang that they are growing more like white men,—less naïve and less grotesque. Still, I think there is enough of it to last, and that their joyous buoyancy, at least, will hold out while life does.

"As for our destination, our greatest fear is of finding ourselves posted at Hilton Head and going no farther. As a dashing Irish officer remarked the other day, 'If we are ordered away anywhere, I hope it will be either to go to Florida or else stay here!' "

"February 18, 1864.

"Sublime uncertainties again!

"After being ordered in from picket, under marching orders; after the subsequent ten days of uncertainty; after watching every steamboat that came up the river, to see if the Fourth New Hampshire was on board,—at last the regiment came.

"Then followed another break; there was no transportation to take us. At last a boat was notified.

"Then General Saxton, as anxious to keep us as was the regiment to go, played his last card in small-pox, telegraphing to department head-quarters that we had it dangerously in the regiment. (N. B. All varioloid, light at that, and besides, we always have it.)

"Then the order came to leave behind the sick and those who had been peculiarly exposed, and embark the rest next day.

"Great was the jubilee! The men were up, I verily believe, by three in the morning, and by eight the whole camp was demolished or put in wagons, and we were on our way. The soldiers of the Fourth New Hampshire swarmed in; every board was swept away by them; there had been a time when colored boards (if I may delicately so express myself) were repudiated by white soldiers, but that epoch had long since passed. I gave my new tent-frame, even the latch, to Colonel Bell; ditto Lieutenant-Colonel to Lieutenant-Colonel.

"Down we marched, the men singing 'John Brown' and 'Marching Along' and 'Gwine in de Wilderness'; women in tears and smiles lined the way. We halted opposite the dear General's; we cheered, he speeched, I speeched, we all embraced symbolically, and cheered some more. Then we went to work at the wharf; vast wagon-loads of tents, rations, ordnance, and what-not disappeared in the capacious maw of the Delaware. In the midst of it all came riding down General Saxton with a despatch from Hilton Head:—

"'If you think the amount of small-pox in the First South Carolina Volunteers sufficient, the order will be countermanded.'

"'What shall I say?' quoth the guilty General, perceiving how preposterously too late the negotiation was reopened.

"'Say, sir?' quoth I. 'Say that we are on board already and the small-pox left behind. Say we had only thirteen cases, chiefly varioloid, and ten almost well.'

"Our blood was up with a tremendous morning's work done, and, rather than turn back, we felt ready to hold down Major-General Gillmore, commanding department, and all his staff upon the wharf, and vaccinate them by main force.

"So General Saxton rode away, and we worked away. Just as the last wagon-load but one was being transferred to the omnivorous depths of the Delaware,—which I should think would have been filled ten times over with what we had put into it,—down rode the General with a fiendish joy in his bright eyes and held out a paper,—one of the familiar rescripts from headquarters.

" 'The marching orders of the First South Carolina Volunteers are hereby countermanded.'

" 'Major Trowbridge,' said I, 'will you give my compliments to Lieutenant Hooper, somewhere in the hold of that steamer, and direct him to set his men at work to bring out every individual article which they have carried in.' And I sat down on a pile of boards.

" 'You will return to your old camping-ground, Colonel,' said the General, placidly. 'Now,' he added, with serene satisfaction, 'we will have some brigade drills!'

"Brigade drills! Since Mr. Pickwick, with his heartless tomato-sauce and warming-pans, there had been nothing so aggravating as to try to solace us, who were as good as on board ship and under way,—nay, in imagination as far up the St. John's as Pilatka at least,—with brigade drills! It was very kind and flattering in him to wish to keep us. But unhappily we had made up our minds to go.

"Never did officer ride at the head of a battalion of more wo-begone, spiritless wretches than I led back from Beaufort that day. 'When I march down to de landin',' said one of the men after-wards, 'my knapsack full of feathers. Comin' back, *he lead!*' And the lead, instead of the feathers, rested on the heart of every one.

"As if the disappointment itself were not sufficient, we had to return to our pretty camp, accustomed to its drawing-room order, and find it a desert. Every board gone from the floors, the screens torn down from the poles, all the little conveniences scattered, and, to crown all, a cold breeze such as we had not known since New-Year's Day blowing across the camp and flooding every-thing with dust. I sincerely hope the regiment would never behave after a defeat as they behaved then. Every man seemed crushed, officers and soldiers alike; when they broke ranks, they went and lay down like sheep where their tents used to be, or wandered disconsolately about, looking for their stray belongings. The scene was so infinitely dolorous that it gradually put me in the highest spirits; the ludicrousness of the whole affair was so complete, there was nothing to do but laugh. The horrible dust blew till every officer had some black spot on his nose which paralyzed pathos. Of course the only way was to set them all at work as soon as possible; and work them we did,—I at the camp and the Major at the wharf,—loading and unloading wagons and just reversing all which the morning had done.

"The New Hampshire men were very considerate, and gave back most of what they had taken, though many of our men were really too delicate or proud to ask or even take what they had once given to soldiers or to the colored people. I had no such delicacy about my tentframe, and by night things had resumed something of their old aspect, and cheerfulness was in part restored. Yet long after this I found one first sergeant absolutely in tears,—a Florida man, most of whose kindred were up the St. John's. It was very natural that the men from that region should feel thus bitterly, but it shows how much of the habit of soldiers they have all acquired, that the South Carolina men, who were leaving the neighborhood of their families for an indefinite time, were just as eager to go, and not one deserted, though they knew it for a week beforehand. No doubt my precarious health makes it now easier for me personally to remain here—easier on reflection at least—than for the others. At the same time Florida is fascinating, and offers not only adventure, but the command of a brigade. Certainly at the last moment there was not a sacrifice I would not have made rather than wrench myself and others away from the expedition. We are, of course, thrown back into the old uncertainty, and if the small-pox subsides (and it is really diminishing decidedly) we may yet come in at the wrong end of the Florida affair."

"February 19.

"Not a bit of it! This morning the General has ridden up radiant, has seen General Gillmore, who has decided not to order us to Florida at all, nor withdraw any of this garrison. Moreover, he says that all which is intended in Florida is done,—that there will be no advance to Tallahassee, and General Seymour will establish a camp of instruction in Jacksonville. Well, if that is all, it is a lucky escape."

We little dreamed that on that very day the march toward Olustee was beginning. The battle took place next day, and I add one more extract to show how the news reached Beaufort.

"February 23, 1864.

"There was the sound of revelry by night at a ball in Beaufort last night, in a new large building beautifully decorated. All the collected flags of the garrison hung round and over us, as if the stars and stripes were devised for an ornament alone. The array of uniforms was such that a civilian became a distinguished object, much more a lady. All would have gone according to the proverbial marriage-bell, I suppose, had there not been a slight palpable shadow over all of us from hearing vague stories of a lost battle in Florida, and from the thought that perhaps the very ambulances in which we rode to the ball were ours only until the wounded or the dead might tenant them.

"General Gillmore only came, I supposed, to put a good face upon the matter. He went away soon, and General Saxton went; then came a rumor that the Cosmopolitan had actually arrived with wounded, but still the dance went on. There was nothing unfeeling about it,—one gets used to things,—when suddenly, in the midst of the 'Lancers,' there came a perfect hush, the music ceasing, a few surgeons went hastily to and fro, as if conscience-stricken (I should think they might have been),—then there 'waved a mighty shadow in,' as in Uhland's 'Black Knight,'² and as we all stood wondering we were 'ware of General Saxton, who strode hastily down the hall, his pale face very resolute, and looking almost sick with anxiety. He had just been on board the steamer; there were two hundred and fifty wounded men just arrived, and the ball must end. Not that there was anything for us to do; but the revel was mistimed, and must be ended; it was wicked to be dancing, with such a scene of suffering near by.

"Of course the ball was instantly broken up, though with some murmurings and some longings of appetite, on the part of some, toward the wasted supper.

"Later, I went on board the boat. Among the long lines of wounded, black and white intermingled, there was the wonderful quiet which usually prevails on such occasions. Not a sob nor a groan, except from those undergoing removal. It is not self-control, but chiefly the shock to the system produced by severe wounds, especially gunshot wounds, and which usually keeps the patient stiller at first than at any later time.

"A company from my regiment waited on the wharf, in their

accustomed dusky silence, and I longed to ask them what they thought of our Florida disappointment now? In view of what they saw, did they still wish we had been there? I confess that in presence of all that human suffering, I could not wish it. But I would not have suggested any such thought to them.

"I found our kind-hearted ladies, Mrs. Chamberlin and Mrs. Dewhurst, on board the steamer, but there was nothing for them to do, and we walked back to camp in the radiant moonlight; Mrs. Chamberlin more than ever strengthened in her blushing woman's philosophy, 'I don't care who wins the laurels, provided we don't!'"

"February 29.

"But for a few trivial cases of varioloid, we should certainly have been in that disastrous fight. We were confidently expected for several days at Jacksonville, and the commanding general told Colonel Hallowell that we, being the oldest colored regiment, would have the right of the line. This was certainly to miss danger and glory very closely."

CHAPTER XII

The Negro as a Soldier

There was in our regiment a very young recruit, named Sam Roberts, of whom Trowbridge used to tell this story. Early in the war Trowbridge had been once sent to Amelia Island with a squad of men, under direction of Commodore Goldsborough, to remove the negroes from the island. As the officers stood on the beach, talking to some of the older freedmen, they saw this urchin peeping at them from front and rear in a scrutinizing way, for which his father at last called him to account, as thus:—

"Hi! Sammy, what you's doin', chile?"

"Daddy," said the inquisitive youth, "don't you know mas'r tell us Yankee hab tail? I don't see no tail, daddy!"

There were many who went to Port Royal during the war, in civil or military positions, whose previous impressions of the colored race were about as intelligent as Sam's view of themselves. But, for one, I had always had so much to do with fugitive slaves, and had studied the whole subject with such interest, that I found not much to learn or unlearn as to this one point. Their courage I had before seen tested; their docile and lovable qualities I had known; and the only real surprise that experience brought me was in finding them so little demoralized. I had not allowed for the extreme remoteness and seclusion of their lives, especially among the Sea Islands. Many of them had literally spent their whole existence on some lonely island or remote plantation, where the master never came, and the overseer only once or twice a week. With these exceptions, such persons had never seen a white face, and of the excitements or sins of larger communities they had not a conception. My friend Colonel Hallowell, of the Fifty-Fourth Massachusetts, told me that he had among his men some of the worst reprobates of Northern cities. While I had some men who were unprincipled and troublesome, there was not one whom I could call a hardened villain. I was constantly expecting to find male Topsies,[1] with no notions of good and plenty of evil. But I never found one. Among the most ignorant there was very often a childlike absence of vices, which was rather to be classed as inexperience than as innocence, but which had some of the advantages of both.

Apart from this, they were very much like other men. General Saxton, examining with some impatience a long list of questions from some philanthropic Commission at the North, respecting the traits and habits of the freedmen, bade some staff-officer answer them all in two words,—"Intensely human." We all admitted that it was a striking and comprehensive description.

For instance, as to courage. So far as I have seen, the mass of men are naturally courageous up to a certain point. A man seldom runs away from danger which he ought to face, unless others run; each is apt to keep with the mass, and colored soldiers have more than usual of this gregariousness. In almost every regiment, black or white, there are a score or two of men who are naturally daring, who really hunger after dangerous adventures, and are happiest when allowed to seek them. Every commander gradually finds out who these men are, and habitually uses them; certainly I had such, and I remember with delight their bearing, their coolness, and their dash. Some of them were negroes, some mulattoes. One of them would have passed for white, with brown hair and blue eyes, while others were so black you could hardly see their features. These picked men varied in other respects too; some were neat and well-drilled soldiers, while others were slovenly, heedless fellows,—the despair of their officers at inspection, their pride on a raid. They were the natural scouts and rangers of the regiment; they had the two-o'clock-in-the-morning courage, which Napoleon thought so rare. The mass of the regiment rose to the same level under excitement, and were more excitable, I think, than whites, but neither more nor less courageous.

Perhaps the best proof of a good average of courage among them was in the readiness they always showed for any special enterprise. I do not remember ever to have had the slightest difficulty in obtaining volunteers, but rather in keeping down the number. The previous pages include many illustrations of this, as well as of their endurance of pain and discomfort. For instance, one of my lieutenants, a very daring Irishman, who had served for eight years as a sergeant of regular artillery in Texas, Utah, and South Carolina, said he had never been engaged in anything so risky as our raid up the St. Mary's. But in truth it seems to me a mere absurdity to deliberately argue the question of courage, as applied to men among whom I waked and slept, day and night, for so many months together. As well might he who has been wandering for years upon the desert, with a Bedouin escort, discuss the courage of the men whose tents have been his shelter and whose spears his guard. We, their officers, did not go there to teach lessons, but to receive them. There were more than a hundred men in the ranks who had voluntarily met more dangers in their escape from slavery than any of my young captains had incurred in all their lives.

There was a family named Wilson, I remember, of which we had several representatives. Three or four brothers had planned an escape from the interior to our lines; they finally decided that the youngest should stay and take care of the old mother; the rest, with their sister and her children, came in a "dug-out" down one of the rivers. They were fired upon, again and again, by the pickets along the banks, until finally every man on board was wounded; and still they got safely through. When the bullets began to fly about them, the woman shed tears, and her little girl of nine said to her, "Don't cry, mother, Jesus will help you," and then the child began praying as the wounded men still urged the boat along. This the mother told me, but I had previously heard it from an officer who was on the gunboat that picked them up,—a big, rough man, whose voice fairly broke as he described their appearance. He said that the mother and child had been hid for nine months in the woods before attempting their escape, and the child would speak to no one,—indeed, she hardly would when she came to our camp. She was almost white, and this officer wished to adopt her, but the mother said, "I would do anything but that for *oonah*,"—this being a sort of Indian formation of the second-person-plural, such as they sometimes use. This same officer afterwards saw a reward offered for this family in a Savannah paper.

I used to think that I should not care to read "Uncle Tom's Cabin" in our camp; it would have seemed tame. Any group of men in a tent would have had more exciting tales to tell. I needed

no fiction when I had Fanny Wright, for instance, daily passing
to and fro before my tent, with her shy little girl clinging to her
skirts. Fanny was a modest little mulatto woman, a soldier's wife,
and a company laundress. She had escaped from the main-land in
a boat, with that child and another. Her baby was shot dead in
her arms, and she reached our lines with one child safe on earth
and the other in heaven. I never found it needful to give any
elementary instructions in courage to Fanny's husband, you may
be sure.

There was another family of brothers in the regiment named
Miller. Their grandmother, a fine-looking old woman, nearly seventy, I should think, but erect as a pine-tree, used sometimes to
come and visit them. She and her husband had once tried to escape
from a plantation near Savannah. They had failed, and had been
brought back; the husband had received five hundred lashes, and
while the white men on the plantation were viewing the punishment, she was collecting her children and grandchildren, to the
number of twenty-two, in a neighboring marsh, preparatory to
another attempt that night. They found a flat-boat which had been
rejected as unseaworthy, got on board,—still under the old woman's orders,—and drifted forty miles down the river to our lines.
Trowbridge happened to be on board the gunboat which picked
them up, and he said that when the "flat" touched the side of the
vessel, the grandmother rose to her full height, with her youngest
grandchild in her arms, and said only, "My God! are we free?"
By one of those coincidences of which life is full, her husband
escaped also, after his punishment, and was taken up by the same
gunboat.

I hardly need point out that my young lieutenants did not have
to teach the principles of courage to this woman's grandchildren.

I often asked myself why it was that, with this capacity of
daring and endurance, they had not kept the land in a perpetual
flame of insurrection; why, especially since the opening of the
war, they had kept so still. The answer was to be found in the
peculiar temperament of the races, in their religious faith, and in
the habit of patience that centuries had fortified. The shrewder
men all said substantially the same thing. What was the use of
insurrection, where everything was against them? They had no

knowledge, no money, no arms, no drill, no organization,—above all, no mutual confidence. It was the tradition among them that all insurrections were always betrayed by somebody. They had no mountain passes to defend like the Maroons of Jamaica,—no impenetrable swamps, like the Maroons of Surinam. Where they had these, even on a small scale, they had used them,—as in certain swamps round Savannah and in the everglades of Florida, where they united with the Indians, and would stand fire—so I was told by General Saxton, who had fought them there—when the Indians would retreat.

It always seemed to me that, had I been a slave, my life would have been one long scheme of insurrection. But I learned to respect the patient self-control of those who had waited till the course of events should open a better way. When it came they accepted it. Insurrection on their part would at once have divided the Northern sentiment; and a large part of our army would have joined with the Southern army to hunt them down. By their waiting till we needed them, their freedom was secured.

Two things chiefly surprised me in their feeling toward their former masters,—the absence of affection and the absence of revenge. I expected to find a good deal of the patriarchal feeling. It always seemed to me a very ill-applied emotion, as connected with the facts and laws of American slavery,—still I expected to find it. I suppose that my men and their families and visitors may have had as much of it as the mass of freed slaves; but certainly they had not a particle. I never could cajole one of them, in his most discontented moment, into regretting "ole mas'r time" for a single instant. I never heard one speak of the masters except as natural enemies. Yet they were perfectly discriminating as to individuals; many of them claimed to have had kind owners, and some expressed great gratitude to them for particular favors received. It was not the individuals, but the ownership, of which they complained. That they saw to be a wrong which no special kindnesses could right. On this, as on all points connected with slavery, they understood the matter as clearly as Garrison² or Phillips; the wisest philosophy could teach them nothing as to that, nor could any false philosophy befog them. After all, personal experience is the best logician.

Certainly this indifference did not proceed from any want of personal affection, for they were the most affectionate people among whom I had ever lived. They attached themselves to every officer who deserved love, and to some who did not; and if they failed to show it to their masters, it proved the wrongfulness of the mastery. On the other hand, they rarely showed one gleam of revenge, and I shall never forget the self-control with which one of our best sergeants pointed out to me, at Jacksonville, the very place where one of his brothers had been hanged by the whites for leading a party of fugitive slaves. He spoke of it as a historic matter, without any bearing on the present issue.

But side by side with this faculty of patience, there was a certain tropical element in the men, a sort of fiery ecstasy when aroused, which seemed to link them by blood with the French Turcos, and made them really resemble their natural enemies, the Celts, far more than the Anglo-Saxon temperament. To balance this there were great individual resources when alone,—a sort of Indian wiliness and subtlety of resource. Their gregariousness and love of drill made them more easy to keep in hand than white American troops, who rather like to straggle or go in little squads, looking out for themselves, without being bothered with officers. The blacks prefer organization.

The point of inferiority that I always feared, though I never had occasion to prove it, was that they might show less fibre, less tough and dogged resistance, than whites, during a prolonged trial,—a long, disastrous march, for instance, or the hopeless defence of a besieged town. I should not be afraid of their mutinying or running away, but of their drooping and dying. It might not turn out so; but I mention it for the sake of fairness, and to avoid overstating the merits of these troops. As to the simple general fact of courage and reliability I think no officer in our camp ever thought of there being any difference between black and white. And certainly the opinions of these officers, who for years risked their lives every moment on the fidelity of their men, were worth more than those of all the world beside.

No doubt there were reasons why this particular war was an especially favorable test of the colored soldiers. They had more to fight for than the whites. Besides the flag and the Union, they had home and wife and child. They fought with ropes round their necks, and when orders were issued that the officers of colored troops should be put to death on capture, they took a grim satisfaction. It helped their *esprit de corps* immensely. With us, at least, there was to be no play-soldier. Though they had begun with a slight feeling of inferiority to the white troops, this compliment substituted a peculiar sense of self-respect. And even when the new colored regiments began to arrive from the North my men still pointed out this difference,—that in case of ultimate defeat, the Northern troops, black or white, would go home, while the First South Carolina must fight it out or be re-enslaved. This was one thing that made the St. John's River so attractive to them and even to me;—it was so much nearer the everglades. I used seriously to ponder, during the darker periods of the war, whether I might not end my days as an outlaw,—a leader of Maroons.

Meanwhile, I used to try to make some capital for the Northern troops, in their estimate, by pointing out that it was a disinterested thing in these men from the free States, to come down there and fight, that the slaves might be free. But they were apt keenly to reply, that many of the white soldiers disavowed this object, and said that that was not the object of the war, nor even likely to be its end. Some of them even repeated Mr. Seward's unfortunate words to Mr. Adams,[3] which some general had been heard to quote. So, on the whole, I took nothing by the motion, as was apt to be the case with those who spoke a good word for our Government, in those vacillating and half proslavery days.

At any rate, this ungenerous discouragement had this good effect, that it touched their pride; they would deserve justice, even if they did not obtain it. This pride was afterwards severely tested during the disgraceful period when the party of repudiation in Congress temporarily deprived them of their promised pay. In my regiment the men never mutinied, nor even threatened mutiny; they seemed to make it a matter of honor to do their part, even if the Government proved a defaulter; but one third of them, including the best men in the regiment, quietly refused to take a dollar's pay, at the reduced price. "We 'se gib our sogerin' to de Guv'-ment, Cunnel," they said, "but we won't 'spise ourselves so much for take de seben dollar." They even made a contemptuous ballad, of which I once caught a snatch.

> "Ten dollar a month!
> Tree ob dat for clothin'!
> Go to Washington
> Fight for Linkum's darter!"

This "Lincoln's daughter" stood for the Goddess of Liberty, it would seem. They would be true to her, but they would not take the half-pay. This was contrary to my advice, and to that of their other officers; but I now think it was wise. Nothing less than this would have called the attention of the American people to this outrageous fraud.*

The same slow forecast had often marked their action in other ways. One of our ablest sergeants, Henry McIntyre, who had earned two dollars and a half per day as a master-carpenter in Florida, and paid one dollar and a half to his master, told me that he had deliberately refrained from learning to read, because that knowledge exposed the slaves to so much more watching and suspicion. This man and a few others had built on contract the greater part of the town of Micanopy in Florida, and was a thriving man when his accustomed discretion failed for once, and he lost all. He named his child William Lincoln, and it brought upon him such suspicion that he had to make his escape.

I cannot conceive what people at the North mean by speaking of the negroes as a bestial or brutal race. Except in some insensibility to animal pain, I never knew of an act in my regiment which I should call brutal. In reading Kay's "Condition of the English Peasantry"[4] I was constantly struck with the unlikeness of my men to those therein described. This could not proceed from my prejudices as an abolitionist, for they would have led me the other way, and indeed I had once written a little essay to show the brutalizing influences of slavery. I learned to think that we abolitionists had underrated the suffering produced by slavery among the negroes, but had overrated the demoralization. Or rather, we did not know how the religious temperament of the negroes had checked the demoralization. Yet again, it must be admitted that this temperament, born of sorrow and oppression, is far more marked in the slave than in the native African.

*See Appendix.

Theorize as we may, there was certainly in our camp an average tone of propriety which all visitors noticed, and which was not created, but only preserved by discipline. I was always struck, not merely by the courtesy of the men, but also by a certain sober decency of language. If a man had to report to me any disagreeable fact, for instance, he was sure to do it with gravity and decorum, and not blurt it out in an offensive way. And it certainly was a significant fact that the ladies of our camp, when we were so fortunate as to have such guests,—the young wives, especially, of the adjutant and quartermaster,—used to go among the tents when the men were off duty, in order to hear their big pupils read and spell, without the slightest fear of annoyance. I do not mean direct annoyance or insult, for no man who valued his life would have ventured that in presence of the others, but I mean the annoyance of accidentally seeing or hearing improprieties not intended for them. They both declared that they would not have moved about with anything like the same freedom in any white camp they had ever entered, and it always roused their indignation to hear the negro race called brutal or depraved.

This came partly from natural good manners, partly from the habit of deference, partly from ignorance of the refined and ingenious evil which is learned in large towns; but a large part came from their strongly religious temperament. Their comparative freedom from swearing, for instance,—an abstinence which I fear military life did not strengthen,—was partly a matter of principle. Once I heard one of them say to another, in a transport of indignation, "Ha-a-a, boy, s'pose I no be a Christian, I cuss you so!"—which was certainly drawing pretty hard upon the bridle. "Cuss," however, was a generic term for all manner of evil speaking; they would say, "He cuss me fool," or "He cuss me coward," as if the essence of propriety were in harsh and angry speech,— which I take to be good ethics. But certainly, if Uncle Toby[5] could have recruited his army in Flanders from our ranks, their swearing would have ceased to be historic.

It used to seem to me that never, since Cromwell's time,[6] had there been soldiers in whom the religious element held such a place. "A religious army," "a gospel army," were their frequent phrases. In their prayer-meetings there was always a mingling, often quaint enough, of the warlike and the pious. "If each one of us was a praying man," said Corporal Thomas Long in a sermon, "it appears to me that we could fight as well with prayers as with bullets,—for the Lord has said that if you have faith even as a grain of mustard-seed cut into four parts, you can say to the sycamore-tree, Arise, and it will come up." And though Corporal Long may have got a little perplexed in his botany, his faith proved itself by works, for he volunteered and went many miles on a solitary scouting expedition into the enemy's country in Florida, and got back safe, after I had given him up for lost.

The extremes of religious enthusiasm I did not venture to encourage, for I could not do it honestly; neither did I discourage them, but simply treated them with respect, and let them have their way, so long as they did not interfere with discipline. In general they promoted it. The mischievous little drummer-boys, whose scrapes and quarrels were the torment of my existence, might be seen kneeling together in their tents to say their prayers at night, and I could hope that their slumbers were blessed by some spirit of peace, such as certainly did not rule over their waking. The most reckless and daring fellows in the regiment were perfect fatalists in their confidence that God would watch over them, and that if they died, it would be because their time had come. This almost excessive faith, and the love of freedom and of their families, all co-operated with their pride as soldiers to make them do their duty. I could not have spared any of these incentives. Those of our officers who were personally the least influenced by such considerations, still saw the need of encouraging them among the men.

I am bound to say that this strongly devotional turn was not always accompanied by the practical virtues; but neither was it strikingly divorced from them. A few men, I remember, who belonged to the ancient order of hypocrites, but not many. Old Jim Cushman was our favorite representative scamp. He used to vex his righteous soul over the admission of the unregenerate to prayer-meetings, and went off once shaking his head and muttering, "Too much goat shout wid de sheep." But he who objected to this profane admixture used to get our mess-funds far more hopelessly mixed with his own, when he went out to buy us chickens. And I remember that, on being asked by our Major, in that semi-Ethiopian dialect into which we sometimes slid, "How much wife you got, Jim?" the veteran replied, with a sort of penitence for lost opportunities, "On'y but four, Sah!"

Another man of somewhat similar quality went among us by the name of Henry Ward Beecher,[7] from a remarkable resemblance in face and figure to that sturdy divine. I always felt a sort of admiration for this worthy, because of the thoroughness with which he outwitted me, and the sublime impudence in which he culminated. He got a series of passes from me, every week or two, to go and see his wife on a neighboring plantation, and finally, when this resource seemed exhausted, he came boldly for one more pass, that he might go and be married.

We used to quote him a good deal, also, as a sample of a certain Shakespearian boldness of personification in which the men sometimes indulged. Once, I remember, his captain had given him a fowling-piece to clean. Henry Ward had left it in the captain's tent, and the latter, finding it, had transferred the job to some one else.

Then came a confession, in this precise form, with many dignified gesticulations:—

"Cappen! I took dat gun, and I put him in Cappen tent. Den I look, and de gun not dar! Den Conscience say, Cappen mus' hab gib dat gun to somebody else for clean. Den I say, Conscience, you reason correck!"

Compare Lancelot Gobbo's soliloquy[8] in the "Two Gentlemen of Verona!"

Still, I maintain that, as a whole, the men were remarkably free from inconvenient vices. There was no more lying and stealing than in average white regiments. The surgeon was not much troubled by shamming sickness, and there were not a great many complaints of theft. There was less quarrelling than among white soldiers, and scarcely ever an instance of drunkenness. Perhaps the influence of their officers had something to do with this; for not a ration of whiskey was ever issued to the men, nor did I ever touch it, while in the army, nor approve a requisition for any of the officers, without which it could not easily be obtained. In this respect our surgeons fortunately agreed with me, and we never had reason to regret it. I believe the use of ardent spirits to be as useless and injurious in the army as on board ship, and among the colored troops, especially, who had never been accustomed to it, I think that it did only harm.

The point of greatest laxity in their moral habits—the want of a high standard of chastity—was not one which affected their camp life to any great extent, and it therefore came less under my observation. But I found to my relief that, whatever their deficiency in this respect, it was modified by the general quality of their temperament, and indicated rather a softening and relaxation than a hardening and brutalizing of their moral natures. Any insult or violence in this direction was a thing unknown. I never heard of an instance. It was not uncommon for men to have two or three wives in different plantations,—the second, or remoter, partner being called a " 'broad wife,"—i.e. wife abroad. But the whole tendency was toward marriage, and this state of things was only regarded as a bequest from "mas'r time."

I knew a great deal about their marriages, for they often consulted me, and took my counsel as lovers are wont to do,—that is, when it pleased their fancy. Sometimes they would consult their captains first, and then come to me in despairing appeal. "Cap'n Scroby [Trowbridge] he acvise me not for marry dis lady, 'cause she hab seben chil'en. What for use? Cap'n Scroby can't lub for me. I mus' lub for myself, and I lub he." I remember that on this occasion "he" stood by, a most unattractive woman, jet black, with an old pink muslin dress, torn white cotton gloves, and a very flowery bonnet, that must have descended through generations of tawdry mistresses.

I felt myself compelled to reaffirm the decision of the inferior court. The result was as usual. They were married the next day, and I believe that she proved an excellent wife, though she had seven children, whose father was also in the regiment. If she did not, I know many others who did, and certainly I have never seen more faithful or more happy marriages than among that people.

The question was often asked, whether the Southern slaves or the Northern free blacks made the best soldiers. It was a compliment to both classes that each officer usually preferred those whom he had personally commanded. I preferred those who had been slaves, for their greater docility and affectionateness, for the powerful stimulus which their new freedom gave, and for the fact that they were fighting, in a manner, for their own homes and firesides. Every one of these considerations afforded a special aid to discipline, and cemented a peculiar tie of sympathy between them and their officers. They seemed like clansmen, and had a more confiding and filial relation to us than seemed to me to exist in the Northern colored regiments.

So far as the mere habits of slavery went, they were a poor preparation for military duty. Inexperienced officers often assumed that, because these men had been slaves before enlistment, they would bear to be treated as such afterwards. Experience proved the contrary. The more strongly we marked the difference between the slave and the soldier, the better for the regiment. One half of military duty lies in obedience, the other half in self-respect. A soldier without self-respect is worthless. Consequently there were no regiments in which it was so important to observe the courtesies and proprieties of military life as in these. I had to caution the officers to be more than usually particular in returning the salutations of the men; to be very careful in their dealings with those on picket or guard-duty; and on no account to omit the titles of the non-commissioned officers. So, in dealing out punishments, we had carefully to avoid all that was brutal and arbitrary, all that savored of the overseer. Any such dealing found them as obstinate and contemptuous as was Topsy when Miss Ophelia undertook to chastise her. A system of light punishments, rigidly administered according to the prescribed military forms, had more weight with them than any amount of angry severity. To make them feel as remote as possible from the plantation, this was essential. By adhering to this, and constantly appealing to their pride as soldiers and their sense of duty, we were able to maintain a high standard of discipline,—so, at least, the inspecting officers said,—and to get rid, almost entirely, of the more degrading class of punishments,—standing on barrels, tying up by the thumbs, and the ball and chain.

In all ways we had to educate their self-respect. For instance, at first they disliked to obey their own non-commissioned officers. "I don't want him to play de white man ober me," was a sincere objection. They had been so impressed with a sense of inferiority that the distinction extended to the very principles of honor. "I ain't got colored-man principles," said Corporal London Simmons, indignantly defending himself from some charge before me. "I'se got white-gemman principles. I'se do my best. If Cap'n tell me to take a man, s'pose de man be as big as a house, I'll clam hold on him till I die, inception [excepting] I'm sick."

But it was plain that this feeling was a bequest of slavery, which military life would wear off. We impressed it upon them that they did not obey their officers because they were white, but because they were their officers, just as the Captain must obey me, and I the General; that we were all subject to military law, and protected by it in turn. Then we taught them to take pride in having good material for non-commissioned officers among themselves, and in obeying them. On my arrival there was one white first sergeant, and it was a question whether to appoint others. This I prevented, but left that one, hoping the men themselves would at last petition for his removal, which at length they did. He was at once detailed on other duty. The picturesqueness of the regiment suffered, for he was very tall and fair, and I liked to see him step forward in the centre when the line of first sergeants came together at dress-parade. But it was a help to discipline to eliminate the Saxon, for it recognized a principle.

Afterwards I had excellent battalion-drills without a single white officer, by way of experiment; putting each company under a sergeant, and going through the most difficult movements, such as division-columns and oblique-squares. And as to actual discipline, it is doing no injustice to the line-officers of the regiment to say that none of them received from the men more implicit obedience than Color-Sergeant Rivers. I should have tried to obtain commissions for him and several others before I left the regiment, had their literary education been sufficient; and such an attempt was finally made by Lieutenant-Colonel Trowbridge, my successor in immediate command, but it proved unsuccessful. It always seemed to me an insult to those brave men to have novices put over their heads, on the ground of color alone; and the men felt it the more keenly as they remained longer in service. There were more than seven hundred enlisted men in the regiment, when mustered out after more than three years' service. The ranks had been kept full by enlistment, but there were only fourteen line-officers instead of the full thirty. The men who should have filled those vacancies were doing duty as sergeants in the ranks.

In what respect were the colored troops a source of disappointment? To me in one respect only,—that of health. Their health improved, indeed, as they grew more familiar with military life; but I think that neither their physical nor moral temperament gave them that toughness, that obstinate purpose of living, which sustains the more materialistic Anglo-Saxon. They had not, to be sure, the same predominant diseases, suffering in the pulmonary, not in the digestive organs; but they suffered a good deal. They felt malaria less, but they were more easily choked by dust and made ill by dampness. On the other hand, they submitted more readily to sanitary measures than whites, and, with efficient officers, were more easily kept clean. They were injured throughout the army by an undue share of fatigue duty, which is not only exhausting but demoralizing to a soldier; by the unsuitableness of the rations, which gave them salt meat instead of rice and hominy; and by the lack of good medical attendance. Their childlike constitutions peculiarly needed prompt and efficient surgical care; but almost all the colored troops were enlisted late in the war, when it was hard to get good surgeons for any regiments, and especially for these. In this respect I had nothing to complain of, since there were no surgeons in the army for whom I would have exchanged my own.

And this late arrival on the scene affected not only the medical supervision of the colored troops, but their opportunity for a career. It is not my province to write their history, nor to vindicate them, nor to follow them upon those larger fields compared with which the adventures of my regiment appear but a partisan warfare. Yet this, at least, may be said. The operations on the South Atlantic coast, which long seemed a merely subordinate and incidental part of the great contest, proved to be one of the final pivots on which it turned. All now admit that the fate of the Confederacy was decided by Sherman's march to the sea. Port Royal was the objective point to which he marched, and he found the Department of the South, when he reached it, held almost exclusively by colored troops. Next to the merit of those who made the march was that of those who held open the door. That service will always remain among the laurels of the black regiments.

CHAPTER XIII

Conclusion

My personal forebodings proved to be correct, and so were the threats of the surgeons. In May, 1864, I went home invalided, was compelled to resign in October from the same cause, and never saw the First South Carolina again. Nor did any one else see it under that appellation, for about that time its name was changed to the Thirty-Third United States Colored Troops, "a most vague and heartless baptism,"[1] as the man in the story says. It was one of those instances of injudicious sacrifice of *esprit de corps* which were so frequent in our army. All the pride of my men was centred in "de Fus' Souf"; the very words were a recognition of the loyal South as against the disloyal. To make the matter worse, it had been originally designed to apply the new numbering only to the new regiments, and so the early numbers were all taken up before the older regiments came in. The governors of States, by especial effort, saved their colored troops from this chagrin; but we found here, as more than once before, the disadvantage of having no governor to stand by us. "It's a far cry to Loch Awe," said the Highland proverb. We knew to our cost that it was a far cry to Washington in those days, unless an officer left his duty and stayed there all the time.

In June, 1864, the regiment was ordered to Folly Island, and remained there and on Cole's Island till the siege of Charleston was done. It took part in the battle of Honey Hill, and in the capture of a fort on James Island, of which Corporal Robert Vendross wrote triumphantly in a letter, "When we took the pieces we found that we recapt our own pieces back that we lost on Willtown Revear (River) and thank the Lord did not lose but seven men out of our regiment."

In February, 1865, the regiment was ordered to Charleston to do provost and guard duty, in March to Savannah, in June to Hamburg and Aiken, in September to Charleston and its neighborhood, and was finally mustered out of service—after being detained beyond its three years, so great was the scarcity of troops—on the 9th of February, 1866. With dramatic fitness this muster-out took place at Fort Wagner, above the graves of Shaw and his men. I give in the Appendix the farewell address of Lieutenant-Colonel Trowbridge, who commanded the regiment from the time I left it. Brevet Brigadier-General W. T. Bennett, of the One Hundred and Second United States Colored Troops, who was assigned to the command, never actually held it, being always in charge of a brigade.

The officers and men are scattered far and wide. One of our captains was a member of the South Carolina Constitutional Convention, and is now State Treasurer; three of our sergeants were in that Convention, including Sergeant Prince Rivers; and he and Sergeant Henry Hayne are still members of the State Legislature. Both in that State and in Florida the former members of the regiment are generally prospering, so far as I can hear. The increased self-respect of army life fitted them to do the duties of civil life. It is not in nature that the jealousy of race should die out in this generation, but I trust they will not see the fulfilment of Corporal Simon Crum's prediction. Simon was one of the shrewdest old fellows in the regiment, and he said to me once, as he was jogging out of Beaufort behind me, on the Shell Road, "I'se goin' to leave de Souf, Cunnel, when de war is over. I'se made up my mind dat dese yer Secesh will neber be cibilized in my time."

The only member of the regiment whom I have seen since leaving it is a young man, Cyrus Wiggins, who was brought off from the main-land in a dug-out, in broad day, before the very eyes of the rebel pickets, by Captain James S. Rogers, of my regiment. It was one of the most daring acts I ever saw, and as it happened under my own observation I was glad when the Captain took home with him this "captive of his bow and spear" to be educated under his eye in Massachusetts. Cyrus has done credit to his friends, and will be satisfied with nothing short of a college-training at Howard University. I have letters from the men, very quaint in handwriting and spelling; but he is the only one whom I have seen. Some time I hope to revisit those scenes, and shall feel, no doubt, like a bewildered Rip Van Winkle who once wore uniform.

We who served with the black troops have this peculiar satisfaction, that, whatever dignity or sacredness the memories of the war may have to others, they have more to us. In that contest all the ordinary ties of patriotism were the same, of course, to us as to the rest; they had no motives which we had not, as they have now no memories which are not also ours. But the peculiar privilege of associating with an outcast race, of training it to defend its rights, and to perform its duties, this was our especial meed. The vacillating policy of the Government sometimes filled other officers with doubt and shame; until the negro had justice, they were but defending liberty with one hand and crushing it with the other. From this inconsistency we were free. Whatever the Government did, we at least were working in the right direction. If this was not recognized on our side of the lines, we knew that it was admitted on the other. Fighting with ropes round our necks, denied the ordinary courtesies of war till we ourselves compelled their concession, we could at least turn this outlawry into a compliment. We had touched the pivot of the war. Whether this vast and dusky mass should prove the weakness of the nation or its strength, must depend in great measure, we knew, upon our efforts. Till the blacks were armed, there was no guaranty of their freedom. It was their demeanor under arms that shamed the nation into recognizing them as men.

Appendix

APPENDIX A

Roster of Officers

FIRST SOUTH CAROLINA VOLUNTEERS,
Afterwards Thirty-Third United States Colored Troops.

Colonels

T. W. HIGGINSON, 51st Mass. Vols., Nov. 10, 1862; Resigned, Oct. 27, 1864.

WM. T. BENNETT, 102d U. S. C. T., Dec. 18, 1864; Mustered out with regiment.

Lieutenant-Colonels

LIBERTY BILLINGS, Civil Life, Nov. 1, 1862; Dismissed by Examining Board, July 28, 1863.

JOHN D. STRONG, Promotion, July 28, 1863; Resigned, Aug. 15, 1864.

CHAS. T. TROWBRIDGE, Promotion, Dec. 9, 1864; Mustered out, &c.

Majors

JOHN D. STRONG, Civil Life, Oct. 21, 1862; Lt.-Col., July 28, 1863.

CHAS. T. TROWBRIDGE, Promotion, Aug. 11, 1863; Lt.-Col., Dec. 9, 1864.

H. A. WHITNEY, Promotion, Dec. 9, 1864; Mustered out, &c.

Surgeons

SETH ROGERS, Civil Life, Dec. 2, 1862; Resigned, Dec. 21, 1863.

WM. B. CRANDALL, 29th Ct., June 8, 1864; Mustered out, &c.

Assistant Surgeons

J. M. HAWKS, Civil Life, Oct. 20, 1862; Surgeon 3d S. C. Vols., Oct. 29, 1863.

THOS. T. MINOR, 7th Ct., Jan. 8, 1863; Resigned, Nov. 21, 1864.

E. S. STUARD, Civil Life, Sept. 4, 1865; Mustered out, &c.

Chaplain

JAS. H. FOWLER, Civil Life, Oct. 24, 1862; Mustered out, &c.

Captains

CHAS. T. TROWBRIDGE, N. Y. Vol. Eng., Oct. 13, 1862; Major, Aug. 11, 1863.

WM. JAMES, 100th Pa., Oct. 13, 1862; Mustered out, &c.

W. J. RANDOLPH, 100th Pa., Oct. 13, 1862; Resigned, Jan. 29, 1864.

H. A. WHITNEY, 8th Me., Oct. 13, 1862; Major, Dec. 9, 1864.

ALEX. HEASLEY, 100th Pa., Oct. 13, 1862; Killed at Augusta, Ga., Sept. 6, 1865.

GEORGE DOLLY, 8th Me., Nov. 1, 1862; Resigned, Oct. 30, 1863.

L. W. METCALF, 8th Me., Nov. 11, 1862; Mustered out, &c.

JAS. H. TONKING, N. Y. Vol. Eng., Nov. 17, 1862; Resigned, July 28, 1863.

JAS. S. ROGERS, 51st Mass., Dec. 6, 1862; Resigned, Oct. 20, 1863.

J. H. THIBADEAU, Promotion, Jan. 10, 1863; Mustered out, &c.

GEORGE D. WALKER, Promotion, July 28, 1863; Resigned, Sept. 1, 1864.

WM. H. DANILSON, Promotion, July 28, 1863; Major 128th U. S. C. T., May, 1865 [Now 1st Lt. 40th U. S. Infantry].

WM. W. SAMPSON, Promotion, Nov. 5, 1863; Mustered out, &c.

JOHN M. THOMPSON, Promotion, Nov. 7, 1863; Mustered out, &c. [Now 1st Lt. and Bvt. Capt. 38th U. S. Inf'y].

ABR. W. JACKSON, Promotion, April 30, 1864; Resigned, Aug. 15, 1865.

NILES G. PARKER, Promotion, Feb., 1865; Mustered out, &c.

CHAS. W. HOOPER, Promotion, Sept., 1865; Mustered out, &c.

E. C. MERRIAM, Promotion, Sept., 1865; Resigned, Dec. 4, 1865.

E. W. ROBBINS, Promotion, Nov. 1, 1865; Mustered out, &c.

N. S. WHITE, Promotion, Nov. 18, 1865; Mustered out, &c.

First Lieutenants

G. W. DEWHURST (Adjutant), Civil Life, Oct. 20, 1862; Resigned, Aug. 31, 1865.

J. M. BINGHAM (Quartermaster), Civil Life, Oct. 20, 1862; Died from effect of exhaustion on a military expedition, July 20, 1863.

G. M. CHAMBERLIN (Quartermaster), 11th Mass. Battery, Aug. 29, 1863; Mustered out, &c.

GEO. D. WALKER, N. Y. Vol. Eng., Oct. 13, 1862; Captain, Aug. 11, 1863.

W. H. DANILSON, 48th N. Y., Oct. 18, 1862; Captain, July 26, 1863.

J. H. THIBADEAU, 8th Me., Oct. 18, 1862; Captain, Jan. 10, 1863.

EPHRAIM P. WHITE, 8th Me., Nov. 14, 1862; Resigned, March 9, 1864.

JAS. POMEROY, 100th Pa., Oct. 13, 1862; Resigned, Feb. 9, 1863.

JAS. F. JOHNSTON, 100th Pa., Oct. 13, 1862; Resigned, March 26, 1863.

JESSE FISHER, 48th N. Y., Oct. 13, 1862; Resigned, Jan. 26, 1863.

CHAS. I. DAVIS, 8th Me., Oct. 13, 1862; Resigned, Feb. 28, 1863.

WM. STOCKDALE, 8th Me., Oct. 13, 1862; Resigned, May 2, 1863.

JAS. B. O'NEIL, Promotion, Jan. 10, 1863; Resigned, May 2, 1863.

W. W. SAMPSON, Promotion, Jan. 10, 1863; Captain, Oct. 30, 1863.

J. M. THOMPSON, Promotion, Jan. 27, 1863; Captain, Oct. 30, 1863.

R. M. GASTON, Promotion, April 15, 1863; Killed at Coosaw Ferry, S. C., May 27, 1863.

JAS. B. WEST, Promotion, Feb. 28, 1863; Resigned, June 14, 1865.

N. G. PARKER, Promotion, May 5, 1863; Captain, Feb., 1865.

W. H. HYDE, Promotion, May 5, 1863; Resigned, April 3, 1865.

HENRY A. STONE, 8th Me., June 26, 1863; Resigned, Dec. 16, 1864.

J. A. TROWBRIDGE, Promotion, Aug. 11, 1863; Resigned, Nov. 29, 1864.

A. W. JACKSON, Promotion, Aug. 26, 1863; Captain, April 30, 1864.

CHAS. E. PARKER, Promotion, Aug. 26, 1863; Resigned, Nov. 29, 1864.

CHAS. W. HOOPER, Promotion, Nov. 8, 1863; Captain, Sept., 1865.

E. C. MERRIAM, Promotion, Nov. 19, 1863; Captain, Sept., 1865.

HENRY A. BEACH, Promotion, April 30, 1864; Resigned, Sept. 23, 1864.

E. W. ROBBINS, Promotion, April 30, 1864: Captain, Nov. 1, 1865.

ASA CHILD, Promotion, Sept., 1865; Mustered out, &c.

N. S. WHITE, Promotion, Sept., 1865; Captain, Nov. 18, 1865.

F. S. GOODRICH, Promotion, Oct., 1865; Mustered out, &c.

E. W. HYDE, Promotion, Oct. 27, 1865; Mustered out, &c.

HENRY WOOD, Promotion, Nov., 1865; Mustered out, &c.

Second Lieutenants

J. A. TROWBRIDGE, N. Y. Vol. Eng., Oct. 18, 1862; First Lt., Aug. 11, 1863.

JAS. B. O'NEIL, 1st U. S. Art'y, Oct. 13, 1862; First Lt., Jan. 10, 1863.

W. W. SAMPSON, 8th Me., Oct. 13, 1862; First Lt., Jan. 10, 1863.

J. M. THOMPSON, 7th N. H., Oct. 13, 1862; First Lt., Jan. 27, 1863.

R. M. GASTON, 100th Pa., Oct. 13, 1862; First Lt., April 15, 1863.

W. H. HYDE, 6th Ct., Oct. 13, 1862; First Lt., May 5, 1863.

JAS. B. WEST, 100th Pa., Oct. 13, 1862; First Lt., Feb. 28, 1863.

HARRY C. WEST, 100th Pa., Oct. 13, 1862; Resigned, Nov. 4, 1864.

E. C. MERRIAM, 8th Me., Nov. 17, 1862; First Lt., Nov. 19, 1863.

CHAS. E. PARKER, 8th Me., Nov. 17, 1862; First Lt., Aug. 26, 1863.

C. W. HOOPER, N. Y. Vol. Eng., Feb. 17, 1863; First Lt., April 15, 1863.

N. G. PARKER, 1st Mass. Cavalry, March, 1863; First Lt., May 5, 1863.

A. H. TIRRELL, 1st Mass. Cav., March 6, 1863; Resigned, July 22, 1863.

A. W. JACKSON, 8th Me., March 6, 1863; First Lt., Aug. 26, 1863.

HENRY A. BEACH, 48th N. Y., April 5, 1863; First Lt., April 30, 1864.

E. W. ROBBINS, 8th Me., April 5, 1863; First Lt., April 30, 1864.

A. B. BROWN, Civil Life, April 17, 1863; Resigned, Nov. 27, 1863.

F. M. GOULD, 3d R. I. Battery, June 1, 1863; Resigned, June 8, 1864.

ASA CHILD, 8th Me., Aug. 7, 1863; First Lt., Sept., 1865.

JEROME T. FURMAN, 52d Pa., Aug. 30, 1863; Killed at Walhalla, S. C., Aug. 26, 1865.

JOHN W. SELVAGE, 48th N. Y., Sept. 10, 1863; First Lt. 36th U. S. C. T., March, 1865.

MIRAND W. SAXTON, Civil Life, Nov. 19, 1863; Captain 128th U. S. C. T., June 25, 1864 [now Second Lt. 38th U. S. Infantry].

NELSON S. WHITE, Dec. 22, 1863; First Lt., Sept., 1865.

EDW. W. HYDE, Civil Life, May 4, 1864; First Lt., Oct. 27, 1865.

F. S. GOODRICH, 115th N. Y., May, 1864; First Lt., Oct., 1865.

B. H. MANNING, Aug. 11, 1864; Capt. 128th U. S. C. T., March 17, 1865.

R. M. DAVIS, 4th Mass. Cavalry, Nov. 19, 1864; Capt. 104th U. S. C. T., May 11, 1865.

HENRY WOOD, N. Y. Vol. Eng., Aug., 1865; First Lt., Nov., 1865.

JOHN M. SEARLES, 1st N. Y. Mounted Rifles, June 15, 1865; Mustered out, &c.

APPENDIX B

The First Black Soldiers

It is well known that the first systematic attempt to organize colored troops during the war of the rebellion was the so-called "Hunter Regiment." The officer originally detailed to recruit for this purpose was Sergeant C. T. Trowbridge, of the New York Volunteer Engineers (Col. Serrell). His detail was dated May 7, 1862, S. O. 84 Dept. South.

Enlistments came in very slowly, and no wonder. The white officers and soldiers were generally opposed to the experiment, and filled the ears of the negroes with the same tales which had been told them by their masters,—that the Yankees really meant to sell them to Cuba, and the like. The mildest threats were that they would be made to work without pay (which turned out to be the case), and that they would be put in the front rank in every battle. Nobody could assure them that they and their families would be freed by the Government, if they fought for it, since no such policy had been adopted. Nevertheless, they gradually enlisted, the most efficient recruiting officer being Sergeant William Bronson, of Company A, in my regiment, who always prided himself on this service, and used to sign himself by the very original title, "No. 1, African Foundations" in commemoration of his deeds.

By patience and tact these obstacles would in time have been overcome. But before long, unfortunately, some of General Hunter's staff became impatient, and induced him to take the position that the blacks *must* enlist. Accordingly, squads of soldiers were sent to seize all the able-bodied men on certain plantations, and bring them to the camp. The immediate consequence was a renewal of the old suspicion, ending in a wide-spread belief that they were to be sent to Cuba, as their masters had predicted. The ultimate result was a habit of distrust, discontent, and desertion, that it was almost impossible to surmount. All the men who knew anything about General Hunter believed in him; but they all knew that there were bad influences around him, and that the Government had repudiated his promises. They had been kept four months in service, and then had been dismissed without pay. That having been the case, why should not the Government equally repudiate General Saxton's promises or mine? As a matter of fact, the Government did repudiate these pledges for years, though we had its own written authority to give them. But that matter needs an appendix by itself.

The "Hunter Regiment" remained in camp on Hilton Head Island until the beginning of August, 1862, kept constantly under drill, but much demoralized by desertion. It was then disbanded except one company That company, under command of Sergeant Trowbridge, then acting as Captain, but not commissioned, was kept in service, and was sent (August 5, 1862) to garrison St. Simon's Island, on the coast of Georgia. On this island (made famous by Mrs. Kemble's description) there were then five hundred colored people, and not a single white man.

The black soldiers were sent down on the Ben De Ford, Captain Hallett. On arriving, Trowbridge was at once informed by Commodore Goldsborough, naval commander at that station, that there was a party of rebel guerillas on the island, and was asked whether he would trust his soldiers in pursuit of them. Trowbridge gladly assented; and the Commodore added, "If you should capture them, it will be a great thing for you."

They accordingly went on shore, and found that the colored men of the island had already undertaken the enterprise. Twenty-five of them had armed themselves, under the command of one of their own number, whose name was John Brown. The second in command was Edward Gould, who was afterwards a corporal in my own regiment. The rebel party retreated before these men, and drew them into a swamp. There was but one path, and the negroes entered single file. The rebels lay behind a great log, and fired upon them. John Brown, the leader, fell dead within six feet of the log,—probably the first black man who fell under arms in the war,—several others were wounded, and the band of raw recruits retreated; as did also the rebels, in the opposite direction. This was the first armed encounter, so far as I know, between the rebels and their former slaves; and it is worth noticing that the attempt was a spontaneous thing, and not accompanied by any white man. The men were not soldiers, nor in uniform, though some of them afterwards enlisted in Trowbridge's company.

The father of this John Brown was afterwards a soldier in my regiment; and, after his discharge for old age, was, for a time, my servant. "Uncle York," as we called him, was as good a specimen of a saint as I have ever met, and was quite the equal of Mrs. Stowe's "Uncle Tom." He was a fine-looking old man, with dignified and courtly manners, and his gray head was a perfect benediction, as he sat with us on the platform at our Sunday meetings. He fully believed, to his dying day, that the "John Brown Song" related to his son, and to him only.

Trowbridge, after landing on the island, hunted the rebels all day with his colored soldiers, and a posse of sailors. In one place, he found by a creek a canoe, with a tar-kettle, and a fire burning; and it was afterwards discovered that, at that very moment, the guerrillas were hid in a dense palmetto thicket, near by, and so eluded pursuit. The rebel leader was one Miles Hazard, who had a plantation on the island, and the party escaped at last through the aid of his old slave, Henry, who found them a boat. One of my sergeants, Clarence Kennon, who had not then escaped from slavery, was present when they reached the main-land; and he described them as being tattered and dirty from head to foot, after their efforts to escape their pursuers.

When the troops under my command occupied Jacksonville, Fla., in March of the following year, we found at the railroad station, packed for departure, a box of papers, some of them valuable. Among them was a letter from this very Hazard to some friend, describing the perils of that adventure, and saying, "If you wish to know hell before your time, go to St. Simon's and be hunted ten days by niggers."

I have heard Trowbridge say that not one of his men flinched; and they seemed to take delight in the pursuit, though the weather was very hot, and it was fearfully exhausting.

This was early in August; and the company remained two months at St. Simon's, doing picket duty within hearing of the rebel drums, though not another scout ever ventured on the island, to their knowledge. Every Saturday Trowbridge summoned the island people to drill with his soldiers: and they came in hordes, men, women, and children, in every imaginable garb, to the number of one hundred and fifty or two hundred.

His own men were poorly clothed and hardly shod at all; and, as no new supply of uniform was provided, they grew more and more ragged. They got poor rations, and no pay; but they kept up their spirits. Every week or so some of them would go on scouting excursions to the main-land; one scout used to go regularly to his old mother's hut, and keep himself hid under her bed, while she collected for him all the latest news of rebel movements. This man never came back without bringing recruits with him.

At last the news came that Major-General Mitchell had come to relieve General Hunter, and that Brigadier-General Saxton had gone North; and Trowbridge went to Hilton Head in some anxiety to see if he and his men were utterly forgotten. He prepared a report, showing the services and claims of his men, and took it with him. This was early in October, 1862. The first person he met was Brigadier-General Saxton, who informed him that he had authority to organize five thousand colored troops, and that he (Trowbridge) should be senior captain of the first regiment.

This was accordingly done; and Company A of the First South Carolina could honestly claim to date its enlistment back to May, 1862, although they never got pay for that period of their service, and their date of muster was November 15, 1862.

The above facts were written down from the narration of Lieutenant-Colonel Trowbridge, who may justly claim to have been the first white officer to recruit and command colored troops in this war. He was constantly in command of them from May 9, 1862, to February 9, 1866.

Except the Louisiana soldiers mentioned in the Introduction, —of whom no detailed reports have, I think, been published,— my regiment was unquestionably the first mustered into the service of the United States; the first company muster bearing date, November 7, 1862, and the others following in quick succession.

The second regiment in order of muster was the "First Kansas Colored," dating from January 13, 1863. The first enlistment in the Kansas regiment goes back to August 6, 1862; while the earliest technical date of enlistment in my regiment was October 19, 1862, although, as was stated above, one company really dated its organization back to May, 1862. My muster as colonel dates back to November 10, 1862, several months earlier than any other of which I am aware, among colored regiments, except that of Colonel Stafford (First Louisiana Native Guards), September 27, 1862. Colonel Williams, of the "First Kansas Colored," was mustered as lieutenant-colonel on January 13, 1863; as colonel, March 8, 1863. These dates I have (with the other facts relating to the regiment) from Colonel R. J. Hinton, the first officer detailed to recruit it.

To sum up the above facts: my late regiment had unquestioned priority in muster over all but the Louisiana regiments. It had priority over those in the actual organization and term of service of one company. On the other hand, the Kansas regiment had the priority in average date of enlistment, according to the muster-rolls.

The first detachment of the Second South Carolina Volunteers (Colonel Montgomery) went into camp at Port Royal Island, February 23, 1863, numbering one hundred and twenty men. I do not know the date of his muster; it was somewhat delayed, but was probably dated back to about that time.

Recruiting for the Fifty-Fourth Massachusetts (colored) began on February 9, 1863, and the first squad went into camp at Readville, Massachusetts, on February 21, 1863, numbering twenty-five men. Colonel Shaw's commission (and probably his muster) was dated April 17, 1863. (Report of Adjutant-General of Massachusetts for 1863, pp. 896–899.)

These were the earliest colored regiments, so far as I know.

APPENDIX C

General Saxton's Instructions

[THE following are the instructions under which my regiment was raised. It will be seen how unequivocal were the provisions in respect to pay, upon which so long and weary a contest was waged by our friends in Congress, before the fulfilment of the contract could be secured.]

WAR DEPARTMENT, WASHINGTON CITY, D. C.,
August 25, 1862.

GENERAL,—Your despatch of the 16th has this moment been received. It is considered by the Department that the instructions given at the time of your appointment were sufficient to enable you to do what you have now requested authority for doing. But in order to place your authority beyond all doubt, you are hereby authorized and instructed,

1st, To organize in any convenient organization, by squads, companies, battalions, regiments, and brigades, or otherwise, colored persons of African descent for volunteer laborers, to a number not exceeding fifty thousand, and muster them into the service of the United States for the term of the war, at a rate of compensation not exceeding five dollars per month for common laborers, and eight dollars per month for mechanical or skilled laborers, and assign them to the Quartermaster's Department, to do and perform such laborer's duty as may be required during the present war, and to be subject to the rules and articles of war.

2d The laboring forces herein authorized shall, under the order of the General-in-Chief, or of this Department, be detailed by the Quartermaster-General for laboring service with the armies of the United States; and they shall be clothed and subsisted, after enrollment, in the same manner as other persons in the Quartermaster's service.

3d. In view of the small force under your command, and the inability of the Government at the present time to increase it, in order to guard the plantations and settlements occupied by the United States from invasion, and protect the inhabitants thereof from captivity and murder by the enemy, you are also authorized to arm, uniform, equip, and receive into the service of the United

States, such number of volunteers of African descent as you may deem expedient, not exceeding five thousand, and may detail officers to instruct them in military drill, discipline, and duty, and to command them. The persons so received into service, and their officers, to be entitled to, and receive, the same pay and rations as are allowed, by law, to volunteers in the service.

4th. You will occupy, if possible, all the islands and plantations heretofore occupied by the Government, and secure and harvest the crops, and cultivate and improve the plantations.

5th. The population of African descent that cultivate the lands and perform the labor of the rebels constitute a large share of their military strength, and enable the white masters to fill the rebel armies, and wage a cruel and murderous war against the people of the Northern States. By reducing the laboring strength of the rebels, their military power will be reduced. You are therefore authorized by every means in your power, to withdraw from the enemy their laboring force and population, and to spare no effort, consistent with civilized warfare, to weaken, harass, and annoy them, and to establish the authority of the Government of the United States within your Department.

6th. You may turn over to the navy any number of colored volunteers that may be required for the naval service.

7th. By recent act of Congress, all men and boys received into the service of the United States, who may have been the slaves of rebel masters, are, with their wives, mothers, and children, declared to be forever free. You and all in your command will so treat and regard them.

Yours truly,
EDWIN M. STANTON,
Secretary of War.

Brigadier-General Saxton.

APPENDIX D

The Struggle for Pay

The story of the attempt to cut down the pay of the colored troops is too long, too complicated, and too humiliating, to be here narrated. In the case of my regiment there stood on record the direct pledge of the War Department to General Saxton that their pay should be the same as that of whites. So clear was this that our kind paymaster, Major W. J. Wood, of New Jersey, took upon himself the responsibility of paying the price agreed upon, for five months, till he was compelled by express orders to reduce it from thirteen dollars per month to ten dollars, and from that to seven dollars,—the pay of quartermaster's men and day-laborers. At the same time the "stoppages" from the pay-rolls for the loss of all equipments and articles of clothing remained the same as for all other soldiers, so that it placed the men in the most painful and humiliating condition. Many of them had families to provide for, and between the actual distress, the sense of wrong, the taunts of those who had refused to enlist from the fear of being cheated, and the doubt how much farther the cheat might be carried, the poor fellows were goaded to the utmost. In the Third South Carolina regiment, Sergeant William Walker was shot, by order of court-martial, for leading his company to stack arms before their captain's tent, on the avowed ground that they were released from duty by the refusal of the Government to fulfil its share of the contract. The fear of such tragedies spread a cloud of solicitude over every camp of colored soldiers for more than a year, and the following series of letters will show through what wearisome labors the final triumph of justice was secured. In these labors the chief credit must be given to my admirable Adjutant, Lieutenant G. W. Dewhurst. In the matter of bounty justice is not yet obtained; there is a discrimination against those colored soldiers who were slaves on April 19, 1861. Every officer, who through indolence or benevolent design claimed on his muster-rolls that all his men had been free on that day, secured for them the bounty; while every officer who, like myself, obeyed orders and told the truth in each case, saw his men and their families suffer for it, as I have done. A bill to abolish this distinction was introduced by Mr. Wilson at the last session, but failed to pass the House. It is hoped that next winter may remove this last vestige of the weary contest.

To show how persistently and for how long a period these claims had to be urged on Congress, I reprint such of my own printed letters on the subject as are now in my possession. There are one or two of which I have no copies. It was especially in the

Senate that it was so difficult to get justice done; and our thanks will always be especially due to Hon. Charles Sumner and Hon. Henry Wilson for their advocacy of our simple rights. The records of those sessions will show who advocated the fraud.

To the Editor of the New York Tribune:

SIR,—No one can overstate the intense anxiety with which the officers of colored regiments in this Department are awaiting action from Congress in regard to arrears of pay of their men.

It is not a matter of dollars and cents only; it is a question of common honesty,—whether the United States Government has sufficient integrity for the fulfilment of an explicit business contract.

The public seems to suppose that all required justice will be done by the passage of a bill equalizing the pay of all soldiers for the future. But, so far as my own regiment is concerned, this is but half the question. My men have been nearly sixteen months in the service, and for them the immediate issue is the question of arrears.

They understand the matter thoroughly, if the public do not. Every one of them knows that he volunteered under an explicit *written assurance* from the War Department that he should have the pay of a white soldier. He knows that for five months the regiment received that pay, after which it was cut down from the promised thirteen dollars per month to ten dollars, for some reason to him inscrutable.

He does *not* know—for I have not yet dared to tell the men —that the Paymaster has been already reproved by the Pay Department for fulfilling even in part the pledges of the War Department; that at the next payment the ten dollars are to be further reduced to seven; and that, to crown the whole, all the previous overpay is to be again deducted or "stopped" from the future wages, thus leaving them a little more than a dollar a month for six months to come, unless Congress interfere!

Yet so clear were the terms of the contract that Mr. Solicitor Whiting, having examined the original instructions from the War Department issued to Brigadier-General Saxton, Military Governor, admits to me (under date of December 4, 1863,) that "the faith of the Government was thereby pledged to every officer and soldier enlisted under that call."

He goes on to express the generous confidence that "the pledge will be honorably fulfilled." I observe that every one at the North seems to feel the same confidence, but that, meanwhile, the pledge is unfulfilled. Nothing is said in Congress about fulfilling it. I have not seen even a proposition in Congress to pay the colored soldiers, *from date of enlistment*, the same pay with white soldiers; and yet anything short of that is an unequivocal breach of contract, so far as this regiment is concerned.

Meanwhile, the land sales are beginning, and there is danger of every foot of land being sold from beneath my soldiers' feet, because they have not the petty sum which Government first promised, and then refused to pay.

The officers' pay comes promptly and fully enough, and this makes the position more embarrassing. For how are we to explain to the men the mystery that Government can afford us a hundred or two dollars a month, and yet must keep back six of the poor thirteen which it promised them? Does it not naturally suggest the most cruel suspicions in regard to us? And yet nothing but their childlike faith in their officers, and in that incarnate soul of honor, General Saxton, has sustained their faith, or kept them patient, thus far.

There is nothing mean or mercenary about these men in general. Convince them that the Government actually needs their money, and they would serve it barefooted and on half-rations, and without a dollar—for a time. But, unfortunately, they see white soldiers beside them, whom they know to be in no way their superiors for any military service, receiving hundreds of dollars for re-enlisting from this impoverished Government, which can only pay seven dollars out of thirteen to its black regiments. And they see, on the other hand, those colored men who refused to volunteer as soldiers, and who have found more honest paymasters than the United States Government, now exulting in well-filled pockets, and able to buy the little homesteads the soldiers need, and to turn the soldiers' families into the streets. Is this a school for self-sacrificing patriotism?

I should not speak thus urgently were it not becoming manifest that there is to be no promptness of action in Congress, even as regards the future pay of colored soldiers,—and that there is especial danger of the whole matter of *arrears* going by default. Should it be so, it will be a repudiation more ungenerous than any which Jefferson Davis advocated or Sydney Smith denounced.[1] It will sully with dishonor all the nobleness of this opening page of history, and fix upon the North a brand of meanness worse than either Southerner or Englishman has yet dared to impute. The mere delay in the fulfilment of this contract has already inflicted untold suffering, has impaired discipline, has relaxed loyalty, and has begun to implant a feeling of sullen distrust in the very regiments whose early career solved the problem of the nation, created a new army and made peaceful emancipation possible.

T. W. HIGGINSON,
Colonel commanding 1st S. C. Vols.
BEAUFORT, S. C., January 22, 1864.

HEADQUARTERS FIRST SOUTH CAROLINA VOLUNTEERS.
BEAUFORT, S. C., Sunday, February 14, 1864.
To the Editor of the New York Times:

May I venture to call your attention to the great and cruel injustice which is impending over the brave men of this regiment?

They have been in military service for over a year, having volunteered, every man, without a cent of bounty, on the written pledge of the War Department that they should receive the same pay and rations with white soldiers.

This pledge is contained in the written instructions of Brigadier-General Saxton, Military Governor, dated August 25, 1862. Mr. Solicitor Whiting, having examined those instructions, admits to me that "the faith of the Government was thereby pledged to every officer and soldier under that call."

Surely, if this fact were understood, every man in the nation would see that the Government is degraded by using for a year the services of the brave soldiers, and then repudiating the contract under which they were enlisted. This is what will be done, should Mr. Wilson's bill, legalizing the back pay of the army, be defeated.

We presume too much on the supposed ignorance of these

men. I have never yet found a man in my regiment so stupid as not to know when he was cheated. If fraud proceeds from Government itself, so much the worse, for this strikes at the foundation of all rectitude, all honor, all obligation.

Mr. Senator Fessenden said, in the debate on Mr. Wilson's bill, January 4, that the Government was not bound by the unauthorized promises of irresponsible recruiting officers. But is the Government itself an irresponsible recruiting officer? and if men have volunteered in good faith on the written assurances of the Secretary of War, is not Congress bound, in all decency, either to fulfil those pledges or to disband the regiments?

Mr. Senator Doolittle argued in the same debate that white soldiers should receive higher pay than black ones, because the families of the latter were often supported by Government. What an astounding statement of fact is this! In the white regiment in which I was formerly an officer (the Massachusetts Fifty-First) nine tenths of the soldiers' families, in addition to the pay and bounties, drew regularly their "State aid." Among my black soldiers, with half-pay and no bounty, not a family receives any aid. Is there to be no limit, no end to the injustice we heap upon this unfortunate people? Cannot even the fact of their being in arms for the nation, liable to die any day in its defence, secure them ordinary justice? Is the nation so poor, and so utterly demoralized by its pauperism, that after it has had the lives of these men, it must turn round to filch six dollars of the monthly pay which the Secretary of War promised to their widows? It is even so, if the excuses of Mr. Fessenden and Mr. Doolittle are to be accepted by Congress and by the people.

Very respectfully, your obedient servant,

T. W. HIGGINSON,
Colonel commanding 1st S. C. Volunteers.

New Victories and Old Wrongs

To the Editors of the Evening Post:

On the 2d of July, at James Island, S. C., a battery was taken by three regiments, under the following circumstances:

The regiments were the One Hundred and Third New York (white), the Thirty-Third United States (formerly First South Carolina Volunteers), and the Fifty-Fifth Massachusetts, the two last being colored. They marched at one A. M., by the flank, in the above order, hoping to surprise the battery. As usual the rebels were prepared for them, and opened upon them as they were deep in one of those almost impassable Southern marshes. The One Hundred and Third New York, which had previously been in twenty battles, was thrown into confusion; the Thirty-Third United States did better, being behind; the Fifty-Fifth Massachusetts being in the rear, did better still. All three formed in line, when Colonel Hartwell, commanding the brigade, gave the order to retreat. The officer commanding the Fifty-Fifth Massachusetts, either misunderstanding the order, or hearing it countermanded, ordered his regiment to charge. This order was at once repeated by Major Trowbridge, commanding the Thirty-Third United States, and by the commander of the One Hundred and Third New York, so that the three regiments reached the fort in reversed order. The color-bearers of the Thirty-Third United States and of the Fifty-Fifth Massachusetts had a race to be first in, the latter winning. The One Hundred and Third New York entered the battery immediately after.

These colored regiments are two of the five which were enlisted in South Carolina and Massachusetts, under the written pledge of the War Department that they should have the same pay and allowances as white soldiers. That pledge has been deliberately broken by the War Department, or by Congress, or by both, except as to the short period, since last New-Year's Day. Every one of those killed in this action from these two colored regiments— under a fire before which the veterans of twenty battles recoiled —*died defrauded by the Government of nearly one half his petty pay.*

Mr. Fessenden, who defeated in the Senate the bill for the fulfilment of the contract with these soldiers, is now Secretary of the Treasury. Was the economy of saving six dollars per man worth to the Treasury the ignominy of the repudiation?

Mr. Stevens, of Pennsylvania, on his triumphal return to his constituents, used to them this language: "He had no doubt whatever as to the final result of the present contest between liberty and slavery. The only doubt he had was whether the nation had yet been satisfactorily chastised for their cruel oppression of a harmless and long-suffering race." Inasmuch as it was Mr. Stevens himself who induced the House of Representatives, most unexpectedly to all, to defeat the Senate bill for the fulfilment of the national contract with these soldiers, I should think he had excellent reasons for the doubt.

Very respectfully,
T. W. HIGGINSON,
Colonel 1st S. C. Vols. (now 33d U. S.)
July 10, 1864.

To the Editor of the New York Tribune:

No one can possibly be so weary of reading of the wrongs done by Government toward the colored soldiers as am I of writing about them. This is my only excuse for intruding on your columns again.

By an order of the War Department, dated August 1, 1864, it is at length ruled that colored soldiers shall be paid the full pay of soldiers from date of enlistment, provided they were free on April 19, 1861,—not otherwise; and this distinction is to be noted on the pay-rolls. In other words, if one half of a company escaped from slavery on April 18, 1861, they are to be paid thirteen dollars per month and allowed three dollars and a half per month for clothing. If the other half were delayed two days, they receive seven dollars per month and are allowed three dollars per month for precisely the same articles of clothing. If one of the former class is made first sergeant, his pay is put up to twenty-one dollars per month; but if he escaped two days later, his pay is still estimated at seven dollars.

It had not occurred to me that anything could make the pay-rolls of these regiments more complicated than at present, or the men more rationally discontented. I had not the ingenuity to imagine such an order. Yet it is no doubt in accordance with the spirit, if not with the letter, of the final bill which was adopted by Congress under the lead of Mr. Thaddeus Stevens.

The ground taken by Mr. Stevens apparently was that the country might honorably save a few dollars by docking the promised pay of those colored soldiers whom the war had made free. *But the Government should have thought of this before it made the contract with these men and received their services.* When the War Department instructed Brigadier-General Saxton, August 25,

1862, to raise five regiments of negroes in South Carolina, it was known very well that the men so enlisted had only recently gained their freedom. But the instructions said: "The persons so received into service, and their officers, to be entitled to and receive the same pay and rations as are allowed by law to volunteers in the service." Of this passage Mr. Solicitor Whiting wrote to me: "I have no hesitation in saying that the faith of the Government was thereby pledged to every officer and soldier enlisted under that call." Where is that faith of the Government now?

The men who enlisted under the pledge were volunteers, every one; they did not get their freedom by enlisting; they had it already. They enlisted to serve the Government, trusting in its honor. Now the nation turns upon them and says: Your part of the contract is fulfilled; we have had your services. If you can show that you had previously been free for a certain length of time, we will fulfil the other side of the contract. If not, we repudiate it. Help yourselves, if you can.

In other words, a freedman (since April 19, 1861) has no rights which a white man is bound to respect. He is incapable of making a contract. No man is bound by a contract made with him. Any employer, following the example of the United States Government, may make with him a written agreement, receive his services, and then withhold the wages. He has no motive to honest industry, or to honesty of any kind. He is virtually a slave, and nothing else, to the end of time.

Under this order, the greater part of the Massachusetts colored regiments will get their pay at last, and be able to take their wives and children out of the almshouses, to which, as Governor Andrew informs us, the gracious charity of the nation has consigned so many. For so much I am grateful. But toward my regiment, which had been in service and under fire, months before a Northern colored soldier was recruited, the policy of repudiation has at last been officially adopted. There is no alternative for the officers of South Carolina regiments but to wait for another session of Congress, and meanwhile, if necessary, act as executioners for those soldiers who, like Sergeant Walker, refuse to fulfil their share of a contract where the Government has openly repudiated the other share. If a year's discussion, however, has at length secured the arrears of pay for the Northern colored regiments, possibly two years may secure it for the Southern.

T. W. HIGGINSON,
Colonel 1st S. C. Vols. (now 33d U. S.)
August 12, 1864.

Justice Not Done Yet

To the Editor of the New York Tribune:

SIR,—An impression seems to prevail in the newspapers that the lately published "opinion" of Attorney-General Bates (dated in July last) at length secures justice to the colored soldiers in respect to arrears of pay. This impression is a mistake.

That "opinion" does indeed show that there never was any excuse for refusing them justice; but it does not, of itself, secure justice to them.

It *logically* covers the whole ground, and was doubtless intended to do so; but *technically* it can only apply to those soldiers who were free at the commencement of the war. For it was only about these that the Attorney-General was officially consulted.

Under this decision the Northern colored regiments have already got their arrears of pay,—and those few members of the Southern regiments who were free on April 19, 1861. But in the South Carolina regiments this only increases the dissatisfaction among the remainder, who volunteered under the same pledge of full pay from the War Department, and who do not see how the question of their *status* at some antecedent period can affect an express contract. If, in 1862, they were free enough to make a bargain with, they were certainly free enough to claim its fulfilment.

The unfortunate decision of Mr. Solicitor Whiting, under which all our troubles arose, is indeed superseded by the reasoning of the Attorney-General. But unhappily that does not remedy the evil, which is already embodied in an Act of Congress, making the distinction between those who were and those who were not free on April 19, 1861.

The question is, whether those who were not free at the breaking out of the war are still to be defrauded, after the Attorney-General has shown that there is no excuse for defrauding them?

I call it defrauding, because it is not a question of abstract justice, but of the fulfilment of an express contract.

I have never met with a man, whatever might be his opinions as to the enlistment of colored soldiers, who did not admit that if they had volunteered under the direct pledge of full pay from the War Department, they were entitled to every cent of it. That these South Carolina regiments had such direct pledge is undoubted, for it still exists in writing, signed by the Secretary of War, and has never been disputed.

It is therefore the plain duty of Congress to repeal the law which discriminates between different classes of colored soldiers, or at least so to modify it as to secure the fulfilment of actual contracts. Until this is done the nation is still disgraced. The few thousand dollars in question are nothing compared with the absolute wrong done and the discredit it has brought, both here and in Europe, upon the national name.

T. W. HIGGINSON,
Late Col. 1st S. C. Vols. (now 3d U. S. C. T.)
NEWPORT, R. I., December 8, 1864.

Petition

"To the Honorable Senate and House of Representatives of the United States in Congress assembled:—

"The undersigned respectfully petitions for the repeal of so much of Section IV. of the Act of Congress making appropriations for the army and approved July 4, 1864, as makes a distinction, in respect of pay due, between those colored soldiers who were free on or before April 19, 1861, and those who were not free until a later date;

"Or at least that there may be such legislation as to secure the fulfilment of pledges of full pay from date of enlistment, made by direct authority of the War Department to the colored soldiers of South Carolina, on the faith of which pledges they enlisted.

"THOMAS WENTWORTH HIGGINSON,
Late Colonel 1st S. C. Vols. (now 33d U. S. C. Vols.)
"NEWPORT, R. I., December 9, 1864."

APPENDIX E

Farewell Address of Lt.-Col. Trowbridge

HEADQUARTERS 33D UNITED STATES COLORED TROOPS,
LATE 1ST SOUTH CAROLINA VOLUNTEERS,
MORRIS ISLAND, S. C.,
February 9, 1866.

GENERAL ORDERS, NO. 1.

COMRADES,—The hour is at hand when we must separate forever, and nothing can ever take from us the pride we feel, when we look back upon the history of the First South Carolina Volunteers,—the first black regiment that ever bore arms in defence of freedom on the continent of America.

On the ninth day of May, 1862, at which time there were nearly four millions of your race in a bondage sanctioned by the laws of the land, and protected by our flag,—on that day, in the face of floods of prejudice, that wellnigh deluged every avenue to manhood and true liberty, you came forth to do battle for your country and your kindred. For long and weary months without pay, or even the privilege of being recognized as soldiers, you labored on, only to be disbanded and sent to your homes, without even a hope of reward. And when our country, necessitated by the deadly struggle with armed traitors, finally granted you the opportunity *again* to come forth in defence of the nation's life, the alacrity with which you responded to the call gave abundant evidence of your readiness to strike a manly blow for the liberty of your race. And from that little band of hopeful, trusting, and brave men, who gathered at Camp Saxton, on Port Royal Island, in the fall of 1862, amidst the terrible prejudices that then surrounded us, has grown an army of a hundred and forty thousand black soldiers, whose valor and heroism has won for your race a name which will live as long as the undying pages of history shall endure; and by whose efforts, united with those of the white man, armed rebellion has been conquered, the millions of bondmen have been emancipated, and the fundamental law of the land has been so altered as to remove forever the possibility of human slavery being re-established within the borders of redeemed America. The flag of our fathers, restored to its rightful significance, now floats over every foot of our territory, from Maine to

California, and beholds only freemen! The prejudices which formerly existed against you are wellnigh rooted out.

Soldiers, you have done your duty, and acquitted yourselves like men, who, actuated by such ennobling motives, could not fail; and as the result of your fidelity and obedience, you have won your freedom. And O, how great the reward!

It seems fitting to me that the last hours of our existence as a regiment should be passed amidst the unmarked graves of your comrades,—at Fort Wagner. Near you rest the bones of Colonel Shaw, buried by an enemy's hand, in the same grave with his black soldiers, who fell at his side; where, in future, your children's children will come on pilgrimages to do homage to the ashes of those that fell in this glorious struggle.

The flag which was presented to us by the Rev. George B. Cheever and his congregation, of New York City, on the first of January, 1863,—the day when Lincoln's immortal proclamation of freedom was given to the world,—and which you have borne so nobly through the war, is now to be rolled up forever, and deposited in our nation's capital. And while there it shall rest, with the battles in which you have participated inscribed upon its folds, it will be a source of pride to us all to remember that it has never been disgraced by a cowardly faltering in the hour of danger or polluted by a traitor's touch.

Now that you are to lay aside your arms, and return to the peaceful avocations of life, I adjure you, by the associations and history of the past, and the love you bear for your liberties, to harbor no feelings of hatred toward your former masters, but to seek in the paths of honesty, virtue, sobriety, and industry, and by a willing obedience to the laws of the land, to grow up to the full stature of American citizens. The church, the school-house, and the right forever to be free are now secured to you, and every prospect before you is full of hope and encouragement. The nation guarantees to you full protection and justice, and will require from you in return that respect for the laws and orderly deportment which will prove to every one your right to all the privileges of freemen.

To the officers of the regiment I would say, your toils are ended, your mission is fulfilled, and we separate forever. The fidelity, patience, and patriotism with which you have discharged your duties, to your men and to your country, entitle you to a far higher tribute than any words of thankfulness which I can give you from the bottom of my heart. You will find your reward in the proud conviction that the cause for which you have battled so nobly has been crowned with abundant success.

Officers and soldiers of the Thirty-Third United States Colored Troops, once the First South Carolina Volunteers, I bid you all farewell!

By order of Lt.-Col. C. T. Trowbridge, commanding Regiment.

E. W. HYDE,
Lieutenant and Acting Adjutant.

RELATED READINGS

A Visit to John Brown's Household in 1859[1]

THE traveler into the enchanted land of the Adirondacks has his choice of two routes from Keeseville to the Lower Saranac Lake, where his outdoor life is to begin. The one least frequented and most difficult should be selected, for it has the grandest mountain pass that the Northern States can show. After driving twenty-two miles of mountain road from Keeseville, past wild summits bristling with stumps, and through villages where every other man is black from the iron foundry, and every alternate one black from the charcoal pit, your pathway makes a turn at the little hamlet of Wilmington, and you soon find yourself facing a wall of mountain, with only glimpses of one wild gap, through which you must penetrate. In two miles more you have passed the last house this side the Notch, and you then drive on over a rugged way, constantly ascending, with no companion but the stream which ripples and roars below. Soon the last charcoal clearing is past, and thick woods of cedar and birch close around you: the high mountain on your right comes nearer and nearer, and close beside, upon your left, are glimpses of a wall, black and bare as iron, rising sheer for four hundred feet above your head. Coming from the soft marble country of Vermont, and from the pale granite of Massachusetts, there seems something weird and forbidding in this utter blackness. On your left the giant wall now appears nearer—now retreats again; on your right foams the merry stream, breaking into graceful cascades—and across it the great mountain Whiteface, seamed with slides. Now the woods upon your left are displaced by the wall, almost touching the roadside; against its steep abruptness scarcely a shrub can cling, scarcely a fern flutter—it takes your breath away; but five miles of perilous driving conduct you through it; and beyond this stern passway, this cave of iron, lie the lovely lakes and mountains of the Adirondacks, and the homestead of John Brown.

The Notch seems beyond the world, North Elba and its half-dozen houses are beyond the Notch, and there is a wilder little mountain road which rises beyond North Elba. But the house we seek is not even on that road, but behind it and beyond it; you ride a mile or two, then take down a pair of bars; beyond the bars, faith takes you across a half-cleared field, through the most difficult of wood paths, and after half a mile of forest you come out upon a clearing. There is a little frame house, unpainted, set in a girdle of black stumps, and with all heaven about it for a wider girdle; on a high hill-side, forests on north and west,—the glorious line of the Adirondacks on the east, and on the south one slender road leading off to Westport,—a road so straight that you could sight a United States marshal for five miles.

There stands the little house with no ornament or relief about it—it needs none with the setting of mountain horizon. Yes, there is one decoration which at once takes the eye, and which, stern and misplaced as it would seem elsewhere, seems appropriate here. It is a strange thing to see any thing so old, where all the works of man are new! but it is an old, mossy, time-worn tombstone— not marking any grave, not set in the ground, but resting against the house as if its time were either past or not yet come. Both are true—it has a past duty and a future one. It bears the name of Captain John Brown, who died during the Revolution, eighty-three years ago; it was brought hither by his grandson bearing the same name and title; the latter caused to be inscribed upon it, also, the name of his son Frederick, "murdered at Osawatomie for his adherence to the cause of freedom" (so reads the inscription); and he himself has said, for years, that no other tombstone should mark his own grave.

For two years, now, that stone has stood there. No oath has been taken upon it, no curses been invoked upon it. It marks the abode of a race who do not curse. But morning and noon, as the sons have gone out to their work on that upland farm, they have passed by it; the early light over the Adirondacks has gilded it, the red reflection of sunset has glowed back upon it; its silent appeal has perpetually strengthened and sanctified that home— and as the two lately wedded sons went forth joyfully on their father's call to keep their last pledge at Harper's Ferry, they issued from that doorway between their weeping wives on the one side and that ancestral stone upon the other.

The farm is a wild place, cold and bleak. It is too cold to raise corn there; they can scarcely, in the most favorable seasons, obtain a few ears for roasting. Stock must be wintered there nearly six months in every year. I was there on the first of November; the ground was snowy, and winter had apparently begun, and it would last till the middle of May. They never raise anything to sell off that farm, except sometimes a few fleeces. It was well, they said, if they raised their own provisions, and could spin their own wool for clothing.

Do you ask why they live in such a bleak spot? With John Brown and his family there is a reason for everything, and it is always the same reason. Strike into their lives anywhere, and you find the same firm purpose at bottom, and to the widest questioning the same prompt answer comes ringing back,—the very motto of the tombstone,—"For adherence to the cause of freedom." The same purpose, nay, the selfsame project that sent John Brown to Harper's Ferry sent him to the Adirondacks.

Twenty years ago John Brown made up his mind that there was an irrepressible conflict between freedom and slavery, and that in that conflict he must take his share. He saw at a glance, moreover, what the rest of us are only beginning to see, even now—that slavery must be met, first or last, on its own ground. The time has come to tell the whole truth now—that John Brown's whole Kansas life was the result of this self-imposed mission, not the cause of it. Let us do this man justice; he was not a vindictive guerrilla, nor a maddened Indian; nor was he of so shallow a nature that it took the death of a son to convince him that right was right, and wrong was wrong. He had long before made up his mind to sacrifice every son he ever had, if necessary, in fighting slavery. If it was John Brown against the world, no matter; for, as his friend Frederick Douglass had truly said, "In the right *one* is a majority." On this conviction, therefore, he deliberately determined, twenty years ago this summer, that at some future period he would organize an armed party, go into a slave State, and liberate a large number of slaves. Soon after, surveying professionally in the mountains of Virginia, he chose the very ground for his purpose. Visiting Europe afterwards, he studied military strategy for this purpose, even making designs (which I have seen) for a new style of forest fortification, simple and ingenious, to be used by parties of fugitive slaves when brought to bay. He knew the ground, he knew his plans, he knew himself; but where should he find his men? He came to the Adirondacks to look for them.

Ten years ago Gerrit Smith gave to a number of colored men tracts of ground in the Adirondack Mountains. The emigrants were grossly defrauded by a cheating surveyor, who, being in advance of his age, practically anticipated Judge Taney's[2] opinion, that black men have no rights which white men are bound to respect. By his villainy the colony was almost ruined in advance; nor did it ever recover itself; though some of the best farms which I have seen in that region are still in the hands of colored men. John Brown heard of this; he himself was a surveyor, and he would have gone to the Adirondacks, or anywhere else, merely to right this wrong. But he had another object—he thought that among these men he should find coadjutors in his cherished plan. He was not wholly wrong, and yet he afterwards learned something more. Such men as he needed are not to be found ordinarily; they must be reared. John Brown did not merely look for men, therefore; he reared them in his sons. During long years of waiting and postponement, he found others; but his sons and their friends (the Thompsons) formed the nucleus of his force in all his enterprises. What services the women of his family may have rendered it is not yet time to tell; but it is a satisfaction to think that he was repaid for his early friendship to these New York colored men by some valuable aid from freed slaves and fugitive slaves at Harper's Ferry; especially from Dangerfield Newby, who, poor fellow! had a slave wife and nine slave children to fight for, all within thirty miles of that town.

To appreciate the character of the family, it is necessary to know these things; to understand that they have all been trained from childhood on this one principle, and for this one special project; taught to believe in it as they believed in their God or their father. It has given them a wider perspective than the Adirondacks. Five years before, when they first went to Kansas, the father and sons had a plan of going to Louisiana, trying this same project, and then retreating into Texas with the liberated slaves. Nurtured on it so long, for years sacrificing to it all the other objects of life, the thought of its failure never crossed their minds;

and it is an extraordinary fact that when the disastrous news first came to North Elba, the family utterly refused to believe it and were saved from suffering by that incredulity till the arrival of the next weekly mail.

I had left the world outside, to raise the latch of this humble door amid the mountains; and now my pen falters on the threshold, as my steps did then. This house is a home of sacred sorrow. How shall we enter it? Its inmates are bereft and ruined men and women, as the world reckons; what can we say to them? Do not shrink; you are not near the world; you are near John Brown's household. "In the world ye shall have tribulation; but be of good cheer: they have overcome the world."

It had been my privilege to live in the best society all my life —namely, that of abolitionists and fugitive slaves. I had seen the most eminent persons of the age: several men on whose heads tens of thousands of dollars had been set; a black woman, who, after escaping from slavery herself, had gone back secretly eight times into the jaws of death to bring out persons whom she had never seen; and a white man, who, after assisting away fugitives by the thousand, had twice been stripped of every dollar of his property in fines, and, when taunted by the court, had mildly said, "Friend, if thee knows any poor fugitive in need of a breakfast, send him to Thomas Garrett's door." I had known these, and such as these; but I had not known the Browns. Nothing short of knowing them can be called a liberal education. Lord Byron could not help clinging to Shelley, because he said he was the only person in whom he saw anything like disinterested benevolence. He really believed that Shelley would give his life for another. Poor Byron! he might well have exchanged his wealth, his peerage, and his genius for a brief training at North Elba.

Let me pause a moment, and enumerate the members of the family. John Brown was born in 1800, and his wife in 1816, though both might have been supposed older than the ages thus indicated. He has had in all twenty children—seven being the offspring of his first wife, thirteen of his second. Four of each race are living—eight in all. The elder division of the surviving family comprises John and Jason, both married, and living in Ohio; Owen, unmarried, who escaped from Harper's Ferry, and Ruth, the wife of Henry Thompson, who lives on an adjoining farm at

North Elba, an intelligent and noble woman. The younger division consists of Salmon, aged twenty-three, who resides with his young wife in his mother's house, and three unmarried daughters, Anne (sixteen), Sarah (thirteen), and Ellen (five). In the same house dwell also the widows of the two slain sons—young girls, aged but sixteen and twenty. The latter is the sister of Henry Thompson, and of the two Thompsons who were killed at Harper's Ferry; they also lived in the same vicinity, and one of them also has left a widow. Thus complicated and intertangled is this genealogy of sorrow.

All these young men went deliberately from North Elba for no other purpose than to join in this enterprise. "They could not," they told their mother and their wives, "live for themselves alone;" and so they went. One young wife, less submissive than the others, prevailed on her husband to remain; and this is the only reason why Salmon Brown survives. Oliver Brown, the youngest son, only twenty, wrote back to his wife from Harper's Ferry in a sort of premonition of what was coming, "If I can do a single good action, my life will not have been all a failure."[3]

Having had the honor of Captain Brown's acquaintance for some years, I was admitted into the confidence of the family, though I could see them observing me somewhat suspiciously as I approached the door. Everything that was said of the absent father and husband bore testimony to the same simple, upright character. Though they had been much separated from him for the last few years, they all felt it to be a necessary absence, and had not only no complaint to make, but cordially approved it. Mrs. Brown had been always the sharer of his plans. "Her husband always believed," she said, "that he was to be an instrument in the hands of Providence," and she believed it too. "This plan had occupied his thoughts and prayers for twenty years." "Many a night he had lain awake, and prayed concerning it." "Even now," she did not doubt, "he felt satisfied because he thought it would be overruled by Providence for the best." "For herself," she said, "she had always prayed that her husband might be killed in fight rather than fall alive into the hands of slaveholders; but she could not regret it now, in view of the noble words of freedom which it had been his privilege to utter." When, the next day, on the railway, I was compelled to put into her hands the newspaper containing the death warrant of her husband, I felt no fears of her exposing herself to observation by any undue excitement. She read it, and then the tall, strong woman bent her head for a few minutes on the back of the seat before us; then she raised it, and spoke calmly as before.

I thought that I had learned the lesson once for all in Kansas, which no one ever learns from books of history alone, of the readiness with which danger and death fit into the ordinary grooves of daily life, so that on the day of a battle, for instance, all may go on as usual,—breakfast and dinner are provided, children cared for, and all external existence has the same smoothness that one observes at Niagara, just above the American Fall; but it impressed me anew on visiting this household at this time. Here was a family out of which four young men had within a fortnight been killed. I say nothing of a father under sentence of death, and a brother fleeing for his life, but only speak of those killed. Now that word "killed" is a word which one hardly cares to mention in a mourning household circle, even under all mitigating circumstances, when sad unavailing kisses and tender funeral rites have softened the last memories; how much less here, then, where it suggested not merely wounds and terror, and agony, but also coffinless graves in a hostile land, and the last ignominy of the dissecting-room.

Yet there was not one of that family who could not pronounce that awful word with perfect quietness; never, of course, lightly, but always quietly. For instance, as I sat that evening, with the women busily sewing around me, preparing the mother for her sudden departure with me on the morrow, some daguerreotypes were brought out to show me and some one said, "This is Oliver, one of those who were killed at Harper's Ferry." I glanced up sidelong at the young, fair-haired girl, who sat near me by the little table—a wife at fifteen, a widow at sixteen; and this was her husband, and he was killed. As the words were spoken in her hearing, not a muscle quivered, and her finger did not tremble as she drew the thread. Her life had become too real to leave room for wincing at mere words. She had lived through, beyond the word, to the sterner fact, and having confronted that, language

was an empty shell. To the Browns, killing means simply dying
—nothing more; one gate into heaven, and that one a good deal
frequented by their family; that is all.

There was no hardness about all this, no mere stoicism of will;
only God had inured them to the realities of things. They were
not supported by any notions of worldly honor or applause, nor
by that chilly reflection of it, the hope of future fame. In con-
versing with the different members of this family, I cannot recall
a single instance of any heroics of that description. There, in that
secluded home among the mountains, what have they to do with
the world's opinion, even now, still less next century? You
remember Carlyle and his Frenchman, to whom he was endeavoring to expound the Scottish Covenanters. "These poor, perse-
cuted people," said Carlyle,—"they made their appeal." "Yes,"
interrupted the Frenchman, "they appealed to posterity, no
doubt." "Not a bit of it," quoth Carlyle,—"they appealed to the
Eternal God!" So with these whom I visited. I was the first person
who had penetrated their solitude from the outer world since the
thunderbolt had fallen. Do not imagine that they asked, What is
the world saying of us? Will justice be done to the memory of
our martyrs? Will men build the tombs of the prophets? Will the
great thinkers of the age affirm that our father "makes the gallows
glorious like the cross?"[4] Not at all; they asked but one question
after I had told them how little hope there was of acquittal or
rescue. "Does it seem as if freedom were to gain or lose by this?"
That was all. Their mother spoke the spirit of them all to me, next
day, when she said, "I have had thirteen children, and only four
are left; but if I am to see the ruin of my house, I cannot but hope
that Providence may bring out of it some benefit to the poor
slaves."

No; this family works for a higher price than fame. You know
it is said that in all Wellington's dispatches you never meet with
the word Glory; it is always Duty. In Napoleon's you never meet
with the word Duty; it is always Glory. The race of John Brown
is of the Wellington type. Principle is the word I brought away
with me as most familiar in their vocabulary. That is their standard
of classification. A man may be brave, ardent, generous; no
matter—if he is not all this from principle, it is nothing. The
daughters, who knew all the Harper's Ferry men, had no confi-

dence in Cook because "he was not a man of principle." They
would trust Stevens round the world, because "he was a man of
principle." "He tries the hardest to be good," said Annie Brown,
in her simple way, "of any man I ever saw."

It is pleasant to add that this same brave-hearted girl, who had
known most of her father's associates, recognized them all but
Cook as being men of principle. "People are surprised," she said,
"at father's daring to invade Virginia with only twenty-three men;
but I think if they knew what sort of men they were, there would
be less surprise. I never saw such men."

And it pleases me to remember that since this visit, on the day
of execution, while our Worcester bells were tolling their melancholy refrain, I took from the post-office a letter from this same
young girl, expressing pity and sorrow for the recreant Cook, and
uttering the hope that allowances might be made for his conduct,
"though she could not justify it." And on the same day I read
that infuriated letter of Mrs. Mahala Doyle[5]—a letter which common charity bids us suppose a forgery, uttering fiendish revenge
in regard to a man against whom, by her own showing, there is
not one particle of evidence to identify him with her wrongs.
Nothing impressed me more in my visit to the Brown family, and
in subsequent correspondence with them, than the utter absence
of the slightest vindictive spirit, even in words.

The children spoke of their father as a person of absolute rectitude, thoughtful kindness, unfailing foresight, and inexhaustible
activity. On his flying visits to the farm, every moment was used;
he was "up at three A. M., seeing to everything himself," providing
for everything, and giving heed to the minutest points. It was
evident that some of the older ones had stood a little in awe of
him in their childish years. "We boys felt a little pleased sometimes, after all," said the son, "when father left the farm for a few
days." "We girls never did," said the married daughter, reproachfully, the tears gushing to her eyes. "Well," said the brother, re-
penting, "we were always glad to see the old man come back
again; for if we did get more holidays in his absence, we always
missed him."

Those dramatic points of character in him, which will of course
make him the favorite hero of all American romance hereafter, are
nowhere appreciated more fully than in his own family. In the

midst of all their sorrow, their strong and healthy hearts could enjoy the record of his conversations with the Virginians, and applaud the keen, wise, simple answers which I read to them, selecting here and there from the ample file of newspapers I carried with me. When, for instance, I read the inquiry, "Did you go out under the auspices of the Emigrant Aid Society?" and the answer, "No, sir; I went out under the auspices of John Brown," three voices eagerly burst in with, "That's true," and "That's so." And when it was related that the young Virginia volunteer taxed him with want of military foresight in bringing so small a party to conquer Virginia, and the veteran imperturbably informed the young man that probably their views on military matters would materially differ, there was a general delighted chorus of, "That sounds just like father." And his sublimer expressions of faith and self-devotion produced no excitement or surprise among them,— since they knew in advance all which we now know of him—and these things only elicited, at times, a half-stifled sigh as they reflected that they might never hear that beloved voice again.

References to their father were constant. This book he brought them; the one sitting-room had been plastered with the last money he sent; that desk, that gun, were his; this was his daguerreotype; and at last the rosy little Ellen brought me, with reverent hands, her prime treasure. It was a morocco case, inclosing a small Bible; and in the beginning, written in the plain, legible hand I knew so well, the following inscription, which would alone (in its touching simplicity) have been worthy the pilgrimage to North Elba to see.

This Bible, presented to my dearly beloved daughter Ellen Brown, is not intended for common use, but to be carefully preserved *for her* and *by her*, in remembrance of her father (of whose care and attentions she was deprived in her infancy), he being absent in the territory of Kansas from the summer of 1855.

May the Holy Spirit of God incline your heart, *in earliest childhood*, "to receive the truth in the love of it," and to form your thoughts, words, and actions by its wise and holy precepts, is *my best wish* and *most earnest* prayer to Him in whose care I leave you. Amen.

From your affectionate father,

JOHN BROWN.

April 2, 1857.

This is dated two years ago; but the principles which dictated it were permanent. Almost on the eve of his last battle, October 1, 1859, he wrote home to his daughter Anne, in a letter which I saw, "Anne, I want you first of all to become a sincere, humble, and consistent Christian, and then [this is characteristic], to acquire good and efficient business habits. Save this to remember your father by, Anne. God Almighty bless and save you all."

John Brown is almost the only radical abolitionist I have ever known who was not more or less radical in religious matters also. His theology was Puritan, like his practice; and accustomed as we now are to see Puritan doctrines and Puritan virtues separately exhibited, it seems quite strange to behold them combined in one person again. He and his wife were regular communicants of the Presbyterian church; but it tried his soul to see the juvenile clerical gentlemen who came into the pulpits up that way, and dared to call themselves Presbyterians—preachers of the gospel with all the hard applications left out. Since they had lived in North Elba, his wife said, but twice had the slave been mentioned in the Sunday services, and she had great doubts about the propriety of taking part in such worship as that. But when the head of the family made his visits home from Kansas, he commonly held a Sunday meeting in the little church, "under the auspices of John Brown," and the Lord heard the slave mentioned pretty freely then.

In speaking of religious opinions, Mrs. Brown mentioned two preachers whose sermons her sons liked to read, and "whose anti-slavery principles she enjoyed, though she could not agree with all their doctrines." She seemed to regard their positions as essentially the same. I need not say who the two are—the thunders of Brooklyn and of Boston acquire much the same sound as they roll up among the echoes of the Adirondacks.

In respect to politics, Mrs. Brown told me that her husband had taken little interest in them since the election of Jackson, because he thought that politics merely followed the condition of public sentiment on the slavery question, and that this public sentiment was mainly created by actual collisions between slavery and freedom. Such, at least, was the view which I was led to attribute to him, by combining this fact which she mentioned with my own personal knowledge of his opinions. He had an almost exaggerated aversion to words and speeches, and a profound conviction of the importance of bringing all questions to a direct issue, and subjecting every theory to the test of practical application.

I did not, of course, insult Mrs. Brown by any reference to that most shallow charge of insanity against her husband, which some even of his friends have, with what seems most cruel kindness, encouraged,—thereby doing their best to degrade one of the age's prime heroes into a mere monomaniac,—but it may be well to record that she spoke of it with surprise, and said that if her husband were insane, he had been consistent in his insanity from the first moment she knew him.

Now that all is over, and we appear to have decided, for the present, not to employ any carnal weapons, such as steel or iron, for the rescue of John Brown, but only to use the safer metals of gold and silver for the aid of his family, it may be natural for those who read this narrative to ask, What is the pecuniary condition[6] of this household? It is hard to answer, because the whole standard is different, as to such matters, in North Elba and in Massachusetts. The ordinary condition of the Brown family may be stated as follows: They own the farm, such as it is, without incumbrance, except so far as unfelled forest constitutes one. They have ordinarily enough to eat of what the farm yields, namely, bread and potatoes, pork and mutton—not any great abundance of these, but ordinarily enough. They have ordinarily enough to wear, at least of woolen clothing, spun by themselves. And they have absolutely no money. When I say this I do not merely mean that they have no superfluous cash to go shopping with, but I mean almost literally that they have none. For nearly a whole winter, Mrs. Brown said, they had no money with which to pay postage, except a tiny treasury which the younger girls had earned for that express object, during the previous summer, by picking berries for a neighbor three miles off.

The reason of these privations simply was, that it cost money to live in Kansas in "adherence to the cause of freedom" (see the tombstone inscription again), but not so much to live at North Elba; and therefore the women must stint themselves that the men might continue their Kansas work. When the father came upon his visits he never came empty-handed, but brought a little money, some plain household stores, flour, sugar, rice, salt fish; tea and coffee they do not use. But what their standard of expense is may be seen from the fact that Mrs. Brown seemed to speak as if her youngest widowed daughter were not totally and absolutely destitute, because her husband had left a property of five sheep, which would belong to her. These sheep, I found on inquiry, were worth, at that place and season, two dollars apiece: a child of sixteen, left a widow in the world, with an estate amounting to ten dollars! The immediate financial anxieties of Mrs. Brown herself seemed chiefly to relate to a certain formidable tax bill, due at New Year's time; if they could only weather that, all was clear for the immediate future. How much was it, I asked, rather surprised that that wild country should produce a high rate of taxation. It was from eight to ten dollars, she gravely said; and she had put by ten dollars for the purpose, but had had occasion to lend most of it to a poor black woman, with no great hope of repayment. And one of the first things done by her husband, on recovering his money in Virginia, was to send her, through me, fifteen dollars, to make sure of that tax bill.

I see, on looking back, how bare and inexpressive this hasty narrative is; but I could not bear to suffer such a privilege as this visit to pass away unrecorded. I spent but one night at the house, and drove away with Mrs. Brown, in the early frosty morning, from that breezy mountain home, which her husband loved (as one of them told me) "because he seemed to think there was something romantic in that kind of scenery." There was, indeed, always a sort of thrill in John Brown's voice when he spoke of mountains. I never shall forget the quiet way in which he once told me that "God had established the Alleghany Mountains from the foundation of the world that they might one day be a refuge for fugitive slaves." I did not then know that his own home was among the Adirondacks.

Just before we went, I remember, I said something or other to Salmon Brown about the sacrifices of their family; and he looked up in a quiet, manly way, which I shall never forget, and said briefly, "I sometimes think that is what we came into the world for —to make sacrifices." And I know that the murmuring echo of those words went with me all that day, as we came down from the mountains, and out through the iron gorge; and it seemed to me that any one must be very unworthy the society I had been permitted to enter who did not come forth from it a wiser and a better man.

Nat Turner's Insurrection

DURING the year 1831, up to the twenty-third of August, the Virginia newspapers were absorbed in the momentous problems which then occupied the minds of intelligent American citizens: —What General Jackson should do with the scolds, and what with the disreputables,—Should South Carolina be allowed to nullify? and would the wives of Cabinet Ministers call on Mrs. Eaton? It is an unfailing opiate, to turn over the drowsy files of the "Richmond Enquirer," until the moment when those dry and dusty pages are suddenly kindled into flame by the torch of Nat Turner. Then the terror flares on increasing, until the remotest Southern States are found shuddering at nightly rumors of insurrection,—until far-off European colonies, Antigua, Martinique, Caraccas, Tortola, recognize by some secret sympathy the same epidemic alarms,—until the very boldest words of freedom are reported as uttered in the Virginia House of Delegates with unclosed doors,—until an obscure young man named Garrison is indicted at Common Law in North Carolina, and has a price set upon his head by the Legislature of Georgia. The insurrection revived in one agonizing reminiscence all the distresses of Gabriel's Revolt, thirty years before; and its memory endures still fresh, now that thirty added years have brought the more formidable presence of General Butler.[1] It is by no means impossible that the very children or even confederates of Nat Turner may be included at this moment among the contraband articles of Fort Monroe.

Near the southeastern border of Virginia, in Southampton County, there is a neighborhood known as "The Cross Keys." It lies fifteen miles from Jerusalem, the county-town or "courthouse," seventy miles from Norfolk, and about as far from Richmond. It is some ten or fifteen miles from Murfreesboro' in North Carolina, and about twenty-five from the Great Dismal Swamp. Up to Sunday, the twenty-first of August, 1831, there was nothing to distinguish it from any other rural, lethargic, slipshod Virginia neighborhood, with the due allotment of mansion-houses and log-huts, tobacco-fields and "old-fields," horses, dogs, negroes, "poor white folks," so called, and other white folks, poor without being called so. One of these last was Joseph Travis, who had recently married the widow of one Putnam Moore, and had unfortunately wedded to himself her negroes also.

In the woods on the plantation of Joseph Travis, upon the Sunday just named, six slaves met at noon for what is called in the Northern States a picnic and in the Southern a barbecue. The bill of fare was to be simple: one brought a pig, and another some brandy, giving to the meeting an aspect so cheaply convivial that no one would have imagined it to be the final consummation of a conspiracy which had been for six months in preparation. In this plot four of the men had been already initiated,—Henry, Hark or Hercules, Nelson, and Sam. Two others were novices, Will and Jack by name. The party had remained together from twelve to three o'clock, when a seventh man joined them,—a short, stout, powerfully built person, of dark mulatto complexion and strongly-marked African features, but with a face full of expression and resolution. This was Nat Turner.

He was at this time nearly thirty-one years old, having been born on the second of October, 1800. He had belonged originally to Benjamin Turner,—whence his last name, slaves having usually no patronymic,—had then been transferred to Putnam Moore, and then to his present owner. He had, by his own account, felt himself singled out from childhood for some great work; and he had some peculiar marks on his person, which, joined to his great mental precocity, were enough to occasion, among his youthful companions, a superstitious faith in his gifts and destiny. He had great mechanical ingenuity also, experimentalized very early in making paper, gunpowder, pottery, and in other arts which in later life he was found thoroughly to understand. His moral faculties were very strong, so that white witnesses admitted that he had never been known to swear an oath, to drink a drop of spirits, or to commit a theft. And in general, so marked were his early peculiarities, that people said "he had too much sense to be raised, and if he was, he would never be of any use as a slave." This impression of personal destiny grew with his growth;—he fasted, prayed, preached, read the Bible, heard voices when he walked behind his plough, and communicated his revelations to the awe-struck slaves. They told him in return, that, "if they had his sense, they would not serve any master in the world."

The biographies of slaves can hardly be individualized; they belong to the class. We know bare facts; it is only the general experience of human beings in like condition which can clothe them with life. The outlines are certain, the details are inferential. Thus, for instance, we know that Nat Turner's young wife was a slave; we know that she belonged to a different master from him-self; we know little more than this, but this is much. For this is equivalent to saying that by day or by night that husband had no more power to protect her than the man who lies bound upon a plundered vessel's deck has power to protect his wife on board the pirate-schooner disappearing in the horizon; she may be rev-erenced, she may be outraged; it is in the powerlessness that the agony lies. There is, indeed, one thing more which we do know of this young woman: the Virginia newspapers state that she was tortured under the lash, after her husband's execution, to make her produce his papers: this is all.

What his private experiences and special privileges or wrongs may have been, it is therefore now impossible to say. Travis was declared to be "more humane and fatherly to his slaves than any man in the county"; but it is astonishing how often this phenom-enon occurs in the contemporary annals of slave insurrections. The chairman of the county court also stated, in pronouncing sentence, that Nat Turner had spoken of his master as "only too indulgent"; but this, for some reason, does not appear in his printed Confession, which only says, "He was a kind master, and placed the greatest confidence in me." It is very possible that it may have been so, but the printed accounts of Nat Turner's per-son look suspicious: he is described in Governor Floyd's procla-mation as having a scar on one of his temples, also one on the back of his neck, and a large knot on one of the bones of his right arm, produced by a blow; and although these were explained away in Virginia newspapers as being produced by fights with his com-panions, yet such affrays are entirely foreign to the admitted habits of the man. It must, therefore, remain an open question, whether the scars and the knot were produced by black hands or by white.

Whatever Nat Turner's experiences of slavery might have been, it is certain that his plans were not suddenly adopted, but that he had brooded over them for years. To this day there are traditions among the Virginia slaves of the keen devices of "Prophet Nat." If he was caught with lime and lamp-black in hand, conning over a half-finished county-map on the barn-door, he was always "planning what to do, if he were blind," or "studying how to get to Mr. Francis's house." When he had called a meeting of slaves, and some poor whites came eavesdropping, the poor whites at once became the subjects for discussion; he incidentally mentioned that the masters had been heard threatening to drive them away; one slave had been ordered to shoot Mr. Jones's pigs, another to tear down Mr. Johnson's fences. The poor whites, Johnson and Jones, ran home to see to their homesteads, and were better friends than ever to Prophet Nat.

He never was a Baptist preacher, though such vocation has often been attributed to him. The impression arose from his having immersed himself, during one of his periods of special enthusiasm, together with a poor white man named Brantley. "About this time," he says in his Confession, "I told these things to a white man, on whom it had a wonderful effect, and he ceased from his wickedness, and was attacked immediately with a cutaneous eruption, and the blood oozed from the pores of his skin, and after praying and fasting nine days he was healed. And the Spirit appeared to me again, and said, as the Saviour had been baptized, so should we be also; and when the white people would not let us be baptized by the Church, we went down into the water together, in the sight of many who reviled us, and were baptized by the Spirit. After this I rejoiced greatly and gave thanks to God."

The religious hallucinations narrated in his Confession seem to have been as genuine as the average of such things, and are very well expressed. It reads quite like Jacob Behmen. He saw white spirits and black spirits contending in the skies, the sun was darkened, the thunder rolled. "And the Holy Ghost was with me, and said, 'Behold me as I stand in the heavens!' And I looked and saw the forms of men in different attitudes. And there were lights in the sky, to which the children of darkness gave other names than what they really were; for they were the lights of the Saviour's hands, stretched forth from east to west, even as they were extended on the cross on Calvary, for the redemption of sinners." He saw drops of blood on the corn: this was Christ's blood, shed for man. He saw on the leaves in the woods letters and numbers and figures of men,—the same symbols which he had seen in the skies. On May 12, 1828, the Holy Spirit appeared to him and proclaimed that the yoke of Jesus must fall on him, and he must fight against the Serpent when the sign appeared. Then came an eclipse of the sun in February, 1831: this was the sign; then he must arise and prepare himself, and slay his enemies with their own weapons; then also the seal was removed from his lips, and then he confided his plans to four associates.

When he came, therefore, to the barbecue on the appointed Sunday, and found, not these four only, but two others, his first question to the intruders was, How they came thither. To this Will answered manfully, that his life was worth no more than the others, and "his liberty was as dear to him." This admitted him to confidence, and as Jack was known to be entirely under Hark's influence, the strangers were no bar to their discussion. Eleven hours they remained there, in anxious consultation: one can imagine those terrible dusky faces, beneath the funereal woods, and amid the flickering of pine-knot torches, preparing that stern revenge whose shuddering echoes should ring through the land so long. Two things were at last decided: to begin their work that night, and to begin it with a massacre so swift and irresistible as to create in a few days more terror than many battles, and so spare the need of future bloodshed. "It was agreed that we should commence at home on that night, and, until we had armed and equipped ourselves and gained sufficient force, neither age nor sex was to be spared: which was invariably adhered to."

John Brown invaded Virginia with nineteen men, and with the avowed resolution to take no life but in self-defence. Nat Turner attacked Virginia from within, with six men, and with the determination to spare no life until his power was established. John Brown intended to pass rapidly through Virginia, and then retreat to the mountains. Nat Turner intended to "conquer Southampton

County as the white men did in the Revolution, and then retreat, if necessary, to the Dismal Swamp." Each plan was deliberately matured; each was in its way practicable; but each was defeated by a single false step, as will soon appear.

We must pass over the details of horror, as they occurred during the next twenty-four hours. Swift and stealthy as Indians, the black men passed from house to house,—not pausing, not hesitating, as their terrible work went on. In one thing they were humaner than Indians or than white men fighting against Indians,—there was no gratuitous outrage beyond the death-blow itself, no insult, no mutilation; but in every house they entered, that blow fell on man, woman, and child,—nothing that had a white skin was spared. From every house they took arms and ammunition, and from a few, money; on every plantation they found recruits: those dusky slaves, so obsequious to their master the day before, so prompt to sing and dance before his Northern visitors, were all swift to transform themselves into fiends of retribution now; show them sword or musket and they grasped it, though it were an heirloom from Washington himself. The troop increased from house to house,—first to fifteen, then to forty, then to sixty. Some were armed with muskets, some with axes, some with scythes; some came on their masters' horses. As the numbers increased, they could be divided, and the awful work was carried on more rapidly still. The plan then was for an advanced guard of horsemen to approach each house at a gallop, and surround it till the others came up. Meanwhile what agonies of terror must have taken place within, shared alike by innocent and by guilty! what memories of wrongs inflicted on those dusky creatures, by some,—what innocent participation, by others, in the penance! The outbreak lasted for but forty-eight hours; but during that period fifty-five whites were slain, without the loss of a single slave.

One fear was needless, which to many a husband and father must have intensified the last struggle. These negroes had been systematically brutalized from childhood; they had been allowed no legalized or permanent marriage; they had beheld around them an habitual licentiousness, such as can scarcely exist except in a Slave State; some of them had seen their wives and sisters habitually polluted by the husbands and the brothers of these fair white women who were now absolutely in their power. Yet I have looked through the Virginia newspapers of that time in vain for one charge of an indecent outrage on a woman against these triumphant and terrible slaves. Wherever they went, there went death, and that was all. Compare this with ordinary wars; compare it with the annals of the French Revolution. No one, perhaps, has yet painted the wrongs of the French populace so terribly as Dickens in his "Tale of Two Cities"; yet what man, conversant with slave-biographies, can read that narrative without feeling it weak beside the provocations to which fugitive slaves testify? It is something for human nature that these desperate insurgents revenged such wrongs by death alone. Even that fearful penalty was to be inflicted only till the object was won. It was admitted in the "Richmond Enquirer" of the time, that "indiscriminate massacre was not their intention, after they obtained foothold, and was resorted to in the first instance to strike terror and alarm. Women and children would afterwards have been spared, and men also who ceased to resist."

It is reported by some of the contemporary newspapers, that a portion of this abstinence was the result of deliberate consultation among the insurrectionists; that some of them were resolved on taking the white women for wives, but were overruled by Nat Turner. If so, he is the only American slave-leader of whom we know certainly that he rose above the ordinary level of slave vengeance, and Mrs. Stowe's picture[2] of Dred's purposes is then precisely typical of his. "Whom the Lord saith unto us, 'Smite,' them will we smite. We will not torment them with the scourge and fire, nor defile their women as they have done with ours. But we will slay them utterly, and consume them from off the face of the earth."

When the number of adherents had increased to fifty or sixty, Nat Turner judged it time to strike at the county-seat, Jerusalem. Thither a few white fugitives had already fled, and couriers might thence be despatched for aid to Richmond and Petersburg, unless promptly intercepted. Besides, he could there find arms, ammunition, and money; though they had already obtained, it is dubiously reported, from eight hundred to one thousand dollars. On the way it was necessary to pass the plantation of Mr. Parker, three miles from Jerusalem. Some of the men wished to stop here and enlist some of their friends. Nat Turner objected, as the delay might prove dangerous; he yielded at last, and it proved fatal.

He remained at the gate with six or eight men; thirty or forty went to the house, half a mile distant. They remained too long, and he went alone to hasten them. During his absence a party of eighteen white men came up suddenly, dispersing the small guard left at the gate; and when the main body of slaves emerged from the house, they encountered, for the first time, their armed masters. The blacks halted, the whites advanced cautiously within a hundred yards and fired a volley; on its being returned, they broke into disorder, and hurriedly retreated, leaving some wounded on the ground. The retreating whites were pursued, and were saved only by falling in with another band of fresh men from Jerusalem, with whose aid they turned upon the slaves, who in their turn fell into confusion. Turner, Hark, and about twenty men on horseback retreated in some order; the rest were scattered. The leader still planned to reach Jerusalem by a private way, thus evading pursuit; but at last decided to stop for the night, in the hope of enlisting additional recruits.

During the night the number increased again to forty, and they encamped on Major Ridley's plantation. An alarm took place during the darkness,—whether real or imaginary does not appear,—and the men became scattered again. Proceeding to make fresh enlistments with the daylight, they were resisted at Dr. Blunt's house, where his slaves, under his orders, fired upon them, and this, with a later attack from a party of white men near Captain Harris's, so broke up the whole force that they never reunited. The few who remained together agreed to separate for a few hours to see if anything could be done to revive the insurrection, and meet again that evening at their original rendezvous. But they never reached it.

Sadly came Nat Turner at nightfall into those gloomy woods where forty-eight hours before he had revealed the details of his terrible plot to his companions. At the outset all his plans had succeeded; everything was as he predicted: the slaves had come readily at his call, the masters had proved perfectly defenceless. Had he not been persuaded to pause at Parker's plantation, he would have been master before now of the arms and ammunition at Jerusalem; and with these to aid, and the Dismal Swamp for a refuge, he might have sustained himself indefinitely against his pursuers.

Now the blood was shed, the risk was incurred, his friends were killed or captured, and all for what? Lasting memories of terror, to be sure, for his oppressors; but on the other hand, hopeless failure for the insurrection, and certain death for him. What a watch he must have kept that night! To that excited imagination, which had always seen spirits in the sky and blood-drops on the corn and hieroglyphic marks on the dry leaves, how full the lonely forest must have been of signs and solemn warnings! Alone with the fox's bark, the rabbit's rustle, and the screech-owl's scream, the self-appointed prophet brooded over his despair. Once creeping to the edge of the wood, he saw men stealthily approach on horseback. He fancied them some of his companions; but before he dared to whisper their ominous names, "Hark" or "Dred,"— for the latter was the name, since famous, of one of his more recent recruits,—he saw them to be white men, and shrank back stealthily beneath his covert.

There he waited two weary days and two melancholy nights, —long enough to satisfy himself that no one would rejoin him, and that the insurrection had hopelessly failed. The determined, desperate spirits who had shared his plans were scattered forever, and longer delay would be destruction for him also. He found a spot which he judged safe, dug a hole under a pile of fence-rails in a field, and lay there for six weeks, only leaving it for a few moments at midnight to obtain water from a neighboring spring. Food he had previously provided, without discovery, from a house near by.

Meanwhile an unbounded variety of rumors went flying through the State. The express which first reached the Governor announced that the militia were retreating before the slaves. An express to Petersburg further fixed the number of militia at three hundred, and of blacks at eight hundred, and invented a convenient shower of rain to explain the dampened ardor of the whites. Later reports described the slaves as making three desperate attempts to cross the bridge over the Nottoway between Cross Keys and Jerusalem, and stated that the leader had been shot in the attempt. Other accounts put the number of negroes at three hundred, all well mounted and armed, with two or three white men as leaders. Their intention was supposed to be to reach the Dismal Swamp, and they must be hemmed in from that side.

Indeed, the most formidable weapon in the hands of slave-insurgents is always this blind panic they create, and the wild exaggerations which follow. The worst being possible, every one takes the worst for granted. Undoubtedly a dozen armed men could have stifled this insurrection, even after it had commenced operations; but it is the fatal weakness of a slaveholding community, that it can never furnish men promptly for such a purpose. "My first intention was," says one of the most intelligent newspaper narrators of the affair, "to have attacked them with thirty or forty men; but those who had families here were strongly opposed to it."

As usual, each man was pinioned to his own hearth-stone. As usual, aid had to be summoned from a distance, and, as usual, the United States troops were the chief reliance. Colonel House, commanding at Fort Monroe, sent at once three companies of artillery under Lieutenant-Colonel Worth, and embarked them on board the steamer Hampton for Suffolk. These were joined by detachments from the United States ships Warren and Natchez, the whole amounting to nearly eight hundred men. Two volunteer companies went from Richmond, four from Petersburg, one from Norfolk, one from Portsmouth, and several from North Carolina. The militia of Norfolk, Nansemond, and Princess Anne Counties, and the United States troops at Old Point Comfort, were ordered to scour the Dismal Swamp, where it was believed that two or three thousand fugitives were preparing to join the insurgents. It was even proposed to send two companies from New York and one from New London to the same point.

When these various forces reached Southampton County, they found all labor paralyzed and whole plantations abandoned. A letter from Jerusalem, dated August 24th, says, "The oldest inhabitant of our county has never experienced such a distressing time as we have had since Sunday night last. . . . Every house, room, and corner in this place is full of women and children, driven from home, who had to take the woods until they could get to this place." "For many miles around their track," says another, "the county is deserted by women and children." Still another writes, "Jerusalem is full of women, most of them from the

other side of the river,—about two hundred at Vix's." Then follow descriptions of the sufferings of these persons, many of whom
had lain night after night in the woods. But the immediate danger
was at an end, the short-lived insurrection was finished, and now
the work of vengeance was to begin. In the frank phrase of a
North Carolina correspondent,—"The massacre of the whites was
over, and the white people had commenced the destruction of the
negroes, which was continued after our men got there, from time
to time, as they could fall in with them, all day yesterday." A
postscript adds, that "passengers by the Fayetteville stage say,
that, by the latest accounts, one hundred and twenty negroes had
been killed,"—this being little more than one day's work.

These murders were defended as Nat Turner defended his:
a fearful blow must be struck. In shuddering at the horrors of
the insurrection, we have forgotten the far greater horrors of its
suppression.

The newspapers of the day contain many indignant protests
against the cruelties which took place. "It is with pain," says a
correspondent of the "National Intelligencer," September 7, 1831,
"that we speak of another feature of the Southampton Rebellion;
for we have been most unwilling to have our sympathies for the
sufferers diminished or affected by their misconduct. We allude
to the slaughter of many blacks without trial and under circumstances of great barbarity. . . . We met with an individual of intelligence who told us that he himself had killed between ten and
fifteen. . . . We [the Richmond troop] witnessed with surprise the
sanguinary temper of the population, who evinced a strong disposition to inflict immediate death on every prisoner."

There is a remarkable official document from General Eppes,
the officer in command, to be found in the "Richmond Enquirer"
for September 6, 1831. It is an indignant denunciation of precisely
these outrages; and though he refuses to give details, he supplies
their place by epithets: "revolting,"—"inhuman and not to be
justified,"—"acts of barbarity and cruelty,"—"acts of atrocity,"
—"this course of proceeding dignifies the rebel and the assassin
with the sanctity of martyrdom." And he ends by threatening
martial law upon all future transgressors. Such general orders are
not issued except in rather extreme cases. And in the parallel columns of the newspaper the innocent editor prints equally indig-

nant descriptions of Russian atrocities in Lithuania, where the Poles were engaged in active insurrection, amid profuse sympathy from Virginia.

The truth is, it was a Reign of Terror. Volunteer patrols rode in all directions, visiting plantations. "It was with the greatest difficulty," said General Brodnax before the House of Delegates, "and at the hazard of personal popularity and esteem, that the coolest and most judicious among us could exert an influence sufficient to restrain an indiscriminate slaughter of the blacks who were suspected." A letter from the Rev. G. W. Powell declares, "There are thousands of troops searching in every direction, and many negroes are killed every day: the exact number will never be ascertained." Petition after petition was subsequently presented to the legislature, asking compensation for slaves thus assassinated without trial.

Men were tortured to death, burned, maimed, and subjected to nameless atrocities. The overseers were called on to point out any slaves whom they distrusted, and if any tried to escape, they were shot down. Nay, worse than this. "A party of horsemen started from Richmond with the intention of killing every colored person they saw in Southampton County. They stopped opposite the cabin of a free colored man, who was hoeing in his little field. They called out, 'Is this Southampton County?' He replied, 'Yes, Sir, you have just crossed the line, by yonder tree.' They shot him dead and rode on." This is from the narrative of the editor of the "Richmond Whig," who was then on duty in the militia, and protested manfully against these outrages. "Some of these scenes," he adds, "are hardly inferior in barbarity to the atrocities of the insurgents."

These were the masters' stories. If even these conceded so much, it would be interesting to hear what the slaves had to report. I am indebted to my honored friend, Lydia Maria Child,[3] for some vivid recollections of this terrible period, as noted down from the lips of an old colored woman, once well known in New York, Charity Bowery. "At the time of the old Prophet Nat," she said, "the colored folks was afraid to pray loud; for the whites threatened to punish 'em dreadfully, if the least noise was heard. The patrols was low drunken whites, and in Nat's time, if they heard any of the colored folks praying or singing a hymn, they would fall upon 'em and abuse 'em, and sometimes kill 'em, afore master or missis could get to 'em. The brightest and best was killed in Nat's time. The whites always suspect such ones. They killed a great many at a place called Duplon. They killed Antonio, a slave of Mr. J. Stanley, whom they shot; then they pointed their guns at him, and told him to confess about the insurrection. He told 'em he didn't know anything about any insurrection. They shot several balls through him, quartered him, and put his head on a pole at the fork of the road leading to the court." (This is no exaggeration, if the Virginia newspapers may be taken as evidence.) "It was there but a short time. He had no trial. They never do. In Nat's time, the patrols would tie up the free colored people, flog 'em, and try to make 'em lie against one another, and often killed them before anybody could interfere. Mr. James Cole, High Sheriff, said, if any of the patrols came on his plantation, he would lose his life in defence of his people. One day he heard a patroller boasting how many niggers he had killed. Mr. Cole said, 'If you don't pack up, as quick as God Almighty will let you, and get out of this town, and never be seen in it again, I'll put you where dogs won't bark at you.' He went off, and wasn't seen in them parts again."

These outrages were not limited to the colored population; but other instances occurred which strikingly remind one of more recent times. An Englishman, named Robinson, was engaged in selling books at Petersburg. An alarm being given, one night, that five hundred blacks were marching towards the town, he stood guard, with others, on the bridge. After the panic had a little subsided, he happened to remark, that "the blacks, as men, were entitled to their freedom, and ought to be emancipated." This led to great excitement, and he was warned to leave town. He took passage in the stage, but the stage was intercepted. He then fled to a friend's house; the house was broken open, and he was dragged forth. The civil authorities, being applied to, refused to interfere. The mob stripped him, gave him a great number of lashes, and sent him on foot, naked, under a hot sun, to Richmond, whence he with difficulty found a passage to New York.

Of the capture or escape of most of that small band who met with Nat Turner in the woods upon the Travis plantation little can now be known. All appear among the list of convicted, except

Henry and Will. General Moore, who occasionally figures as second in command, in the newspaper narratives of that day, was probably the Hark or Hercules before mentioned; as no other of the confederates had belonged to Mrs. Travis, or would have been likely to bear her previous name of Moore. As usual, the newspapers state that most, if not all the slaves, were "the property of kind and indulgent masters." Whether in any case they were also the sons of those masters is a point ignored; but from the fact that three out of the seven were at first reported as being white men by several different witnesses,—the whole number being correctly given, and the statement therefore probably authentic,—one must suppose that there was an admixture of patrician blood in some of these conspirators.

The subordinate insurgents sought safety as they could. A free colored man, named Will Artist, shot himself in the woods, where his hat was found on a stake and his pistol lying by him; another was found drowned; others were traced to the Dismal Swamp; others returned to their homes, and tried to conceal their share in the insurrection, assuring their masters that they had been forced, against their will, to join,—the usual defence in such cases. The number shot down at random must, by all accounts, have amounted to many hundreds, but it is past all human registration now. The number who had a formal trial, such as it was, is officially stated at fifty-five; of these, seventeen were convicted and hanged, twelve convicted and transported, twenty acquitted, and four free colored men sent on for further trial and finally acquitted. "Not one of those known to be concerned escaped." Of those executed, one only was a woman: "Lucy, slave of John T. Barrow": that is all her epitaph, shorter even than that of Wordsworth's more famous Lucy;⁴—but whether this one was old or young, pure or wicked, lovely or repulsive, octroon or negro, a Cassy, an Emily, or a Topsy, no information appears; she was a woman, she was a slave, and she died.

There is one touching story, in connection with these terrible retaliations, which rests on good authority, that of the Rev. M. B. Cox, a Liberian missionary, then in Virginia. In the hunt which followed the massacre, a slaveholder went into the woods, accompanied by a faithful slave, who had been the means of saving his life during the insurrection. When they had reached a retired

place in the forest, the man handed his gun to his master, inform-
ing him that he could not live a slave any longer, and requesting
him either to free him or shoot him on the spot. The master took
the gun, in some trepidation, levelled it at the faithful negro, and
shot him through the heart. It is probable that this slaveholder
was a Dr. Blunt,—his being the only plantation where the slaves
were reported as thus defending their masters. "If this be true,"
said the "Richmond Enquirer," when it first narrated this instance of loyalty, "great will be the desert of these noble-minded
Africans." This "noble-minded African," at least, estimated his
own desert at a high standard: he demanded freedom,—and obtained it.

Meanwhile the panic of the whites continued; for, though all
others might be disposed of, Nat Turner was still at large. We
have positive evidence of the extent of the alarm, although great
efforts were afterwards made to represent it as a trifling affair. A
distinguished citizen of Virginia wrote three months later to the
Hon. W. B. Seabrook of South Carolina,—"From all that has
come to my knowledge during and since that affair, I am convinced most fully that every black preacher in the country east of
the Blue Ridge was in the secret." "There is much reason to believe," says the Governor's message on December 6th, "that the
spirit of insurrection was not confined to Southampton. Many
convictions have taken place elsewhere, and some few in distant
counties." The withdrawal of the United States troops, after some
ten days' service, was a signal for fresh excitement, and an address,
numerously signed, was presented to the United States Government, imploring their continued stay. More than three weeks after
the first alarm, the Governor sent a supply of arms into Prince
William, Fauquier, and Orange Counties. "From examinations
which have taken place in other counties," says one of the best
newspaper historians of the affair, (in the "Richmond Enquirer"
of September 6th,) "I fear that the scheme embraced a wider
sphere than I at first supposed." Nat Turner himself, intentionally
or otherwise, increased the confusion by denying all knowledge
of the North Carolina outbreak, and declaring that he had communicated his plans to his four confederates within six months;
while, on the other hand, a slave-girl, sixteen or seventeen years
old, belonging to Solomon Parker, testified that she had heard the

subject discussed for eighteen months, and that at a meeting held during the previous May some eight or ten had joined the plot.

It is astonishing to discover, by laborious comparison of newspaper files, how vast was the immediate range of these insurrectionary alarms. Every Southern State seems to have borne its harvest of terror. On the Eastern shore of Maryland great alarm was at once manifested, especially in the neighborhood of Easton and Snowhill; and the houses of colored men were searched for arms even in Baltimore. In Delaware, there were similar rumors through Sussex and Dover Counties; there were arrests and executions; and in Somerset County great public meetings were held, to demand additional safeguards. On election-day; in Seaford, Del., some young men, going out to hunt rabbits, discharged their guns in sport; the men being absent, all the women in the vicinity took to flight; the alarm spread like the "Ipswich Fright"; soon Seaford was thronged with armed men; and when the boys returned from hunting, they found cannon drawn out to receive them.

In North Carolina, Raleigh and Fayetteville were put under military defence, and women and children concealed themselves in the swamps for many days. The rebel organization was supposed to include two thousand. Forty-six slaves were imprisoned in Union County, twenty-five in Sampson County, and twenty-three at least in Duplin County, some of whom were executed. The panic also extended into Wayne, New Hanover, and Lenoir Counties. Four men were shot without trial in Wilmington,— Nimrod, Abraham, Prince, and "Dan the Drayman," the latter a man of seventy,—and their heads placed on poles at the four corners of the town. Nearly two months afterwards the trials were still continuing; and at a still later day, the Governor in his proclamation recommended the formation of companies of volunteers in every county.

In South Carolina, General Hayne issued a proclamation "to prove the groundlessness of the existing alarms,"—thus implying that serious alarms existed. In Macon, Georgia, the whole population were roused from their beds at midnight by a report of a large force of armed negroes five miles off. In an hour, every woman and child was deposited in the largest building of the town, and a military force hastily collected in front. The editor of the Macon "Messenger" excused the poor condition of his paper, a few days afterwards, by the absorption of his workmen in patrol duties, and describes "dismay and terror" as the condition of the people, of "all ages and sexes." In Jones, Twiggs, and Monroe Counties, the same alarms were reported; and in one place "several slaves were tied to a tree, while a militia captain hacked at them with his sword."

In Alabama, at Columbus and Fort Mitchell, a rumor was spread of a joint conspiracy of Indians and negroes. At Claiborne the panic was still greater; the slaves were said to be thoroughly organized through that part of the State, and multitudes were imprisoned; the whole alarm being apparently founded on one stray copy of the "Liberator."[5]

In Tennessee, the Shelbyville "Freeman" announced that an insurrectionary plot had just been discovered, barely in time for its defeat, through the treachery of a female slave. In Louisville, Kentucky, a similar organization was discovered or imagined, and arrests were made in consequence. "The papers, from motives of policy, do not notice the disturbance," wrote one correspondent to the Portland "Courier." "Pity us!" he added.

But the greatest bubble burst in Louisiana. Captain Alexander, an English tourist, arriving in New Orleans at the beginning of September, found the whole city in tumult. Handbills had been issued, appealing to the slaves to rise against their masters, saying that all men were born equal, declaring that Hannibal was a black man, and that they also might have great leaders among them. Twelve hundred stand of weapons were said to have been found in a black man's house; five hundred citizens were under arms, and four companies of regulars were ordered to the city, whose barracks Alexander himself visited.

If such were the alarm in New Orleans, the story, of course, lost nothing by transmission to other Slave States. A rumor reached Frankfort, Kentucky, that the slaves already had possession of the coast, both above and below New Orleans. But the most remarkable circumstance is, that all this seems to have been a mere revival of an old terror, once before excited and exploded. The following paragraph had appeared in the Jacksonville (Georgia) "Observer," during the spring previous:—

"FEARFUL DISCOVERY. We were favored, by yesterday's mail,

with a letter from New Orleans, of May 1st, in which we find that an important discovery had been made a few days previous in that city. The following is an extract:—'Four days ago, as some planters were digging under ground, they found a square room containing eleven thousand stand of arms and fifteen thousand cartridges, each of the cartridges containing a bullet.' It is said the negroes intended to rise as soon as the sickly season began, and obtain possession of the city by massacring the white population. The same letter states that the mayor had prohibited the opening of Sunday-schools for the instruction of blacks, under a penalty of five hundred dollars for the first offence, and for the second, death."

Such were the terrors that came back from nine other Slave States, as the echo of the voice of Nat Turner; and when it is also known that the subject was at once taken up by the legislatures of other States, where there was no public panic, as in Missouri and Tennessee,—and when, finally, it is added that reports of insurrection had been arriving all that year from Rio Janeiro, Martinique, St. Jago, Antigua, Caraccas, and Tortola, it is easy to see with what prolonged distress the accumulated terror must have weighed down upon Virginia, during the two months that Nat Turner lay hid.

True, there were a thousand men in arms in Southampton County, to inspire security. But the blow had been struck by only seven men before; and unless there were an armed guard in every house, who could tell but any house might at any moment be the scene of new horrors? They might kill or imprison unresisting negroes by day, but could they resist their avengers by night? "The half cannot be told," wrote a lady from another part of Virginia, at this time, "of the distresses of the people. In Southampton County, the scene of the insurrection, the distress beggars description. A gentleman who has been there says that even here, where there has been great alarm, we have no idea of the situation of those in that county. . . . . I do not hesitate to believe that many negroes around us would join in a massacre as horrible as that which has taken place, if an opportunity should offer."

Meanwhile the cause of all this terror was made the object of desperate search. On September 17th the Governor offered a reward of five hundred dollars for his capture, and there were other

rewards swelling the amount to eleven hundred dollars,—but in
vain. No one could track or trap him. On September 30th a minute account of his capture appeared in the newspapers, but it was
wholly false. On October 7th there was another, and on October
18th another; yet all without foundation. Worn out by confine-
ment in his little cave, Nat Turner grew more adventurous, and
began to move about stealthily by night, afraid to speak to any
human being, but hoping to obtain some information that might
aid his escape. Returning regularly to his retreat before daybreak,
he might possibly have continued this mode of life until pursuit
had ceased, had not a dog succeeded where men had failed. The
creature accidentally smelt out the provisions hid in the cave, and
finally led thither his masters, two negroes, one of whom was
named Nelson. On discovering the terrible fugitive, they fled pre-
cipitately, when he hastened to retreat in an opposite direction.
This was on October 15th, and from this moment the neighborhood was all alive with excitement, and five or six hundred men
undertook the pursuit.

It shows a more than Indian adroitness in Nat Turner to have
escaped capture any longer. The cave, the arms, the provisions
were found; and lying among them the notched stick of this mis-
erable Robinson Crusoe, marked with five weary weeks and six
days. But the man was gone. For ten days more he concealed
himself among the wheat-stacks on Mr. Francis's plantation, and
during this time was reduced almost to despair. Once he decided
to surrender himself, and walked by night within two miles of
Jerusalem before his purpose failed him. Three times he tried to
get out of that neighborhood, but in vain: travelling by day was,
of course, out of the question, and by night he found it impossible
to elude the patrol. Again and again, therefore, he returned to his
hiding-place, and during his whole two months' liberty never
went five miles from the Cross Keys. On the 25th of October, he
was at last discovered by Mr. Francis, as he was emerging from a
stack. A load of buckshot was instantly discharged at him, twelve
of which passed through his hat as he fell to the ground. He
escaped even then, but his pursuers were rapidly concentrating
upon him, and it is perfectly astonishing that he could have eluded
them for five days more.

On Sunday, October 30th, a man named Benjamin Phipps, going out for the first time on patrol duty, was passing at noon a clearing in the woods where a number of pine-trees had long since been felled. There was a motion among their boughs; he stopped to watch it; and through a gap in the branches he saw, emerging from a hole in the earth beneath, the face of Nat Turner. Aiming his gun instantly, Phipps called on him to surrender. The fugitive, exhausted with watching and privation, entangled in the branches, armed only with a sword, had nothing to do but to yield; sagaciously reflecting, also, as he afterwards explained, that the woods were full of armed men, and that he had better trust fortune for some later chance of escape, instead of desperately attempting it then. He was correct in the first impression, since there were fifty armed scouts within a circuit of two miles. His insurrection ended where it began; for this spot was only a mile and a half from the house of Joseph Travis.

Torn, emaciated, ragged, "a mere scarecrow," still wearing the hat perforated with buckshot, with his arms bound to his sides, he was driven before the levelled gun to the nearest house, that of a Mr. Edwards. He was confined there that night; but the news had spread so rapidly that within an hour after his arrival a hundred persons had collected, and the excitement became so intense "that it was with difficulty he could be conveyed alive to Jerusalem." The enthusiasm spread instantly through Virginia; Mr. Trezvant, the Jerusalem postmaster, sent notices of it far and near; and Governor Floyd himself wrote a letter to the "Richmond Enquirer" to give official announcement of the momentous capture.

When Nat Turner was asked by Mr. T. R. Gray, the counsel assigned him, whether, although defeated, he still believed in his own Providential mission, he answered, as simply as one who came thirty years after him, "Was not Christ crucified?" In the same spirit, when arraigned before the court, "he answered, 'Not guilty,' saying to his counsel that he did not feel so." But apparently no argument was made in his favor by his counsel, nor were any witnesses called,—he being convicted on the testimony of Levi Waller, and upon his own confession, which was put in by Mr. Gray, and acknowledged by the prisoner before the six justices composing the court, as being "full, free, and voluntary." He was therefore placed in the paradoxical position of conviction by his own confession, under a plea of "Not guilty." The arrest took place on the thirtieth of October, 1831, the confession on the first of November, the trial and conviction on the fifth, and the execution on the following Friday, the eleventh of November, precisely at noon. He met his death with perfect composure, declined addressing the multitude assembled, and told the sheriff in a firm voice that he was ready. Another account says that he "betrayed no emotion, and even hurried the executioner in the performance of his duty." "Not a limb nor a muscle was observed to move. His body, after his death, was given over to the surgeons for dissection."

This last statement merits remark. There would be no evidence that this formidable man was not favored during his imprisonment with that full measure of luxury which slave-jails afford to slaves, but for a rumor which arose after the execution, that he was compelled to sell his body in advance, for purposes of dissection, in exchange for food. But it does not appear probable, from the known habits of Southern anatomists, that any such bargain could have been needed. For in the circular of the South Carolina Medical School for that very year I find this remarkable suggestion:
—"Some advantages of a peculiar character are connected with this institution. No place in the United States affords so great opportunities for the acquisition of medical knowledge, subjects being obtained among the colored population in sufficient number for every purpose, and proper dissections carried on without offending any individual." What a convenience, to possess for scientific purposes a class of population sufficiently human to be dissected, but not human enough to be supposed to take offence at it! And as the same arrangement may be supposed to have existed in Virginia, Nat Turner would hardly have gone through the formality of selling his body for food to those who claimed its control at any rate.

The Confession of the captive was published under authority of Mr. Gray, in a pamphlet, at Baltimore. Fifty thousand copies of it are said to have been printed, and it was "embellished with an accurate likeness of the brigand, taken by Mr. John Crawley, portrait-painter, and lithographed by Endicott & Swett, at Baltimore." The newly published "Liberator" said of it, at the time, that it would "only serve to rouse up other leaders, and hasten other insurrections," and advised grand juries to indict Mr. Gray. I have never seen a copy of the original pamphlet, it is not to be found in any of our public libraries, and I have heard of but one as still existing, although the Confession itself has been repeatedly reprinted. Another small pamphlet, containing the main features of the outbreak, was published at New York during the same year, and this is in my possession. But the greater part of the facts which I have given were gleaned from the contemporary newspapers.

Who now shall go back thirty years and read the heart of this extraordinary man, who, by the admission of his captors, "never was known to swear an oath or drink a drop of spirits,"—who, on the same authority, "for natural intelligence and quickness of apprehension was surpassed by few men," "with a mind capable of attaining anything,"—who knew no book but his Bible, and that by heart,—who devoted himself soul and body to the cause of his race, without a trace of personal hope or fear,—who laid his plans so shrewdly that they came at last with less warning than any earthquake on the doomed community around,—and who, when that time arrived, took the life of man, woman, and child, without a throb of compunction, a word of exultation, or an act of superfluous outrage? Mrs. Stowe's "Dred" seems dim and melodramatic beside the actual Nat Turner. De Quincey's "Avenger"[6] is his only parallel in imaginative literature: similar wrongs, similar retribution. Mr. Gray, his self-appointed confessor, rises into a sort of bewildered enthusiasm, with the prisoner before him. "I shall not attempt to describe the effect of his narrative, as told and commented on by himself, in the condemned-hole of the prison. The calm, deliberate composure with which he spoke of his late deeds and intentions, the expression of his fiend-like face when excited by enthusiasm, still bearing the stains of the blood of helpless innocence about him, clothed with rags and covered with chains, yet daring to raise his manacled hands to heaven, with a spirit soaring above the attributes of man,—I looked on him, and the blood curdled in my veins."

But the more remarkable the personal character of Nat Turner, the greater the amazement felt that he should not have appreciated the extreme felicity of his position as a slave. In all insurrections, the standing wonder seems to be that the slaves most trusted and best used should be most deeply involved. So in this case, as usual, they resorted to the most astonishing theories of the origin of the affair. One attributed it to Free-Masonry, and another to free whiskey,—liberty appearing dangerous, even in these forms. The poor whites charged it upon the free colored people, and urged their expulsion, forgetting that in North Carolina the plot was betrayed by one of this class, and that in Virginia there were but two engaged, both of whom had slave-wives. The slaveholding clergymen traced it to want of knowledge of the Bible, forgetting that Nat Turner knew scarcely anything else. On the other hand, "a distinguished citizen of Virginia" combined in one sweeping denunciation "Northern incendiaries, tracts, Sunday-schools, religion, reading, and writing."

But whether the theories of its origin were wise or foolish, the insurrection made its mark, and the famous band of Virginia emancipationists who all that winter made the House of Delegates ring with unavailing eloquence—till the rise of slave-exportation to new cotton regions stopped their voices—were but the unconscious mouth-pieces of Nat Turner. In January, 1832, in reply to a member who had called the outbreak a "petty affair," the eloquent James McDowell thus described the impression it left behind:—

"Now, Sir, I ask you, I ask gentlemen, in conscience to say, was that a 'petty affair' which startled the feelings of your whole population,—which threw a portion of it into alarm, a portion of it into panic,—which wrung out from an affrighted people the thrilling cry, day after day, conveyed to your executive, *We are in peril of our lives; send us an army for defence*'? Was that a 'petty affair' which drove families from their homes,—which assembled women and children in crowds, without shelter, at places of common refuge, in every condition of weakness and infirmity, under every suffering which want and terror could inflict, yet willing to endure all, willing to meet death from famine, death from climate, death from hardships, preferring anything rather than the horrors of meeting it from a domestic assassin? Was that a 'petty affair' which erected a peaceful and confiding portion of the State into a military camp,—which outlawed from pity the unfortunate beings whose brothers had offended,—which barred every door, penetrated every bosom with fear or suspicion,—which so banished every sense of security from every man's dwelling, that, let but a hoof or horn break upon the silence of the night, and an aching throb would be driven to the heart, the husband would look to his weapon, and the mother would shudder and weep upon her cradle? Was it the fear of Nat Turner, and his deluded, drunken handful of followers, which produced such effects? Was it this that induced distant counties, where the very name of Southampton was strange, to arm and equip for a struggle? No, Sir, it was the suspicion eternally attached to the slave himself,—the suspicion that a Nat Turner might be in every family,—that the same bloody deed might be acted over at any time and in any place,—that the materials for it were spread through the land, and were always ready for a like explosion. Nothing but the force of this withering apprehension,—nothing but the paralyzing and deadening weight with which it falls upon and prostrates the heart of every man who has helpless dependants to protect,—nothing but this could have thrown a brave people into consternation, or could have made any portion of this powerful Commonwealth, for a single instant, to have quailed and trembled."

While these things were going on, the enthusiasm for the Polish Revolution was rising to its height. The nation was ringing with a peal of joy, on hearing that at Frankfort the Poles had killed fourteen thousand Russians. "The Southern Religious Telegraph" was publishing an impassioned address to Kosciusko;[7] standards were being consecrated for Poland in the larger cities; heroes, like Skrzynecki, Czartoryski, Rozyski, Kaminski, were choking the trump of Fame with their complicated patronymics. These are all forgotten now; and this poor negro, who did not even possess a name, beyond one abrupt monosyllable,—for even the name of Turner was the master's property,—still lives a memory of terror and a symbol of retribution triumphant.

Letter to a Young Contributor

My dear young gentleman or young lady,—for many are the Cecil Dreemes of literature who superscribe their offered manuscripts with very masculine names in very feminine handwriting,—it seems wrong not to meet your accumulated and urgent epistles with one comprehensive reply, thus condensing many private letters into a printed one. And so large a proportion of "Atlantic" readers either might, would, could, or should be "Atlantic" contributors also, that this epistle will be sure of perusal, though Mrs. Stowe remain uncut and the Autocrat[1] go for an hour without readers.

Far from me be the wild expectation that every author will not habitually measure the merits of a periodical by its appreciation of his or her last manuscript. I should as soon ask a young lady not to estimate the management of a ball by her own private luck in respect to partners. But it is worth while at least to point out that in the treatment of every contribution the real interests of editor and writer are absolutely the same, and any antagonism is merely traditional, like the supposed hostility between France and England, or between England and Slavery. No editor can ever afford the rejection of a good thing, and no author the publication of a bad one. The only difficulty lies in drawing the line. Were all offered manuscripts unequivocally good or bad, there would be no great trouble; it is the vast range of mediocrity which perplexes: the majority are too bad for blessing and too good for banning; so that no conceivable reason can be given for either fate, save that upon the destiny of any single one may hang that of a hundred others just like it. But whatever be the standard fixed, it is equally for the interest of all concerned that it be enforced without flinching.

Nor is there the slightest foundation for the supposed editorial prejudice against new or obscure contributors. On the contrary, every editor is always hungering and thirsting after novelties. To take the lead in bringing forward a new genius is as fascinating a privilege as that of the physician who boasted to Sir Henry Halford of having been the first man to discover the Asiatic cholera and to communicate it to the public. It is only stern necessity which compels the magazine to fall back so constantly on the regular old staff of contributors, whose average product has been gauged already; just as every country-lyceum attempts annually to arrange an entirely new list of lecturers, and ends with no bolder experiment than to substitute Chapin and Beecher in place of last year's Beecher and Chapin.

Of course no editor is infallible, and the best magazine contains an occasional poor article. Do not blame the unfortunate conductor. He knows it as well as you do,—after the deed is done. The newspapers kindly pass it over, still preparing their accustomed opiate of sweet praises, so much for each contributor, so much for the magazine collectively,—like a hostess with her tea-making, a spoonful for each person and one for the pot. But I can tell you that there is an official person who meditates and groans, meanwhile, in the night-watches, to think that in some atrocious moment of good-nature or sleepiness he left the door open and let that ungainly intruder in. Do you expect him to acknowledge the blunder, when you tax him with it? Never,—he feels it too keenly. He rather stands up stoutly for the surpassing merits of the misshapen thing, as a mother for her deformed child; and as the mother is nevertheless inwardly imploring that there may never be such another born to her, so be sure that it is not by reminding the editor of this calamity that you can allure him into risking a repetition of it.

An editor thus shows himself to be but human; and it is well enough to remember this fact, when you approach him. He is not a gloomy despot, no Nemesis or Rhadamanthus, but a bland and virtuous man, exceedingly anxious to secure plenty of good subscribers and contributors, and very ready to perform any acts of kindness not inconsistent with this grand design. Draw near him, therefore, with soft approaches and mild persuasions. Do not treat him like an enemy, and insist on reading your whole manuscript aloud to him, with appropriate gestures. His time has some value, if yours has not; and he has therefore educated his eye till it has become microscopic, like a naturalist's, and can classify nine out of ten specimens by one glance at a scale or a feather. Fancy an ambitious echinoderm claiming a private interview with Agassiz, to demonstrate by verbal arguments that he is a mollusk! Besides, do you expect to administer the thing orally to each of the two hundred thousand, more or less, who turn the leaves of the "Atlantic"? You are writing for the average eye, and must submit to its verdict. "Do not trouble yourself about the light on your statue; it is the light of the public square which must test its value."

Do not despise any honest propitiation, however small, in dealing with your editor. Look to the physical aspect of your manuscript, and prepare your page so neatly that it shall allure instead of repelling. Use good pens, black ink, nice white paper and plenty of it. Do not emulate "paper-sparing Pope," whose chaotic manuscript of the "Iliad," written chiefly on the backs of old letters, still remains in the British Museum. If your document be slovenly, the presumption is that its literary execution is the same, Pope to the contrary notwithstanding. An editor's eye becomes carnal, and is easily attracted by a comely outside. If you really wish to obtain his good-will for your production, do not first tax his time for deciphering it, any more than in visiting a millionnaire to solicit a loan you would begin by asking him to pay for the hire of the carriage which takes you to his door.

On the same principle, send your composition in such a shape that it shall not need the slightest literary revision before printing. Many a bright production dies discarded which might have been made thoroughly presentable by a single day's labor of a competent scholar, in shaping, smoothing, dovetailing, and retrenching. The revision seems so slight an affair that the aspirant cannot conceive why there should be so much fuss about it.

> "The piece, you think, is incorrect; why,
>   take it;
>   I'm all submission; what you'd have it,
>   make it."

But to discharge that friendly office no universal genius is salaried; and for intellect in the rough there is no market.

Rules for style, as for manners, must be chiefly negative: a positively good style indicates certain natural powers in the individual, but an unexceptionable style is merely a matter of culture and good models. Dr. Channing established in New England a standard of style which really attained almost the perfection of the pure and the colorless, and the disciplinary value of such a literary influence, in a raw and crude nation, has been very great; but the defect of this standard is that it ends in utterly renouncing all the great traditions of literature, and ignoring the magnificent mystery of words. Human language may be polite and powerless in itself, uplifted with difficulty into expression by the high thoughts it utters, or it may in itself become so saturated with warm life and delicious association that every sentence shall palpitate and thrill with the mere fascination of the syllables. The statue is not more surely included in the block of marble than is all conceivable splendor of utterance in "Worcester's Unabridged." And as Ruskin says of painting that it is in the perfection and precision of the instantaneous line that the claim to immortality is made, so it is easy to see that a phrase may outweigh a library. Keats heads the catalogue of things real with "sun, moon, and passages of Shakspeare"; and Keats himself has left behind him winged wonders of expression which are not surpassed by Shakspeare, or by any one else who ever dared touch the English tongue. There may be phrases which shall be palaces to dwell in, treasure-houses to explore; a single word may be a window from which one may perceive all the kingdoms of the earth and the glory of them. Oftentimes a word shall speak what accumulated volumes have labored in vain to utter: there may be years of crowded passion in a word, and half a life in a sentence.

Such being the majesty of the art you seek to practise, you can at least take time and deliberation before dishonoring it. Disabuse yourself especially of the belief that any grace or flow of style can come from writing rapidly. Haste can make you slipshod, but it can never make you graceful. With what dismay one reads of the wonderful fellows in fashionable novels, who can easily dash off a brilliant essay in a single night! When I think how slowly my poor thoughts come in, how tardily they connect themselves, what a delicious prolonged perplexity it is to cut and contrive a decent clothing of words for them, as a little girl does for her doll,—nay, how many new outfits a single sentence sometimes costs before it is presentable, till it seems at last, like our army on the Potomac, as if it never could be thoroughly clothed,—I certainly should never dare to venture into print, but for the confirmed suspicion that the greatest writers have done even so. I can hardly believe that there is any autograph in the world so precious or instructive as that scrap of paper, still preserved at Ferrara, on which Ariosto wrote in sixteen different revisions one of his most famous stanzas. Do you know, my dear neophyte, how Balzac used to compose? As a specimen of the labor that sometimes goes to make an effective style, the process is worth recording. When Balzac had a new work in view, he first spent weeks in studying from real life for it, haunting the streets of Paris by day and night, note-book in hand. His materials gained, he shut himself up till the book was written, perhaps two months, absolutely excluding everybody but his publisher. He emerged pale and thin, with the complete manuscript in his hand,—not only written, but almost rewritten, so thoroughly was the original copy altered, interlined, and rearranged. This strange production, almost illegible, was sent to the unfortunate printers; with infinite difficulty a proof-sheet was obtained, which, being sent to the author, was presently returned in almost as hopeless a chaos of corrections as the manuscript first submitted. Whole sentences were erased, others transposed, everything modified. A second and a third followed, alike torn to pieces by the ravenous pen of Balzac. The despairing printers labored by turns, only the picked men of the office being equal to the task, and they relieving each other at hourly intervals, as beyond that time no one could endure the fatigue. At last, by the fourth proof-sheet, the author too was wearied out, though not contented. "I work ten hours out of the twenty-four," said he, "over the elaboration of my unhappy style, and I am never satisfied, myself, when all is done."

Do not complain that this scrupulousness is probably wasted, after all, and that nobody knows. The public knows. People criticize higher than they attain. When the Athenian audience hissed a public speaker for a mispronunciation, it did not follow that any one of the malcontents could pronounce as well as the orator. In our own lyceum-audiences there may not be a man who does not yield to his own private eccentricities of dialect, but see if they do not appreciate elegant English from Phillips or Everett! Men talk of writing down to the public taste who have never yet written up to that standard. "There never yet was a good tongue," said old Fuller, "that wanted ears to hear it." If one were expecting to be judged by a few scholars only, one might hope somehow to cajole them; but it is this vast, unimpassioned, unconscious tribunal, this average judgment of intelligent minds, which is truly formidable,—something more undying than senates and more omnipotent than courts, something which rapidly cancels all transitory reputations, and at last becomes the organ of eternal justice and infallibly awards posthumous fame.

The first demand made by the public upon every composition is, of course, that it should be attractive. In addressing a miscellaneous audience, whether through eye or ear, it is certain that no man living has a right to be tedious. Every editor is therefore compelled to insist that his contributors should make themselves agreeable, whatever else they may do. To be agreeable, it is not necessary to be amusing; an essay may be thoroughly delightful without a single witticism, while a monotone of jokes soon grows tedious. Charge your style with life, and the public will not ask for conundrums. But the profounder your discourse, the greater must necessarily be the effort to refresh and diversify. I have observed, in addressing audiences of children in schools and elsewhere, that there is no fact so grave, no thought so abstract, but you can make it very interesting to the small people, if you will only put in plenty of detail and illustration; and I have not observed that in this respect grown men are so very different. If, therefore, in writing, you find it your mission to be abstruse, fight to render your statement clear and attractive, as if your life depended on it: your literary life does depend on it, and, if you fail, relapses into a dead language, and becomes, like that of Coleridge, only a *Biographia Literaria*. Labor, therefore, not in thought alone, but in utterance; clothe and reclothe your grand conception twenty times, until you find some phrase that with its grandeur shall be lucid also. It is this unwearied literary patience that has enabled Emerson not merely to introduce, but even to popularize, thoughts of such a quality as never reached the popular mind before. And when such a writer, thus laborious to do his utmost for his disciples, becomes after all incomprehensible, we can try to believe that it is only that inevitable obscurity of vast thought which Coleridge said was a compliment to the reader.

In learning to write availably, a newspaper-office is a capital preparatory school. Nothing is so good to teach the use of materials, and to compel to pungency of style. Being always at close quarters with his readers, a journalist must shorten and sharpen his sentences, or he is doomed. Yet this mental alertness is bought at a severe price; such living from hand to mouth cheapens the whole mode of intellectual existence, and it would seem that no successful journalist could ever get the newspaper out of his blood, or achieve any high literary success.

For purposes of illustration and elucidation, and even for amplitude of vocabulary, wealth of accumulated materials is essential; and whether this wealth be won by reading or by experience makes no great difference. Coleridge attended Davy's chemical lectures to acquire new metaphors, and it is of no consequence whether one comes to literature from a library, a machine-shop, or a forecastle, provided he has learned to work with thoroughness the soil he knows. After all is said and done, however, books remain the chief quarries. Johnson declared, putting the thing perhaps too mechanically, "The greater part of an author's time is spent in reading in order to write; a man will turn over half a library to make one book." Addison collected three folios of materials before publishing the first number of the "Spectator." Remember, however, that copious preparation has its perils also, in the crude display to which it tempts. The object of high culture is not to exhibit culture, but its results. You do not put guano on your garden that your garden may blossom guano. Indeed, even for the proper subordination of one's own thoughts the same self-control is needed; and there is no severer test of literary training than in the power to prune out one's most cherished sentence, when it grows obvious that the sacrifice will help the symmetry or vigor of the whole.

Be noble both in the affluence and the economy of your diction; spare no wealth that you can put in, and tolerate no superfluity that can be struck out. Remember the Lacedemonian who was fined for saying that in three words which might as well have been expressed in two. Do not throw a dozen vague epithets at a thing, in the hope that some one of them will fit; but study each phrase so carefully that the most ingenious critic cannot alter it without spoiling the whole passage for everybody but himself. For the same reason do not take refuge, as was the practice a few years since, in German combinations, heart-utterances, soul-sentiments, and hyphenized phrases generally; but roll your thought into one good English word. There is no fault which seems so hopeless as commonplaceness, but it is really easier to elevate the commonplace than to reduce the turgid. How few men in all the pride of culture can emulate the easy grace of a bright woman's letter!

Have faith enough in your own individuality to keep it resolutely down for a year or two. A man has not much intellectual capital who cannot treat himself to a brief interval of modesty. Premature individualism commonly ends either in a reaction against the original whims, or in a mannerism which perpetuates them. For mannerism no one is great enough, because, though in the hands of a strong man it imprisons us in novel fascination, yet we soon grow weary, and then hate our prison forever. How sparkling was Reade's crisp brilliancy in "Peg Woffington"!—but into what disagreeable affectations it has since degenerated! Carlyle was a boon to the human race, amid the tameness into which English style was declining; but who is not tired of him and his catchwords now? He was the Jenner of our modern style, inoculating and saving us all by his quaint frank Germanism, then dying of his own disease. Now the age has outgrown him, and is approaching a mode of writing which unites the smoothness of the eighteenth century with the vital vigor of the seventeenth, so that Sir Thomas Browne and Andrew Marvell seem quite as near to us as Pope or Addison,—a style penetrated with the best spirit of Carlyle, without a trace of Carlylism.

Be neither too lax nor too precise in your use of language: the one fault ends in stiffness, the other in slang. Some one told the Emperor Tiberius that he might give citizenship to men, but not to words. To be sure, Louis XIV, in childhood, wishing for a carriage, called for *mon carrosse,* and made the former feminine a masculine to all future Frenchmen. But do not undertake to exercise these prerogatives of royalty until you are quite sure of being crowned. The only thing I remember of our college textbook of Rhetoric is one admirable verse of caution which it quoted:—

> "In words, as fashions, the same rule will hold,
>   Alike fantastic, if too new or old;
>   Be not the first by whom the new are tried,
>   Nor yet the last to lay the old aside."

Especially do not indulge any fantastic preference for either Latin or Anglo-Saxon, the two great wings on which our magnificent English soars and sings; we can spare neither. The combination gives us an affluence of synonymes and a delicacy of discrimination such as no unmixed idiom can show.

While you utterly shun slang, whether native- or foreign-born,—(at present, by the way, our popular writers use far less slang than the English,)—yet do not shrink from Americanisms, so they be good ones. American literature is now thoroughly out of leading-strings; and the nation which supplied the first appreciative audience for Carlyle, Tennyson, and the Brownings, can certainly trust its own literary instincts to create the new words it needs. To be sure, the inelegancies with which we are chiefly reproached are not distinctively American: Burke uses "pretty considerable"; Miss Burney says, "I trembled a few"; the English Bible says "reckon," Locke has "guess," and Southey "realize," in the exact senses in which one sometimes hears them used colloquially here. Nevertheless such improprieties are of course to be avoided; but whatever good Americanisms exist, let us hold to them by all means. The diction of Emerson alone is a sufficient proof, by its unequalled range and precision, that no people in the world ever had access to a vocabulary so rich and copious as we are acquiring. To the previous traditions and associations of the English tongue we add resources of contemporary life such as England cannot rival. Political freedom makes every man an individual; a vast industrial activity makes every man an inventor, not merely of labor-saving machines, but of labor-saving words; universal schooling popularizes all thought and sharpens the edge of all language. We unconsciously demand of our writers the same dash and the same accuracy which we demand in railroading or dry-goods-jobbing. The mixture of nationalities is constantly coining and exchanging new felicities of dialect: Ireland, Scotland, Germany, Africa are present everywhere with their various contributions of wit and shrewdness, thought and geniality; in New York and elsewhere one finds whole thoroughfares of France, Italy, Spain, Portugal; on our Western railways there are placards printed in Swedish; even China is creeping in. The colonies of England are too far and too provincial to have had much reflex influence on her literature, but how our phraseology is already amplified by our relations with Spanish-America! The life-blood of Mexico flowed into our newspapers while the war was in progress; and the gold of California glitters in our primers. Many foreign cities may show a greater variety of mere national costumes, but the representative value of our immigrant tribes is far greater from the very fact that they merge their mental costume in ours. Thus the American writer finds himself among his phrases like an American sea-captain amid his crew: a medley of all nations, waiting for the strong organizing New-England mind to mould them into a unit of force.

There are certain minor matters, subsidiary to elegance, if not elegancies, and therefore worth attention. Do not habitually prop your sentences on crutches, such as Italics and exclamation-points, but make them stand without aid; if they cannot emphasize themselves, these devices are commonly but a confession of helplessness. Do not leave loose ends as you go on, straggling things, to be caught up and dragged along uneasily in foot-notes, but work them all in neatly, as Biddy at her bread-pan gradually kneads in all the outlying bits of dough, till she has one round and comely mass. Reduce yourself to short allowance of parentheses and dashes; if you employ them merely from clumsiness, they will lose all their proper power in your hands. Economize quotation-marks also, clear that dust from your pages, assume your readers to be acquainted with the current jokes and the stock epithets: all persons like the compliment of having it presumed that they know something, and prefer to discover the wit or beauty of your allusion without a guide-board.

The same principle applies to learned citations and the results of study. Knead these thoroughly in, supplying the maximum of desired information with a minimum of visible schoolmaster. It requires no pedantic mention of Euclid to indicate a mathematical

mind, but only the habitual use of clear terms and close connec-
tions. To employ in argument the forms of Whately's Logic
would render it probable that you are juvenile and certain that
you are tedious; wreathe the chain with roses. The more you have
studied foreign languages, the more you will be disposed to keep
Ollendorff in the background: the proper result of such acquire-
ments is visible in a finer ear for words; so that Goethe said, the
man who had studied but one language could not know that one.
But spare the raw material; deal as cautiously in Latin as did General Jackson when Jack Downing[2] was out of the way; and avoid
French as some fashionable novelists avoid English.

Thus far, these are elementary and rather technical suggestions,
fitted for the very opening of your literary career. Supposing you
fairly in print, there are needed some further counsels.

Do not waste a minute, not a second, in trying to demonstrate
to others the merit of your own performance. If your work does
not vindicate itself, you cannot vindicate it, but you can labor
steadily on to something which needs no advocate but itself. It
was said of Haydon, the English artist, that, if he had taken half
the pains to paint great pictures that he took to persuade the public he had painted them, his fame would have been secure. Similar
was the career of poor Horne, who wrote the farthing epic of
"Orion" with one grand line in it, and a prose work without any,
on "The False Medium excluding Men of Genius from the Public." He spent years in ineffectually trying to repeal the exclusion
in his own case, and has since manfully gone to the grazing
regions in Australia, hoping there at least to find the sheep and
the goats better discriminated. Do not emulate these tragedies.
Remember how many great writers have created the taste by
which they were enjoyed, and do not be in a hurry. Toughen
yourself a little, and perform something better. Inscribe above
your desk the words of Rivarol, "Genius is only great patience."
It takes less time to build an avenue of shingle palaces than to
hide away unseen, block by block, the vast foundation-stones of
an observatory. Most by-gone literary fames have been very
short-lived in America, because they have lasted no longer than
they deserved. Happening the other day to recur to a list of Cambridge lyceum-lecturers in my boyish days, I find with dismay
that the only name now popularly remembered is that of Emer-

son: death, oblivion, or a professorship has closed over all the rest, while the whole standard of American literature has been vastly raised meanwhile, and no doubt partly through their labors. To this day, some of our most gifted writers are being dwarfed by the unkind friendliness of too early praise. It was Keats, the most precocious of all great poets, the stock victim of critical assassination,—though the charge does him utter injustice,—who declared that "nothing is finer for purposes of production than a very gradual ripening of the intellectual powers."

Yet do not be made conceited by obscurity, any more than by notoriety. Many fine geniuses have been long neglected; but what would become of us, if all the neglected were to turn out geniuses? It is unsafe reasoning from either extreme. You are not necessarily writing like Holmes because your reputation for talent began in college, nor like Hawthorne because you have been before the public ten years without an admirer. Above all, do not seek to encourage yourself by dwelling on the defects of your rivals: strength comes only from what is above you. Northcote, the painter, said, that, in observing an inferior picture, he always felt his spirits droop, with the suspicion that perhaps he deceived himself and his own paintings were no better; but the works of the mighty masters always gave him renewed strength, in the hope that perhaps his own had in their smaller way something of the same divine quality.

Do not complacently imagine, because your first literary attempt proved good and successful, that your second will doubtless improve upon it. The very contrary sometimes happens. A man dreams for years over one projected composition, all his reading converges to it, all his experience stands related to it, it is the net result of his existence up to a certain time, it is the cistern into which he pours his accumulated life. Emboldened by success, he mistakes the cistern for a fountain, and instantly taps his brain again. The second production, as compared with the first, costs but half the pains and attains but a quarter part of the merit; a little more of fluency and facility perhaps,—but the vigor, the wealth, the originality, the head of water, in short, are wanting. One would think that almost any intelligent man might write one good thing in a lifetime, by reserving himself long enough: it is the effort after quantity which proves destructive. The greatest man has passed his zenith, when he once begins to cheapen his style of work and sink into a book-maker: after that, though the newspapers may never hint at it, nor his admirers own it, the decline of his career is begun.

Yet the author is not alone to blame for this, but also the world which first tempts and then reproves him. Goethe says, that, if a person once does a good thing, society forms a league to prevent his doing another. His seclusion is gone, and therefore his unconsciousness and his leisure; luxuries tempt him from his frugality, and soon he must toil for luxuries; then, because he has done one thing well, he is urged to squander himself and do a thousand things badly. In this country especially, if one can learn languages, he must go to Congress; if he can argue a case, he must become agent of a factory: out of this comes a variety of training which is very valuable, but a wise man must have strength to call in his resources before middle-life, prune off divergent activities, and concentrate himself on the main work, be it what it may. It is shameful to see the indeterminate lives of many of our gifted men, unable to resist the temptations of a busy land, and so losing themselves in an aimless and miscellaneous career.

Yet it is unjust and unworthy in Marsh to disfigure his fine work on the English language by traducing all who now write that tongue. "None seek the audience, fit, though few, which contented the ambition of Milton, and all writers for the press now measure their glory by their gains," and so indefinitely onward, —which is simply cant. Does Sylvanus Cobb, Jr., who honestly earns his annual five thousand dollars from the "New York Ledger," take rank as head of American literature by virtue of his salary? Because the profits of true literature are rising,—trivial as they still are beside those of commerce or the professions,—its merits do not necessarily decrease, but the contrary is more likely to happen; for in this pursuit, as in all others, cheap work is usually poor work. None but gentlemen of fortune can enjoy the bliss of writing for nothing and paying their own printer. Nor does the practice of compensation by the page work the injury that has often been ignorantly predicted. No contributor need hope to cover two pages of a periodical with what might be adequately said in one, unless he assumes his editor to be as foolish as himself. The Spartans exiled Ctesiphon for bragging that he could speak the whole day on any subject selected; and a modern magazine is of little value, unless it has a Spartan at its head.

Strive always to remember—though it does not seem intended that we should quite bring it home to ourselves—that "To-Day is a king in disguise," and that this American literature of ours will be just as classic a thing, if we do our part, as any which the past has treasured. There is a mirage over all literary associations. Keats and Lamb seem to our young people to be existences as remote and legendary as Homer, yet it is not an old man's life since Keats was an awkward boy at the door of Hazlitt's lecture-room, and Lamb was introducing Talfourd to Wordsworth as his own only admirer. In reading Spence's "Anecdotes," Pope and Addison appear no farther off; and wherever I open Bacon's "Essays," I am sure to end at last with that one magical sentence, annihilating centuries, "When I was a child, and Queen Elizabeth was in the flower of her years."

And this imperceptible transformation of the commonplace present into the storied past applies equally to the pursuits of war and to the serenest works of peace. Be not misled by the excitements of the moment into overrating the charms of military life. In this chaos of uniforms, we seem to be approaching times such as existed in England after Waterloo, when the splenetic Byron declared that the only distinction was to be a little undistinguished. No doubt, war brings out grand and unexpected qualities, and there is a perennial fascination in the Elizabethan Raleighs and Sidneys, alike heroes of pen and sword. But the fact is patent, that there is scarcely any art whose rudiments are so easy to acquire as the military; the manuals of tactics have no difficulties comparable to those of the ordinary professional text-books; and any one who can drill a boat's crew or a ballclub can learn in a very few weeks to drill a company or even a regiment. Given in addition the power to command, to organize, and to execute,—high qualities, though not rare in this community,—and you have a man needing but time and experience to make a general. More than this can be acquired only by an exclusive absorption in this one art; as Napoleon said, that, to have good soldiers, a nation must be always at war.

If, therefore, duty and opportunity call, count it a privilege to obtain your share in the new career; throw yourself into it as resolutely and joyously as if it were a summer-campaign in the Adirondack, but never fancy for a moment that you have discovered any grander or manlier life than you might be leading every day at home. It is not needful here to decide which is intrinsically the better thing, a column of a newspaper or a column of attack, Wordsworth's "Lines on Immortality" or Wellington's Lines of Torres Vedras; each is noble, if nobly done, though posterity seems to remember literature the longest. The writer is not celebrated for having been the favorite of the conqueror, but sometimes the conqueror only for having favored or even for having spurned the writer. "When the great Sultan died, his power and glory departed from him, and nothing remained but this one fact, that he knew not the worth of Ferdousi." There is a slight delusion in this dazzling glory. What a fantastic whim the young lieutenants thought it, when General Wolfe, on the eve of battle, said of Gray's "Elegy," "Gentlemen, I would rather have written that poem than have taken Quebec." Yet, no doubt, it is by the memory of that remark that Wolfe will live the longest,—aided by the stray line of another poet, still reminding us, not needlessly, that "Wolfe's great name's cotemporal with our own."

Once the poets and the sages were held to be pleasing triflers, fit for hours of relaxation in the lulls of war. Now the pursuits of peace are recognized as the real, and war as the accidental. It interrupts all higher avocations, as does the cry of fire: when the fire is extinguished, the important affairs of life are resumed. Six years ago the London "Times" was bewailing that all thought and culture in England were suspended by the Crimean War. "We want no more books. Give us good recruits, at least five feet seven, a good model for a floating-battery, and a gun to take effect at five thousand yards,—and Whigs and Tories, High and Low Church, the poets, astronomers, and critics, may settle it among themselves." How remote seems that epoch now! and how remote will the present soon appear! while art and science will resume their sway serene, beneath skies eternal. Yesterday I turned from treatises on gunnery and fortification to open Milton's Latin Poems, which I had never read, and there, in the "Sylvarum Liber," I came upon a passage as grand as anything in "Paradise Lost," —his description of Plato's archetypal man, the vast ideal of the human race, eternal, incorrupt, coeval with the stars, dwelling either in the sidereal spaces, or among the Lethean mansions of souls unborn, or pacing the unexplored confines of the habitable globe. There stood the majestic image, veiled in a dead language, yet still visible; and it was as if one of the poet's own sylvan groves had been suddenly cut down, and opened a view of Olympus. Then all these present fascinating trivialities of war and diplomacy ebbed away, like Greece and Rome before them, and there seemed nothing real in the universe but Plato's archetypal man.

Indeed, it is the same with all contemporary notorieties. In all free governments, especially, it is the habit to overrate the *dramatis personœ* of the hour. How empty to us are now the names of the great politicians of the last generation, as Crawford and Lowndes!—yet it is but a few years since these men filled in the public ear as large a space as Clay or Calhoun afterwards, and when they died, the race of the giants was thought ended. The path to oblivion of these later idols is just as sure; even Webster will be to the next age but a mighty tradition, and all that he has left will seem no more commensurate with his fame than will his statue by Powers. If anything preserves the statesmen of to-day, it will be only because we are coming to a contest of more vital principles, which may better embalm the men. Of all gifts, eloquence is the most short-lived. The most accomplished orator fades forgotten, and his laurels pass to some hoarse, inaudible Burke,[3] accounted rather a bore during his lifetime, and possessed of a faculty of scattering, not convincing, the members of the House. "After all," said the brilliant Choate, with melancholy foreboding, "a book is the only immortality."

So few men in any age are born with a marked gift for literary expression, so few of this number have access to high culture, so few even of these have the personal nobleness to use their powers well, and this small band is finally so decimated by disease and manifold disaster, that it makes one shudder to observe how little of the embodied intellect of any age is left behind. Literature is attar of roses, one distilled drop from a million blossoms. Think how Spain and Portugal once divided the globe between them in a treaty, when England was a petty kingdom of illiterate tribes! —and now all Spain is condensed for us into Cervantes, and all Portugal into the fading fame of the unread Camoens. The long magnificence of Italian culture has left us only *I Quattro Poeti*,

the Four Poets.[4] The difference between Shakspeare and his contemporaries is not that he is read twice, ten times, a hundred times
as much as they: it is an absolute difference; he is read, and they
are only printed.

Yet, if our life be immortal, this temporary distinction is of
little moment, and we may learn humility, without learning despair, from earth's evanescent glories. Who cannot bear a few disappointments, if the vista be so wide that the mute inglorious
Miltons of this sphere may in some other sing their Paradise as
Found? War or peace, fame or forgetfulness, can bring no real
injury to one who has formed the fixed purpose to live nobly day
by day. I fancy that in some other realm of existence we may look
back with some kind interest on this scene of our earlier life, and
say to one another,—"Do you remember yonder planet, where
once we went to school?" And whether our elective study here
lay chiefly in the fields of action or of thought will matter little
to us then, when other schools shall have led us through other
disciplines.

Some War Scenes Revisited

NOTHING in actual life can come so near the experience of Rip Van Winkle as to revisit war scenes after a dozen years of peace. Alice's adventures in Wonderland, when she finds herself dwarfed after eating the clover leaf,[1] do not surpass the sense of insignificance that comes over any one who once wore uniform when he enters, as a temporary carpet-bagger, some city which he formerly ruled or helped to rule with absolute sway. An ex-commander of colored troops has this advantage, that the hackmen and longshore-men may remember him if nobody else does; and he at once possesses that immense practical convenience which comes only from a personal acquaintance with what are called the humbler classes. In a strange place, if one can establish relations with a black waiter or a newspaper correspondent, all doors fly open. The patronage of the great is powerless in comparison.

When I had last left Jacksonville, Florida, in March, 1864, the town was in flames: the streets were full of tongues of fire creeping from house to house; the air was dense with lurid smoke. Our steamers dropped rapidly down the river, laden to the gunwale with the goods of escaping inhabitants. The black soldiers, guiltless of all share in the flames, were yet excited by the occasion, recalled their favorite imagery of the Judgment Day, and sang and shouted without ceasing. I never saw a wilder scene. Fourteen years after, the steamboat came up to the same wharf, and I stepped quietly ashore into what seemed a summer watering-place: the roses were in bloom, the hotel verandas were full of guests, there were gay shops in the street, the wharves were covered with merchandise and with people. The delicious air was the same, the trees were the same; all else was changed. The earthworks we had built were leveled and overgrown; there was a bridge at the ford we used to picket; the church in whose steeple we built a lookout was still there, but it had a new tower, planned for peaceful purposes only. The very railroad along which we

287

skirmished almost daily was now torn up, and a new track entered the town at a different point. I could not find even the wall which one of our men clambered over, loading and firing, with a captured goose between his legs. Only the blue sky and the soft air, the lovely atmosphere of Florida, remained; the distant line of woods had the same outlook, and when the noon guns began to be fired for Washington's birthday I could hardly convince myself that the roar was not that of our gunboats, still shelling the woods as they had done so many years before. Then the guns ceased; the past withdrew into yet deeper remoteness. It seemed as if I were the only man left on earth to recall it. An hour later, the warm grasp of some of my old soldiers dispelled the dream of oblivion.

I had a less vivid sense of change at Beaufort, South Carolina, so familiar to many during the war. The large white houses still look peacefully down the placid river, but there are repairs and paint everywhere, and many new houses or cabins have been built. There is a new village, called Port Royal, at the railroad terminus, about a mile from my first camp at Old Fort plantation; and there is also a station near Beaufort itself, approached by a fine shell-road. The fortifications on the old shell-road have almost disappeared; the freedmen's village near them, named after the present writer, blew away one day in a tornado, and returned no more. A great national cemetery is established near its site. There are changes enough, and yet the general effect of the town is unaltered; there is Northern energy there, and the discovery of valuable phosphates has opened a new branch of industry; but after all it is the same pleasant old sleepy Beaufort, and no military Rip Van Winkle need feel himself too rudely aroused.

However, I went South not to see places, but people. On the way from Washington I lingered for a day or two to visit some near kinsfolk in Virginia, formerly secessionists to a man, or, to be more emphatic, to a woman. Then I spent a Sunday in Richmond, traversed rapidly part of North Carolina and Georgia, spent a day and two nights in Charleston, two days at Beaufort, and visited various points in Florida, going as far as St. Augustine. I had not set foot in the Southern States for nearly fourteen years, but I remembered them vividly across that gap of time, and also recalled very distinctly a winter visit to Virginia during college days. With these memories ever present, it was to me a matter of great interest to observe the apparent influence of freedom on the colored people, and the relation between them and the whites.

And first, as to the material condition of the former slaves. Sydney Smith, revisiting Edinburgh in 1821, after ten years' absence, was struck with the "wonderful increase of shoes and stockings, streets and houses." The change as to the first item, in South Carolina, tells the story of social progress since emancipation. The very first of my old acquaintances whom I met in that region was the robust wife of one of my soldiers. I found her hoeing in a field, close beside our old camp-ground. I had seen that woman hoeing in the same field fifteen years before. The same sky was above her, the same soil beneath her feet; but the war was over, slavery was gone. The soil that had been her master's was now her own by purchase; and the substantial limbs that trod it were no longer bare and visibly black, but incased in red-striped stockings of the most conspicuous design. "Think of it!" I said to a clever Massachusetts damsel in Washington, "the whole world so changed, and yet that woman still hoes." "In hose," quoth the lively maiden; and I preserve for posterity the condensed epigram.

Besides the striped stockings, which are really so conspicuous that the St. Augustine light-house is painted to match them, one sees a marked, though moderate progress in all the comforts of life. Formerly the colored people of the sea islands, even in their first days of freedom, slept very generally on the floor; and when our regimental hospital was first fitted up, the surgeon found with dismay that the patients had regarded the beds as merely beautiful ornaments, and had unanimously laid themselves down in the intervening spaces. Now I noticed bedstead and bedding in every cabin I visited in South Carolina and Florida. Formerly the cabins often had no tables, and families rarely ate together, each taking food as was convenient; but now they seemed to have family meals, a step toward decent living. This progress they themselves recognized. Moreover, I often saw pictures from the illustrated papers on the wall, and the children's school-books on the shelf. I rarely met an ex-soldier who did not own his house and ground, the inclosures varying from five to two hundred acres; and I found one man on the St. John's who had been offered $3000 for his real estate. In many cases these homesteads had been bought within a few years, showing a steady progress in self-elevation.

I do not think the world could show a finer sample of self-respecting peasant life than a colored woman, with whom I came down the St. John's River to Jacksonville, from one of the little settlements along that magnificent stream. She was a freed slave, the wife of a former soldier, and was going to market, basket in hand, with her little boy by her side. She had the tall erect figure, clear black skin, thin features, fine teeth, and intelligent bearing that marked so many of my Florida soldiers. She was dressed very plainly, but with scrupulous cleanliness: a rather faded gingham dress, well-worn tweed sack, shoes and stockings, straw hat with plain black ribbon, and neat white collar and cuffs. She told me that she and her husband owned one hundred and sixty acres of land, bought and paid for by their own earnings, at $1.25 per acre; they had a log-house, and were going to build a frame-house; they raised for themselves all the food they needed, except meat and flour, which they bought in Jacksonville. They had a church within reach (Baptist); a school-house of forty pupils, taught by a colored teacher; her husband belonged to the Good Templars, as did all the men in their neighborhood. For miles along the St. John's, a little back from the river, such settlements are scattered; the men cultivating their own plots of ground, or working on the steam-boats, or fishing, or lumbering. What more could be expected of any race, after fifteen years of freedom? Are the Irish voters of New York their superiors in condition, or the factory operatives of Fall River?

I met perhaps a hundred men, in different places, who had been under my command, and whose statements I could trust. Only one of these complained of poverty; and he, as I found, earned good wages, had neither wife nor child to support, and was given to whisky. There were some singular instances of prosperity among these men. I was told in Jacksonville that I should find Corporal McGill "de most populous man in Beaufort." When I got there, I found him the proprietor of a livery stable populous with horses at any rate; he was worth $3000 or $4000, and was cordial and hospitable to the last degree. At parting, he drove me to the station with his best carriage and horses; and I regret to add that while he was refusing all compensation his young steeds ran away, and as the train whirled off I saw my "populous" cor-

poral double-quick down the shell-road, to recapture his equip-
age. I found Sergeant Hodges a master carpenter at Jacksonville;
Corporal Hicks was a preacher there, highly respected; and I
heard of Corporal Sutton as a traveling minister farther up the
river. Sergeant Shemeltella, a fine-looking half-Spaniard from St.
Augustine, now patrols, with gun in hand, the woods which we
once picketed at Port Royal Ferry, and supplies game to the mar-
kets of Charleston and Savannah. And without extending the list
I may add that some of these men, before attaining prosperity,
had to secure, by the severest experience, the necessary judgment
in business affairs. It will hardly be believed that the men of my
regiment alone sunk $30,000 in an impracticable building associ-
ation, and in the purchase of a steamboat which was lost unin-
sured. One of the shrewdest among them, after taking his share
of this, resolved to be prudent, put $750 in the Freedmen's Bank,[2]
and lost that too. Their present prosperity must be judged in the
light of such formidable calamities as these.

I did not hear a single charge of laziness made against the freed
colored people in the States I visited. In Virginia it was admitted
that they would work wherever they were paid, but that many
were idle for want of employment. Rev. Dr. Pinckney, in a recent
address before the Charleston Historical Society, declares that the
negroes "do not refuse to work; all are planting;" and he only
complains that they work unskillfully. A rice-planter in Georgia
told me that he got his work done more efficiently than under
the slave system. Men and women worked well for seventy-five
cents a day; many worked under contract, which at first they did
not understand or like. On the other hand, he admitted, the planters did not at once learn how to manage them as freedmen, but
had acquired the knowledge by degrees; so that even the strikes
at harvest-time, which had at first embarrassed them, were now
avoided. Another Georgia planter spoke with much interest of an
effort now making by the colored people in Augusta to establish
a cotton factory of their own, in emulation of the white factories
which have there been so successful. He said that this proposed
factory was to have a capital of fifty thousand dollars in fifty
dollar shares, and that twenty-eight thousand dollars of it were
already raised. The white business agent of one of the existing
factories was employed, he said, as the adviser of those organizing

this. He spoke of it with interest as a proper outlet for the industry of the better class of colored people, who were educated rather above field labor. He also spoke with pride of the normal school for colored people at Atlanta.

The chief of police in Beaufort, South Carolina, a colored man, told me that the colored population there required but little public assistance, though two thousand of them had removed from the upper parts of the State within a year and a half, thinking they could find better wages at Beaufort. This removal struck me as being of itself a favorable indication, showing that they were now willing to migrate, whereas they were once hopelessly fixed to the soil, and therefore too much in the power of the land owners. The new industry of digging phosphates for exportation to England employs a good many in Beaufort County, and they earn by this from seventy-five cents to a dollar a day. Others are employed in loading vessels at the new settlement of Port Royal; but the work is precarious and insufficient, and I was told that if they made two dollars a week they did well. But it must be remembered that they have mostly little patches of land of their own, and can raise for themselves the corn and vegetables on which they chiefly live. I asked an old man if he could supply his family from his own piece of ground. "Oh, yes, mars'r," he said (the younger men do not say "mars'r," but "boss"), and then he went on, with a curious accumulation of emphasis: "I raise plenty too, much more dan I destroy,"—meaning simply "very much more."

The price of cotton is now very low, and the sea-island cotton has lost forever, perhaps, its place in the English market. Yet Rev. Dr. Pinckney, in the address just quoted, while lamenting the ravages of war in the sea islands, admits that nearly half as much cotton was raised in them in 1875 as in 1860, and more than half as much corn, the population being about the same, and the area cultivated less than one third. To adopt his figures, the population in 1860 was 40,053; acres under cultivation, 274,015; corn, 618,959 bushels; cotton, 19,121 bales. In 1875 the population was 43,060; acres under cultivation, 86,449; corn, 314,271 bushels; cotton, 8199 bales.

When we consider the immense waste of war, the destruction of capital, the abandonment of estates by those who yet refuse to sell them, and the partial introduction of industry other than agricultural, this seems to me a promising exhibit. And when we observe how much more equitable than formerly is now the distribution of the products between capitalist and laborer, the case is still better. Dr. Pinckney's utmost complaint in regard to South Carolina is that the result of the war "has been injurious to the whites, and not beneficial to the blacks." Even he, a former slave-holder, does not claim that it has injured the blacks; and this, from his point of view, is quite a concession. Twenty years hence he may admit that whatever the result of war may have been, that of peace will be beneficial to both races.

In observing a lately emancipated race, it is always harder to judge as to the condition of the women than of the men, especially where the men alone have been enfranchised. My friend the judge, in Virginia, declared that the colored men and women were there so unlike that they seemed like different races: the men had behaved "admirably," he said; the women were almost hopelessly degraded. On the other hand, my white friends of both sexes at Beaufort took just the opposite view, and thought the women there quite superior to the men, especially in respect to whisky. Perhaps the influences of the two regions may have made the difference, as the sea islands have had the presence, ever since the beginning of the war, of self-devoted and well-educated teachers, mostly women, while such teachers have been much rarer in Virginia. They have also been rare in Florida; but then the Florida negroes are a superior class.

Certainly it was pleasant to me to hear favorable accounts of this and that particular colored woman of whom I had known something in war times. Almost the first old acquaintance named to me on the sea islands, for instance, was one Venus, whose marriage to a soldier of my regiment I chronicled in war times. "Now, cunnel," said that soldier in confidence, "I want for get me one good lady." And when I asked one of his friends about the success of the effort, he said triumphantly, "John's gwine for marry Venus." Now the record of Venus as a good lady was so very questionable in her earlier incarnations that the name was not encouraging; but I was delighted to hear of the goddess, fifteen years later, as a most virtuous wife and a very efficient teacher of sewing in Miss Botume's school. Her other sewing-teacher, by the way, is Juno.

I went into schools, here and there; the colored people seemed to value them very much, and to count upon their own votes as a means of securing these advantages, instead of depending, as formerly, on Northern aid. The schools I visited did not seem to me so good as those kept by Northern ladies during the war, at Port Royal; but the present schools form a part of a public system, and are in that respect better, while enough of the Northern teachers still remain to exert a beneficial influence, at least on the sea islands. I was sorry to be in Charleston only on Saturday, when the Shaw Memorial School was not in session. This is a large wooden building, erected on land bought with part of a fund collected in the colored regiments for a monument to Colonel Shaw. This school has an average attendance of five hundred and twenty, with twelve teachers, white and black. The Morris Street School for colored children, in Charleston, has fourteen hundred pupils. These two schools occupy nearly half of the four columns given by the Charleston News and Courier of April 12, 1878, to the annual exhibition of public schools. The full programme of exercises is given, with the names of the pupils receiving prizes and honors; and it seems almost incredible that the children whose successes are thus proudly recorded can be the sons and daughters of freed slaves. And I hold it utterly ungenerous, in view of such facts, to declare that the white people of the South have learned nothing by experience, and are "incapable of change."

Public officials at Beaufort told me that in that place most of the men could now sign their names,—certainly a great proof of progress since war times. I found some of my friends anxious lest school should unfit the young people for the hard work of the field; but I saw no real proof of this, nor did the parents confirm it. Miss Botume, however, said that the younger women now thought that, after marriage, they ought to be excused from field labor, if they took care of their homes and children; a proposal so directly in the line of advancing civilization that one can hardly object to it. The great solicitude of some of the teachers in that region relates to the passage of some congressional bill which shall set aside the tax sales under which much real estate is now held; but others think that there is no fear of this, even under a democratic administration.

This leads naturally to the question, What is to be the relation between the two races in those Southern States of which I speak? I remember that Corporal Simon Crier, one of the oddities of my regiment, used to declare that when the war was over, he should go to "Libery;"[3] and, when pressed for a reason, used to say, "Dese yer secesh will neber be cibilized in my time." Yet Simon Crier's time is not ended, for I heard of him as peacefully dwelling near Charleston, and taking no part in that insignificant colonization movement of which we hear so much more at the North than at the South. Taking civilization in his sense,—a fair enough sense,—we shall find Virginia, South Carolina, and Florida holding an intermediate position; being probably behind North Carolina, West Virginia, and the border States, but decidedly in advance of Georgia, Alabama, and Mississippi.

It is certain that there is, in the States I visited, a condition of outward peace and no conspicuous outrages; and that this has now been the case for many months. All will admit that this state of things must be a blessing, unless there lies beneath it some covert plan for crushing or reënslaving the colored race. I know that a few good men at the North honestly believe in the existence of some such plan; I can only say that I thoroughly disbelieve in it. Taking the nature of the Southern whites as these very men describe it,—impulsive and ungoverned,—it is utterly inconceivable that such a plan, if formed, should not show itself in some personal ill usage of the blacks, in the withdrawal of privileges, in legislation endangering their rights. I can assert that, carrying with me the eyes of a tolerably suspicious abolitionist, I saw none of these indications. During the war, I could hardly go anywhere within the Union lines for twenty-four hours without being annoyed by some sign of race hostility, or being obliged to interfere for the protection of some abused man or woman. During this trip, I had absolutely no occasion for any such attitude. The change certainly has not resulted from any cringing demeanor on the part of the blacks, for they show much more manhood than they once did. I am satisfied that it results from the changed feeling created towards a race of freedmen and voters. How can we ask more of the States formerly in rebellion than that they should be abreast of New England in granting rights and privileges to the colored race? Yet this is now the case in the three States I name; or at least if they fall behind at some points, they lead at some points. Let us look at a few instances.

The republican legislature of Connecticut has just refused to incorporate a colored military company; but the colored militia regiment of Charleston was reviewed by General Hampton and his staff just before my visit. One of the colored officers told me that there was absolutely no difference in the treatment accorded this regiment and that shown toward the white militia, who were reviewed the day before; and Messrs. Whipper and Jones, the only dissatisfied republican leaders whom I saw, admitted that there was no opposition whatever to this arming of the blacks. I may add that while I was in Virginia a bill was reported favorably in the legislature for the creation of a colored militia company, called the State Guard, under control of their own officers, and reporting directly to the adjutant-general.

I do not know a Northern city which enrolls colored citizens in its police, though this may here and there have happened. I saw colored policemen in Charleston, Beaufort, and Jacksonville, though the former city is under democratic control; and I was told by a leading colored man that the number had lately been increased in Charleston, and that one lieutenant of police was of that race. The republican legislature of Rhode Island has just refused once more to repeal the bill prohibiting intermarriages, while the legislature of South Carolina has refused to pass such a bill. I can remember when Frederick Douglas was ejected from the railway cars in Massachusetts, because of his complexion; and it is not many years since one of the most cultivated and lady-like colored teachers in the nation was ejected from a street car in Philadelphia, her birthplace, for the same reason. But I rode with colored people in first-class cars throughout Virginia and South Carolina, and in street cars in Richmond and Charleston. I am told that this last is the case also in Savannah and New Orleans, but can testify only to what I have seen. In Georgia, I was told, the colored people were not allowed in first-class cars; but they had always a decent second-class car, opening from the smoking-car, with the door usually closed between.

All these things may be true, and still a great deal may remain to be done; but it is idle to declare that the sun has not risen because we do not yet see it in the zenith. Even the most extreme Southern newspapers constantly contain paragraphs that amaze us, not only in contrast to slavery times, but in contrast to the times immediately following the war. While I was in South Carolina the Charleston News and Courier published, with commendation, the report of a bill, passed by the Maryland legislature, admitting colored lawyers to practice, after the court of appeals had excluded them; and it copied with implied approval the remark of the Baltimore Gazette: "Raise the educational test, the rigidity of the examinations for admission, or the moral test as high as you please, but let us have done with the color test."

It is certain that every republican politician whom I saw in South Carolina, black or white, spoke well of Governor Hampton, with two exceptions,—Mr. W. J. Whipper, whom Governor Chamberlain refused to commission as judge, and Mr. Jones, who was clerk of the house of delegates through its most corrupt period. I give their dissent for what it is worth, but the opinion of others was as I have said. "We have no complaint to make of Governor Hampton; he has kept his pledges," was the general remark. For instance, a bill passed both houses by a party vote, requiring able-bodied male prisoners, under sentence in county jails, to work on the public roads and streets. The colored people remonstrated strongly, regarding it as aimed at them. Governor Hampton vetoed the bill, and the house, on reflection, sustained the veto by a vote of one hundred and two to ten. But he is not always so strong in influence: there is a minority of "fire-eaters" who resist him; he is denounced by the "upcountry people" as an aristocrat; and I was told that he might yet need the colored vote to sustain him against his own party. Grant that this assumes him to be governed by self-interest; that strengthens the value of this evidence. We do not expect that saints will have the monopoly of government at South or North; what we need is to know that the colored vote in South Carolina makes itself felt as a power, and secures its rightful ends.

The facts here stated are plain and unquestionable. When we come to consider the political condition of the former slaves, we find greater difficulties in taking in the precise position. First, it must be remembered that even at the North the practical antagonism towards colored voters lasted long after their actual enfranchisement, and has worn out only by degrees. Samuel Breck, in his very entertaining reminiscences, tells us that in Philadelphia, in the early part of this century, the colored voters seldom dared to come to the polls, for fear of ill usage. Then we must remember that in South Carolina, the State which has been most under discussion in this essay, the colored voters were practically massed, for years, under the banner of spoliation, and the antagonism created was hardly less intense than that created by the Tweed dynasty in New York. As far as I can judge, neither the "carpet-bag" frauds nor the "Ku-Klux" persecutions have been exaggerated, and they certainly kept each other alive, and have, at least temporarily, ceased together. No doubt the atrocities committed by the whites were the worst, inasmuch as murder is worse than robbery, but few in South Carolina will now deny that the provocation was simply enormous.

And it is moreover true that this state of things left bad blood behind it, which will long last. It has left jealousies which confound the innocent with the guilty. Judging the future by the past, the white South Carolinian finds it almost impossible to believe that a republican state administration can be decently honest. This is a feeling quite apart from any national attitude, and quite consistent with a fair degree of loyalty. Nor does it take the form of resistance to colored voters as such. The Southern whites accept them precisely as Northern men in cities accept the ignorant Irish vote,—not cheerfully, but with acquiescence in the inevitable; and when the strict color-line is once broken they are just as ready to conciliate the negro as the Northern politician to flatter the Irishman. Any powerful body of voters may be cajoled to-day and intimidated to-morrow and hated always, but it can never be left out of sight. At the South, politics are an absorbing interest: people are impetuous; they divide and subdivide on all local issues, and each faction needs votes. Two men are up for mayor or sheriff, or what not: each conciliates every voter he can reach, and each finds it for his interest to stand by those who help him. This has been long predicted by shrewd observers, and is beginning to happen all over the South. I heard of a dozen instances of it. Indeed, the vote of thanks passed by the Mississippi legislature to its colored senator, Mr. Bruce, for his vote on the silver bill was only the same thing on a larger scale. To praise him was to censure Mr. Lamar.

It may be said, "Ah, but the real test is, Will the black voters be allowed to vote for the republican party?" To assert this crowning right will undoubtedly demand a good deal of these voters; it will require courage, organization, intelligence, honesty, and leaders. Without these, any party, in any State, will sooner or later go to the wall. As to South Carolina, I can only say that one of the ablest republican lawyers in the State, a white man, unsuspected of corruption, said to me, "This is a republican State, and to prove it such we need only to bring out our voters. For this we do not need troops, but that half a dozen well-known Northern republicans should canvass the State, just as if it were a Northern State. The colored voters need to know that the party at the North has not, as they have been told, deserted them. With this and a perfectly clean list of nominees, we can carry the legislature, making no nominations against Hampton." "But," I asked, "would not these meetings be broken up?" "Not one of them," he said. "They will break up our local meetings, but not those held by speakers from other States. It would ruin them with the nation." And this remark was afterwards indorsed by others, white and black. When I asked one of the few educated colored leaders in the State, "Do you regret the withdrawal[4] of the troops by President Hayes?" "No," he said; "the only misfortune was that they were not withdrawn two years earlier. That would have put us on our good behavior, obliged us to command respect, and made it easier to save the republican party. But it can still be saved."

There is no teacher so wholesome as personal necessity. In South Carolina a few men and many women cling absolutely to the past, learning nothing, forgetting nothing.[5] But the bulk of thinking men see that the old Southern society is as absolutely annihilated as the feudal system, and that there is no other form of society now possible except such as prevails at the North and West. "The purse-proud Southerner," said Rev. Dr. Pinckney, in his address at Charleston, "is an institution which no longer exists. The race has passed away as completely as the Saurian tribes, whose bones we are now digging from the fossil beds of the Ashley." "The Yankees ought to be satisfied," said one gentleman to me: "every live man at the South is trying with all his might to be a Yankee." Business, money, financial prosperity,—these now form the absorbing Southern question. At the Exchange Hotel in Richmond, where I spent a Sunday, the members of the Assembly were talking all day about the debt,—how to escape bankruptcy. I did not overhear the slightest allusion to the negro or the North. It is likely enough that this may lead to claims on the national treasury, but it tends to nothing worse. The dream of reënslaving the negro, if it ever existed, is like the negro's dream, if he ever had it, of five acres and a mule[6] from the government. Both races have long since come down to the stern reality of self-support. No sane Southerner would now take back as slaves, were they offered, a race of men who have been for a dozen years freemen and voters.

Every secessionist risked his all upon secession, and has received as the penalty of defeat only poverty. It is the mildest punishment ever inflicted after an unsuccessful civil war, and it proves in this case a blessing in disguise. Among Southern young men it has made energy and industry fashionable. Formerly, if a Southern planter wished to travel, he borrowed money on his coming crop, or sold a slave or two. Now he must learn what John Randolph, of Roanoke, once announced as the philosopher's stone, to "pay as you go." The Northern traveler asks himself, Where are the white people of the South? You meet few in public conveyances; you see no crowd in the streets. In the hotels of Washington you rarely hear the Southern accent, and, indeed, my Virginia friends declared that some of its more marked intonations were growing unfashionable. Out of one hundred and three Southern representatives in Congress, only twenty-three have their families with them. On one of the few day trains from Washington to Richmond, there was but one first-class car, and there were not twenty passengers, mostly from the Northern States. Among some fifty people on the steamboat from Savannah to Jacksonville, there were not six Southerners. Everywhere you hear immigration desired and emigration recognized as a fact. My friend the judge talked to me eloquently about the need of more Northern settlers, and the willingness of all to receive them; the plantations would readily be broken up to accommodate any purchaser who had money. But within an hour, his son, a young law student, told me that as soon as he was admitted to the bar he should go West.

The first essential to social progress at the South is that each State should possess local self-government. The States have been readmitted as States, and can no more be treated as Territories than you can replace a bird in the egg. They must now work out their own salvation, just as much as Connecticut and New Jersey. If any abuses exist, the remedy is not to be found in federal interference, except in case of actual insurrection, but in the voting power of the blacks, so far as they have strength or skill to assert it; and where that fails, in their power of locomotion. They must leave those counties or States which ill-use them for others which treat them better. If a man is dissatisfied with the laws of Massachusetts, and cannot get them mended, he can at least remove into Rhode Island or Connecticut, and the loss of valuable citizens will soon make itself felt.

This is the precise remedy possessed by the colored people at the South, with the great advantage that they have the monopoly of all the leading industries, and do not need the whites more, on the whole, than the whites need them. They have reached the point where civilized methods begin to prevail. When they have once enlisted the laws of political economy on their side, this silent ally will be worth more than an army with banners.

Emily Dickinson's Letters

Few events in American literary history have been more curious than the sudden rise of Emily Dickinson into a posthumous fame only more accentuated by the utterly recluse character of her life and by her aversion to even a literary publicity. The lines which form a prelude to the published volume of her poems are the only ones that have yet come to light indicating even a temporary desire to come in contact with the great world of readers; she seems to have had no reference, in all the rest, to anything but her own thought and a few friends. But for her only sister, it is very doubtful if her poems would ever have been printed at all; and when published,[1] they were launched quietly and without any expectation of a wide audience; yet the outcome of it is that six editions of the volume have been sold within six months, a suddenness of success almost without a parallel in American literature.

One result of this glare of publicity has been a constant and earnest demand by her readers for further information in regard to her; and I have decided with much reluctance to give some extracts from her early correspondence with one whom she always persisted in regarding—with very little ground for it—as a literary counselor and confidant.

It seems to be the opinion of those who have examined her accessible correspondence most widely, that no other letters bring us quite so intimately near to the peculiar quality and aroma of her nature; and it has been urged upon me very strongly that her readers have the right to know something more of this gifted and most interesting woman.

On April 16, 1862, I took from the post office in Worcester, Mass., where I was then living, the following letter:—

MR. HIGGINSON,—Are you too deeply occupied to say if my verse is alive?

The mind is so near itself it cannot see distinctly, and I have none to ask.

Should you think it breathed, and had you the leisure to tell me, I should feel quick gratitude.

If I make the mistake, that you dared to tell me would give me sincerer honor toward you.

I inclose my name, asking you, if you please, sir, to tell me what is true?

That you will not betray me it is needless to ask, since honor is its own pawn.

The letter was postmarked "Amherst," and it was in a handwriting so peculiar that it seemed as if the writer might have taken her first lessons by studying the famous fossil bird-tracks in the museum of that college town. Yet it was not in the slightest degree illiterate, but cultivated, quaint, and wholly unique. Of punctuation there was little; she used chiefly dashes, and it has been thought better, in printing these letters, as with her poems, to give them the benefit in this respect of the ordinary usages; and so with her habit as to capitalization, as the printers call it, in which she followed the Old English and present German method of thus distinguishing every noun substantive. But the most curious thing about the letter was the total absence of a signature. It proved, however, that she had written her name on a card, and put it under the shelter of a smaller envelope inclosed in the larger; and even this name was written—as if the shy writer wished to recede as far as possible from view—in pencil, not in ink. The name was Emily Dickinson. Inclosed with the letter were four poems, two of which have been already printed,—"Safe in their alabaster chambers" and "I'll tell you how the sun rose," together with the two that here follow. The first comprises in its eight lines a truth so searching that it seems a condensed summary of the whole experience of a long life:—

> We play at paste
> Till qualified for pearl;
> Then drop the paste
> And deem ourself a fool.

The shapes, though, were similar
And our new hands
Learned gem-tactics,
Practicing sands.

Then came one which I have always classed among the most
exquisite of her productions, with a singular felicity of phrase and
an aerial lift that bears the ear upward with the bee it traces:—

The nearest dream recedes unrealized.
The heaven we chase,
Like the June bee
Before the schoolboy,
Invites the race,
Stoops to an easy clover,
Dips—evades—teases—deploys—
Then to the royal clouds
Lifts his light pinnace,
Heedless of the boy
Staring, bewildered, at the mocking sky.

Homesick for steadfast honey,—
Ah! the bee flies not
Which brews that rare variety.

The impression of a wholly new and original poetic genius was
as distinct on my mind at the first reading of these four poems as
it is now, after thirty years of further knowledge; and with it came
the problem never yet solved, what place ought to be assigned in
literature to what is so remarkable, yet so elusive of criticism. The
bee himself did not evade the schoolboy more than she evaded
me; and even at this day I still stand somewhat bewildered, like
the boy.

Circumstances, however, soon brought me in contact with an
uncle[2] of Emily Dickinson, a gentleman not now living; a prominent citizen of Worcester, a man of integrity and character, who
shared her abruptness and impulsiveness but certainly not her poetic temperament, from which he was indeed singularly remote.
He could tell but little of her, she being evidently an enigma to

him, as to me. It is hard to tell what answer was made by me, under these circumstances, to this letter. It is probable that the adviser sought to gain time a little and find out with what strange creature he was dealing. I remember to have ventured on some criticism which she afterwards called "surgery," and on some questions, part of which she evaded, as will be seen, with a naïve skill such as the most experienced and worldly coquette might envy. Her second letter (received April 26, 1862), was as follows:—

MR. HIGGINSON,—Your kindness claimed earlier gratitude, but I was ill, and write to-day from my pillow.

Thank you for the surgery; it was not so painful as I supposed. I bring you others, as you ask, though they might not differ. While my thought is undressed, I can make the distinction; but when I put them in the gown, they look alike and numb.

You asked how old I was? I made no verse, but one or two, until this winter, sir.

I had a terror since September, I could tell to none; and so I sing, as the boy does of the burying ground, because I am afraid.

You inquire my books. For poets, I have Keats, and Mr. and Mrs. Browning. For prose, Mr. Ruskin, Sir Thomas Browne, and the Revelations. I went to school, but in your manner of the phrase had no education. When a little girl, I had a friend who taught me Immortality; but venturing too near, himself, he never returned. Soon after my tutor died, and for several years my lexicon was my only companion. Then I found one more, but he was not contented I be his scholar, so he left the land.

You ask of my companions. Hills, sir, and the sundown, and a dog large as myself, that my father bought me. They are better than beings because they know, but do not tell; and the noise in the pool at noon excels my piano.

I have a brother and sister; my mother does not care for thought, and father,[3] too busy with his briefs to notice what we do. He buys me many books, but begs me not to read them, because he fears they joggle the mind. They are religious, except me, and address an eclipse, every morning, whom they call their "Father."

But I fear my story fatigues you. I would like to learn. Could you tell me how to grow, or is it unconveyed, like melody or witchcraft?

You speak of Mr. Whitman.[4] I never read his book, but was told that it was disgraceful.

I read Miss Prescott's *Circumstance*,[5] but it followed me in the dark, so I avoided her.

Two editors of journals came to my father's house this winter, and asked me for my mind, and when I asked them "why" they said I was penurious, and they would use it for the world.

I could not weigh myself, myself. My size felt small to me. I read your chapters in the Atlantic, and experienced honor for you. I was sure you would not reject a confiding question.

Is this, sir, what you asked me to tell you? Your friend,

E. DICKINSON.

It will be seen that she had now drawn a step nearer, signing her name, and as my "friend." It will also be noticed that I had sounded her about certain American authors, then much read; and that she knew how to put her own criticisms in a very trenchant way. With this letter came some more verses, still in the same birdlike script, as for instance the following:—

> Your riches taught me poverty,
>   Myself a millionaire
> In little wealths, as girls could boast,
>   Till, broad as Buenos Ayre,
> You drifted your dominions
>   A different Peru,
> And I esteemed all poverty
>   For life's estate, with you.
>
> Of mines, I little know, myself,
>   But just the names of gems,
> The colors of the commonest,
>   And scarce of diadems
> So much that, did I meet the queen
>   Her glory I should know;
> But this must be a different wealth,
>   To miss it, beggars so.

I'm sure 't is India, all day,
 To those who look on you
Without a stint, without a blame,
 Might I but be the Jew!
I'm sure it is Golconda
 Beyond my power to deem,
To have a smile for mine, each day,
 How better than a gem!

At least, it solaces to know
 That there exists a gold
Although I prove it just in time
 It distance to behold;
Its far, far treasure to surmise
 And estimate the pearl
That slipped my simple fingers through
 While just a girl at school!

Here was already manifest that defiance of form, never through carelessness, and never precisely from whim, which so marked her. The slightest change in the order of words—thus, "While yet at school, a girl"—would have given her a rhyme for this last line; but no; she was intent upon her thought, and it would not have satisfied her to make the change. The other poem further showed, what had already been visible, a rare and delicate sympathy with the life of nature:—

A bird came down the walk;
He did not know I saw;
He bit an angle-worm in halves
And ate the fellow raw.

And then he drank a dew
From a convenient grass,
And then hopped sidewise to a wall,
To let a beetle pass.

He glanced with rapid eyes
That hurried all around;
They looked like frightened beads, I

thought;
He stirred his velvet head

Like one in danger, cautious.
I offered him a crumb,
And he unrolled his feathers
And rowed him softer home

Than oars divide the ocean,
Too silver for a seam—
Or butterflies, off banks of noon,
Leap, plashless as they swim.

It is possible that in a second letter I gave more of distinct praise or encouragement, for her third is in a different mood. This was received June 8, 1862. There is something startling in its opening image; and in the yet stranger phrase that follows, where she apparently uses "mob" in the sense of chaos or bewilderment:—

DEAR FRIEND,—Your letter gave no drunkenness, because I tasted rum before. Domingo comes but once; yet I have had few pleasures so deep as your opinion, and if I tried to thank you, my tears would block my tongue.

My dying tutor told me that he would like to live till I had been a poet, but Death was much of mob as I could master, then. And when, far afterward, a sudden light on orchards, or a new fashion in the wind troubled my attention, I felt a palsy, here, the verses just relieve.

Your second letter surprised me, and for a moment, swung. I had not supposed it. Your first gave no dishonor, because the true are not ashamed I thanked you for your justice, but could not drop the bells whose jingling cooled my tramp. Perhaps the balm seemed better, because you bled me first. I smile when you suggest that I delay "to publish," that being foreign to my thought as firmament to fin.

If fame belonged to me, I could not escape her; if she did not, the longest day would pass me on the chase, and the approbation of my dog would forsake me then. My barefoot rank is better.

You think my gait "spasmodic." I am in danger, sir. You think me "uncontrolled." I have no tribunal.

Would you have time to be the "friend" you should think I need? I have a little shape: it would not crowd your desk, nor make much racket as the mouse that dents your galleries.

If I might bring you what I do—not so frequent to trouble you—and ask you if I told it clear, 't would be control to me. The sailor cannot see the North, but knows the needle can. The "hand you stretch me in the dark" I put mine in, and turn away. I have no Saxon now:—

> As if I asked a common alms,
> And in my wondering hand
> A stranger pressed a kingdom,
> And I, bewildered, stand;
> As if I asked the Orient
> Had it for me a morn,
> And it should lift its purple dikes
> And shatter me with dawn!

But, will you be my preceptor, Mr. Higginson?

With this came the poem already published in her volume and entitled Renunciation; and also that beginning "Of all the sounds dispatched abroad," thus fixing approximately the date of those two. I must soon have written to ask her for her picture, that I might form some impression of my enigmatical correspondent. To this came the following reply, in July, 1862:—

Could you believe me without? I had no portrait, now, but am small, like the wren; and my hair is bold, like the chestnut bur; and my eyes, like the sherry in the glass, that the guest leaves. Would this do just as well?

It often alarms father. He says death might occur, and he has moulds of all the rest, but has no mould of me; but I noticed the quick wore off those things, in a few days, and forestall the dishonor. You will think no caprice of me.

You said "Dark." I know the butterfly, and the lizard, and the orchis. Are not those *your* countrymen?

I am happy to be your scholar, and will deserve the kindness I cannot repay.

If you truly consent, I recite now. Will you tell me my fault, frankly as to yourself, for I had rather wince than die. Men do not call the surgeon to commend the bone, but to set it, sir, and fracture within is more critical. And for this, preceptor, I shall bring you obedience, the blossom from my garden, and every gratitude I know.

Perhaps you smile at me. I could not stop for that. My business is circumference. An ignorance, not of customs, but if caught with the dawn, or the sunset see me, myself the only kangaroo among the beauty, sir, if you please, it afflicts me, and I thought that instruction would take it away.

Because you have much business, beside the growth of me, you will appoint, yourself, how often I shall come, without your inconvenience.

And if at any time you regret you received me, or I prove a different fabric to that you supposed, you must banish me.

When I state myself, as the representative of the verse, it does not mean me, but a supposed person.

You are true about the "perfection." To-day makes Yesterday mean.

You spoke of Pippa Passes.[6] I never heard anybody speak of Pippa Passes before. You see my posture is benighted.

To thank you baffles me. Are you perfectly powerful? Had I a pleasure you had not, I could delight to bring it.

YOUR SCHOLAR.

This was accompanied by this strong poem, with its breathless conclusion. The title is of my own giving:—

THE SAINTS' REST

Of tribulation, these are they,
    Denoted by the white;
The spangled gowns, a lesser rank
    Of victors designate.

All these did conquer; but the ones
   Who overcame most times,
Wear nothing commoner than snow,
   No ornaments but palms.

"Surrender" is a sort unknown
   On this superior soil;
"Defeat" an outgrown anguish,
   Remembered as the mile

Our panting ancle barely passed
   When night devoured the road;
But we stood whispering in the house,
   And all we said, was "Saved!"

[Note by the writer of the verses.] I
spelled ankle wrong.

It would seem that at first I tried a little,—a very little—to lead her in the direction of rules and traditions; but I fear it was only perfunctory, and that she interested me more in her—so to speak—unregenerate condition. Still, she recognizes the endeavor. In this case, as will be seen, I called her attention to the fact that while she took pains to correct the spelling of a word, she was utterly careless of greater irregularities. It will be seen by her answer that with her usual naïve adroitness she turns my point:—

DEAR FRIEND,—Are these more orderly? I thank you for the truth.

I had no monarch in my life, and cannot rule myself; and when I try to organize, my little force explodes and leaves me bare and charred.

I think you called me "wayward." Will you help me improve?

I suppose the pride that stops the breath, in the core of woods, is not of ourself.

You say I confess the little mistake, and omit the large. Because I can see orthography; but the ignorance out of sight is my preceptor's charge.

Of "shunning men and women," they talk of hallowed things, aloud, and embarrass my dog. He and I don't object to them, if they'll exist their side. I think Carl would please you. He is dumb, and brave. I think you would like the chestnut tree I met in my walk. It hit my notice suddenly, and I thought the skies were in blossom.

Then there's a noiseless noise in the orchard that I let persons hear.

You told me in one letter you could not come to see me "now," and I made no answer; not because I had none, but did not think myself the price that you should come so far.

I do not ask so large a pleasure, lest you might deny me.

You say, "Beyond your knowledge." You would not jest with me, because I believe you; but, preceptor, you cannot mean it?

All men say "What" to me, but I thought it a fashion.

When much in the woods, as a little girl, I was told that the snake would bite me, that I might pick a poisonous flower, or goblins kidnap me; but I went along and met no one but angels, who were far shyer of me than I could be of them, so I have n't that confidence in fraud which many exercise.

I shall observe your precept, though I don't understand it, always.

I marked a line in one verse, because I met it after I made it, and never consciously touch a paint mixed by another person.

I do not let go it, because it is mine. Have you the portrait of Mrs. Browning?

Persons sent me three. If you had none, will you have mine?

YOUR SCHOLAR.

A month or two after this I entered the volunteer army of the civil war, and must have written to her during the winter of 1862–3 from South Carolina or Florida, for the following reached me in camp:—

AMHERST.

DEAR FRIEND,—I did not deem that planetary forces annulled, but suffered an exchange of territory, or world.

I should have liked to see you before you became improbable. War feels to me an oblique place. Should there be other summers, would you perhaps come?

I found you were gone, by accident, as I find systems are, or seasons of the year, and obtain no cause, but suppose it a treason of progress that dissolves as it goes. Carlo still remained, and I told him

> Best gains must have the losses' test,
> To constitute them gains.

My shaggy ally assented.

Perhaps death gave me awe for friends, striking sharp and early, for I held them since in a brittle love, of more alarm than peace. I trust you may pass the limit of war; and though not reared to prayer, when service is had in church for our arms, I include yourself. . . . I was thinking to-day, as I noticed, that the "Supernatural" was only the Natural disclosed.

> Not "Revelation" 't is that waits,
> But our unfurnished eyes.

But I fear I detain you. Should you, before this reaches you, experience immortality, who will inform me of the exchange? Could you, with honor, avoid death, I entreat you, sir. It would bereave   YOUR GNOME.

I trust the "Procession of Flowers"[7] was not a premonition.

I cannot explain this extraordinary signature, substituted for the now customary "Your Scholar," unless she imagined her friend to be in some incredible and remote condition, imparting its strangeness to her. Mr. Howells[8] reminds me that Swedenborg[9] somewhere has an image akin to her "oblique place," where he symbolizes evil as simply an oblique angle. With this letter came verses, most refreshing in that clime of jasmines and mocking-birds, on the familiar robin:—

THE ROBIN

> The robin is the one
> That interrupts the morn
> With hurried, few, express reports
> When March is scarcely on.

The robin is the one
That overflows the noon
With her cherubic quantity,
An April but begun.

The robin is the one
That, speechless from her nest,
Submits that home and certainty
And sanctity are best.

In the summer of 1863 I was wounded, and in hospital for a time, during which came this letter in pencil, written from what was practically a hospital for her, though only for weak eyes:—

DEAR FRIEND,—Are you in danger? I did not know that you were hurt. Will you tell me more? Mr. Hawthorne died.[10]

I was ill since September, and since April in Boston for a physician's care. He does not let me go, yet I work in my prison, and make guests for myself.

Carlo did not come, because that he would die in jail; and the mountains I could not hold now, so I brought but the Gods.

I wish to see you more than before I failed. Will you tell me your health? I am surprised and anxious since receiving your note.

The only news I know
Is bulletins all day
From Immortality.

Can you render my pencil? The physician has taken away my pen.

I inclose the address from a letter, lest my figures fail.

Knowledge of your recovery would excel my own.

                                        E. DICKINSON.

Later this arrived:—

DEAR FRIEND,—I think of you so wholly that I cannot resist to write again, to ask if you are safe? Danger is not at first, for then we are unconscious, but in the after, slower days.

Do not try to be saved, but let redemption find you, as it certainly will. Love is its own rescue; for we, at our supremest, are but its trembling emblems.

YOUR SCHOLAR.

These were my earliest letters from Emily Dickinson, in their order. From this time and up to her death (May 15, 1886) we corresponded at varying intervals, she always persistently keeping up this attitude of "Scholar," and assuming on my part a preceptorship which it is almost needless to say did not exist. Always glad to hear her "recite," as she called it, I soon abandoned all attempt to guide in the slightest degree this extraordinary nature, and simply accepted her confidences, giving as much as I could of what might interest her in return.

Sometimes there would be a long pause, on my part, after which would come a plaintive letter, always terse, like this:—

"Did I displease you? But won't you tell me how?"

Or perhaps the announcement of some event, vast to her small sphere, as this:

AMHERST.

Carlo died.   E. DICKINSON.
Would you instruct me now?

Or sometimes there would arrive an exquisite little detached strain, every word a picture, like this:—

THE HUMMING-BIRD

A route of evanescence
With a revolving wheel;
A resonance of emerald;
A rush of cochineal.
And every blossom on the bush
Adjusts its tumbled head;—
The mail from Tunis, probably,
An easy morning's ride.

Nothing in literature, I am sure, so condenses into a few words that gorgeous atom of life and fire of which she here attempts the description. It is, however, needless to conceal that many of her brilliant fragments were less satisfying. She almost always grasped whatever she sought, but with some fracture of grammar and dictionary on the way. Often, too, she was obscure and sometimes inscrutable; and though obscurity is sometimes, in Coleridge's phrase, a compliment to the reader, yet it is never safe to press this compliment too hard.

Sometimes, on the other hand, her verses found too much favor for her comfort, and she was urged to publish. In such cases I was sometimes put forward as a defense; and the following letter was the fruit of some such occasion:—

DEAR FRIEND,—Thank you for the advice. I shall implicitly follow it.

The one who asked me for the lines I had never seen.

He spoke of "a charity." I refused, but did not inquire. He again earnestly urged, on the ground that in that way I might "aid unfortunate children." The name of "child" was a snare to me, and I hesitated, choosing my most rudimentary, and without criterion.

I inquired of you. You can scarcely estimate the opinion to one utterly guideless. Again thank you.

YOUR SCHOLAR.

Again came this, on a similar theme:

DEAR FRIEND,—Are you willing to tell me what is right? Mrs. Jackson,[11] of Colorado ["H. H.," her early schoolmate], was with me a few moments this week, and wished me to write for this. [A circular of the "No Name Series" was inclosed.] I told her I was unwilling, and she asked me why? I said I was incapable, and she seemed not to believe me and asked me not to decide for a few days. Meantime, she would write me. She was so sweetly noble, I would regret to estrange her, and if you would be willing to give me a note saying you disapproved it, and thought me unfit, she would believe you. I am sorry to flee so often to my safest friend, but hope he permits me.

In all this time—nearly eight years—we had never met, but she had sent invitations like the following:—

AMHERST

DEAR FRIEND,—Whom my dog understood could not elude others.

I should be so glad to see you, but think it an apparitional pleasure, not to be fulfilled. I am uncertain of Boston.

I had promised to visit my physician for a few days in May, but father objects because he is in the habit of me.

Is it more far to Amherst?

You will find a minute host, but a spacious welcome. . . .

If I still entreat you to teach me, are you much displeased? I will be patient, constant, never reject your knife, and should my slowness goad you, you knew before myself that

> Except the smaller size
> No lives are round.
> These hurry to a sphere
> And show and end.
> The larger slower grow
> And later hang;
> The summers of Hesperides
> Are long.

Afterwards, came this:—

AMHERST.

DEAR FRIEND,—A letter always feels to me like immortality because it is the mind alone without corporeal friend. Indebted in our talk to attitude and accent, there seems a spectral power in thought that walks alone. I would like to thank you for your great kindness, but never try to lift the words which I cannot hold.

Should you come to Amherst, I might then succeed, though gratitude is the timid wealth of those who have nothing. I am sure that you speak the truth, because the noble do, but your letters always surprise me.

My life has been too simple and stern to embarrass any. "Seen of Angels," scarcely my responsibility.

It is difficult not to be fictitious in so fair a place, but tests' severe repairs are permitted all.

When a little girl I remember hearing that remarkable passage and preferring the "Power," not knowing at the time that "Kingdom" and "Glory" were included.

You noticed my dwelling alone. To an emigrant, country is idle except it be his own. You speak kindly of seeing me; could it please your convenience to come so far as Amherst, I should be very glad, but I do not cross my father's ground to any house or town.

Of our greatest acts we are ignorant. You were not aware that you saved my life. To thank you in person has been since then one of my few requests. . . . You will excuse each that I say, because no one taught me.

At last, after many postponements, on August 16, 1870, I found myself face to face with my hitherto unseen correspondent. It was at her father's house, one of those large, square, brick mansions so familiar in our older New England towns, surrounded by trees and blossoming shrubs without, and within exquisitely neat, cool, spacious, and fragrant with flowers. After a little delay, I heard an extremely faint and pattering footstep like that of a child, in the hall, and in glided, almost noiselessly, a plain, shy little person, the face without a single good feature, but with eyes, as she herself said, "like the sherry the guest leaves in the glass," and with smooth bands of reddish chestnut hair. She had a quaint and nun-like look, as if she might be a German canoness of some religious order, whose prescribed garb was white piqué, with a blue net worsted shawl. She came toward me with two day-lilies, which she put in a childlike way into my hand, saying softly, under her breath, "These are my introduction," and adding, also, under her breath, in childlike fashion, "Forgive me if I am frightened; I never see strangers, and hardly know what I say." But soon she began to talk, and thence-forward continued almost constantly; pausing sometimes to beg that I would talk instead, but readily recommencing when I evaded. There was not a trace of affectation in all this; she seemed to speak absolutely for her own relief, and wholly without watching its effect on her hearer. Led on by me, she told much about her early life, in which her father was always the chief figure,—evidently a man of the old type, *la vieille roche*[12] of Puritanism—a man who, as she said, read on Sunday "lonely and rigorous books;" and who had from childhood inspired her with such awe, that she never learned to tell time by the clock till she was fifteen, simply because he had tried to explain it to her when she was a little child, and she had been afraid to tell him that she did not understand, and also afraid to ask any one else lest he should hear of it. Yet she had never heard him speak a harsh word, and it needed only a glance at his photograph to see how truly the Puritan tradition was preserved in him. He did not wish his children, when little, to read anything but the Bible; and when, one day, her brother brought her home Longfellow's Kavanagh,[13] he put it secretly under the pianoforte cover, made signs to her, and they both afterwards read it. It may have been before this, however, that a student of her father's was amazed to find that she and her brother had never heard of Lydia Maria Child, then much read, and he brought Letters from New York,[14] and hid it in the great bush of old-fashioned tree-box beside the front door. After the first book she thought in ecstasy, "This, then, is a book, and there are more of them." But she did not find so many as she expected, for she afterwards said to me, "When I lost the use of my eyes, it was a comfort to think that there were so few real books that I could easily find one to read me all of them." Afterwards, when she regained her eyes, she read Shakespeare, and thought to herself, "Why is any other book needed?"

She went on talking constantly and saying, in the midst of narrative, things quaint and aphoristic. "Is it oblivion or absorption when things pass from our minds?" "Truth is such a rare thing, it is delightful to tell it." "I find ecstacy in living; the mere sense of living is joy enough." When I asked her if she never felt any want of employment, not going off the grounds and rarely seeing a visitor, she answered, "I never thought of conceiving that I could ever have the slightest approach to such a want in all future time;" and then added, after a pause, "I feel that I have not expressed myself strongly enough," although it seemed to me that she had. She told me of her household occupations, that she made all their bread, because her father liked only hers; then saying shyly, "And people must have puddings," this very timidly and suggestively, as if they were meteors or comets. Interspersed with these confidences came phrases so emphasized as to seem the very wantonness of over-statement, as if she pleased herself with putting into words what the most extravagant might possibly think without saying, as thus: "How do most people live without any thoughts? There are many people in the world,—you must have noticed them in the street,—how do they live? How do they get strength to put on their clothes in the morning?" Or this crowning extravaganza: "If I read a book and it makes my whole body so cold no fire can ever warm me, I know that is poetry. If I feel physically as if the top of my head were taken off, I know that is poetry. These are the only ways I know it. Is there any other way?"

I have tried to describe her just as she was, with the aid of notes taken at the time; but this interview left our relation very much what it was before;—on my side an interest that was strong and even affectionate, but not based on any thorough comprehension; and on her side a hope, always rather baffled, that I should afford some aid in solving her abstruse problem of life.

The impression undoubtedly made on me was that of an excess of tension, and of an abnormal life. Perhaps in time I could have got beyond that somewhat overstrained relation which not my will, but her needs, had forced upon us. Certainly I should have been most glad to bring it down to the level of simple truth and every-day comradeship; but it was not altogether easy. She was much too enigmatical a being for me to solve in an hour's interview, and an instinct told me that the slightest attempt at direct cross-examination would make her withdraw into her shell; I could only sit still and watch, as one does in the woods; I must name my bird without a gun, as recommended by Emerson.[15] Under this necessity I had no opportunity to see that human and humorous side of her which is strongly emphasized by her nearer friends, and which shows itself in her quaint and unique description of a rural burglary, contained in the volume of her poems. Hence, even her letters to me show her mainly on her *exaltée* side; and should a volume of her correspondence ever be printed, it is very desirable that it should contain some of her letters to friends of closer and more familiar intimacy.

After my visit came this letter:—

Enough is so vast a sweetness, I suppose it never occurs, only pathetic counterfeits.

Fabulous to me as the men of the Revelations who "shall not hunger any more." Even the possible has its insoluble particle.

After you went, I took Macbeth and turned to "Birnam Wood." Came twice "To Dunsinane." I thought and went about my work. . . .

The vein cannot thank the artery, but her solemn indebtedness to him, even the stolidest admit, and so of me who try, whose effort leaves no sound.

You ask great questions accidentally. To answer them would be events. I trust that you are safe.

I ask you to forgive me for all the ignorance I had. I find no nomination sweet as your low opinion.

Speak, if but to blame your obedient child.

You told me of Mrs. Lowell's poems.[16] Would you tell me where I could find them, or are they not for sight? An article of yours, too, perhaps the only one you wrote that I never knew. It was about a "Latch." Are you willing to tell me? [Perhaps "A Sketch."]

If I ask too much, you could please refuse. Shortness to live has made me bold.

Abroad is close to-night and I have but to lift my hands to touch the "Heights of Abraham."[17]   DICKINSON.

When I said, at parting, that I would come again some time, she replied, "Say, in a long time; that will be nearer. Some time is no time." We met only once again, and I have no express record of the visit. We corresponded for years, at long intervals, her side of the intercourse being, I fear, better sustained; and she sometimes wrote also to my wife, inclosing flowers or fragrant leaves with a verse or two. Once she sent her one of George Eliot's books, I think Middlemarch, and wrote, "I am bringing you a little granite book for you to lean upon." At other times she would send single poems, such as these:—

THE BLUE JAY

No brigadier throughout the year
So civic as the jay.
A neighbor and a warrior too,
With shrill felicity
Pursuing winds that censure us
A February Day,
The brother of the universe
Was never blown away.
The snow and he are intimate;
I've often seen them play
When heaven looked upon us all
With such severity
I felt apology were due
To an insulted sky
Whose pompous frown was nutriment
To their temerity.
The pillow of this daring head
Is pungent evergreens;
His larder—terse and militant—
Unknown, refreshing things;
His character—a tonic;
His future—a dispute;
Unfair an immortality
That leaves this neighbor out.

THE WHITE HEAT

Dare you see a soul at the white heat?
   Then crouch within the door;
Red is the fire's common tint,
   But when the vivid ore

Has sated flame's conditions,
   Its quivering substance plays
Without a color, but the light
   Of unanointed blaze.

Least village boasts its blacksmith,
   Whose anvil's even din

> Stands symbol for the finer forge
>   That soundless tugs within,
>
> Refining these impatient ores
>   With hammer and with blaze,
> Until the designated light
>   Repudiate the forge.

Then came the death of her father, that strong Puritan father who had communicated to her so much of the vigor of his own nature, and who bought her many books, but begged her not to read them. Mr. Edward Dickinson, after service in the national House of Representatives and other public positions, had become a member of the lower house of the Massachusetts legislature. The session was unusually prolonged, and he was making a speech upon some railway question at noon, one very hot day (July 16, 1874), when he became suddenly faint and sat down. The house adjourned, and a friend walked with him to his lodgings at the Tremont House; where he began to pack his bag for home, after sending for a physician, but died within three hours. Soon afterwards, I received the following letter:—

The last afternoon that my father lived, though with no premonition, I preferred to be with him, and invented an absence for mother, Vinnie [her sister] being asleep. He seemed peculiarly pleased, as I oftenest stayed with myself; and remarked, as the afternoon withdrew, he "would like it to not end."

His pleasure almost embarrassed me, and my brother coming, I suggested they walk. Next morning I woke him for the train, and saw him no more.

His heart was pure and terrible, and I think no other like it exists.

I am glad there is immortality, but would have tested it myself, before entrusting him. Mr. Bowles was with us. With that exception, I saw none. I have wished for you, since my father died, and had you an hour unengrossed, it would be almost priceless. Thank you for each kindness. . . .

Later she wrote:—

When I think of my father's lonely life and lonelier death, there is this redress—

> Take all away;
> The only thing worth larceny
> Is left—the immortality.

My earliest friend wrote me the week before he died, "If I live, I will go to Amherst; if I die, I certainly will."

Is your house deeper off?

YOUR SCHOLAR.

A year afterwards came this:—

DEAR FRIEND,—Mother was paralyzed Tuesday, a year from the evening father died. I thought perhaps you would care.

YOUR SCHOLAR.

With this came the following verse, having a curious seventeenth-century flavor:—

> A death-blow is a life-blow to some,
> Who, till they died, did not alive become;
> Who, had they lived, had died, but when
> They died, vitality begun.

And later came this kindred memorial of one of the oldest and most faithful friends of the family, Mr. Samuel Bowles of the Springfield Republican:—

DEAR FRIEND,—I felt it shelter to speak to you.

My brother and sister are with Mr. Bowles, who is buried this afternoon.

The last song that I heard—that was, since the birds—was "He leadeth me,[18] he leadeth me; yea, though I walk"—then the voices stooped, the arch was so low.

After this added bereavement the inward life of the diminished household became only more concentrated, and the world was held farther and farther away. Yet to this period belongs the following letter, written about 1880, which has more of what is commonly called the objective or external quality than any she ever wrote me; and shows how close might have been her observation and her sympathy, had her rare qualities taken a somewhat different channel:—

DEAR FRIEND,—I was touchingly reminded of [a child who had died] this morning by an Indian woman with gay baskets and a dazzling baby, at the kitchen door. Her little boy "once died," she said, death to her dispelling him. I asked her what the baby liked, and she said "to step." The prairie before the door was gay with flowers of hay, and I led her in. She argued with the birds, she leaned on clover walls and they fell, and dropped her. With jargon sweeter than a bell, she grappled buttercups, and they sank together, the buttercups the heaviest. What sweetest use of days! 'T was noting some such scene made Vaughan humbly say, "My days that are at best but dim and hoary." I think it was Vaughan. . . .[19]

And these few fragmentary memorials—closing, like every human biography, with funerals, yet with such as were to Emily Dickinson only the stately introduction to a higher life—may well end with her description of the death of the very summer she so loved.

As imperceptibly as grief
The summer lapsed away,
Too imperceptible at last
To feel like perfidy.

A quietness distilled,
As twilight long begun,
Or Nature spending with herself
Sequestered afternoon.

The dusk drew earlier in,
The morning foreign shone,

A courteous yet harrowing grace
As guest that would be gone.

And thus without a wing
Or service of a keel
Our summer made her light escape
Into the Beautiful.

Explanatory Notes

These notes are intended to explain to modern readers allusions that Higginson might reasonably have expected the *Atlantic Monthly* reader of his own day to recognize. Many, such as the paraphrases which interlard "Letter to a Young Contributor," are self-explanatory—or nearly so. Higginson was, however, enormously well read, and the present notes have not attempted to cover Higginson's more deliberately esoteric references. For a systematic view of literature in the Civil War, see Wilson (listed in *Suggestions for Further Reading*), and for the war itself see Geoffrey C. Ward, *The Civil War: An Illustrated History* (New York: Alfred A. Knopf, 1990). These notes have been compiled with the assistance of David Bruce Noble.

ARMY LIFE IN A BLACK REGIMENT
Chapter I: Introductory

1. *Kalmuck Tartars:* Asian nomads living south of the Altai Mountains and east of the Caspian Sea.

2. *Kansas troubles:* The Kansas-Nebraska Act of 1854 was designed as a compromise measure guaranteeing self-determination to the territories most likely to become the next two states. But Kansas itself became a bloody arena where outside agitators competed for influence.

3. *John Brown:* Hanged for leading an abolitionist attack on Harpers Ferry, Brown (1800–1859) gained almost instant martyr status in the north.

Chapter II: Camp Diary

1. *Stedman:* In 1772 John Gabriel Stedman (1744–97) accompanied a Dutch expedition to subdue slaves in revolt in Surinam.

2. *double, double:* Cf. *Macbeth*, IV, i, 10–11.

3. *Harriet Tubman:* After escaping from slavery on Maryland's Eastern Shore, Tubman (1821?–1913) led more than three hundred slaves to freedom on the Underground Railroad.

4. *Gough:* John B. Gough (1817–86), temperance lecturer.

5. *beyond Molière:* Jean-Baptiste Poquelin (1622–73), French comic playwright.

6. *Dr. Zachos:* John Zachos, Greek by origin, was superintendent of Paris Island under the Freedmen's organization.

7. *Dwelling in tents:* Cf. Hebrews 11:9.

8. *Among the Pines:* An 1862 secessionist novel by "Edmund Kirke" (James R. Gilmore).

9. *Fremont's time:* John C. Frémont (1813–90), explorer, abolitionist, and soldier, and first Republican candidate for president, in 1856.

10. *Haroun Alraschid:* Caliph of Baghdad, principle character in the *Arabian Nights*.

11. *Hungary:* The movement for Hungarian freedom under Louis Kossuth (1802–94) peaked with the declaration of independence in 1849, but the country was soon overrun by Russia.

12. *"Scottish Border Minstrelsy":* Sir Walter Scott (1771–1832) published his *Minstrelsy of the Scottish Border*, a collection of traditional lyrics heavily edited by himself, in 1802–3.

13. *Toussaint:* Toussaint L'Ouverture (1743?–1803) led a successful slave revolt to make Haiti the first free republic in the western hemisphere.

14. *J.R.L.:* James Russell Lowell (1819–91), poet and editor.

15. *M———'s:* Higginson's first wife, Mary Channing (d. 1877).

Chapter III: Up the St. Mary's

1. *Araucanians:* Inhabitants of southern Chile, named after the coniferous trees among which they lived.

2. *Blackstone:* Generic label for the law, after William Blackstone (1723–80), English jurist.

3. *Lake Quinsigamond:* Elongated lake east of Worcester, Massachusetts.

4. *Mrs. Kemble:* Frances Anne Kemble (1809–93), English actress, married an American named Butler and wrote *Journal of a Residence on a Georgian Plantation in 1838–39* (1863).

5. *Montrose's verse:* James Graham Montrose (1612–50).

6. *let him cast the first stone:* John 8:7.

7. *Scott:* The reference is possibly to Sir Walter Scott's *The Pirate* (1821).

8. *Falstaff's ragged regiment:* Cf. *1 Henry IV*, IV, ii, 11ff.

9. *"Amyas Leigh":* Hero of *Westward Ho!* (1855) by Charles Kingsley (1819–75).

10. *Obadiah Oldbuck:* Probably a misrendering of "Obadiah Oldpath" (J. R. Newhall), who wrote *Lin; or, Jewels of the Third Plantation* (1862).

11. *Ulysses and Rob Roy:* Homer's Ulysses stole sheep from the Cyclops; Scott's outlaw is the title character of *Rob Roy* (1817).

Chapter IV: Up the St. John's

1. *Miles O'Reilly:* Pen name of Charles G. Halpine, whose poem "Sambo's Right to be Kilt" eased acceptance of colored soldiers among the white troops.

2. *Ponce de Leon:* Juan Ponce de León (1460–1521), Spanish explorer who searched for the Fountain of Youth.

3. *Aladdin:* Hero of the oriental tale of the lamp, often confused with the *Arabian Nights*.

4. *Penobscot or Kennebec:* Rivers in Maine.

5. *Wendell Phillips:* American orator and abolitionist (1811–84).

6. *Fifth-Monarchy men:* Extreme Puritan sect during the commonwealth, supporters of Cromwell.

7. *Charles Lamb:* English essayist (1775–1834).

8. *Jean Paul's "Titan":* Johann Paul Friedrich Richter (1763–1825), German novelist.

9. *Suwarrow's:* Aleksandr Vasilyevich Suvorov (1729–1800), Russian general.

10. *Roderick Dhu's:* Character in Scott's *Lady of the Lake* (1810).

11. *Dantean:* Imagery drawn from the *Inferno* of Dante Alighieri (1265–1321).

Chapter V: Out on Picket

1. *Moses, whose Pisgah:* Deuteronomy 34:1.

2. *Thackeray:* William Makepeace Thackeray (1811–63), English novelist of manners.

3. *Henri Larochejaquelein:* A member of the constitutional guard of Louis XVI, Henri (1772–94) later led the loyal peasants of La Vendée.

4. *Robinson Crusoe:* Daniel Defoe's novel of shipwreck and solitude, published 1719.

5. *Kearsarge and Alabama . . . Semmes:* The U.S.S. *Kearsarge* sunk the Confederates States' *Alabama* off Cherbourg, France, in 1864. Raphael Semmes, the commander of the rebel vessel, was rescued by the British yacht *Deerhound* and escaped after apparently surrendering.

6. *not to Hebe, but to Magdalen:* Hebe is a cupbearer to the Greek gods; Mary Magadalen is traditionally associated with the woman in Mark 14:3 and John 12:3.

7. *Scottish moss-trooping:* Probably another reference to sheep-stealing.

8. *Marion's men:* Francis Marion (1732–95), the "Swamp Fox," led a guerrilla war against the British in South Carolina during the American Revolution. He figured largely in the fictional romances of William Gilmore Simms (1806–70), but Higginson's phrase echoes the title of the poem "Song of Marion's Men" (1831) by William Cullen Bryant (1794–1878).

9. *Mr. Pickwick:* Samuel Pickwick, the central character of a series of sketches published by Charles Dickens (1812–70) as *The Pickwick Papers* (1837).

10. *such stuff as dreams are made of:* Cf. *The Tempest*, IV, i, 156–58.

11. *other scenes and encampments new:* Echoing Milton's "Lycidas," "To-morrow to fresh woods, and pastures new."

Chapter VI: A Night in the Water

1. *Saint Somebody:* St. Dionysius the Areopagite.

2. *Plotinus:* Greek Neoplatonic philosopher (203?–62).

3. *Keats:* John Keats (1795–1821), "Lines Written in the Highlands after a Visit to Burns's Country."

4. *That way madness lay:* Cf. *King Lear*, III, iv, 21.

5. *a man and a brother:* Motto from the official medallion of the British Anti-Slavery Society, designed by Josiah Wedgwood: "Am I Not a Man and a Brother?"

6. *Carlyle:* Thomas Carlyle (1795–1881); his *Sartor Resartus* first appeared in book form in Boston in 1836.

Chapter VII: Up the Edisto

1. *Weems:* Mason Locke "Parson" Weems (1759–1825) originated the story of George Washington and the cherry tree in his 1800 biography; his biography of Marion appeared in 1809.

2. *Greeley:* Horace Greeley (1811–72), editor of the New York *Tribune*.

3. *Doré's:* Gustave Doré (1832–83), French illustrator.

4. *Don Quixote . . . Sancho Panza:* Characters in *Don Quixote* (1605, 1615) by Miguel de Cervantes Saavedra (1547–1616).

5. *Rebecca:* Dark heroine of Scott's *Ivanhoe* (1819).

Chapter VIII: The Baby of the Regiment

1. *Raphael:* Raffaello Sanzio (1483–1520), Italian painter. Higginson's possible scorn here may indicate budding Pre-Raphaelitism.

2. *Red-Riding-Hood:* By Charles Perrault (1628–1703).

3. *whatsoever things were pure:* Philipians 4:8.

Chapter IX: Negro Spirituals

1. *Lowell's "Biglow Papers":* The first series was published in book form in 1848; the second was published serially during the war, in 1867. The poems featured the New England dialect of Hosea Biglow and Birdofredom Sawin and satirized pro-slavery sentiment during the Mexican War (first series) and the Civil War (second).

2. *Orientalism:* This fashion was probably initiated by the translation into English of the *Arabian Nights* (1705–8), but mostly was associated in Higginson's day with George Gordon, Lord Byron (1788–1824).

3. *Allan Ramsay:* Ramsay (1686–1758) was probably the most important Scottish poet before Burns.

Chapter X: Life at Camp Shaw

1. *soigné:* Elegant

2. *Kinglake:* Alexander William Kinglake (1809–91), author of *Eothen: or Traces of Travel Brought Home from the East* (1844).

3. *dogs of war:* Cf. *Julius Caesar*, III, i.

4. *pirate-lieutenant:* Another reference to Scott's *The Pirate* (1821).

Chapter XI: Florida Again?

1. *varioloid:* Smallpox.

2. *Uhland's 'Black Knight':* A poem by Johann Ludwig Uhland (1787–1862), German poet.

Chapter XII: The Negro as a Soldier

1. *Topsies:* From the reprobate character Topsy in *Uncle Tom's Cabin* (1852) by Harriet Beecher Stowe (1811–96).

2. *Garrison:* William Lloyd Garrison (1805–79), nonviolent abolitionist and reformer.

3. *Mr. Seward's unfortunate words to Mr. Adams:* William Henry Seward (1801–72); Charles Francis Adams (1807–86). The actual words have not been located.

4. *Kay's "Condition of the English Peasantry":* Joseph Kay (1821–78) wrote *The Condition and Education of Poor Children in English and in German Towns* (1853).

5. *Uncle Toby:* Epitome of amicability in *The Life and Opinions of Tristram Shandy, Gentleman* (1759–67) by Laurence Sterne (1713–68), Toby had remarked on the prodigious swearing by the army in Flanders.

6. *Cromwell's time:* Oliver Cromwell (1599–1658), English soldier and statesman, led the Puritan forces in the English Civil War.

7. *Henry Ward Beecher:* Clergyman and abolitionist (1813–87), younger brother of Harriet Beecher Stowe.

8. *Lancelot Gobbo's soliloquy:* Cf. *Merchant of Venice*, II, ii, 47ff.

Chapter XIII: Conclusion

1. *a most vague and heartless baptism:* Probably another allusion to *Tristram Shandy:* In the fourth volume the narrator is mistakenly baptized "Tristram" instead of "Trismegistus."

Appendix

1. *Jefferson Davis . . . Sydney Smith:* Jefferson Davis (1808–1889), the first (and only) president of the Confederacy; Sydney Smith (1771–1845), cofounder of the *Edinburgh Review.*

RELATED READINGS

A Visit to John Brown's Household in 1859

1. *A Visit:* First published in James Redpath's *The Public Life of Captain John Brown* (Boston: Thayer and Eldridge, 1860).

2. *Judge Taney:* Roger Brooke Taney (1777–1864), Chief Justice of the Supreme Court, defined the legal nonentity of Negroes in the Dred Scott decision (1857).

3. *If I can do:* Cf. Emily Dickinson's "If I can stop one Heart from breaking."

4. *makes the gallows glorious:* A paraphrase of Ralph Waldo Emerson's prediction before the execution of Brown, the "new saint awaiting his martyrdom . . . who, if he shall suffer, will make the gallows glorious like the cross" (Villard, 563).

5. *Mahala Doyle:* In Kansas, Brown had indeed executed Doyle's husband and two sons. Shortly after his capture, she (or an amanuensis) wrote a vengeful letter to Brown, concluding with this postscript: "My son John Doyle whose life I beged of you is now grown up and is very desirous to be at Charlestown on the day of your execution, would certainly be there if his means would permit it that he might adjust the rope around your neck if Gov. Wise would permit it" (Villard, 164).

6. *pecuniary condition:* Redpath's book was published with the specific intention of raising money for the support of Brown's large family.

Nat Turner's Insurrection

1. *Butler:* Frustrated at the illegality of the emancipation of slaves by Union officers, Benjamin Butler (1818–93) decided that if slaves had

to be treated as property, he would "confiscate" them as contraband of war, thus providing provisional emancipation.

2. *Stowe's picture:* In *Dred: a Tale of the Great Dismal Swamp* (1856).

3. *Lydia Maria Child:* American abolitionist and feminist writer (1802–1880.

4. *Wordsworth's . . . Lucy:* William Wordsworth (1770–1850) published four "Lucy Poems" in the *Lyrical Ballads* of 1800; any of these, or a fifth published in 1807, could be construed as an epitaph.

5. *Liberator:* Abolition newspaper founded by Garrison in 1831.

6. *De Quincey's "Avenger":* Thomas De Quincey (1785–1859), author of *Confessions of an English Opium Eater. The Avenger, a Narrative, and Other Papers* was published in Boston by Ticknor and Fields in 1859.

7. *Kosciusko:* Tadeusz Kościuszko (1746–1817), Polish patriot, aided the Americans during the Revolution.

Letter to a Young Contributor

1. *Stowe . . . Autocrat:* Stowe's novel *Agnes of Sorrento* was running serially, as was "The Autocrat of the Breakfast Table" by Oliver Wendell Holmes (1809–94).

2. *General Jackson when Jack Downing:* "Jack Downing" was a generic pen named used by anyone, beginning with Seba Smith (1792–1868), who wanted to attack Andrew Jackson (1767–1845).

3. *hoarse, inaudible Burke:* Edmund Burke (1729–97). The line is a parody of "Elegy written in a Country Church-Yard" (1751) by Thomas Gray (1716–71): "Some mute inglorious Milton here may rest."

4. *the Four Poets:* Dante, Francesco Petrarch (1304–74), Giovanni Boccaccio (1313–75), Torquato Tasso (1544–95).

Some War Scenes Revisited

1. *Alice's . . . clover leaf:* Alice's choices were actually a bottle marked "DRINK ME" (which made her small) and a small cake on which currants spelled out "EAT ME."

2. *Freedmen's Bank:* The "Freedmen's Savings and Trust Company" was founded, in the words of Frederick Douglass, to "furnish a place of security and profit for the hard earnings of the colored people,

especially at the South" (*Life and Times*, p. 400); it failed through overextension and dishonest agents.

3. *Libery:* That is, Liberia, as part of the movement to recolonize freed slaves.

4. *withdrawal:* Federal troops remained in the South after the war until April 1877.

5. *learning nothing, forgetting nothing:* A phrase usually credited to General Dumouriez (1739–1823), quoted by Napoleon on his return from Elba. Also ascribed to Charles-Maurice de Talleyrand-Périgord (1754–1838).

6. *five acres and a mule:* "Forty acres and a mule" was a phrase used to epitomize the freedmen's expectations under Reconstruction. In 1868, Richard H. Cain argued against such large tracts: "The man who can not make his living on five acres, will not do so on twenty-five."

Emily Dickinson's Letters

1. *when published:* In 1890.

2. *an uncle:* William Dickinson.

3. *brother and sister . . . mother . . . father:* Brother, Austin; sister, Lavinia; father, Edward; mother, Emily Norcross.

4. *Whitman:* Walt Whitman (1819–92) had published the third edition of *Leaves of Grass* in 1860.

5. *Miss Prescott's Circumstance:* Harriet Prescott Spofford (1835–1921) published "Circumstance" in the *Atlantic* in 1860.

6. *Pippa Passes:* Poem by Robert Browning (1812–89).

7. *Procession of Flowers:* Higginson published this essay in the *Atlantic* in 1862.

8. *Mr. Howells:* William Dean Howells (1837–1920) edited the *Atlantic* from 1871 to 1881.

9. *Swedenborg:* Emanuel Swedenborg (1688–1772), whose philosophy provided much of the foundation for American Transcendentalism.

10. *Hawthorne:* Nathaniel Hawthorne (1804–64) died on a walking trip in New Hampshire in May.

11. *Mrs. Jackson:* "H. H.," Helen Hunt Jackson (1830–85).

12. *la vieille roche:* "The old rock."

13. *Longfellow's Kavanagh:* Henry Wadsworth Longfellow (1807–1882) published *Kavanagh: A Tale*, his only novel, in 1849.

14. *Letters from New York:* Published in 1843 (first series) and 1845 (second series).

15. *as recommended by Emerson:* Ralph Waldo Emerson (1803–1882).

16. *Mrs. Lowell's poems:* Probably Maria White Lowell (d. 1853), wife of James Russell Lowell.

17. *Heights of Abraham:* Presumably over the Plains of Abraham before Quebec, where British general James Wolfe (1727–59) and Louis-Joseph, Marquis de Montcalm (1712–59) lost their lives.

18. *He leadeth me:* Hymn adapted from Psalm 23.

19. *Vaughan:* Henry Vaughan (1621–95), religious poet.

FOR THE BEST IN PAPERBACKS, LOOK FOR THE 🐧

In every corner of the world, on every subject under the sun, Penguin represents quality and variety—the very best in publishing today.

For complete information about books available from Penguin—including Penguin Classics, Penguin Compass, and Puffins—and how to order them, write to us at the appropriate address below. Please note that for copyright reasons the selection of books varies from country to country.

In the United States: Please write to *Penguin Group (USA), P.O. Box 12289 Dept. B, Newark, New Jersey 07101-5289* or call 1-800-788-6262.

In the United Kingdom: Please write to *Dept. EP, Penguin Books Ltd, Bath Road, Harmondsworth, West Drayton, Middlesex UB7 0DA.*

In Canada: Please write to *Penguin Books Canada Ltd, 90 Eglinton Avenue East, Suite 700, Toronto, Ontario M4P 2Y3.*

In Australia: Please write to *Penguin Books Australia Ltd, P.O. Box 257, Ringwood, Victoria 3134.*

In New Zealand: Please write to *Penguin Books (NZ) Ltd, Private Bag 102902, North Shore Mail Centre, Auckland 10.*

In India: Please write to *Penguin Books India Pvt Ltd, 11 Panchsheel Shopping Centre, Panchsheel Park, New Delhi 110 017.*

In the Netherlands: Please write to *Penguin Books Netherlands bv, Postbus 3507, NL-1001 AH Amsterdam.*

In Germany: Please write to *Penguin Books Deutschland GmbH, Metzlerstrasse 26, 60594 Frankfurt am Main.*

In Spain: Please write to *Penguin Books S. A., Bravo Murillo 19, 1° B, 28015 Madrid.*

In Italy: Please write to *Penguin Italia s.r.l., Via Benedetto Croce 2, 20094 Corsico, Milano.*

In France: Please write to *Penguin France, Le Carré Wilson, 62 rue Benjamin Baillaud, 31500 Toulouse.*

In Japan: Please write to *Penguin Books Japan Ltd, Kaneko Building, 2-3-25 Koraku, Bunkyo-Ku, Tokyo 112.*

In South Africa: Please write to *Penguin Books South Africa (Pty) Ltd, Private Bag X14, Parkview, 2122 Johannesburg.*